QUALITY OF LIF
TENDENC
HYPE

MW01673548

Kanojia Sonal Nandkishor

Contents

Chapter-I

INTRODUCTION

1.0 OVERVIEW:

This is the 21st century, which also known as the smart digital modern era. This century has provided us with a highly flexible way of living. This type of lifestyle has both positive and negative effects on human beings. The positive impact is that it makes our lives easier, smoother, and faster; the adverse effect is that it has a negative impact on our physical and mental health, as well as our social health, in the case of the Covid-19 pandemic. It is associated with a variety of issues, including physical, social, economic, and mental. Cancer, PCOD, hypertension, diabetes, coronary heart disease, obesity, arthritis, and many more illnesses have an impact on our daily lives.

With sixty-seven years having passed since India gained independence from the United Kingdom, it appears that the country's population's health has improved significantly. However, enormous transformations have occurred in the country during the last few decades, and they have had a significant influence on health outcomes. Economic development, nutritional status, and mortality rates have all altered, which has had a significant impact on the illness profile, which has changed significantly. Notwithstanding tremendous progress in the management of infectious illnesses, it has been discovered that they continue to contribute considerably to the overall disease burden in the country, despite these gains. Chronic Non-communicable Illnesses (NCDs) such as cardiovascular disease (CVD), diabetes, chronic obstructive pulmonary disease (COPD), cancer, mental health problems, and injuries have increased in prevalence as a result of the reduction in morbidity and mortality resulting from communicable diseases (Mohan et al., 2011).

Researchers and policymakers all around the globe are increasingly identifying non-communicable diseases (NCDs) as a public health and developmental issue. The most common cause of mortality in the South-East Asian area is non-communicable diseases (NCDs), which claim the lives of 7.9 million people each year (55 % of the total deaths in the region).

Recently, corona disease effect very severely on the whole universe. Many people who have bad health habits they are easy to target for these type of disease, therefore, people who were suffering from these types of disease they have lot of adjustment problem, even they are facing many financial and social problem, including they are suffering from mental problems like stress, anxiety, frustration, traumatic disorder, depression, mood disorder, etc. Sometimes they have a low quality of life & a lack of self-efficacy to committing suicide too. Recently because of covid-19 many people suffering from many health issues like low immunity, cough & cold, fever and many others. In the lockdown period, many people get easily target with diabetes, hypertension and thyroid because of work from home and lack of physical work. Many people suffer from loss of their nearest person, loss of job, lack of money and food; they are suffering from stress, anxiety, PTSD, and severe depression. Some people committed suicide with their family too.

Anyway, the researcher will discuss quality of life, self efficacy, and suicidal tendency & how it affects their diabetes and hypertension and their mental and physical health.

1.1 DIABETES:

Diabetes Mellitus is a major worldwide health issue as well as a significant non-communicable health issue. It is a metabolic disease characterized by a rise in a person's blood glucose level. Diabetes Mellitus affects a large number of people, particularly those who live in cities. Diabetes is becoming more common as a result of population increase, age, urbanization, and rising obesity and physical inactivity rates. "Diabetes prevalence for all age groups was assessed to be 2.8 % in 2000 and is expected to reach 4.4 % in 2030," (Wild et al.,2007).

According to Wild et al. (2004),"the overall number of persons with diabetes is expected to grow from 171 million in 2000 to 366 million in 2030." Between 2000 and 2030, the urban population in emerging nations is expected to double. Type-I and Type-II diabetes are the two types of diabetes. IDDM (Insulin Dependent Diabetes Mellitus), often known as juvenile-onset diabetes, is caused by cellular-mediated autoimmune destruction of the pancreatic -cells. Type 2 Diabetes, commonly known as NIDDM (Non-Insulin Dependent Diabetes Mellitus), affects over 90% of diabetics and includes people with low insulin production or insulin resistance. "These individuals do not require insulin therapy to survive, at least initially and frequently during their lives" (ADA, 2005).

"Oral Hypoglycemic Agents" have long been the mainstay of treatment for Type 2 Diabetes patients, intending to achieve strict blood sugar control and a reduction in a variety of side effects. One of the primary causes of poor glycemic control is noncompliance with Oral Hypoglycemic Agents. Patient noncompliance has always been an issue (Shrestha et al., 2015).

1.1.1 Types of Diabetes:

Type-I Diabetes: Type-I Diabetes is caused by cellular-mediated autoimmune destruction of the pancreatic I^2 cells and accounts for fewer than 10% of all diabetes cases. The breakdown of I^2 occurs rapidly in babies and children but slowly in adults, and this is referred to as "Late-onset Autoimmune Diabetes". In this situation, there is a severe shortage of insulin. Insulin injection is necessary for regulating blood glucose levels, preventing diabetic ketoacidosis, and avoiding deadly consequences. As a result, in the early stages of Type-I Diabetes, a lower dosage is necessary, and the dose may be adjusted later depending on glycemic control.

Type-II Diabetes: of all cases of diabetes mellitus, type 2 diabetes accounts for more than 90%. This is initially characterized by insulin resistance and followed by the failure of I2 cells to compensate for the insulin requirements. Type 2 diabetes mellitus mainly occurs in adults; however, nowadays, because of the change in disease pattern and transition, younger groups are also suffering from the diasease. The significant risk factors associated with type 2 diabetes mellitus are older age, obesity, family history of Diabetes history of gestational diabetes, impairment of glucose metabolism, physical inactivity and race and ethnicity. It is found that in more than half of the affected people, the disease is undiagnosed. Under basal conditions for preventing ketosis, insulin secretion is sufficient; however, ketoacidosis may occur in extreme stress condition.

DM due to secondary causes: DM can be due to other various secondary reasons like from "genetic defects in insulin secretion or action, exocrine pancreatic disease, pancreatectomy, endocrinopathies (e.g., Cushing syndrome, acromegaly) drugs and other syndromes".

Gestational DM: It is found in approximately 4% of all pregnancies and usually resolves after delivery but unfortunately, some women remain at an increased risk of developing Type 2 DM later. All women with gestational diabetes should undergo a 75g oral glucose tolerance test at 6-8 weeks postpartum to determine whether abnormal carbohydrate metabolism has persisted. "Weight loss is encouraged to decrease the likelihood of developing diabetes mellitus after delivery and patients with a history of gestational diabetes should be annually evaluated for onset of diabetes" (Cooper, 2007).

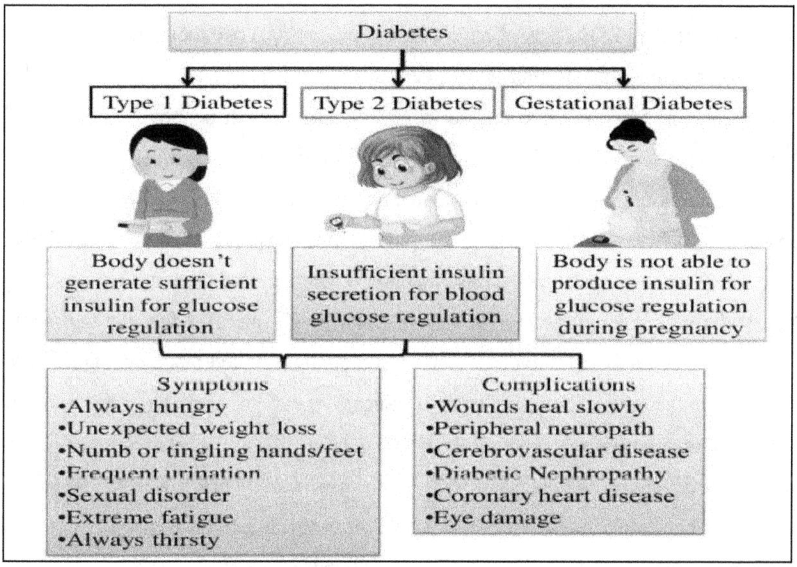

Source: https://www.researchgate.net

1.1.2 Genetics:

Each gene contributes just a little amount to an increased risk of developing type-II diabetes in the vast majority of cases associated with type-II diabetes, with the majority of these cases including a combination of genes. If one identical twin develops diabetes, the chances of the other acquiring diabetes throughout his life are more than 90 %. Still, the risks of developing diabetes in non-identical siblings are between 25 and 50 percent, respectively. As of 2011, more than 36 genes had been identified as having a role in raising the incidence of type-II diabetic complications. Even when all of these genes are taken into consideration, they still only account for

10% of the overall inheritable component of the illness. The TCF7L2 allele, for example, raises the chance of getting diabetes by 1.5 times compared to the other prevalent genetic variations, making it the most dangerous of them all. The majority of the genes associated with diabetes are involved in the beta cell activity (Shoback, 2011).

1.1.3 Lifestyle:

Several variables associated with the development of type-II diabetes have been identified, including obesity, being overweight (defined as having a body mass index of more than 25), a lack of physical exercise, eating a bad diet, stress, and living in urban environments (Herder and Roden, 2011; Shoback, 2011). According to the Centres, increased body fat is related to 30% of instances in people of Chinese and Japanese origin, 60-80% of cases in people of European and African descent, and 100% of cases among Pima Indians and Pacific Islanders for Disease Control and Prevention. A high waist to hip ratio is typical among those who are not fat (Abdullah et al.,2010). Dietary variables can also increase or decrease the likelihood of acquiring type II diabetes. Fats in the diet are also essential, with saturated fats and trans-fatty acids raising the risk and polyunsaturated and monounsaturated fats reducing the risk, as shown in the table (Shoback, 2011). It indicates that consuming large quantities of white rice may potentially increase the risk (Hu et al., 2012). Excessive use of sugar-sweetened beverages is connected with an elevated risk of heart disease and stroke (Riserus et al., 2009; Malik et al., 2010). Lack of physical activity is also suspected of contributing to around seven percent of these instances (Lee et al., 2012).

For future health-care planning, strategy, and delivery, a better understanding of the changeable risk factors and behaviours that cause Type-II Diabetes among this population is required in order to ensure that the inconveniences of disease are treated with as efficiently as possible (Malik et al.,2010).

1.2 HYPERTENSION

The rising burden of hypertension and associated cardiovascular disease in India should be addressed as a public health priority as soon as possible. The most effective way is to employ an optimal context-specific resource-sensitive combination of population and clinical approaches. According to the International Diabetes Federation (2014), hypertension is regarded to be one of the most important non-communicable diseases (NCDs), accounting for significant deaths and disability globally (9.4 million deaths and 7 % of Disability Adjusted Life Years (DALYs) in 2010). There are several obstacles ahead, but there are also multiple chances for mobilizing efforts in order to achieve the WHO-UN target of a 25 % reduction in NCD-related mortality and associated decrease in hypertension by 2025, which is equally encouraging (Alberti et al., 2005).

High blood pressure, often known as hypertension, is a significant public health problem that affects people worldwide. According to World Health Organization standards, hypertension is a person's systolic blood pressure of 140 mmHg or higher and diastolic blood pressure of 90 mmHg or higher, respectively. Using a mercury sphygmomanometer, either the placatory or the auscultator technique is used to determine blood pressure levels in order to diagnose hypertension (Martin, 2008). Hypertension is regarded to be one of the most common non-communicable diseases. The Globe Health Organization reported in 2002 that roughly 600 million individuals were suffering from hypertension globally, which caused an estimated 50 million premature deaths and accounted for 13% of all fatalities globally (Medhi et al., 2006).

According to the World Health Organization's Global Burden of Hypertension study (2002), statistics revealed that more than a quarter of the world's adult population (almost one billion people) had hypertension in 2000, with the number expected to rise by over 60% (1.56 billion people) by 2025. According to the World Health Organization, 26.4 percent of the world's population had hypertension in 2000, and it is projected that by 2025, one in every three individuals over the age of 20 would be affected by this condition (Kearney et al., 2005). It is also believed that the prevalence of hypertension is increasing in developing nations. It is considered among the major causes of death and morbidity among the older population (Murray et al.,

1996). The prevalence of hypertension in Delhi's urban population was found to be 11 % among males and 12 percent among females between 1984 and 1987, according to research conducted during those years (Gopinath et al., 1994; Chadha et al.,1997). After completing an investigation in 2005 on a sample of people aged 40 and under, it was discovered that the prevalence of hypertension in the urban population of Chandigarh was 32.3 % (Kar and Thakur, 2007). Over the previous three decades, the prevalence of hypertension in India has grown by approximately 30 times among urban Indian inhabitants and by approximately 10 times among rural Indian people (Gupta, 2006). Age is a major predictor of the prevalence and severity of hypertension, both of which increase with age (Evans and Rose, 1971). The senior population the fastest increasing group in both developed and developing nations has the highest incidence of hypertension, with the highest prevalence in both developed and developing countries. An investigation by Waldestin et al. (2005) also revealed that the prevalence of hypertension in older persons aged 60 and above was greater than 60% in one research (Oparil 2006). Introduction According to a WHO study published in 2002, the life expectancy of individuals in developing nations has grown, and substantial changes have been seen in the lifestyles and socio-economic conditions of those who live in such countries. There have been reports of people in underdeveloped nations embracing western ways of living. Increasing urbanization, industrialization, and the ageing of the population all had a significant impact on the rising incidence of hypertension (Kornitzer et al., 1999; Erdin and Aran, 2004).

In emerging nations, such as India, there have been substantial changes in people's lives, with falling rates of communicable diseases and rising rates of non-communicable diseases (Erdin and Aran, 2004). However, hypertension is not well controlled because of the acute lack of health-care resources and infrastructure (Kornitzer et al., 1999; Mishra et al., 2006). Researchers have discovered that lifestyle-related risk factors, such as excess body weight, a lack of physical activity, a high intake of fat and salt, and excessive alcohol consumption, can all contribute to the development of hypertension in the north Indian population. Research has identified these risk factors as possible risk factors for the north Indian population (Yadav et al., 2008; Walia et al., 2014).

1.3 QUALITY OF LIFE:

The term "quality of life" is a new moniker for an ancient concept. It's a euphemism for people's "wellbeing" and the environment in which they live. For any individual, Quality of Life refers to a collection of desires that, when met, make the person happy or content. On the other hand, human desires seldom achieve a level of total pleasure, save for a concise period of time, since as one want is gratified, another emerges to take its place. As a result, Quality of Life differs from person to person and from location to place and throughout time.

Despite the obstacles we face, we should not let this dissuade us from our attempts to define and assess the quality of life. A great deal has been accomplished in the last fifteen years in terms of developing reliable measures of wellbeing, understanding how different aspects of life quality are related to one another, and reporting how people from a wide range of national and demographic backgrounds assess their wellbeing in terms of both life as a whole and numerous particular areas of life.

The need to address a basic underlying question becomes increasingly important: How do individuals come to feel the way they do about their wellbeing? While this is a topic that has not yet been thoroughly investigated, at least three distinct approaches have been briefly outlined.

In the early studies of the topic, it was discovered that traditional demographic or social categorization variables—e.g., race and ethnicity—were not predictive of the outcome. When it comes to most self-assessment of life quality, factors such as age, gender, race, educational level, household income, marital status, and stage in the family life cycle have only a minimal, if any, association with it. The relationships that do appear are in the expected directions (e.g., assessments of health decline with age, and evaluations of material wellbeing increase with income), but demographic and social classification factors do not appear to have the potential to be the major explainers of variation in perceived wellbeing. A third strategy is to integrate the ideas of perceived wellbeing developed by the social indicators movement with some of the most promising concepts in psychology. People's sense of wellbeing is something that psychologists are interested in, and they should have something to offer to the discussion.

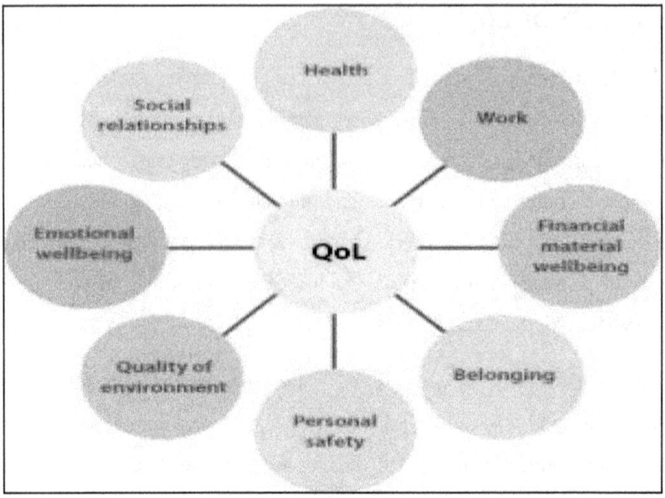

Source: https://www.proyectohuci.com.

According to this viewpoint, there are a number of different areas of living, which leads to a method to measuring the quality of life based on this viewpoint. Individuals' overall perceptions of the quality of their lives are influenced by the domains that they are involved in. Family and friends, job, neighbourhood (shelter), community, health, education, and spirituality are all included in the domains listed above.

Quality of Life (QOL) As a health result in and of itself, quality of life is increasingly recognized as the ultimate goal of all health interventions, and as such, it is becoming increasingly important. According to the World Health Organization, health is characterized by the absence of illness and disability and the presence of physical, mental, and social wellbeing on a person's part. Over the course of more than 50 years, this definition has been in force. When evaluating the efficacy of their interventions, health care providers may be tempted to focus solely on medical outcomes; however, any person with diabetes will tell you that these outcomes are significant only insofar as they affect the physical, emotional, and social wellbeing—that is, the individual's quality of life—of the individual. As Dr. Polonsky points out, the concept of quality of life (QOL) is becoming more and more common as an outcome variable when it comes to biobehavioral research. Although it is a multidimensional and dynamic notion, it is related to, but distinct from other ideas such as well-being, health status, life satisfaction, and hope (KING CR, 1998).

The phrase "health-related quality of life" refers to the level of contentment with one's health that is associated with a particular health condition or set of health conditions or symptoms. It is the monetary value assigned to the duration of life as impacted by impairments, functional states, 31 perceptions, and social opportunities that are altered as a result of illness, injury, treatment, and policy. HRQOL is measured in terms of years of life lived. Shumaker S, Naughton M, and others (Shumaker and Naughton, 1995). When it comes to diabetes, the term "quality of life" (QOL) may be regarded of as an organized way of talking about the human side of diabetes, such as the perceived difficulty of living with the disease (Polonsky W.2004). Different clinical features of diabetes patients, as well as the types of issues they encounter, can all play a role in determining an individual's overall perception of their quality of life. Being diabetic affects not just physical function (for example, decreased energy and physical limitations), but also psychological wellbeing (for example, sadness and stress, as well as overall wellbeing) and social relationships (for example, loneliness and isolation) (Von et al., 2005). The quality of life and the perception of disease in people with diabetes are affected by a variety of factors, including the type of diabetes. The impact of stress on the quality of life (QOL) and other patients' psychological characteristics and conditions is undeniably significant. However, personal sociodemographic characteristics and gender are also significant factors that can interfere at the same time (Wandell, 2000) and are closely associated with self-rated health (Jonnson, P et al., 2001). To achieve this goal, several elements that may influence the quality of life (QOL), such as related and sociodemographic characteristics, are taken into consideration and connected to stress. According to research, the way an individual evaluates their own life circumstances has a substantial influence on the individual's overall quality of life. People's perceptions of the impact of diabetes on their lives and relationships will change as a result of these differences. Health-related quality of life should be evaluated in the context of the patient's assessment of his or her own health and wellbeing, including physical, psychological, and social functioning (Polonsky, 2000).

1.3.1 Diabetes and quality of life:

The rigours of diabetes management can have a significant influence on one's mood, both in the short and long term. Several patients may get persistently disappointed, disheartened, and/or angered as a result of a condition that, despite their best efforts, does not appear to be responding to their efforts. Also possible is a sense of helplessness or despondency over the likelihood of preventing long-term problems. Finding a means to incorporate diabetes in one's life and confronting the sense of death that diabetes may evoke can be a tough and emotional battle for many people. This may be particularly problematic at those specific points in the natural history of the illness when diabetes suddenly appears to be very "real," such as at the time of diagnosis, when insulin is first administered, and when long-term complications begin to manifest themselves, among other things.

In addition, chronically elevated blood glucose levels may lead to persistent fatigue, which can exacerbate depressed mood. Similarly, frequent hypoglycemic episodes can be exhausting, debilitating, discouraging, and potentially quite frightening. Facing a disease that is often difficult and confusing to manage, patients may feel a pervading sense of helplessness that detracts significantly from the overall sense of wellbeing. Patients' reported emotional distress as a result of diabetes-related symptoms, self-care, relevant problematic circumstances, and larger diabetes concerns may be examined in order to measure this component of the patient experience.

1.3.2 Impact of Diabetes on physical functioning of patients:

Diabetes can have a negative impact on physical health in a variety of ways. The development of long-term problems and the implications of these complications are the most well-known. There is a considerable reduction in perceived quality of life when patients suffer from vision impairment, heart illness, end stage renal disease, impotence, or peripheral neuropathy, which can result in chronic discomfort or, in the worst case scenario, an amputation. In addition, the patient's capacity to participate in enjoyable activities will be diminished, and his ability to operate independently may be compromised as well. Gregg and colleagues (2000) have shown that diabetes is a significant cause of physical impairment in adults, and that these disabilities can have a significant impact on their overall quality of life. They discovered that coronary heart disease was the most significant factor to disability, with stroke affecting males more than women. Obesity, on the other hand, was found to be a significant influence, with women being the most affected.

The loss of physical ability in the lower extremities was also a significant factor to the overall decline in quality of life. The second issue to consider is the possibility of short-term problems. Recurrent hypoglycemia episodes or recurrent infections will almost certainly negatively influence one's overall quality of life. Hypoglycemia can cause a variety of adverse symptoms in diabetic patients, including fatigue and dizziness. Researchers have shown that hypoglycemia has a significant negative influence on the wellbeing, productivity, and life quality of persons who have type 2 diabetes. The third main element relates to physical symptoms and lifestyle changes that occur as a result of the diabetes treatment regimen's requirements. Someone who is adhering to a tight insulin regimen may believe that he or she must avoid going out to nightclubs or driving because of recurring hypoglycemia while on insulin. This might lead to treatment dissatisfaction, which can have an impact on how well the condition is managed. This results in poor diabetic management, as well as additional mental discomfort. As a result of the metabolic process, a negative reinforcing loop is created.

1.3.3 Impact of Diabetes on social relationships of patients:

In certain patients, the mere existence of diabetes might have an impact on the quantity and quality of their relationships. As patients begin to make adjustments in their daily routines in order to better control their diabetes, loved ones may become resentful. Alternatively, friends or family members may start to press the patient for self-care adjustments even when the patient is reluctant to do so; this is especially true in the case of a young diabetes patient who is still growing. In any scenario, it is easy to begin to feel isolated by diabetes, to feel different and unsupported, and to believe that no one understands what it is truly like to live with diabetes. Jacobson and colleagues (2004) monitored a group of young individuals with Type I Diabetes for a period of time. These were compared to a sample of people who were similar in age. In general, the diabetic group reported fewer friendships, and they reported less trust and a sense of close friendship in their love connections than the general population.

1.4 SELF EFFICACY:

"Self-efficacy is the conviction in one's own ability to perform well in a particular scenario," according to Bandura (1986); gist (1987). Higher levels of self-efficacy are associated with greater levels of perseverance. Individuals establish and develop a self-perception of competence that is critical to the achievement of their goals and the ability to exert influence over their surroundings, among other things. In turn, their motivation and performance are affected; 'those with high self-efficacy ascribe failure to effort, whereas persons with low self-efficacy attribute failure to ability,' says one researcher. 'Pethe and Dhar (1999)' are two authors who have written about this topic. Individuals have the ability to affect their own behaviour through self-regulation mechanisms, according to Bandura (1986). Self-observation, self-evaluation, and self-reaction are some of the mechanisms used by the brain. The subprocesses of self-concept, self-esteem, and values are all involved in the process of self-evaluation.

Individuals are more likely to engage in tasks in which they feel competent and confident than they are to engage in tasks in which they do not feel competent and confident. It is critical to accurately evaluate the link between self-efficacy, result expectations, and knowledge and competence. The amount to which people feel their actions will result in a specific consequence is referred to as their outcome expectation. An efficacy expectation refers to the extent to which they feel they will be able to achieve a specific result.

Source: https://www.semanticscholar.org

According to Bandura, there is a distinction between thinking that something can happen and believing that one can make it happen (1977). 'Self-efficacy is a more strong predictor of decisions than either predicted results or actual abilities and knowledge relevant to the behaviour in issue,' according to the research. Even though people's knowledge and skills, and even their experiences and expectations, may serve as precursors to and creators of their self-efficacy beliefs, the filtering effect of the created belief ultimately screens, redefines, distorts, or reshapes subsequent efforts and new information, according to Pajaras (2002).

Second, people's self-beliefs influence how much effort they put into a particular activity and how long they are willing to put in to keep going. The stronger the perception of efficacy, the larger the amount of effort expended and the greater the amount of perseverance. This results in a sort of self-fulfilling prophesy since perseverance, which is linked with high efficacy, is likely to lead to improved performance, which enhances the individual's sense of effectiveness. As opposed to this, the giving in that is linked with effectiveness restricts the possibility for enhancing one's own view of oneself. Individuals who are learning a task and those who are practising existing abilities have different effects of effectiveness.

An individual's self-efficacy refers to his or her belief in one's own ability to carry out a certain action. In the words of Bandura (1986), Self-efficacy is defined as "people's assessments of their ability to plan and execute courses of action necessary to achieve specified sorts of performances." Self-Efficacy Comes from a Variety of Places "Beliefs about personal efficacy are learnt from five primary sources: enactive mastery, which is learning by experience; vicarious experience, which is learning via observation of events and/or other people; verbal persuasion; physiological condition; and emotional state" (DeVellis & DeVellis, 2001). The most effective source of efficacy, according to Bandura (1977), is enactive mastery experience, which is learning through personal experience. Enactive mastery experience, or learning by personal experience, is the most authentic proof that one can do the job successfully. It is possible to cognitively analyze both successful and failed experiences, and the way these experiences are perceived can have an impact on one's self-efficacy. Other sources of Self-efficacy include witnessing events or the conduct of others, which Bandura termed "vicarious experience." Another type of efficacy information is verbal persuasion, precisely the correct kind of verbal feedback from a reliable source.

A person's physiological condition may also impact self-efficacy; for example, a highly stimulated bodily state causes one to predict failure. Not only does physical health matter, but a person's mood or affect states can have an impact on their feeling of self-efficacy. A positive mood condition increases a person's perception of self effectiveness, whereas a bad mood state decreases a person's sense of self-efficacy.

1.4.1 Self-efficacy and health

The findings of several studies in the health-related fields have revealed a substantial relationship between self-efficacy and health-promoting behaviour. A variety of theories and models have been developed to examine the relationship between self-efficacy and health-related attitudes and actions.

1. Social Cognitive Theory is a theory that explains how people think and behave. It was in 1986 that Bandura developed and renamed his original theory, which became known as the Social Cognitive Theory. According to Bandura's Social Cognitive Theory (1987), one's own feeling of control has an impact on one's ability to modify health behaviour. Efficacy refers to a person's personal cognitions and ideas about himself or herself that decide whether or not a health-related behaviour change will be begun, how much effort will be necessary, and how long that change will be sustained. It is possible to have both direct and indirect effects on one's own objectives, which can then have an impact on one's health habits. Self-efficacy is a powerful predictor of behaviour in a variety of health-related situations, including weight loss, quitting smoking, and recovery from illness (Seydel, Taal, & Wiegman, 1990; Shiffman et al., 2000), as well as regularly exercising (Schnoll & Zimmerman, 2001; Seydel, Taal, & (Show, Dzewaltowski & McElroy, 1992; Rovnaiak, Anderson, Winett, Stepphens, 2002).

2. According to Rosenstock's Health Belief Model (HBM), a psychological health behaviour change model, people's readiness to engage in health-promoting behaviour is explained by their beliefs about their own health. Later, in 1974, the model's application was extended to predict general compliance with medical advice. In the model, there are four components that together influence the likelihood of taking preventive action:

(1) perceived personal susceptibility to the disease

(2) perceived severity of disease

(3) perceived benefit of preventive action

(4) perceived barriers to taking preventive action

Health-related actions can be explained by any of these beliefs, either alone or in combination. The model has been further developed to include other variables, such as signals to action, motivational factors (age, gender, ethnicity, expertise, personality, and so on), and self efficacy. Rosenstock, Stretcher, and Becker (1988) expanded on the initial four beliefs in the Health Belief Model by include the belief in one's own ability to improve one's health. The majority of the time, people will not participate in something new until they believe or believe they can accomplish it. As a result, self-efficacy, or belief in one's own power to affect change in outcome, is a critical component of health behaviour change.

3. The Protection Motivation (PMT) hypothesis developed by Rogers (1975) seeks to understand the impact of fear appeals. Following this, more study into PMT resulted in the modification of PMT in 1983. According to Protection Motivation theory, various external and intrapersonal sources of information trigger two separate evaluation processes, which are referred to as threat and coping appraisals. Danger appraisal is concerned with an individual's judgments of the severity and vulnerability of a threat, and it is intended to prevent maladaptive behaviour. The presence of intrinsic incentives such as pleasure and extrinsic rewards such as social approbation, on the other hand, might raise the chance of maladaptive behaviours. The coping appraisal is the process of evaluating the coping reactions that the individual has to deal with the danger. Both response efficacy (belief that the recommended response would be effective in decreasing the threat) and Self-efficacy (belief that the individual possesses the ability to carry out the recommended response) have an impact on coping appraisal, which in turn increases the likelihood of an adaptive response. When it comes to forecasting a wide range of health-promoting activities and health compromising habits, this theory is quite

effective (Plotnikoff & Higginbotom, 1995, 1998 & 2002). The majority of the research findings indicated that Self-efficacy was a strong predictor of desire to engage in regular physical activity and consume a low-fat diet. PMT has been utilized in a number of studies in this field, particularly in connection to adherence to a medical regimen (Bennet et al., 1998, Palardy, Greening, Ott, Holderby, & Atchison, 1998, Norman, & Conner, 2003, Rudman et al., 1999).

4. The Theory of Reasoned Action and the Theory of Planned Behavior are two theories that explain why people do what they do. When Fishben and Ajen published their 'Theory of Reasoned Action' in the late 1960s, it was hailed as a breakthrough in the field of social cognition. It holds that a person's "intentions" are accountable for his or her health behaviour, and that intentions are decided by "Attitude" and "Social Norm" concerns held by that individual. A person's attitude toward a health habit can be either positive or negative based on what a person feels would be the likely consequence of individuals engaging in the action and how they evaluate those outcomes. Along with attitude, 'Social Norms,' which refer to societal pressure from significant others, whether or not a person should adopt certain health behaviours, is also a significant deciding factor in a person's intentions. Whether or not a person should adopt certain health behaviours is a big deciding factor behind a person's intentions. For example, a person who wishes to quit smoking must believe in the health advantages of quitting (Attitude), and the society in which the individual lives must disapprove of such conduct. Azen and Madden (1986) later updated and developed this theory, who renamed it the "Theory of Planned Behavior" after the two authors. The initial idea was expanded to include a new dimension called "Perceived Behavioral Control." "Perceived behavioural control" is comprised of two components: "Control beliefs" (how much control the person perceives over the circumstance) and "Self Efficacy" (if the person believes oneself or herself to be capable of doing the activity). It has an impact on health-related behaviour, both directly and indirectly (through intention). As a result, the theory is concerned with understanding the factors that influence specific health-related behaviour.

5. The transtheoretical model presented by Prochaska and DiClemente (1983), which defines the process of health behaviour change, is widely regarded as a

very significant model in the field. This model examines an individual's behavioural changes, his capacity to adjust to new conditions, his health, and his behaviour depending on a variety of factors. It is founded on four fundamental principles:

i) A person's self-efficacy is defined under the idea as their belief in their ability to achieve and maintain a positive change in their lives.

ii) Decisional Balance: In this theory, decisional balance is defined as the understanding that the benefits of engaging in a specific action exceed the disadvantages.

iii) In this section, we'll talk about the stages of change that a person goes through while adopting a healthy habit or choosing to stop engaging in an unhealthy activity. According to the theory, there are six stages: Precontemplation stage (the person is not ready to change and is resentful of suggestion), Contemplation stage (person considers change and welcomes suggestion), Preparation stage (person is actively interested in making change and seeking assistance from a health care provider for that), Action stage (undertaking an attempt to change), Maintenance stage (following a successful attempt to change), and Maintenance stage (following a successful attempt to change) (no temptation left in person for unhealthy behaviour).

iv) The process of change: The phrase "Process of Change" refers to the behavioural methods that may be utilized to bring about and maintain a transformation.

6. The Health Action Process Approach is a method of improving health. Developed by Schwarzer in 1992 and 2008 to describe, explain, and predict the process of health behaviour change, where "health behaviour change" refers to the transition from health-compromising behaviour to health-enhancing behaviour, the Health Action Process Approach is a framework for understanding, explaining, and predicting the process of health behaviour change. It is heavily influenced by Albert Bandura's Social Cognitive Theory. It distinguishes between two periods that adjust the implementation, initiation, and maintenance of health behaviours: the initial and maintenance phases. The

first phase is referred to as the "Motivation Phase," and during this phase, a person must feel motivated to begin a habit. During the motivation phase, risk perception and result expectations are important factors to consider. The second phase is referred to as the "Volitional Phase," and it is separated into three phases: planning, action, and maintenance. During the voluntary phase, a person becomes more inclined toward adopting a healthy behaviour. Distal predictors of conduct include risk perception, result expectations, and self-efficacy; middle-level mediators of intents; and volitional variables, such as action preparation, that are proximal predictors of activity. The idea posits that self-efficacy is vital at all phases but that it takes on different forms and functions at different times, such as fractional self-efficacy, coping self-efficacy, and recovery self-efficacy, among others.

Chronic disease Self-management is defined as a chronic disease patient's "capacity to manage symptoms, therapy, physical and psychological repercussions, and lifestyle modifications" in addition to their "ability to control their condition." Patients with chronic diseases are the primary caretakers for themselves and their families. Self-management, which consists of five core skills – problem solving, decision making, resource utilization, forming a patient–health-care provider partnership, and taking action – has emerged as the cornerstone of hypertension treatment, having been shown to significantly improve health-related behaviour and health status, as well as to reduce health-care utilization and expenditure. The elements that influence self-management, on the other hand, are numerous and complicated. Having a complete knowledge of numerous aspects of self-management has significant implications for the design of self-management therapies and for the overall wellbeing of people with hypertension.

Disease knowledge and social support appear to act as mediators in the self-management of chronic diseases. Disease knowledge may assist patients in better understanding their health issues and treatments, which may result in good changes in health behaviour. Disease knowledge is also crucial in developing self-efficacy abilities. It is defined as companionship, informational, esteem-building, and instrumental resources supplied by a social network consisting of family members and friends to an individual. Preliminary research has demonstrated that social support has the ability to dramatically affect self-management behaviour, either directly or indirectly, through the development of self-efficacy. Although well-intentioned, incorrect counsel from friends and family members may unintentionally negatively impact self-management behaviour, this is not always the case. Supporting the time being, the evidence for connections between disease awareness or social support and self-management behaviour is inconclusive.

1.5 SUICIDAL TENDENCY:

The term 'Suicide' comes from the word 'Suicidium,' which was first used by Desfontaines in the 16th century. Around the same period, the words' Porpriicidium' (Latin) and 'avtoxeipia' (Greek) were also formed. The word 'Suicidium,' according to stietencorn, refers to the act of self-destruction.

For the person who commits suicide, suicide appears to be a permanent solution to a transient issue or life event. The person feels that their pain will continue or worsen, and that they have no other choice than to die. (Department of health, New York State, 2011). The majority of persons who commit suicide feel conflicted about ending their life. When individuals are alone and in a condition of intense psychological suffering and misery, unable to perceive their issues objectively or evaluate other courses of action, they make this irrevocable decision (Carson 2005). Approximately 40% of persons who commit suicide had previously attempted suicide. Suicidal ideation, or thoughts about suicide, is a significant risk factor for suicide. Many people, however, have suicidal thoughts but never commit or attempt suicide. This is especially true for people who are nearing the end of their lives or who are suffering from a terrible chronic condition (Department of health, New York state, 2011).

"Suicide is a deliberate act of self-induced annihilation, best understood as a multifaceted malaise in a needy individual who identifies an issue for which suicide is seen as the greatest solution," writes Edwin Shneidman (1985).

As per the report of the World Health Organization (WHO), more than 800,000 people die by suicide each year, resulting in a global mortality rate of 16 per 100,000, or one suicide death every 40 seconds. 135,000 (17%) of the 800,000 suicides occur in India, a country with 17.5 percent of the world's population. Suicide rates have grown by 60% globally in the previous 45 years. Suicide is one of the three main causes of death among people aged 15-44 years in various countries, with the other two being accidents and HIV, and it is the second leading cause of death among those aged 10-24 years, with accidents being the first. Suicide attempts, which are up to 20 times more common than completed suicides, are not included in these data. In Europe and North America, mental illnesses (especially depression and alcohol use disorders) are considered to be the leading cause of suicide; nevertheless, impulsiveness is a significant component in Asian nations.

1.5.1 Epidemiology of suicide:

Suicide is a worldwide issue that affects people from all walks of life; 75 % of global suicides occur in poor and middle-income nations. Suicide was the 15th most prominent cause of death in the globe, accounting for 1.4 percent of all fatalities.

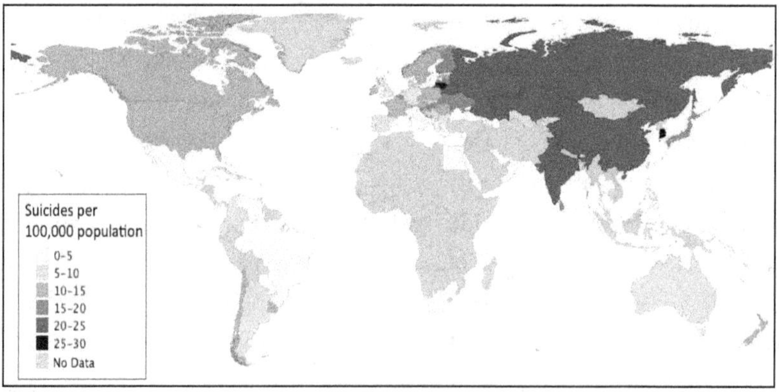

Source: https://www.businessinsider.com

During the decadal period from 2004 to 2014, more than one lakh people in India committed suicide on an annual basis. During the decade (2004–2014), the number of suicides in the country increased by 15.8 percent (1, 31,666 in 2014 from 113,697 in 2004). Each year, a rise in the number of suicides was reported until 2011, after which there was a downward trend. The population has grown by 14.6 percent during the last decade, while the suicide rate has climbed by 1.0 percent (from 10.5 in 2004 to 10.6 in 2014). During the decade, the suicide rate has shown a mixed pattern (2004-2014). Suicide rates, on the other hand, have been falling since 2010.

1.5.2 Suicide case in Gujarat:

Every day throughout the state, news of suicides is reported. Suicides are being reported as a result of a common problem or reason. Suicide data for 2019 have been provided by the National Crime Records Bureau. Gujarat has 7655 persons who have committed suicide in 2019. There are 5168 men and 2486 females in this population. In comparison to 2018, however, there is a 1.8 percent decline in 2019. In 2018, there were 7793 suicides. Family issues accounted for the largest number of suicides in the state, with 2139, followed by 1733 for inexplicable reasons and 1634 for sickness. So far, 106 individuals have died as a result of poverty, 219 as a result of unemployment, and 495 as a result of a love affair.

Due to sickness, including cancer, disability, and mental illness, people of the state committed suicide in 1634, citizens of the state in 2019. There are 1091 men and 543 women among them. 800 people have committed suicide as a result of mental illness, whereas 645 have committed suicide as a result of chronic disease.

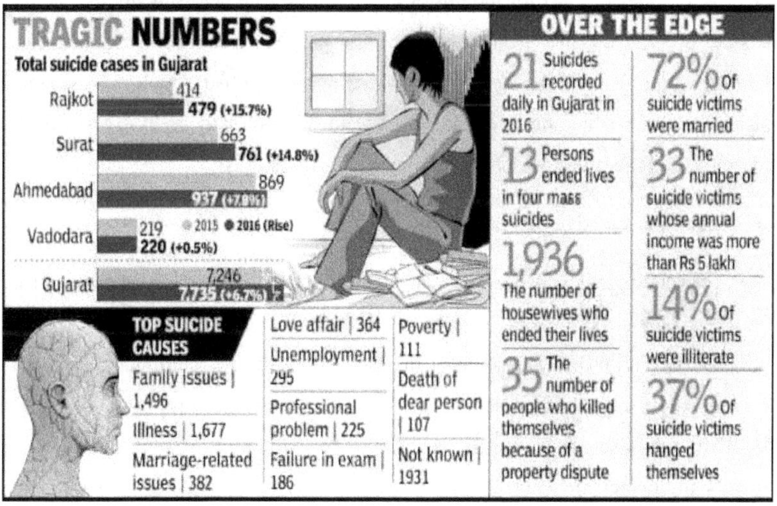

Source: https://www. timesofindia.indiatimes.com.

We must consider Adler's concepts of "style of life" and "inferiority complex" in order to comprehend his explanation of suicide. Those who attempt suicide have a pampered life style, which means they are dependent and incapable of solving their own problems, and they lack in fellow-feeling and social interest. They are unable to confidently resolve their work, friendship, and sexual difficulties. Karen Harney, on the other hand, has adopted Freud's idea of death. She refuses to accept the dynamics as presented by the latter. She believes that society has a significant impact on individuals. If one's neurotic desires to harm others become hard to control, one may destroy oneself.

1.5.3 Psychological aspects of suicide:

According to Shneidman, the pioneer of suicidology, the psychological component of suicide is the problem-solving decision – the best solution to the perceived problem – which is the primary trunk. A self-destructive behaviour is what it is, not a medical condition. It is the tormented and tunnelled reasoning of the persons while they are in a condition of inner-felt, terrible feeling. According to his definition, committing suicide entails a conception of death; it is a mix of an individual's conscious purpose and want to die, as well as his action to carry out that goal. Suicidal crises lasts just a brief period of time, which can be measured in hours or days, and it does not last for months or years at a time. When someone is suicidal, their state of mind is one of ambivalence. The psychological image of a suicidal individual would be that he develops preparations for self-destruction while also fantasizing about rescue and intervention. In a nutshell, he will be torn between the desire to die and the desire to continue living.

1.5.4 Social perspective of suicide:

A psychological as well as a social component to the suicide syndrome exists. Because the human being is a social creature, and without communication, he loses his humanity, social isolation marks the beginning of the culmination of self-destruction because the human being is a social being who loses his humanity (Breed, 1972). Even while social circumstances such as widowhood or marital instability are frequently implicated in feelings of loneliness, it has been said that it is often the psychological makeup of the suicidal people that inhibits the formation of good connections. DL Trout (1980) defined formalized euphemism as People who are vulnerable to prejudice, such as refugees and migrants; indigenous peoples; lesbian, homosexual, bisexual, transgender, and intersex people; and convicts, have higher suicide rates than the general population. In India, unemployment and poverty are both factors that contribute to suicide.

1.5.5 Clinical perspective of suicide:

In DSM IV Suicidal behaviour is seen in the context of a variety of mental disorders, most commonly bipolar disorder, major depressive disorder, schizophrenia, schizoaffective disorder, anxiety disorders (in, panic disorders associated with catastrophic content and PTSD flashbacks), substance use disorders (especially alcohol use disorders), borderline personality disorder, antisocial personality disorder, eating disorders, and adjustment disorders. It rarely manifests in individuals with no discernible pathology, unless, it is undertaken because of a painful medical condition with the intention of drawing attention to martyrdom for political or religious reasons, or in partners in a suicide pact, both of which are excluded from this diagnosis, or when third-party informants wish to conceal the nature of the behavior

1.5.6 Legal perspective of suicide:

Suicide has been a crime in some parts of the world, while suicide has been decriminalized in some western societies, yet the act is still stigmatized and discouraged. In other contexts, such as ancient Rome and medieval Japan, suicide was seen as a defiant act of extreme personal freedom against perceived or actual tyrants (Romero (ed) Smith and Hogan's Criminal Law 2011). Suicide is prohibited in India, and anybody who survives it might face a prison sentence of up to one year and a fine under Section 309 of the Indian Penal Code. There have been several petitions to have the passage removed from various sources. It has also been suggested by the Indian Law Commission that the clause be removed from the statute. A measure in this respect was introduced in the parliament, but it did not become law due to a lack of support.

1.5.7 Models and theories related to suicide:

Historically researchers have proposed several theoretical rationales for suicidal behaviour. As a group, these theories tend to be abstract, even impersonal, and therefore they missed something in depicting the emotional charge of the suicidal behaviour. 1. Social theories of suicide (Durkheim 1897). According to Durkheim (1897), It is possible for people to have a certain amount of commitment to their communities, which he refers to as "social integration." It is possible that individuals with abnormally high or low levels of social integration will experience an increase in suicide rates. Low levels of social integration have this effect because low levels of social integration result in a disorganised society, causing people to turn to suicide as a last resort, whereas high levels cause people to kill themselves in order to avoid becoming a burden on society.

1.5.7.1 Escape theory

(Baumeister 1990). As proposed by Edwin Shneidman, (1985), escape has been recognized as a central driving force underpinning suicidal motives. Baumeister describes, "Suicide as Escape from the Self." Baumeister (1990) Leenaars, (2004) and Williams (2001) have developed models and therapeutic interventions of suicidal behaviour with escape as a key component. Baumeister's main argument was that suicide is the end of a complex series of casual steps driven by an attempt to escape from painful self-awareness.

A negative experience (or a change in the severity of existing or chronic negative experiences) is said to be the catalyst for self and social comparison 17 processes, in which the individual attempts to make sense of why something happened or why circumstances have changed, according to Baumeister (1990). If the resulting negative attributions are internal, they can lead to emotions of blame and negative self-implications, which can then lead to negative self-awareness (such as feelings of inadequacy and guilt) and negative affect (such as depression). It has been characterised as lower level awareness/thinking that leads in "the elimination of higher meanings from awareness" in an attempt to escape these unpleasant cognitions and feelings. Cognitive deconstruction is a technique used to try to escape these painful cognitions and feelings (Baumeister,1990:92). It is believed that, in addition to numbing unpleasant ideas, cognitive deconstruction increases disinhibitions, so that social or moral standards (internal obstacles to action) are reduced or eliminated, increasing the likelihood of suicide.

1.5.7.2 Diathesis Model:

Mann and Arango (1992) proposed a stress–diathesis model based on the integration of neurobiology and psychopathology, which still forms the basis for much of the current research in suicidology. Emphasis; was therefore given to changes in the serotonin system and how these may represent a constitutional risk factor as opposed to a state-dependent risk factor for suicidal behaviour. Psychosocial crises and psychiatric disorders may constitute the stress component of stress–diathesis models of suicidal behavior (Mann et al., 1999). It is difficult to separate the impact of psychosocial adversity from that of psychiatric illness. Psychiatric disorders can lead to job loss, to breakup of marriages or relationships, or to the failure to form such relationships. Moreover, psychiatric illness and psychosocial adversity can combine to increase stress on the person (Mann, 2003). Suicidal individuals may experience suicide-related cognitions, negative effect, and the motivation to engage in suicidal behaviour in the context of a depressive episode and following exposure to triggering life events.

1.5.7.3 Bio-psychosocial theory:

Kinderman (2005) proposed the bio-psychosocial theory, which states that a greater consideration has to be given to the role of psychological processes in the etiology and treatment of mental disorders. He restates Engel's (1980) original formulation that the biological, psychological and social perspectives, which comprise the bio-psychosocial model, are equal partners in the etiology of mental health problems. Rory C.O'Connor (2007) has extended Kinderman's (2005) model to explain suicidal behaviour

1.5.7.4 Interpersonal theory of suicide:

Specifically, the interpersonal-psychological explanation of suicidal behaviour (Joiner, 2005) suggests that an individual will not die by suicide unless and until she or he has both the desire and the ability to do so. According to the idea, when people retain two certain psychological states in their minds at the same time, and when they do so for a long enough period of time, they acquire a wish to die. Perceived burdensomeness and a sense of poor belongingness or social alienation are the two psychological states under consideration. The belief that one's presence is a burden on one's family, friends, and/or society is referred to as perceived burdensomeness. This point of view gives rise to the notion that "my death will be worth more than my life to my family, friends, society, and so on." A poor sense of belongingness is defined as the feeling of being estranged from others and not being a valuable member of a family, circle of friends, or other valued group of individuals.

1.5.8 Prevention of suicide.

In 1999, the U.S.Surgeon General called for the development of a national strategy to prevent suicide, which resulted in a comprehensive plan that includes many levels of prevention. (USDHHS, 2001) This strategy has taken the approach of suicide as a public health problem that needs to be controlled. The plan emphasizes in identifying risk factors, then developing, implementing and evaluating interventions. The United States is not the only country to recognize this problem; nations throughout the world have formulated national strategies for suicide prevention (Beautrais 2005) The U.S. national strategy includes all three approaches to intervention, but many of its goals are oriented toward changing the environment. This program aims to change societal attitudes toward disorders such as depression, which elevate the risk for suicide, and toward seeking mental health care, which decreases risk. Goals also include making the means of suicide less available , such as limiting access to guns and drugs.

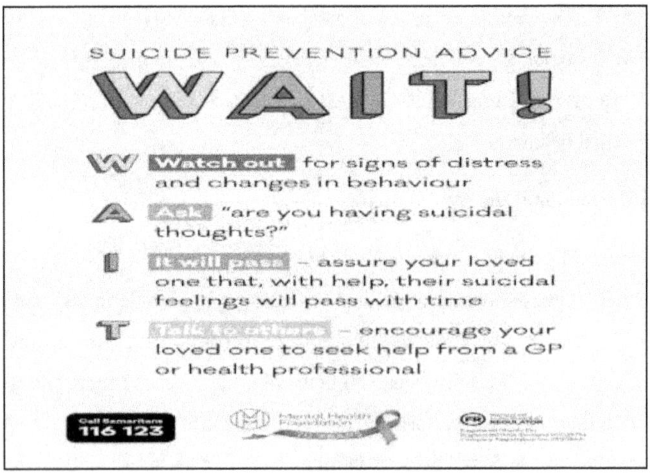

Source: https://lh3.googleusercontent.com/proxy

For young people, suicide is often an impulsive action , and access to a gun makes the chances of death more likely . Restricting access to firearms, especially loaded gun, can be beneficial (Grossman et al., 2005). Training or mandating parents to take precautions with their firearms as well as other strategies to limit access may be helpful. Restricting access to drugs, can also make suicide more difficult.

Individuals who are at risk behavior will be targets for special interventions, as will family and friends of suicide victims. Suicide prevention programs often include training faculty to identify warning signs, forming mental health teams for counseling at-risk students, and developing written formal suicide policies (King,2001).

Other components of school-based interventions include training parents to identify problems in their children. Most of these programs demonstrate an increase in knowledge about suicide, but few have demonstrated lowered suicides or attempts. The signs of Suicide (SOS) were the first school-based prevention program that succeeded in lowering suicide attempts (Aseltine & DeMartino,2004). This program not only teaches suicide awareness but also provides a brief screening for depression, a major risk factor for suicide.

Chapter-II

REVIEW OF LITERATURE

2.1 INTRODUCTION:

A review of literature helps the way for new researches in a particular field and sheds light on various aspects. It provides authenticity to the new research studies. Hence, collection of background information not only facilitates study but also save effort, time and money, also providing valuable and relevant information for further researches.It is necessary to study related research conducted previously before conducting study of various problems in any subject. It makes research work tension free. It relieves the stress of research and serves as a planning tool for researchers. With this goal in mind, the researcher has displayed the findings of earlier studies. "The related literature in any discipline is the basis on which all work is built," states Walter R. Borg (1983) of research and research literature. To make research activity more efficient, a research study is unavoidable. It leads to advancement in life.

It provides synthetic and synoptic understanding of the research works already conducted in the same field over a period of time. It provides some insight regarding strong points and limitations of the previous studies and enables the researcher to improve his own investigation (Panigrahi, 1999). The present review of literature will reflect the conceptual phenomenon as well as the variables under study to measure empirical implication. The present chapter will focus on review of literature related to quality of life, self-efficacy and suicidal tendency of patients with hypertension and diabetes.

2.2 LITERATURE RELATED TO QUALITY OF LIFE:

Rita O Akonoghrere., et al. (2020) carried out a study on 122 people, 72 of whom were men (58.5 %). The mean Physical Component Summary (PCS) of quality of life was 47.75, and the mean Mental Component Summary (MCS) was 46.7.92. The average systolic blood pressure was 139.6mmHg 19.1, with an average diastolic blood pressure of 82.8mmHg 13.3. All of the analyses yielded Beta values greater than 0.05, indicating that there were no significant predictors of quality of life. The quality of life was generally poor, falling short of the 50 percent US benchmark.

However, the physical component scale was the most impacted. The patients' c linical status and socio-demographics were not predictive of their quality of life.

Sholihat, N.K, Utami V.V.F.R,(2020) conducted a study with a aim to assess the health-related quality of life of patients with diabetes and hypertension, The Indonesian version of the EQ-5D-5L was used to conduct a cross-sectional study on 267 diabetic and 349 hypertension patients in six community health clinics. The Indonesian value set, as well as the percentages of the problem in each dimension, were used to generate the EQ-5D-5L utility index. The statistical analyses were done to see if there were any changes in the EQ-5D utility index between diabetes and hypertension, as well as differences in study characteristics. The mean EQ-5D-5L score for diabetic patients was 0.879 0.115, whereas it was 0.879 0.116 for hypertensive patients. The EQ visual analogue scale (EQ-VAS) scores for diabetes and hypertension were 80.030 12.893 and 79.180 14.22, respectively. Pain/discomfort was the most commonly reported condition (67.42 percent in diabetes and 62.75 percent in hypertension), followed by anxiety/depression (36.33 percent in diabetes and 41.11 percent in hypertension). There was no significant difference between diabetic and hypertensive patients' utility index values ($p = 0.056$) or EQ-VAS scores ($p = 0.573$). The occupational status of diabetes patients had a substantial impact on their HRQOL ($p = 0.016$). This study implies that in order to enhance the lives of chronic disease patients, healthcare practitioners should focus more on pain and depression management.

Khoirunnisa, et al. (2020) used a cross-sectional study design to create a descriptive study. The study participants were all hypertensive outpatients from several health centres in Bandar Lampung. The Indonesian SF-36 measure was employed in this study. The patient's demographic information, such as gender, age, education, occupation, and marital status, were collected, as were fields pertaining to the study subjects' health histories, such as the duration of hypertension, complications, and the number of antihypertensive medicines ingested. Age, marital status, and length of hypertension are factors that influence the physical domain, while gender, marital status, duration of hypertension, complications, and the number of medicines are influential factors in the mental domain, according to the results of multivariate analysis.

Azar, F.E, et al. (2020) demonstrated that people with hypertension had a mediocre and unfavourable quality of life. The most closely connected demographic characteristics to patients' quality of life were educational level, occupation, and duration of hypertension. The level of education demonstrated a substantial link with all categories of quality of life among these demographic variables. It is recommended that patients get moral education as a first step toward improving their quality of life.

Abedini, M.R., Bijari, B., Miri, Z. et al.(2020) revealed that Numerous factors, such as sex, career, DM history, and the presence of co-morbidities such as neuropathy and nephropathy, affect the quality of life of people with type-2 diabetes. As a result, considerably more focus should be placed on the primary drivers of HRQoL in order to identify and implement relevant policies for better DM care and, as a result, improved QoL for diabetes patients in this region.

John, R. et al. (2019) concluded in a study that one of the fewer studies in India assessing QoL of diabetics' using an "Indian" instrument. Family history of diabetes, presence of hypertension, BMI, educational status, married status, income status, treatment type, and complications were found to have statistical associations with different QoL domains. They recommend that QoL be assessed as part of a diabetic treatment plan. Although this study shows promising results in Indian patients, more quality-of-life research is needed in the country to further understand the topic and assist policymakers.

Diabetes, according to ***Trikkalinou, A. et al. (2017)***, is still a serious modern epidemic. QoL is a fundamental therapeutic goal in tackling the issues of combating the epidemic. There is still a lot of misunderstanding about what QoL, HRQoL, and diabetes-specific QoL mean. Numerous psychometric techniques have recently been created in order to assess QoL, HRQoL, and diabetes-specific QoL. Although there are variances in ethnicity, environment, gender, socioeconomic situation, culture, career, dietary and lifestyle habits, diabetes affects main components of QoL. More specifically, when dementia is present, there is a cognitive component.

More specifically the physical component, particularly when there are coexisting obes ity complications such as CAD renal failure, diabetic neuropathy, or retinopathy, or c o morbidities; (2) the psychological component, particularly type 1 in younger subject s and when there is depression; (3) the social component by destroying family ties and friendships; and (4) the mental cognitive component, particularly when there are coex isting obesity complications such as CAD renal failure, diabetic neuropathy.

Tirumalesh M, & Chandraiah K (2017) observed that The quality of life experiences of male and female patients were found to be different, but there was no difference in the stress experience. The study also found that there are differences in stress levels between patients with sedentary and non-sedentary employment, but no changes in quality of life. The study also found that type 1 diabetes patients had higher stress levels and lower quality of life than type 2 diabetic patients. The study also found that there are variations in stress levels between patients who exercise and those who do not exercise, but no differences in quality of life.

Ruchira Pangtey (2016) conducted a study on total 269 hypertensive had mean age (58.25 ± 10.35) respectively. Further results indicated statistically significant negative association. Whereas, number of symptoms, systolic blood pressure and duration of illness highlighted statistically significant positive correlation. Female participants had significantly poorer quality of life than male counterparts. Most of the research subjects had an average to poor quality of life. Age, gender, number of symptoms, systolic blood pressure and number of medications may be significant predictors to improve quality of life in patients with hypertension.

Kaliyaperumal, S. et al. (2016) reported that the need of effective therapy and hypertension awareness on the patient's mental and emotional well-being is highlighted. Hypertension is a preventable cause of death, and appropriate treatment can significantly minimize cardiovascular problems. According to our findings, the mental and emotional components of hypertension patients' poor quality of life were more important than physical health in determining their quality of life. Future research could concentrate on proper patient intervention to improve hypertension patients' quality of life. Future research could concentrate on proper patient intervention to improve hypertension patients' quality of life. Doctors, nurses, and other health-care providers.

Bhandari, N. et al. (2016) revealed that in the physical domain, quality of life deteriorated with increasing age, non-formal education, and not cohabiting with a spouse. In the mental realm, however, quality of life was much lower when not living with a partner and having no formal education. The findings imply that hypertension patients receive counselling and detailed information about treatment, as well as signs and symptoms. In hypertension patients, screening for the effects of several variables such as rising age, female sex, not living with spouse, and non-formal education should be investigated. Furthermore, because of the rising morbidity and disability associated with cardio-vascular disorders such as hypertension, stakeholders should be increasingly concerned about policy.

Pichon-Riviere, A., et al.(2015) conducted a cross-sectional analysis of patients with T2DM over 21 years old who had not changed their baseline schedule in the previous 6 months and were treated with either Neutral Protamine Hagedorn insulin or Insulin Glargine. The recruitment took place in nine private diabetic doctors' offices in Buenos Aires, Argentina, between 2006 and 2007. The Audit of Diabetes Dependent Quality of Life (ADDQoL), a standardised diabetes-specific HRQoL questionnaire, was employed. The ADDQoL questionnaire is a tool that can be used in Argentina to evaluate diabetes treatment programmes by measuring the quality of life of individuals with diabetes. The QoL scores in our sample population were comparable to those reported in high-income nations. The findings of this study are expected to raise healthcare providers' knowledge of patients' perceived QoL and assist in overcoming the barriers that delay insulin treatment, primarily clinical inertia and patient resistance.

Ha et al. (2014) determined that hypertension patients residing in a rural area in southern Vietnam had a reasonable quality of life across all dimensions, with the exception of psychological health, which was rather low. Physical activity and marital status were significant independent factors that influenced all QOL dimensions. Physical and psychological health were both linked to poorer QOL as people got older. Women with hypertension rated their psychological health satisfaction lower than men. The presence of co-morbidity in hypertension patients is a significant health concern that influences their physical health satisfaction. In this situation, interventions aimed at enhancing the QOL of disadvantaged patients are required.

According to ***Spasia Ana et al. (2014)***, type 2 diabetic patients have a negative quality of life in all domains. Gender, age, and the presence of co-morbidities all demonstrated statistically significant differences in quality of life. The quality of life in older individuals was lower and was influenced by a variety of factors. Females had a lower quality of life than males, owing to less physical activity and fewer favourable social circumstances. Diabetic patients who were uncontrolled had a lower quality of life than diabetics who were under control. It is critical to improve the quality of life of diabetic people.

Vijayakumar K., Varghese R.T. (2010) indicated that the prevalence of lifestyle diseases such as diabetes is rapidly increasing in developing nations such as India. Given Indians' ethnic predisposition to develop diabetes and have low Health Related Quality of Life (HRQOL), as proven by many research, more efforts must be made to combat diabetes and the burden it imposes. Complications exacerbate the pain, and the rising costs of illness management exacerbate the poor quality of life.

Chouhan, V. L. and Vyas, S. (2006) investigated diabetics' stress and adjustment coping techniques. The sample included 90 people, both male and female, between the ages of 35 and 45 (n=30 in each group). The degree of all four above-mentioned stresses was higher for both high and low blood sugar groups, and average for normal responders, according to mean scores. In comparison to diabetes patients, normal respondents had a higher level of adjustment. The computed F ratio was also found to be substantial, indicating that diabetes has a considerable impact on people's adjustment and stress levels.

2.3 LITERATURE RELATED TO SELF-EFFICACY:

Khairy, S., Aslan, A., Samara, A.M. et al. (2021) observed overweight and obesity, as well as decreased patient-physician communication, were connected to self-efficacy impairment. Furthermore, our findings revealed that poor patient-physician communication was linked to low educational levels and non-city residency types. They urge that policymakers and health-care professionals make the necessary reforms to improve health-care facilities and services, particularly outside of cities. they also recommend providing specialised counselling and training sessions on hypertension management and control.

Seung-Yeon Kong and Mi-Kyoung Cho (2020) indicated that, rather than constant variables like sociodemographic characteristics, self-efficacy and HbA1c, which can be modified through interventions, were the most significant determinants determining self-care in patients with type 2 diabetes. Various issues connected to diabetes care should be investigated in order to improve self-care while allowing diabetic individuals to undertake self-care activities more successfully. Self-efficacy, HbA1c, employment, and smoking should all be taken into account when increasing the degree of self-care in individuals with type 2 diabetes. Additionally, a programme should be established to encourage consistent self-care by developing self-efficacy and establishing patients as the primary agent of self-care through positive achievements.

Medication literacy had a positive influence on medication adherence in individuals with hypertension, according to ***Shen Zhiying, et al. (2020)***. The mechanism underlying this association in hypertensive individuals, however, is poorly understood. In the link between medication literacy and adherence to antihypertensive regimens for hypertensive patients, self-efficacy accounts for 28.7% of the overall mediating effect. More over half of the hypertension patients in the study were noncompliant with their antihypertensive medications. The connection between medicine literacy and medication adherence was partially moderated by self-efficacy. As a result, it was proposed that boosting self-efficacy could improve and drive hypertension patients' medication adherence. It is necessary to create and implement targeted therapies to improve patients' self-efficacy. Furthermore, health care practitioners should be aware of the need of assessing and promoting medication literacy in patients with hypertension.

Lee. MJ, et al. (2019) indicated that self-efficacy is a key element in predicting treatment adherence, yet people with hypertension have low self-efficacy when it comes to managing their hypertension and other comorbid diseases. Patients with hypertension and patients with other chronic diseases had their self-efficacy for managing chronic conditions compared in this study. When compared to the non-hypertension group, the hypertension group had worse self-efficacy in handling everyday activities. Self-efficacy was found to be an indirect predictor of overall quality of life in this hypertension group, mediated by overall physical and mental health.

Fathi, A. et al. (2018) reported about half of the respondents had high levels of self-efficacy and adherence to self-care management, and there was a strong link between selfefficacy and adherence to self-care activities and glycemic control. High levels of diabetes management self-efficacy were found to be substantially linked with educational level and formal diabetes education. Continuous patient education must be considered in a diabetes management plan to improve self-efficacy and adherence to self-care activities.

Albikawi, et al. (2015) indicated that two weeks and three months after the intervention, significant changes in self-care management practises were found. Based on the findings of this study, health personnel can be taught to deliver relevant diabetes therapies based on self self-efficacy theory, and self-efficacy enhancing techniques can be implemented into nursing interventions, education, and research.

Wendling and Beadle (2015) investigated the association between self-efficacy and diabetes patients' foot self-care performance. The level of self-efficacy and the performance of foot self-care behaviours had no significant association. The relationship between foot self-care practises and gender was shown to be statistically significant, with males scoring higher than females.

Manjula and Premkumar (2015) did a cross-sectional study in India with a sample of 150 patients to measure self-efficacy and self-care behaviour of patients with type 2 diabetes mellitus and its connection with sociodemographic and morbidity related variables. In the categories of food, exercise, blood sugar monitoring, medicine and insulin administration, and foot care, the majority of individuals exhibited average selfefficacy and self-care behaviour. Self-efficacy and self-care behaviour were found to have a positive relationship. Increased self-efficacy and self-care behaviour were also linked to lower HbA1c levels. HbA1c and self-efficacy were found to be substantially related to age. HbA1c, self-efficacy, and self-care behaviour were all altered by a family history of diabetes. According to the findings, a rise in self-efficacy leads to an increase in self-care activity. In addition, an increase in self-efficacy and self-care behaviour is associated with a decrease in HbA1c levels.

According to ***Mohebi, Siamak, and colleagues (2013)***, self-efficacy is critical, and diabetic patients should be able to control 95 percent of their condition on their own. At-home care is an important element of caring for these patients, and self-efficacy is crucial here. Motivation for health-promoting behaviour is caused by self-efficacy directly through efficacy expectations. It also influences motivation indirectly through perceived impediments and decision of commitment level or patience in pursuing a performance map. Self-efficacy is defined as a person's assessment and anticipation of their ability to influence a favourite incident through personal struggles. To put it another way, self-efficacy has an impact on motivation. The person is more active and does their best in trial and following a behaviour to reach a goal if their judgement is more powerful. As a result, a person with poor self-efficacy is less likely to try to change a habit or entrenched behaviour. According to the studies, because Self-efficacy influences performance and behaviour, it can be a determining factor in people's success in diabetes patient self-care, particularly in terms of nutritional practises. As a result, Self-efficacy is critical in the diabetes patient's self-care process.

Gao, Wang, et. Al. (2013) found that individuals with higher self-efficacy were more comfortable undertaking diabetic self-care behaviours, which were directly associated to glycemic control, in a study of 222 Chinese adults with type 2 diabetes in one primary care centre.

Warren-Findlow, et al. (2012) carried out a study in which they revealed that in African Americans with hypertension, self-efficacy is strongly linked to compliance with five of the six required self-care tasks. Improving hypertension self-care and blood pressure control requires ensuring that African Americans believe hypertension is a manageable condition and that they are aware about proper self-care habits. Individuals' self-care behaviours should be assessed, and they should be directed toward practical ways to assist them gain confidence in managing their blood pressure.

Al-Khawaldeha, et al. (2012) conducted a cross-sectional study on 223 type 2 diabetes patients (aging above 25 years). Diet self-efficacy and diet self-management behaviour were found to predict improved glycaemic control in the study. Furthermore, subjects with higher self-efficacy report better self-management behaviour in the areas of nutrition, exercise, blood sugar testing, and medication administration.

Mazlooumi et al. (2010) indicated a strong correlation between self-efficacy and predictive behaviours from diabetes type-II.

Shakiba zadeh, et al. (2010) highlighted that self-efficacy directly relates to self-care and 51% of self-care changes are explained by selfefficacy and obstacles.

Cherrington, A., Wallston, K. A., & Rothman, R. L. (2010) reported that individuals with diabetes, depression and low self-efficacy are both linked to poor glycemic control, but the link between these characteristics is unclear. To explore if self-efficacy mediates the relationship between depression and glycemic control, they conducted a cross-sectional study evaluating relationships between depressive symptoms, self-efficacy, and glycemic control among men (n = 64) and women (n = 98) with type 2 diabetes. The association between these three variables was investigated using correlational and mediational analyses for the entire sample and individually by sex. In order to attain glycemic control, they require personalised therapies that boost their self-efficacy. To achieve glycemic control, men with depressive symptoms and type 2 diabetes may require specialised therapies that improve their self-efficacy.

Men had a greater level of self-efficacy, and it was significantly and positively connected with educational level, according to ***Morowati, Sharifabad, and Tonekaboni (2009),*** who investigated the influence of perceived self-efficacy in self-care behaviours among patients with diabetes. In comparison to housewives, female employees had a higher level of self-efficacy. Self-efficacy was found to be positively connected with self-care behaviours, with a 38 percent variance.

2.4 LITERATURE RELATED TO SUICIDAL TENDENCY:

According to ***Zhou, Y., Ren, W., Sun, Q., et al. (2021)***, the prevalence of suicide attempts was 24.28 percent in MDD patients with comorbid anxiety symptoms, which was 9.51 times greater than in MDD patients without anxiety symptoms (3.25 percent). MDD patients with anxiety symptoms who attempted suicide had greater systolic blood pressure, higher levels of thyroid stimulating hormone (TSH), and higher levels of thyroid peroxidases antibody (TPOAb), all of which were associated with suicide attempts in MDD patients with anxiety symptoms. Suicide attempts are associated with concomitant anxiety symptoms in MDD patients. The combination of HAMA score, HAMD score, and TSH could differentiate suicide attempters from non-suicide attempters. In addition, the age of beginning, length of illness, BMI, TSH, and TPOAb levels were linked to the times of suicide attempts in MDD patients with comorbid anxiety symptoms. The findings show that MDD patients with comorbid anxiety symptoms had a significant rate of suicide attempts. Suicide attempts in MDD patients with comorbid anxiety symptoms are influenced by a number of clinical correlates, metabolic factors, and thyroid hormone function.

Dent, K.R. et al. (2020) told that in the field of suicide prevention, emphasise the need of replication. The variations in findings between the Ontario Canada cohort and the VHA cohort could be due to differences in the underlying populations or prescribing procedures. The increased suicide risk among ARB users in Canada, for example, could be due to selection bias, in which ARBs are prescribed only to individuals who are at higher risk of suicide, rather than a pharmacological effect. Selective use of ARBs among seasoned VHA users with a decreased suicide risk, on the other hand, could mask a meaningful pharmacological effect. Information bias and residual confounding are two more major flaws that make analysing links between hypertension medicines and suicide difficult.

Suicide plans were shown to be common among diabetic patients, according to ***Mogesie Necho et al. (2020)*** Unemployment was a risk factor for suicide plan based on sociodemographic variables, poor medication adherence based on clinical variables, and current substance use based on substance related variables. Diabetic patients must be screened and treated early as a standard practise in diabetic clinics.

This study, according to ***Majidi, Shideh, et al. (2020),*** provides preliminary insight into the behaviours and cognitions of youth and young adults with type 1 diabetes who have suicidal and death ideations. During routine type 1 diabetes clinic visits, a comprehensive suicide risk assessment and safety plan can be completed.

Psychological distress had the strongest direct and total effect on suicide ideation, according to ***Ge, D., Zhang, et al. (2019)***. Suicidal ideation was only indirectly influenced by factors such as comorbidities, gender, marital status, economic status, domicile, alcohol consumption, exercise, and hospitalisation. It was discovered that psychological distress had a strong mediation impact on the correlations between suicidal ideation and the aforementioned risk factors like comorbidity, and gender. These path analysis findings will help us better understand the mechanisms underlying the effect of various associated factors on Suicidal ideation in hypertensive individuals, as well as aid in the selection of intervention strategies that target the associated factors in order to prevent subsequent suicidal behaviours.

According to ***Ahmad Nazari M (2019)*** Suicidal ideation was found to be 3.2 percent (n=32) in diabetic patients receiving insulin and 3.1 percent (n=31) in those taking oral medicine treatment, according to Ahmad Nazari M (2019). There was no link found between suicidal ideation and diabetes treatment technique. Suicidal thoughts was more common in illiterate people, although there was no significant link between suicidal ideation and education level. In addition, there was no link between marital status and suicidal ideation. There was no link between suicidal thoughts and the treatment approach (P-value: 0.05). Suicidal ideation is more common in diabetic patients, however there were no differences between the two groups treated with insulin and those treated with oral anti-diabetic drugs.

The prevalence of suicidal attempts among diabetes mellitus patients was found to be high, indicating that diabetes mellitus is a public health concern, according to ***Necho, M., Mekonnen, S., Haile, K., et al. (2019)***. Suicide attempt was found to have a statistically significant relationship with comorbid depression, being female, bad glycemic level, and poor social support. As a result, the findings of this study can aid in the early detection, treatment, and referral of patients who have attempted suicide.

According to ***Brdvik L. (2018)***, depression is a recurrent theme in the articles, and it is also the most common disorder among those who commit suicide. Family history of psychiatric problems, male gender, suicide attempts, more severe depression, hopelessness, and comorbidity were all identified as risk factors in a recent study. Surprisingly, the study on suicide risk in depression could only include 19 studies (28 papers), which is a low quantity given the disorder's significant suicide risk.

Gómez-Peralta et al. (2018) observed in a Mexican community with type 2 diabetes, there was evidence of a significant rate of suicide attempts. Younger age, depression, and a normal BMI, on the other hand, were found to be risk factors for suicide attempt in these patients. Then, to avoid despair and suicide attempts, early psychologic and psychiatric interventions are required. Future studies with bigger sample sizes will be required to replicate these findings.

According to ***Tolstoy et al. (2018)***, those with uncontrolled diabetes are more likely to experience depression and suicidal thoughts than those with well-controlled diabetes. However, there is no statistical link between anxiety and either of the two groups. Interventional trials would reveal the impact of treating both diabetes and depression on one another. Because the link between diabetes and depression is bidirectional, a comprehensive strategy to both is essential to prevent them from worsening.

Bin Wang et al. (2018) conducted a meta analysis that resulted in the inclusion of 54 papers, including 28 studies on the suicide risk linked with diabetes, 47 studies on the suicide incidence rate, and 45 studies on the proportion of deaths due to suicide. Diabetes has been linked to a higher risk of suicide, according to a meta-analysis. A subgroup study revealed that type 1 diabetes was related with a higher risk of suicide. According to this meta-analysis, diabetes can dramatically increase the risk of suicide. Suicide plays a significant role in diabetic patient mortality, particularly among type 1 diabetes patients. Effective strategies to decrease suicide risk and improve mental health outcomes in diabetes patients are needed.

Elamoshy R, Bird Y, Thorpe LU, Moraros J.(2018) discovered that diabetic Aboriginal Canadians living off-reserve have a higher chance of suffering depression symptoms and suicide ideation than non-diabetic Aboriginals. Raising awareness, enhancing health care worker training, and adopting culturally relevant co-screening procedures are all significant steps in reducing the prevalence of depression and suicidality among Aboriginal diabetics. Co-screening activities like these can aid in the early detection and management of these complex cases, reducing the burden of additional disability, hospitalisation, and mortality. Future research is required to elucidate the temporal nature of the association between diabetes, depression, and suicidal ideation among the Aboriginal peoples of Canada.

Conti, C. et al. (2017) concluded that Patients with these characteristics deserve special attention, and health-care practitioners should be aware of the increased suicidal risk in patient subgroups based on clinical characteristics of DM. Clinical management in DM care should include measures to address emotional discomfort in this regard.

Suicidal thoughts and behaviours in diabetic patients are a clinical and public health challenge, according to ***Sarkar, S., and Balhara, Y.S. (2014)***. There are research that imply that diabetes mellitus is linked to a higher rate of suicide thoughts and attempts, but there are also studies that show the opposite. For people with DM, the standardised mortality ratio due to suicide appears to be greater. The availability of fatal measures such as insulin and oral hypoglycemic medications appears to make the endeavour simple. Screening for suicidal thoughts on a regular basis, as well as adequate psychiatric therapy of the symptoms, can assist to prevent potentially deadly outcomes.

Chung, Jae, et al. (2014) examined the mental health of diabetic patients in Korea and compared it to the mental health of the general population. All of the data included in the final analyses came from 34,065 people aged 20 and over who took part in the Korea National Health and Nutrition Examination Survey from 2007 to 2012. (KNHANES). The mental health of 3,846 diabetic patients was compared to the mental health of 30,219 healthy people. 13.6 percent of those with normal glucose tolerance (NGT), 14.3 percent of people with impaired glucose intolerance (IFG), and 17.6 percent of people with diabetes mellitus (DM) reported having a low mood for two weeks or more. Suicidal thoughts were mentioned by 15.3% of people with NGT, 15.6 percent of people with IFG, and 17.6% of people with diabetes. Suicide attempts were recorded by 0.8 percent of NGT patients, 1.0 percent of IFG patients, and 1.3 percent of diabetic patients. The crude odds ratio (OR) for depressive mood was 1.376 (95 percent confidence range [CI]: 1.258–1.504) in DM patients, 1.481 (95 percent CI: 1.361–1.611) for suicidal ideation, and 1.413 (95 percent CI: 1.021–1.956) for suicide attempts. The current investigation discovered that DM was linked to a significant increase in suicidal conduct.

Pompili, Maurizio, et al. (2009) found that internal medicine outpatients had higher levels of despondency and suicidal thoughts. Low self-efficacy, hopelessness, and suicidality were all linked to poor quality of life. Polytherapy and older age were found to predict suicidality in a stepwise multiple regression. Following up on patient samples in the future would be useful in determining how many and which patients engage in fatal and nonfatal suicide conduct, as well as the relationship between these parameters and quality of life.

Chapter-III

METHODOLOGY

3.1 INTRODUCTION:

Research methodology is a method for solving research problems in a meticulous manner. It is a science that entails using a variety of methods and procedures to collect and analyze data, information, and material in order to solve problems that have been identified as requiring study. A study must be planned and the research methodologies and techniques must be understood. Different research methodologies, tools, and procedures can be employed depending on the study problem. A scholarly and systematic search for relevant knowledge on a given topic might be defined as research.

As the title of the present research work advocates the investigator intends to look into the association between quality of life, self-efficacy and suicidal tendency with reference to Types of disease, gender and hereditary status of patients. The present chapter describes the blueprint or plan of the study and displays the details about the research procedure followed in the present research work. It includes information about the population, the sampling method, the nature and form of data collection, tools, methods of collecting data and statistical techniques used for analysis of data etc. In order to accomplish the objectives and the stated corresponding hypotheses, the following plan of the study has been followed.

3.2 STATEMENT OF PROBLEM:

The present research attempts to study ***"Quality of Life, Self-Efficacy & Suicidal Tendency Between Diabetes & Hypertension Patients."***

3.3 SIGNIFICANCE OF THE PROBLEM

Diabetes and hypertension both are key problems of public health issues in the world, and have effects on all domains of life including physical, psychological, mental, cognitive, financial and social. Diabetes type-II and hypertension, in particular, have an effect on patients' psychological well-being, quality of life, and satisfaction with life, as well as their emotions. The recovery plans for diabetic and hypertension patients are greatly influenced by these psychological effects. Diabetic and hypertensive disorders place a psychological burden on the individual and his family for the rest of their lives. Poor psychological functioning can make it difficult to manage diabetes on a daily basis, and it's linked to poor medical results and high costs. Diabetes and hypertension have a significant impact on the patient's psychological well-being, limiting their behaviors and daily activities. Diabetics and hypertensive patients have higher rates of depression and psychological distress than non-diabetics.

The role of psychological factors in diabetes and hypertension has received very little attention in our country. Diabetes type-II and hypertension must be explored in order to get these factors under control. Only through understanding the effects of diabetes type-II and hypertension can these issues be managed, as it is important to provide psychological and emotional support to patients in addition to medication in order to enhance disease management and overall quality of life. Since diabetes and hypertension have such a significant effect on different aspects of life, Thus, deliberately present study was planned. The following are the objectives of the present research:

3.4 OBJECTIVES:

The following objectives were framed as per the nature of the problem.

1. To study and analyze Quality of life factors, Self-efficacy and the Suicidal tendency among diabetes and hypertension patients.
2. To study and analyze the factors of Quality of life, Self-efficacy and the Suicidal tendency among diabetes and hypertension patients with reference to gender.
3. To study and analyze the factors of Quality of life, Self-efficacy and Suicidal tendency among diabetes and hypertension patients with reference to hereditary status.
4. To study and analyze the factors of Quality of life, Self-efficacy and Suicidal tendency among diabetes and hypertension patients with reference to types of disease and Gender.

5. To study and analyze the factors of Quality of life, Self-efficacy and Suicidal tendency among diabetes and hypertension patients with reference to types of disease and hereditary status.

6. To study and analyze the factors of Quality of life, Self-efficacy and Suicidal tendency among diabetes and hypertension patients with reference to Gender and hereditary status.

7. To study and analyze the factors of Quality of life, Self-efficacy and Suicidal tendency among diabetes and hypertension patients with reference to types of disease, Gender and hereditary status.

8. To examine the relationship between factors of Quality of life, Self-efficacy and Suicidal tendency among patients in relation to types of disease.

9. To examine the relationship between factors of Quality of life, Self-efficacy and Suicidal tendency among patients in relation to Gender.

10. To examine the relationship between factors of Quality of life, Self-efficacy and Suicidal tendency among patients in relation to hereditary status.

3.5 HYPOTHESES:

For the present research work, the following null and alternative hypotheses were formulated:

($H0_1$) There will be no significant difference between the mean scores of patients with diabetes and hypertension regarding the dimensions of Quality of life.

($H0_2$) There will be no significant difference between male and female patients' mean scores regarding the dimensions of Quality of life.

($H0_3$) There will be no significant difference between mean scores of patients with and without Hereditary status regarding the dimensions of Quality of life.

($H0_4$) There will be no significant interaction effect between types of disease and gender of patients regarding the dimensions of Quality of life.

($H0_5$) There will be no significant interaction effect between disease types and patients' hereditary status regarding the dimensions of Quality of life.

($H0_6$) There will be no significant interaction effect between gender and hereditary status of patients regarding the dimensions of Quality of life.

($H0_7$) There will be no significant interaction effect between types of disease, Gender and hereditary status of patients regarding the dimensions of Quality of life.

($H0_8$) There will be no significant difference between the mean scores of patients with diabetes and hypertension regarding the factors of Self-efficacy.

($H0_9$) There will be no significant difference between the mean scores of male and female patients regarding the factors of Self-efficacy.

($H0_{10}$) There will be no significant difference between mean scores of patients with and without Hereditary status regarding the factors of Self-efficacy.

($H0_{11}$) There will be no significant interaction effect between types of disease and gender of patients regarding the factors of Self-efficacy.

($H0_{12}$) There will be no significant interaction effect between disease types and patients' hereditary status regarding the factors of Self-efficacy.

($H0_{13}$) There will be no significant interaction effect between gender and hereditary status of patients regarding the factors of Self-efficacy.

($H0_{14}$) There will be no significant interaction effect between types of disease, Gender and hereditary status of patients regarding the traits of Self-efficacy.

($H0_{15}$) There will be no significant difference between the mean scores of patients with diabetes and hypertension regarding the traits of Suicidal tendency.

($H0_{16}$) There will be no significant difference between male and female patients' mean scores regarding the traits of Suicidal tendency.

($H0_{17}$) There will be no significant difference between mean scores of patients with and without Hereditary status regarding the traits of Suicidal tendency.

($H0_{18}$) There will be no significant interaction effect between patients' types of disease and gender regarding the traits of Suicidal tendency.

($H0_{19}$) There will be no significant interaction effect between disease types and patients' hereditary status regarding the traits of Suicidal tendency.

($H0_{20}$) There will be no significant interaction effect between gender and hereditary status of patients regarding the traits of Suicidal tendency.

($H0_{21}$) There will be no significant interaction effect between types of disease, Gender and hereditary status of patients regarding the traits of Suicidal tendency.

(Ha_1) There will be a relationship among factors of Quality of life, Self-efficacy and Suicidal tendency in diabetic patients.

(Ha_2) There will be a relationship among factors of Quality of life, Self-efficacy and Suicidal tendency in hypertension patients.

3.6 RESEARCH DESIGN:

There are several methods of data collection. A systematic and scientific methodology, referred to as research design (Festinger and Katz, 1970), determines the correctness and accuracy of the obtained results.

The 2 X 2 X 2 factorial design of the present study is as under. There are 8 cells in the following table; each cell contains 50 patients.

Table 3.1: Showing 2 X 2 X 2 factorial design of the present study

Groups	**A_1 Patients with diabetes**		**A_2 Patients with hypertension**		**Total**
	B_1 Male	**B_2 Female**	**B_1 Male**	**B_2 Female**	
Patients with heredity C_1	50	50	50	50	200
Patients without heredity C_2	50	50	50	50	200
Total	100	100	100	100	**400**

3.7 VARIABLES:

In the present investigation, types of disease, Gender and hereditary status of patients were taken as Independent Variables. In contrast, dimensions of Quality of life, self-efficacy and suicidal tendency were taken as Dependent Variables.

Table:-3.2 Showing Variables of the study

S. No	Name of Variables	Types of Variables	Grade of Variables	Name of the levels
1	Types of disease	Independent	2	1.Diabetes 2.Hypertension
2	Gender	Independent	2	1.Male 2.Female
3	Hereditary status of patients	Independent	2	1. With Hereditary 2.Without Hereditary
4	Quality of life	Dependent	11	1. Life satisfaction 2. Goals & Motivation 3. Spirituality 4. Happiness 5. Hopes & Wishes 6. Stress reduction 7. Frustration, Depression/ Anxiety 8. Adjustment 9. Physical well-being & Self care 10. Effectiveness/ Efficacy of myself 11.Personal development/ Personal evolution
5	Self-efficacy	Dependent	8	1. Self-Regulatory skill 2. Self influence 3. Self confidence 4. Social achievement 5. Self 6. Self evaluation 7. Self esteem 8. Self cognition
6.	Suicidal tendency	Dependent	4	1.Personality characteristics 2. Emotional disturbance 3. Conflictive thoughts 4. Self- harm tendency

3.8 POPULATION OF THE STUDY:

The research population is also recognized as a well-defined collection of individuals or objects known to have similar characteristics. All individuals or entities within a particular population usually have a common, binding attributes or traits is known as universe o population of the study. The present study population consisted of the patients with diabetes type-II and hypertension from Ahmedabad city of Gujarat State.

3.9 SAMPLE:

For the present study, the researcher has selected 400 patients with diabetes type-II and hypertension from Ahmedabad city of Gujarat State with the help of purposive sampling technique. Further, these patients were classified into two groups, i.e. patients with diabetes type –II (200) and patients with hypertension (200). The categorization and details of sample selection are given in the following chart.

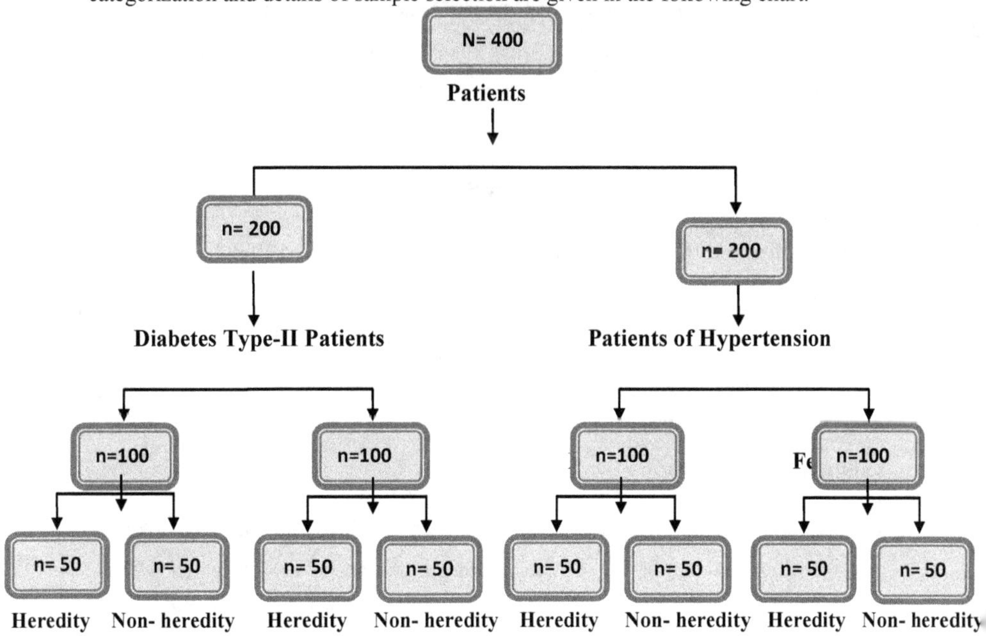

3.10 TOOLS:

3.10.1 Quality of Life Scale:

The Quality of life scale was developed by Sharma, S. and Nasreen, N. in 2014. It consists of a total of 42 (34 positive+8 negatives) statements. It measures the quality of life and consists of 11 dimensions, namely Life Satisfaction, Goals and Motivation, Spirituality, Happiness, Hopes and Wishes, Stress reduction, Frustration/ Depression/ Anxiety, Adjustment, Physical Well-being and Self Care, Effectiveness/ Efficiency of myself and Personal Development/ Personal Evolution.

Reliability:

Cronbach's alpha determined the reliability of the scale. In statistics, Cronbach's alpha is the coefficient of internal consistency. It is commonly used to estimate the reliability of a psychometric test for a sample of examinees. As a result, alpha is most appropriately used when the items measure different substantive areas within a single construct. When the item's set measures more than one construct, coefficient omega hierarchical is more appropriate (McDonald, 1999; Zinberg, Revelle, Yovel& Li, 2005).

Reliability Statistics

Cronbach's Alpha	Cronbach's Alpha Based on Standardized Items	No. of Items
.806	.821	42

Validity:

The scale was carefully examined and given to a group of experts. They were asked to give their judgment about the relevancy, content and language of statements. Thus, for developing the scale for assessing psychological determinants of QOL, face validity and construct validity was assured.

3.10.2 Self-Efficacy Scale:

The Self-Efficacy scale was prepared by Mathur, G.P. &Bhatnagar, R. (2012). It consists of a total of 22 statements. In this scale, items are in two forms, i.e. Positive and negative. It is more appropriate in Indian social conditions; each item describes human self-efficacy in a different social situation. It consists of eight dimensions, namely Self regulatory skills, Self influence, Self-confidence, Social achievement, Self, Self-evaluation, Self-esteem and Self-cognition

Reliability:

The scale's reliability coefficient was measured by test-retest on a 600 (300 male and 300 female) sample. The male ranges between .73 to .81 and in female .79 to .86 and is significant at .01 level of significance.

Validity:

To obtain concurrent validity co-efficient of the self-efficacy scale, the scale was compared with the views of the expert's rating. Validity ranges in male .73 to .81 and in female .76 to .83.

3.10.3 Suicidal Tendency Scale:

The Suicidal Tendency scale was developed by Meghnathi, R. & Bhatt, D. (2002). It consists of 40 items on the base of literature and the judgment of experts. All the items of the scale are presented in a brisk and straightforward style. It consists of four modes, namely Personality Traits, Emotional Disturbances, Conflictive Thoughts and Self-harm Tendency. The scale selected here is a four-point scale bearing the following points as noted against the following statements. Each item of the scale is to be scored from upper to lower in terms of 4,3,2,1. Scores classified to interpret like as 0-40 Normal tendency, 41-80 lower tendency, 81-120 higher tendency, 121-160 savior tendency of suicide.

Reliability:

The split-half reliability has been calculated by the odd-even method. The correlation coefficient was .92, which indicated the STS is highly reliable. The test-retest reliability of this scale has been calculated by administration twice of this scale on a sample of 80 subjects. The reliability coefficient was r=.83.

Validity:

The t-test was applied for the calculation of differences between both groups. There is a significant difference between both groups at a 0.01 level of significance. The abnormal group was significantly higher than the normal group in their suicidal tendency.

3.11 PROCEDURE:

The investigator with great interest planned the data collection soon after selecting the sample and finalizing the research. General and private hospitals were approached and requested to grant permission for data collection. All of them asked about aims and objectives of this research work. After fulfilling some official formalities and conditions, arrangements to meet the patients of diabetic (Type-II) and hypertension were made. Each patient was given a questionnaire and requested to read statements one after the other and give their responses in response column by choosing appropriate response for each statement, whichever they felt correct and appropriate. There was no limitation of time to respond. The respondents were requested not to leave any item unanswered and incomplete. In this way all three questioners were applied in the same sequence to all the subjects.

3.12 STATISTICAL DESIGN:

Statistical techniques were used on the raw scores to make it meaningful and test the scores' significance. Without the use of statistical methods, raw scores did not have their meaning and relevance. In order to study the main and interaction effect on Quality of life, Self-efficacy and Suicidal tendency of the respondents according to type of disease, gender and hereditary status, Two-way Analysis of Variance (ANOVA) with $2 \times 2 \times 2$ Factorial Design was employed using SPSS version 20. Test for homogeneity of variance was employed before conducting Analysis of Variance (ANOVA), the Leven's Test of Homogeneity was used. Similarly, Person r test was used to know the association among various factors of Quality of life, Self-efficacy and Suicidal tendency among patients.

Chapter–IV

RESULTS, INTERPRETATION AND DISCUSSION

4.1 INTRODUCTION:

In the previous chapter, the problem statement, descriptions of tools, and data collection procedure have been written. It has been already stated that this research work aims to study the impact of types of disease, gender and hereditary status of patients in the light of their quality of life, self-efficacy and suicidal tendency. Pauling Young (1956) narrated, "Scientific analysis assess that behind the accumulated data, there is something more important revealing than facts themselves. Through this process, old conceptions can be tested, and the new one can be discovered." In this research, quality of life, self-efficacy and suicidal tendency are the dependent variables, and patients' types of disease, gender and hereditary status have been taken as the independent variable.

This chapter deals with the analysis and interpretation of the data along with discussion of the findings. The Two-Way Analysis of Variance (ANOVA) with 2×2×2 factorial design was employed to study the variables' main effects and interaction effects. It was determined that the hypotheses will be rejected at 0.05 levels of significance. The variables have been compared numerically and presented graphically for ease in understanding the results.

4.2 PRESENTATION AND POSTULATION OF THE STRUCTURAL MODEL OF INDEPENDENT VARIABLES.

Disease (A):
- ✓ A1: Diabetes
- ✓ A2: Hypertension

Gender (B):
- ✓ B1: Male
- ✓ B2: Female

Hereditary status (C) :
- ✓ C1: Patients with hereditary
- ✓ C2: Patients Without hereditary

4.3 RESULT AND DISCUSSION OF ANOVA:

The present section explains the sample details, mean obtained, comparison of score in "F" test and explaining the level of significance.

4.3.1 Result and interpretation of Total score of Quality of life factor:

The score of anxiety was analyzed using a 2 x 2 x 2 factorial design. The ANOVA and the Means are summarized in following tables:

Table-1

Showing ANOVA summary for the quality of life factor- Life satisfaction

Source	Type III Sum of Squares	df	Mean Square	F	Sig. Level
Diseases (A)	252.810	1	252.810	68.790	$p<.01$
Gender (B)	9.000	1	9.000	2.449	NS
Heredity status (C)	46.240	1	46.240	12.582	$p<.01$
Diseases * *Gender* (A*B)	33.640	1	33.640	9.153	$p<.01$
Diseases * *Heredity status* (A*C)	88.360	1	88.360	24.043	$p<.01$
Gender * *Heredity status* (B*C)	5.290	1	5.290	1.439	NS
Diseases * *Gender* * *Heredity status* (A*B*C)	.810	1	.810	.220	NS
Error	1440.640	392	3.675		
Total	37560.000	400			
Corrected Total	1876.790	399			

Levene's Test of Equality of Error Variances[a]

Dependent Variable: Q1

F	df1	df2	Sig.
18.757	7	392	.000

Tests the null hypothesis that the error variance of the dependent variable is equal across groups.

a. Design: Intercept + Diseases + Gender + HS + Diseases * Gender + Diseases * HS + Gender * HS + Diseases * Gender * HS

Table-2

Showing Mean, SD & Mean difference between patients of diabetes and hypertension for quality of life factor- Life satisfaction.

Diseases(A)	N	Mean	SD	Mean Difference
Diabetes A1	200	10.44	1.43	2.19
Hypertension A2	200	8.25	2.47	

Figure no.1

Showing comparison of mean scores between patients of diabetes and hypertension for quality of life factor- Life satisfaction

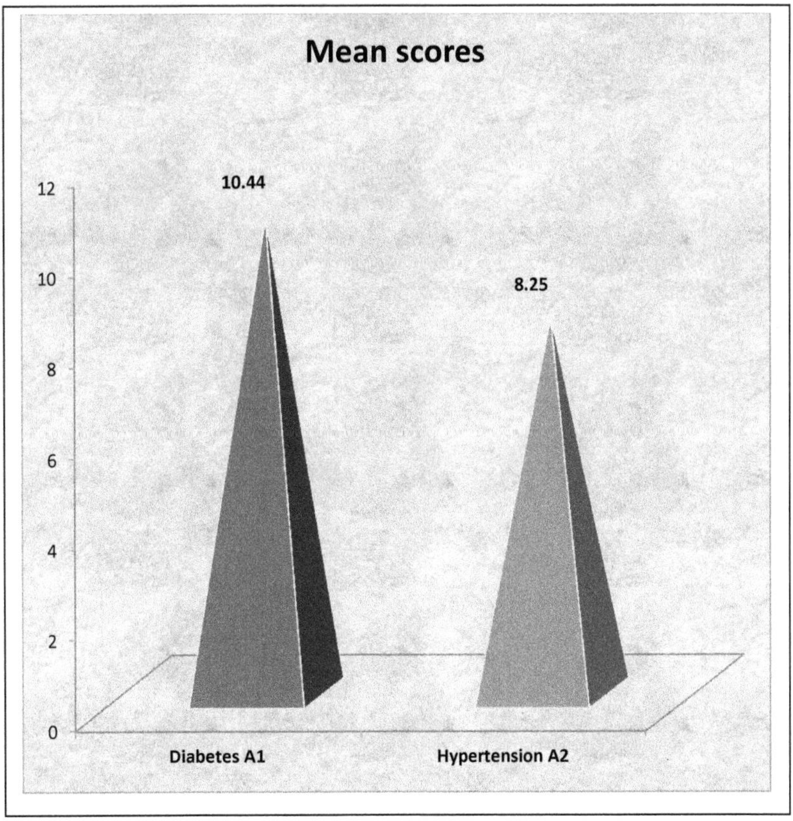

Table-3
Showing Mean, SD & Mean difference between male and female patients with diabetes and hypertension for quality of life factor- Life satisfaction.

Gender (B)	N	Mean	SD	Mean Difference
Male B1	200	9.29	2.36	0.30
Female B2	200	9.59	1.94	

Figure no.2
Showing comparison of mean scores between male and female patients with diabetes and hypertension for quality of life factor- Life satisfaction

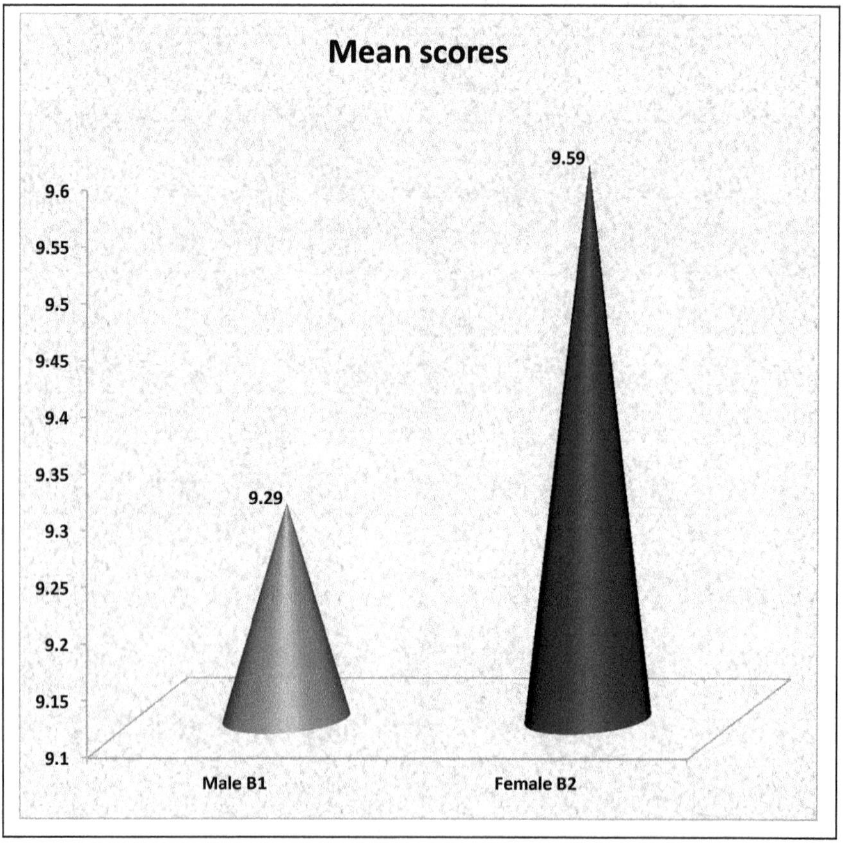

Table-4
Showing Mean, SD & Mean difference between patients with and without hereditary status for the quality of life factor- Life satisfaction.

Hereditary status (C)	N	Mean	SD	Mean Difference
Hereditary C1	200	8.10	2.52	1.68
Non-hereditary C2	200	9.78	1.67	

Figure no. 3
Showing comparison of mean scores between patients with and without hereditary status for the quality of life factor- Life satisfaction.

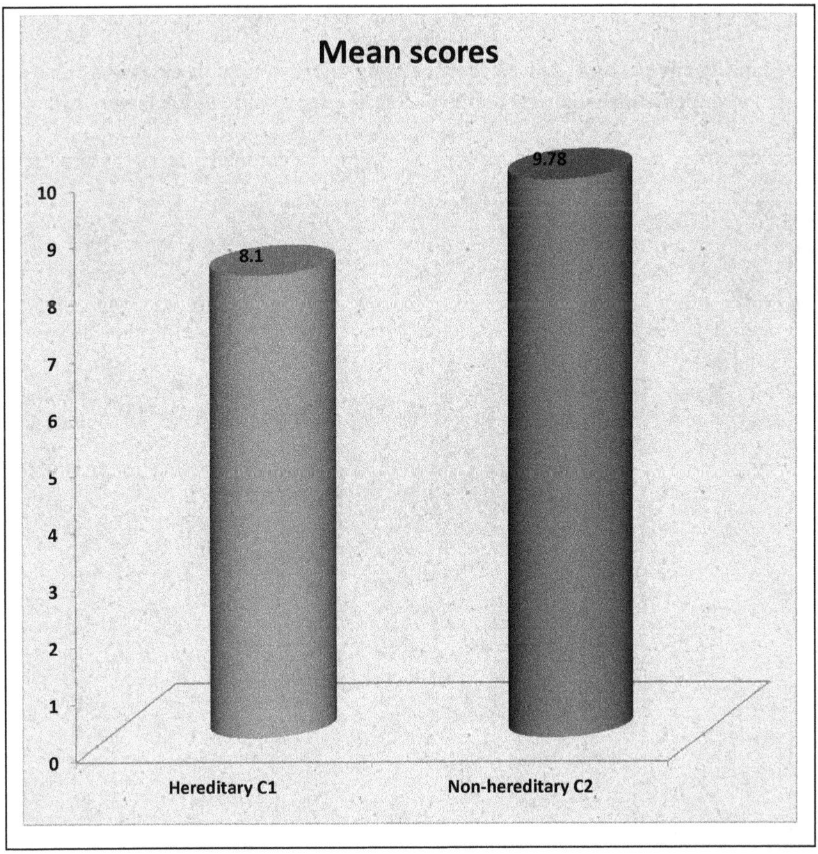

Table-5

Showing Mean, SD & Mean difference among interaction of diseases and Gender of patients with diabetes and hypertension for quality of life factor- Life satisfaction.

Diseases(A)	Gender (B)	N	Mean	SD	Mean Difference
Diabetes A1	Male B1	100	10.38	1.46	0.28
	Female B2	100	10.10	1.39	
Hypertension A2	Male B1	100	8.21	2.59	0.88
	Female B2	100	9.09	2.27	

Figure no. 4

Showing comparison of mean scores among interaction of diseases and Gender of patients with diabetes and hypertension for quality of life factor- Life satisfaction.

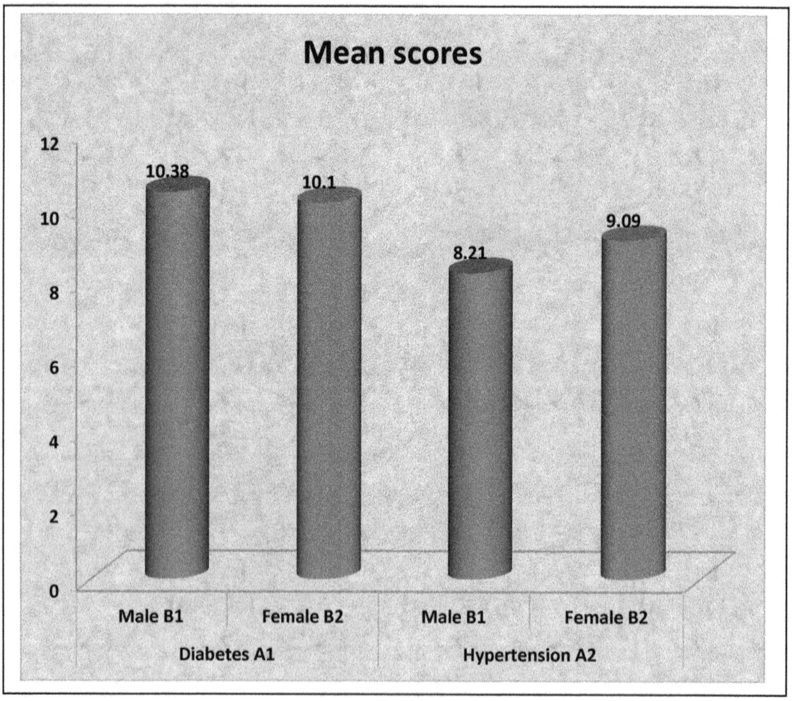

Table-6

Showing Mean, SD & Mean difference among interaction of diseases and hereditary status of patients for the quality of life factor- Life satisfaction.

Diseases(A)	Hereditary (C)	N	Mean	SD	Mean Difference
Diabetes A1	Hereditary *C1*	100	10.37	1.59	0.26
	Non- hereditary *C2*	100	10.11	1.23	
Hypertension A2	Hereditary *C1*	100	7.84	2.65	1.62
	Non- hereditary *C2*	100	9.46	1.97	

Figure no. 5

Showing the comparison of mean scores among interaction of diseases and hereditary status of patients for the quality of life factor- Life satisfaction.

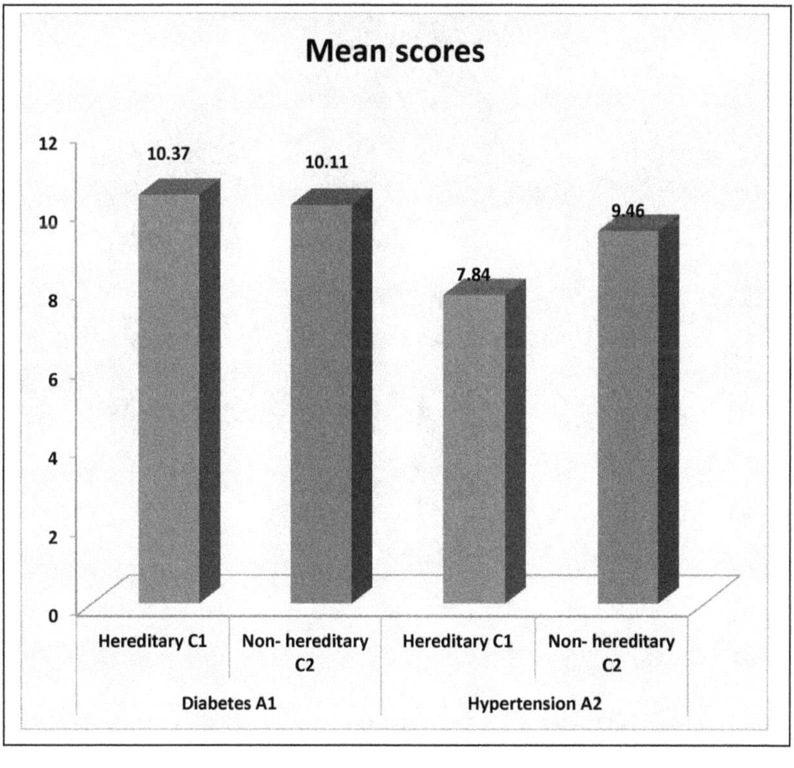

Table-7
Showing Mean, SD & Mean difference among interaction of Gender and hereditary status of patients for the quality of life factor- Life satisfaction.

Gender (B)	Hereditary status (C)	N	Mean	SD	Mean Difference
Male	Hereditary *C1*	100	9.07	2.68	0.45
	Non-hereditary *C2*	100	9.52	1.98	
Female	Hereditary *C1*	100	9.14	2.36	0.91
	Non-hereditary *C2*	100	10.05	1.25	

Figure no. 6
Showing the comparison of mean scores among interaction of Gender and hereditary status of patients for the quality of life factor- Life satisfaction.

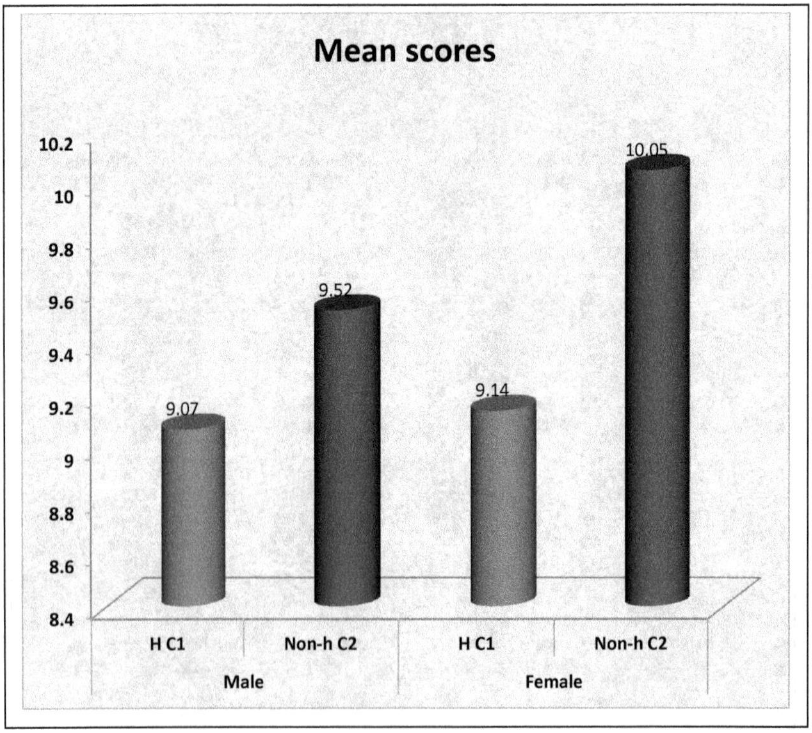

Table 8
Showing Mean, SD & Mean difference among interaction of diseases, gender and hereditary status of patients with diabetes and hypertension for quality of life factor- Life satisfaction.

Diseases (A)	Gender (B)	Hereditary status (C)	N	Mean	SD	Mean Difference
Diabetes A1	*Male B1*	*Hereditary C1*	50	10.58	1.53	0.40
		Non- hereditary C2	50	10.18	1.36	
	Female B2	*Hereditary C1*	50	10.16	1.64	0.14
		Non- hereditary C2	50	10.04	1.10	
Hypertension A2	*Male B1*	*Hereditary C1*	50	7.56	2.74	1.30
		Non- hereditary C2	50	8.86	2.27	
	Female B2	*Hereditary C1*	50	8.12	2.55	1.94
		Non- hereditary C2	50	10.06	1.40	

Figure no. 7
Showing the comparison of mean scores among interaction of diseases, gender and hereditary status of patients with diabetes and hypertension for quality of life factor- Life satisfaction.

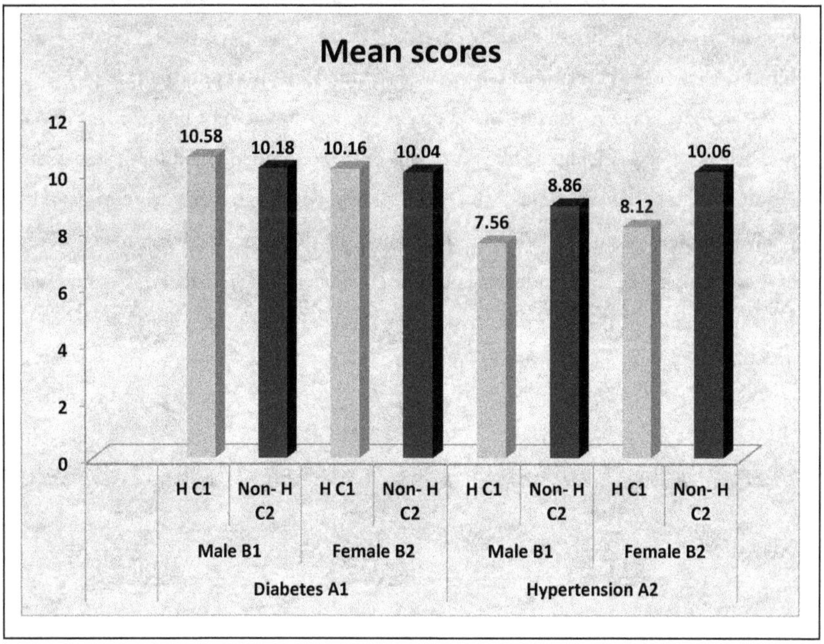

Main Effect:

Quality of life trait life-satisfaction with regard to Types of disease:

When the F test was employed to check the effect of Types of disease on Quality of Life trait life satisfaction among diabetic and hypertension patients, a significant F value was reported. The F value was highlighted F (1, 200) = 68.90, $p<.01$(Table no.1), which was significant. Table 2 and 1 displayed that mean scores of diabetic and hypertension patients are 10.44 (SD = 1.43) and 8.25 (SD = 2.47), respectively, and the difference between the two means is 2.19. On the basis of above results, it can be said that diabetic patients have greater quality of life trait life satisfaction than patients with hypertension.

Quality of life trait life-satisfaction with regard to Gender:

Table no.1 & 3 indicated F value and mean score for the Gender of patients with diabetes and hypertension in which the mean difference and F ratio is reported insignificant F(1,200) = 2.44, p >.05. The mean score obtained by male patients is 9.29 (SD = 2.36) and for female patients is 9.59 (SD = 1.94), whereas the mean difference of both the group is 0.30. This mean difference (Table No3. & Chart No.2) suggested that there is a negligible mean difference among both the groups. It can be concluded that both male and female patients with diabetes and hypertension have more or less equal Quality of life trait life-satisfaction.

Quality of life trait life-satisfaction with regard to Hereditary status:

The calculated F value of Hereditary status was found to be F (1, 200) = 12.58, which was quite significant. Table No. 4 and chart no. 3 highlighted that mean score of patients with hereditary status is 8.10 (SD=2.52), whereas a mean score of patients without hereditary status is 9.78 (SD=1.67), and the difference between mean scores was 1.68, which was very noticeable. It was concluded that hereditary status had an impact on Quality of life trait life satisfaction. Patients without hereditary status have better life satisfaction as compared to patients with hereditary status.

Interaction Effect

Quality of life trait life satisfaction with regard to Types of disease and Gender:

The study's main objective was to examine whether diabetic male and female patients and male and female patients with hypertension differed on Quality of life trait life-satisfaction . Table no.1 displayed that the F value for the interaction of Types of disease and Gender is also observed to be significant F (1,100) = .9.15, *p*< .01. By the same point of view Table no. 5 and chart no. 4 displayed that mean scores of male and female diabetic patients are (M=10.38, SD= 1.46) and (M = 10.10, SD = 1.39) respectively, whereas the mean difference of both the group of patients is 0.28. As again mean scores of male and female patients with hypertension are (M =8.21, SD = 2.59) and (M = 9.09, SD = 2.27), the mean difference of both the group of the patients is 0.28. The mean difference between all four groups highlighted that Types of disease and Gender significantly impact the quality of life trait life satisfaction.

Quality of life trait life satisfaction with regard to Types of disease and Hereditary status:

The F ratio for Types of disease and Hereditary status is F (1, 100) = 24.04, which was significant (*p*<.01). Table no. 6 and chart no.5 depicted the mean score of diabetic patients with hereditary status is 10.37 (SD = 1.59), and the mean score for diabetic patients without genetic status is 10.11 (SD = 1.23). Statistically, the significant mean difference is 0.26. In contrast, the mean of hypertension patients with hereditary status is 7.84 (SD = 2.65) and the mean score of hypertension patients without genetic status is 9.46 (SD = 1.97), the difference between two means is 1.62. It can be concluded that all four groups have a different level of life satisfaction.

Quality of life trait life satisfaction with regard to Gender and Hereditary status:

The calculated value for interaction between Gender and Hereditary status of diabetic and hypertension is found to be F (1, 100) = 1.43, which was quite non-significant. As seen from the Table no.7 and chart, no.6 mean score of male patients with heredity is 9.07 (SD = 2.68), and the mean of male patients without heredity is 9.52 (SD =1.98), whereas the difference of mean scores is 0.45. As again mean score of female patients with heredity is 9.14 (SD = 2.36), and the mean score of female patients without heredity is 10.05 (SD = 1.25). The difference in mean score is 0.91. Almost all four groups have an insignificant mean difference. Thus it can be concluded that all four groups of patients have reported by and large similar quality of life factor life satisfaction.

Quality of life trait life satisfaction with regard to Types of disease, Gender and Hereditary status:

F ratio for Types of disease, Gender and Hereditary status of the patients of diabetes and hypertension is to be reported insignificant $F (1, 50) = .22$, $p > .05$. The mean scores of diabetic male patients with heredity and non-heredity are 10.58 (SD =1.53) and 10.18 (SD =1.36). The mean difference between both groups is 0.40. As again, mean values of diabetic female patients with and without hereditary status are 10.16 (SD = 1.64) &10.04 (SD = 1.10). The mean difference of both the group is 0.14 which was also statistically less. The Table shows that the mean score of hypertension male patients with heredity is 7.56 (SD =2.74), whereas the mean score of hypertension male patients without hereditary status is 8.86 (SD = 2.27). The difference between the mean score is 1.30, which is also statistically not significant. In the same way, the mean score of female hypertension patients with heredity is 8.12 (SD = 2.55) and the mean score of female hypertension patients with non-heredity is 10.06 (SD = 1.40). The mean difference is found at 1.94. All the eight groups of the patients of diabetes and hypertension have more or less equal to quality of life area life satisfaction.

Table-9

Showing ANOVA summary for the quality of life factor- Goals and Motivation

Source	Type III Sum of Squares	df	Mean Square	F	Sig. Level
Diseases (A)	226.502	1	226.502	51.875	p<.01
Gender (B)	6.003	1	6.003	1.375	NS
Heredity status (C)	12.702	1	12.702	2.741	NS
Diseases * *Gender* (A*B)	7.023	1	7.023	1.608	NS
Diseases * *Heredity status* (A*C)	9.302	1	9.302	2.131	NS
Gender * *Heredity status* (B*C)	.023	1	.023	.005	NS
Diseases * *Gender* * *Heredity status* (A*B*C)	.303	1	.303	.069	NS
Error	1711.580	392	4.366		
Total	37797.000	400			
Corrected Total	1981.438	399			

Levene's Test of Equality of Error Variances[a]

Dependent Variable: Q2

F	df1	df2	Sig.
7.085	7	392	.000

Tests the null hypothesis that the error variance of the dependent variable is equal across groups.

a. Design: Intercept + Diseases + Gender + HS + Diseases * Gender + Diseases * HS + Gender * HS + Diseases * Gender * HS

Table-10
Showing Mean, SD & Mean difference between patients of diabetes and hypertension for quality of life factor- Goals and Motivation.

Diseases (A)	N	Mean	SD	Mean Difference
Diabetes A1	200	10.21	1.69	1.50
Hypertension A2	200	8.71	2.43	

Figure no.8
Showing comparison of Mean scores between patients of diabetes and hypertension for quality of life factor- Goals and Motivation.

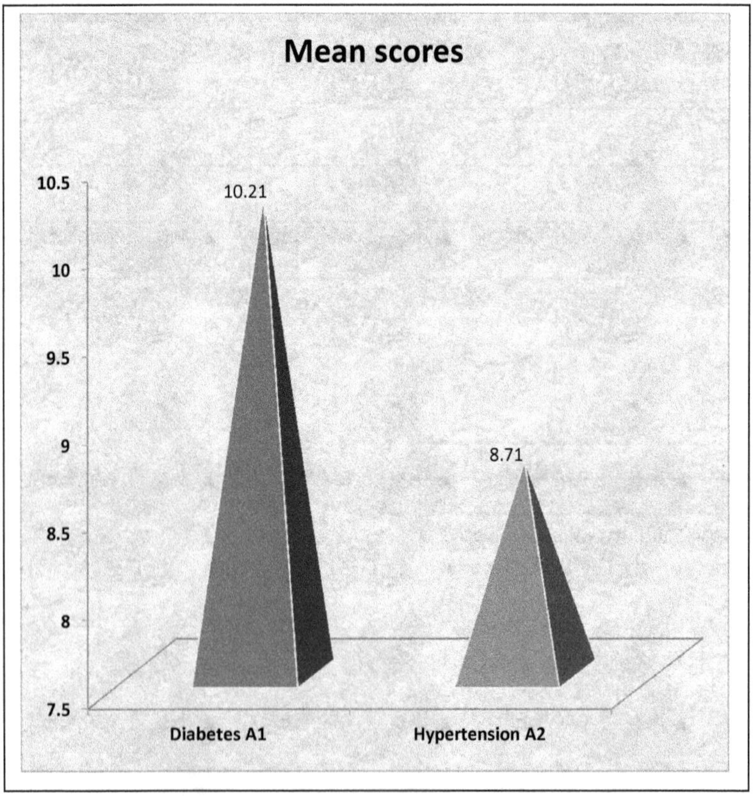

Table-11

Showing Mean, SD & Mean difference between male and female patients with diabetes and hypertension for quality of life factor- Goals and Motivation.

Gender (B)	N	Mean	SD	Mean Difference
Male B1	200	9.34	2.24	0.20
Female B2	200	9.58	2.20	

Figure no.9

Showing comparison of mean score between male and female patients with diabetes and hypertension for quality of life factor- Goals and Motivation.

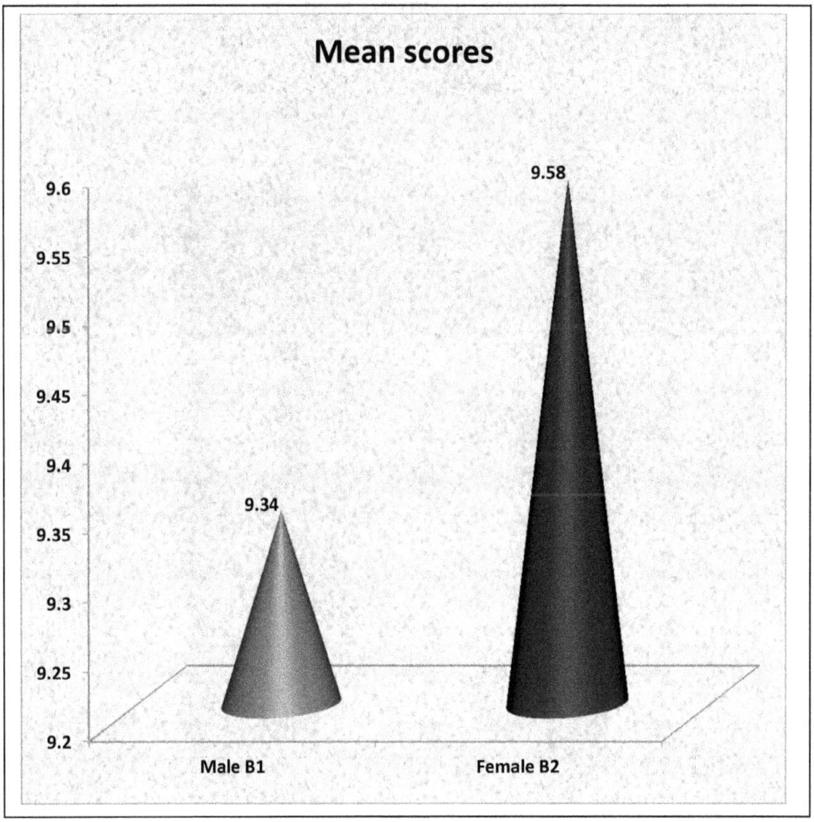

Table-12

Showing Mean, SD & Mean difference between patients with and without hereditary status for quality of life factor- Goals and Motivation.

Hereditary status (C)	N	Mean	SD	Mean Difference
Hereditary C1	200	9.23	2.39	0.46
Non-hereditary C2	200	9.69	2.02	

Figure no. 10

Showing comparisons of mean scores between patients with and without hereditary status for quality of life factor- Goals and Motivation.

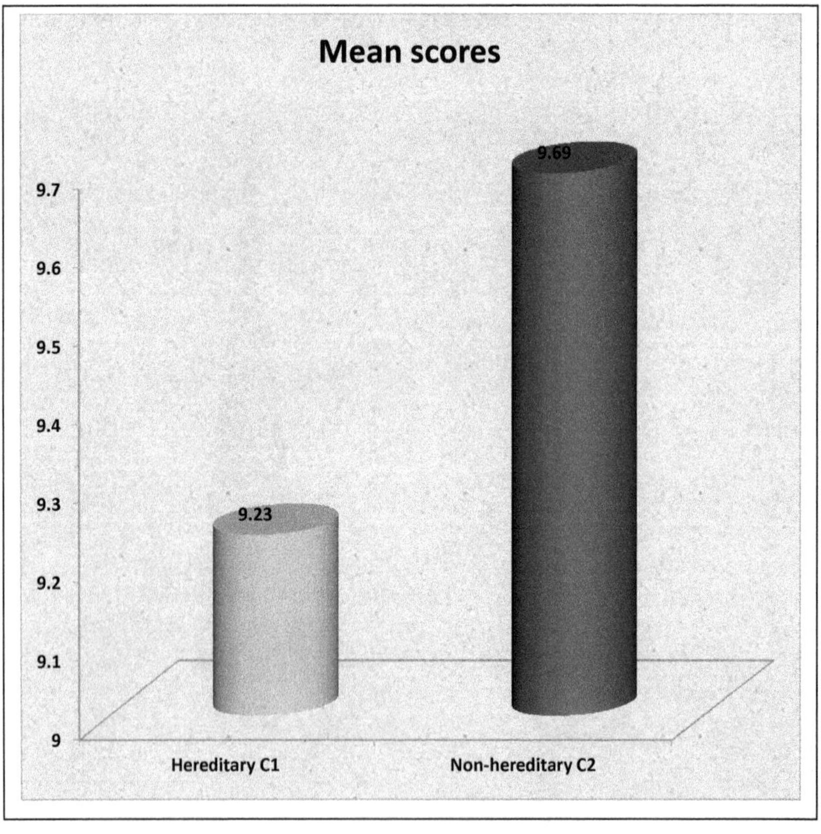

Table 13
Showing Mean, SD & Mean difference among interaction of diseases and Gender of patients with diabetes and hypertension for quality of life factor- Goals and Motivation.

Diseases (A)	Gender (B)	N	Mean	SD	Mean Difference
Diabetes A1	Male B1	100	9.96	1.76	0.51
	Female B2	100	10.47	1.59	
Hypertension A2	Male B1	100	8.72	2.50	0.02
	Female B2	100	8.70	2.38	

Figure no. 11
Showing comparisons of mean scores among interaction of diseases and Gender of patients with diabetes and hypertension for quality of life factor- Goals and Motivation.

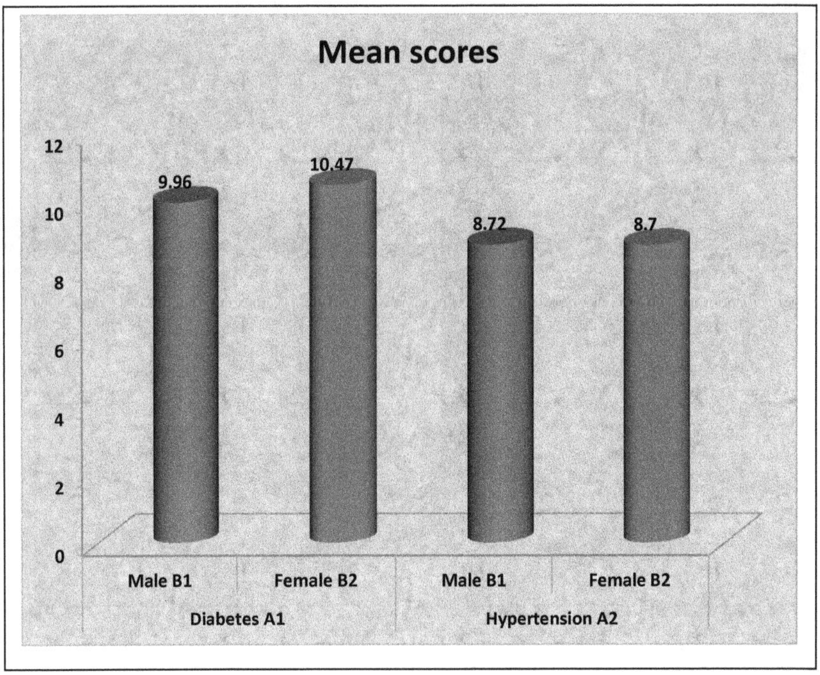

Table 14
Showing Mean, SD & Mean difference among interaction of diseases and hereditary status of patients for quality of life factor- Goals and Motivation.

Diseases (A)	Hereditary (C)	N	Mean	SD	Mean Difference
Diabetes A1	Hereditary *C1*	100	10.14	1.71	0.15
	Non- hereditary *C2*	100	10.29	1.68	
Hypertension A2	Hereditary *C1*	100	8.33	2.63	0.76
	Non- hereditary *C2*	100	9.09	2.17	

Figure no. 12
Showing the comparison of mean scores among interaction of diseases and hereditary status of patients for quality of life factor- Goals and Motivation.

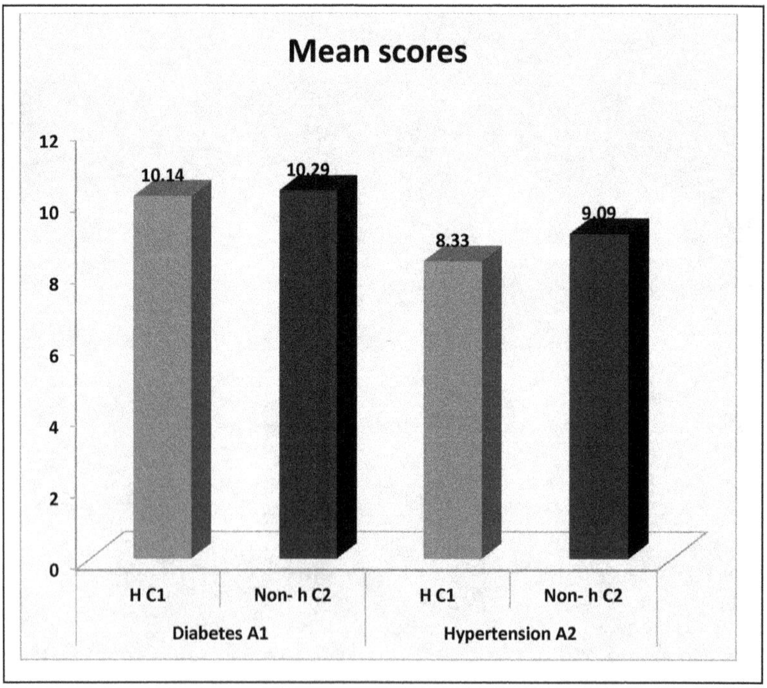

Table 15
Showing Mean, SD & Mean difference among interaction of Gender and hereditary status of patients for quality of life factor- Goals and Motivation.

Gender (B)	Hereditary status (C)	N	Mean	SD	Mean Difference
Male	Hereditary *C1*	100	9.12	2.38	0.44
	Non-hereditary *C2*	100	9.56	2.09	
Female	Hereditary *C1*	100	9.35	2.41	0.47
	Non-hereditary *C2*	100	9.82	1.96	

Figure no. 13
Showing comparisons of mean scores among interaction of Gender and hereditary status of patients for quality of life factor- Goals and Motivation

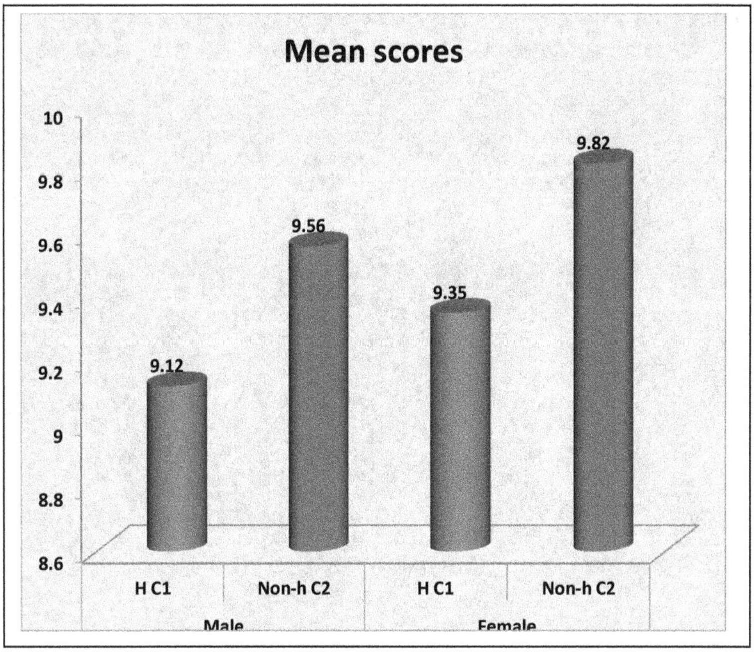

Table 16
Showing Mean, SD & Mean difference among interaction of diseases, gender and hereditary status of patients with diabetes and hypertension for quality of life factor- Goals and Motivation.

Diseases (A)	Gender (B)	Hereditary status (C)	N	Mean	SD	Mean Difference
Diabetes A1	*Male B1*	*Hereditary C1*	50	9.92	1.57	0.08
		Non- hereditary C2	50	10.00	1.94	
	Female B2	*Hereditary C1*	50	10.36	1.82	0.22
		Non- hereditary C2	50	10.58	1.32	
Hypertension A2	*Male B1*	*Hereditary C1*	50	8.32	2.77	0.8
		Non- hereditary C2	50	9.12	2.16	
	Female B2	*Hereditary C1*	50	8.34	2.52	0.72
		Non- hereditary C2	50	9.06	2.19	

Figure no. 14
Showing comparisons of mean scores among interaction of diseases, gender and hereditary status of patients with diabetes and hypertension for quality of life factor- Goals and Motivation.

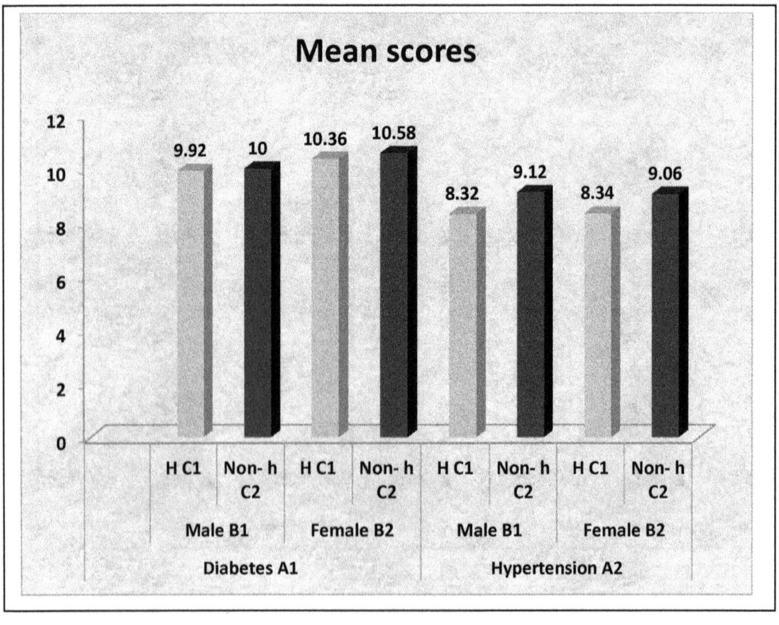

Main Effect:

Quality of life factor goals and motivation with regard to Types of disease:

When the F test was used to investigate the influence of Types of disease on Quality of Life element goals motivation in diabetic and hypertension patients, significant F value was found. The F value was highlighted F (1, 200) = 51.87, $p<.01$(Table no.9), which was significant. Table no.9 and 10 present that mean scores of diabetic and hypertension patients are 10.21 (SD = 1.69) and 8.75 (SD = 2.43), respectively and the difference between two means is 1.50. Based on the above findings, one can well imagine that diabetic patients have a higher quality of life element goals and motivation than hypertensive patients.

Quality of life factor goals and motivation with regard to Gender

Tables 9 and 11 shown the F value and mean score for the gender of diabetic and hypertensive patients. The F ratio was reported to be insignificant F(1,200) = 1.37, p >.05. Mean score acquired by male patients is 9.34 (SD = 2.24) and for female patients is 9.58 (SD = 2.20), whereas the mean difference of both the group is 0.20. This mean difference (Table No.11 & Chart No.9) suggested that there is a nominal mean difference among both the groups. It can be said that both male and female patients with diabetes and hypertension are equal on Quality of life factor goals–motivation.

Quality of life factor goals and motivation with regard to Hereditary status:

The calculated F value of Hereditary status was found to be F (1, 200) = 2.74, which was quite insignificant. Table No. 12 and chart no. 10 highlighted that mean score of patients with hereditary status is 9.23 (SD=2.39), whereas a mean score of patients without hereditary status is 9.69 (SD=2.02), and the difference between mean scores was 0.46, which is very negligible. It can be understood that hereditary status had no impact on Quality of life factor goals motivation. It seems that both the groups of patients have equally motivated towards their goals.

Interaction Effect

Quality of life factor goals and motivation with regard to Types of disease and Gender:

The study's main goal was to see if diabetic male and female patients and male and female patients with hypertension have different Quality of Life factor goals and motivation. Table no. 9 displayed that the F value for the interaction of Types of disease and Gender is also observed to be insignificant F (1,100) = 1.60, *p*> .05. By the same point of view Table no. 13 and chart no.11 displayed that mean scores of male and female diabetic patients are (M=9.96, SD= 1.76) and (M = 10.47, SD = 1.59) respectively, whereas the mean difference of both the group of patients is .051. As again mean scores of male and female patients with hypertension are (M =8.72, SD = 2.50) and (M = 8.70, SD = 2.38), the mean difference of both the group of the patients is 0.02. The insignificant mean difference among four groups revealed that all the groups of patients have similar quality of life factor goals and motivation.

Quality of life trait goals and motivation with regard to Types of disease and Hereditary status:

The F ratio for Types of disease and Hereditary status is F (1, 100) =2.13, which was non-significant (*p* >05). Table no. 14 and chart no.12 represent the mean score of diabetic patients with hereditary status is 10.14 (SD = 1.71), and the mean score for diabetic patients without genetic status is 10.29 (SD 1.68). Statistically, the non-significant mean difference is 0.15, whereas the mean of hypertension patients with hereditary status is 8.33 (SD = 2.63) and the mean score of hypertension patients non hereditary status is 9.09 (SD = 2.17), the difference between two means is 0.76. It can be explained that all four groups have a similar level of goal and motivation.

Quality of life factor-goals and motivation with regard to Gender and Hereditary status:

The calculated value for interaction between Gender and Hereditary status of diabetes and hypertension is found to be F (1, 100) = 0.005, which was quite non-significant. As seen from Table no.15 and chart no.13 mean score of male patients with heredity is 9.12 (SD = 2.38), and the mean of male patients without heredity is 9.56 (SD =2.09), whereas the difference of mean scores is 0.44. Female patients with heredity have a mean score of 9.35 (SD = 2.41), while female patients without heredity have a mean score of 9.82 (SD = 1.96). The mean score difference is 0.47.

The mean difference between almost all four groups is insignificant. As a result, it can be concluded that all four groups of patients reported a similar level of quality of life factor goals and motivation.

Quality of life factor- goals and motivation with regard to Types of disease, Gender and Hereditary status:

The F ratio for Types of disease, Gender, and Hereditary status of diabetic and hypertensive patients is insignificant ($F(1, 50) = 0.06$, $p>.05$). Diabetic male patients with heredity have a mean score of 9.92 (SD =1.57), and non-heredity patients have a mean score of 10.00 (SD =1.94), respectively. The mean difference between both groups is 0.08. As again mean value of diabetic female patients with and without hereditary status are 10.36 (SD = 1.82) &10.58 (SD = 1.32). The mean difference of both the group is 0.22 which was also statistically more negligible. As seen from the table, the mean score of hypertension male patients with heredity is 8.32 (SD =2.77), whereas the mean score of hypertension male patients without hereditary status is 9.12 (SD = 2.16). The difference in average scores is 0.8, which is statistically insignificant. Similarly, the mean score of female hypertension patients with heredity is 8.34 (SD = 2.52), while the mean score of female hypertension patients without heredity is 9.06 (SD = 2.19). The mean difference is calculated to be 0.72. The quality of life factor goals and motivation are similar in all eight groups of diabetic and hypertensive patients.

Table: 17

Showing ANOVA summary for the quality of life factor- Spirituality.

Source	Type III Sum of Squares	df	Mean Square	F	Sig. Level
Diseases (A)	519.840	1	519.840	126.356	$p<.01$
Gender (B)	31.360	1	31.360	7.623	$p<.01$
Heredity status (C)	.010	1	.010	.002	NS
*Diseases * Gender* (A*B)	15.210	1	15.210	3.697	NS
*Diseases * Heredity status* (A*C)	3.240	1	3.240	.788	NS
*Gender * Heredity status* (B*C)	19.360	1	19.360	4.706	$p<.05$
*Diseases * Gender * Heredity status* (A*B*C)	.010	1	.010	.002	NS
Error	1612.720	392	4.114		
Total	34422.000	400			
Corrected Total	2201.750	399			

Levene's Test of Equality of Error Variances[a]

Dependent Variable: Q3

F	df1	df2	Sig.
5.918	7	392	.000

Tests the null hypothesis that the error variance of the dependent variable is equal across groups.

a. Design: Intercept + Diseases + Gender + HS + Diseases * Gender + Diseases * HS + Gender * HS + Diseases * Gender * HS

Table 18
Showing Mean, SD & Mean difference between patients of diabetes and hypertension for quality of life factor- Spirituality.

Diseases (A)	N	Mean	SD	Mean Difference
Diabetes A1	200	10.11	1.68	2.28
Hypertension A2	200	7.83	2.36	

Figure no.15
Showing comparisons of mean scores between patients of diabetes and hypertension for quality of life factor- Spirituality

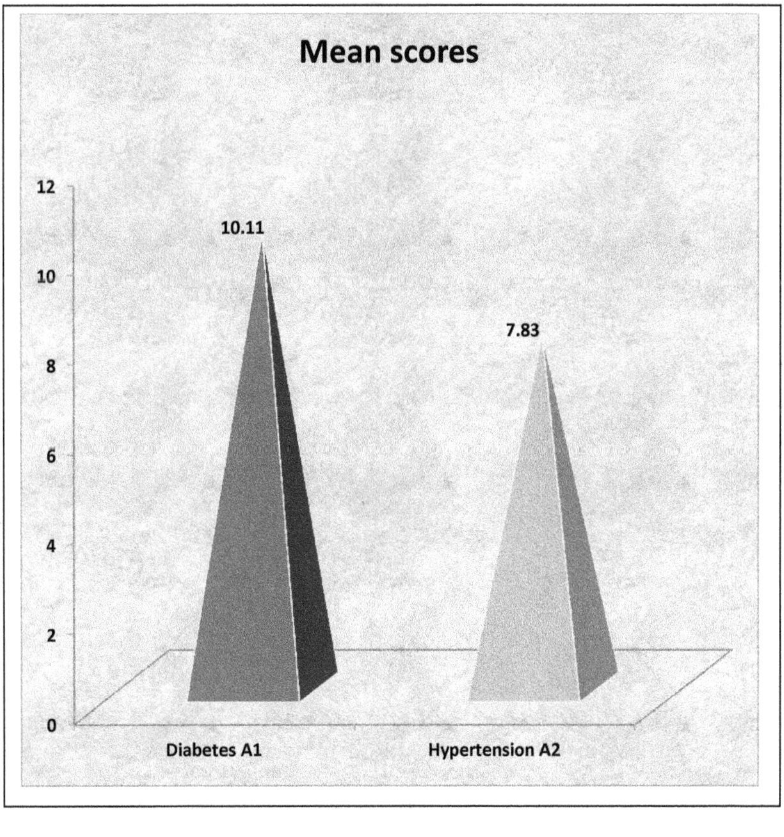

Table 19
Showing Mean, SD & Mean difference between male and female patients with diabetes and hypertension for quality of Spirituality.

Gender (B)	N	Mean	SD	Mean Difference
Male B1	200	8.69	2.42	0.56
Female B2	200	9.25	2.24	

Figure no.16
Showing comparisons of mean scores between male and female patients with diabetes and hypertension for quality of Spirituality.

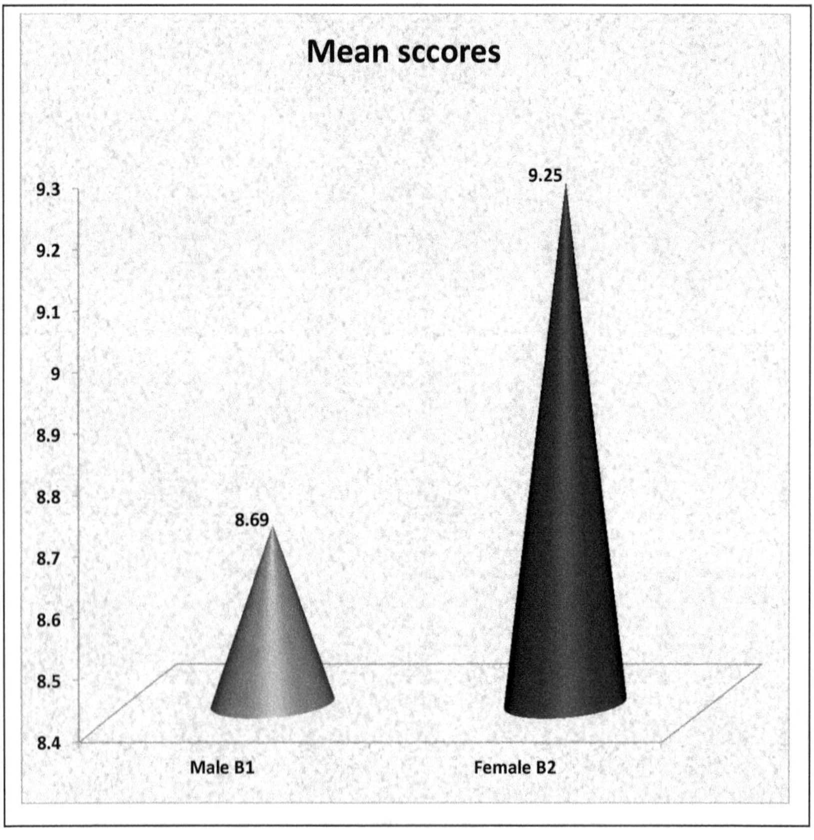

Table 20
Showing Mean, SD & Mean difference between patients with and without hereditary status for quality of life factor- Spirituality.

Hereditary status (C)	N	Mean	SD	Mean Difference
Hereditary C1	200	8.97	2.36	0.01
Non-hereditary C2	200	8.98	2.33	

Figure no. 17
Showing comparisons of mean scores between patients with and without hereditary status for quality of life factor- Spirituality.

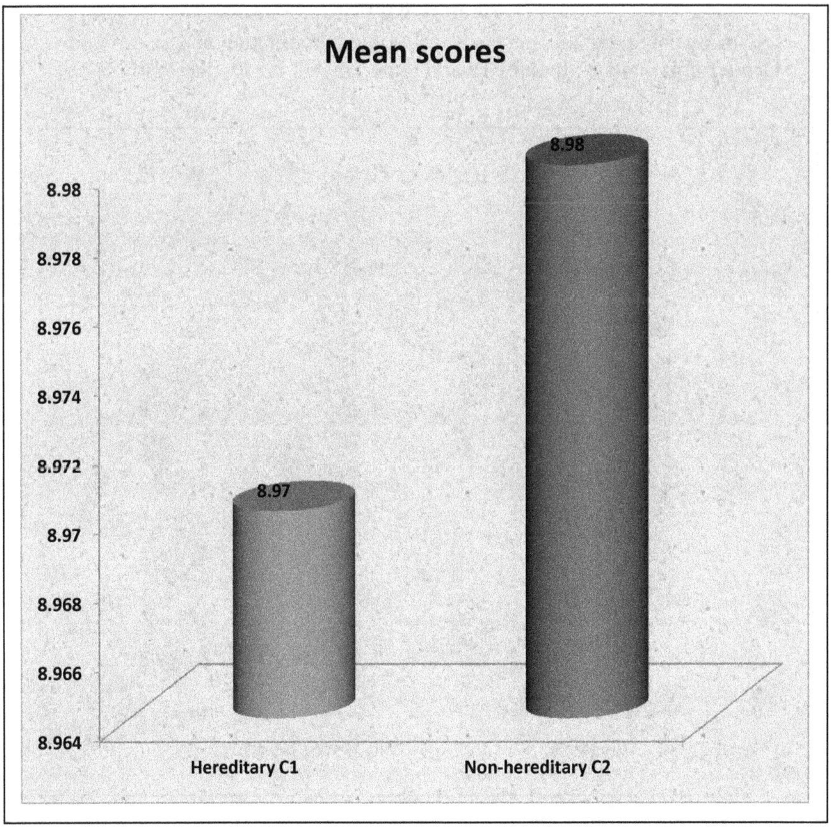

Table 21

Showing Mean, SD & Mean difference among interaction of diseases and Gender of patients with diabetes and hypertension for quality of life factor Spirituality.

Diseases (A)	Gender (B)	N	Mean	SD	Mean Difference
Diabetes A1	Male B1	100	10.03	1.66	0.17
	Female B2	100	10.20	1.71	
Hypertension A2	Male B1	100	7.36	2.32	0.95
	Female B2	100	8.31	2.31	

Figure no. 18

Showing comparisons of mean scores among interaction of diseases and Genderof patients with diabetes and hypertension for quality of life factor Spirituality.

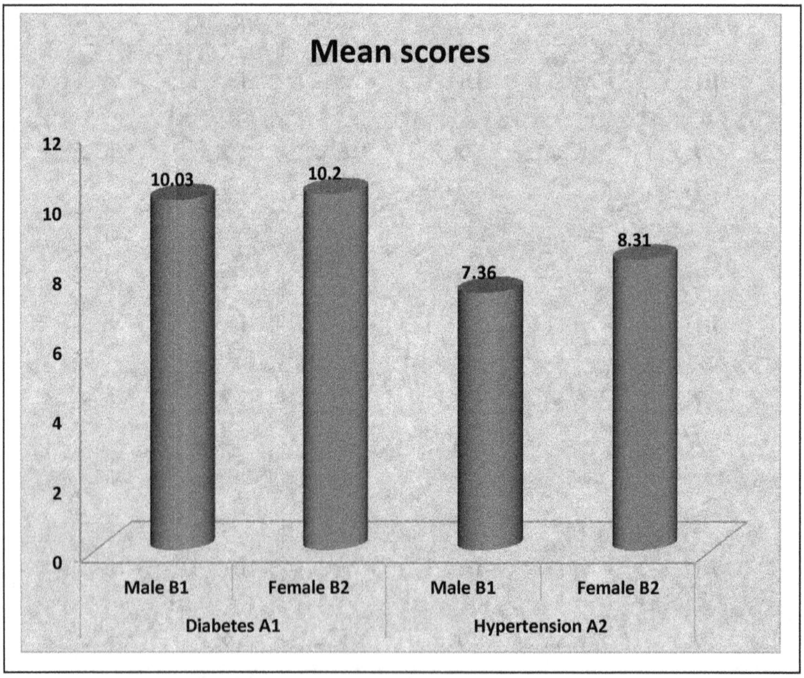

Table 22
Showing Mean, SD & Mean difference among interaction of diseases and hereditary status of patients for quality of life factor- Spirituality.

Diseases (A)	Hereditary (C)	N	Mean	SD	Mean Difference
Diabetes A1	Hereditary *C1*	100	10.20	1.84	0.17
	Non- hereditary *C2*	100	10.03	1.52	
Hypertension A2	Hereditary *C1*	100	7.74	2.18	0.19
	Non- hereditary *C2*	100	7.93	2.53	

Figure no. 19
Showing comparisons of mean scores among interaction of diseases and hereditary status of patients for quality of life factor- Spirituality.

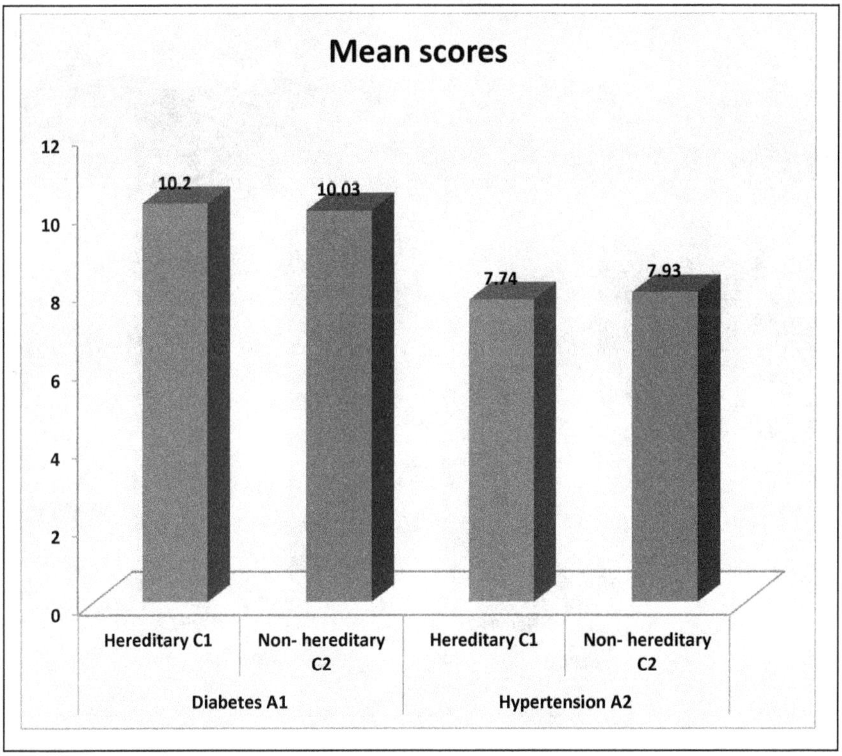

Table 23
Showing Mean, SD & Mean difference among interaction of Gender and hereditary status of patients for quality of life factor- Spirituality.

Gender (B)	Hereditary status (C)	N	Mean	SD	Mean Difference
Male	Hereditary *C1*	100	8.91	2.49	0.43
	Non-hereditary *C2*	100	8.48	2.33	
Female	Hereditary *C1*	100	9.03	2.23	0.45
	Non-hereditary *C2*	100	9.48	2.24	

Figure no. 20
Showing comparisons of mean scores among interaction of Gender and hereditary status of patients for quality of life factor- Spirituality.

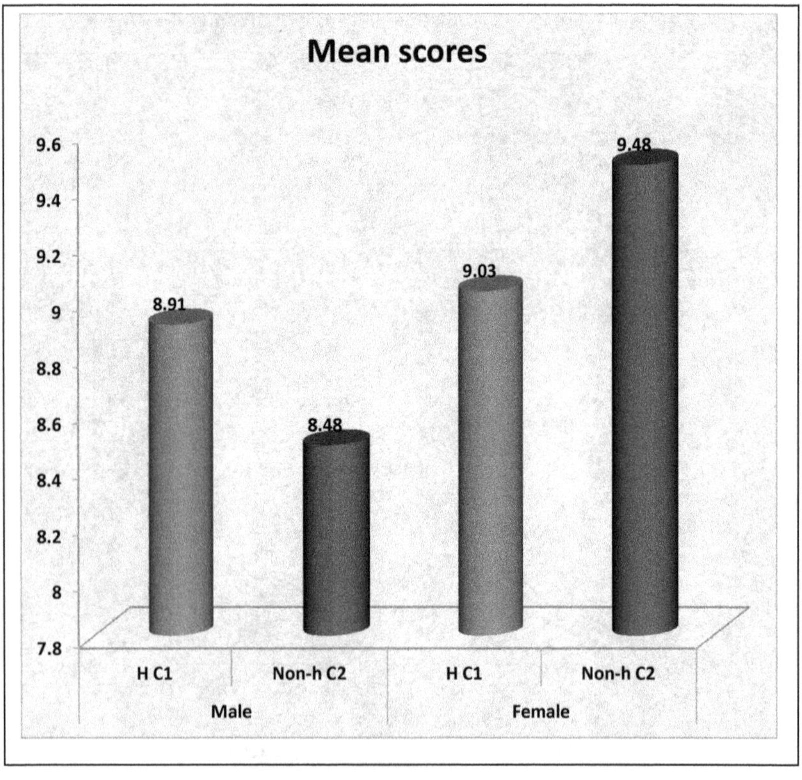

Table 24
Showing Mean, SD & Mean difference among interaction of diseases, gender and hereditary status of patients with diabetes and hypertension for quality of life factor Spirituality.

Diseases (A)	Gender (B)	Hereditary status (C)	N	Mean	SD	Mean Difference
Diabetes A1	*Male B1*	*Hereditary C1*	50	10.34	1.79	0.62
		Non- hereditary C2	50	9.72	1.48	
	Female B2	*Hereditary C1*	50	10.06	1.91	0.28
		Non- hereditary C2	50	10.34	1.50	
Hypertension A2	*Male B1*	*Hereditary C1*	50	7.48	2.28	0.24
		Non- hereditary C2	50	7.24	2.38	
	Female B2	*Hereditary C1*	50	8.00	2.07	0.62
		Non- hereditary C2	50	8.62	2.52	

Figure no. 21
Showing comparisons of mean scores among interaction of diseases, gender and hereditary status of patients with diabetes and hypertension for quality of life factor Spirituality.

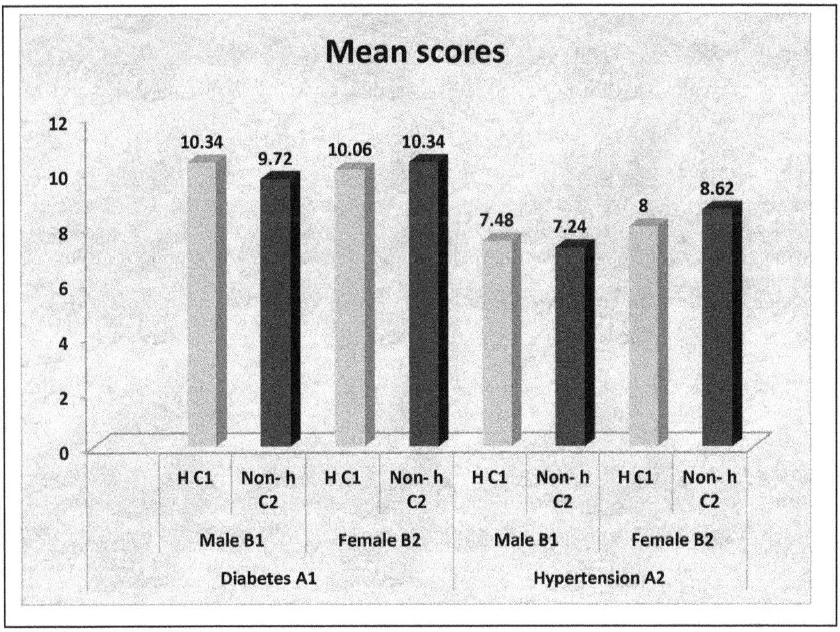

Main Effect:

Quality of life factor spirituality with regard to Types of disease:

A significant F value was found when the F test was used to study the influence of types of disease on the Quality of Life factor spirituality in diabetic and hypertension patients. The significant the F value F (1, 200) = 126.35, p<.01 (Table no.17) was highlighted. Table no.18 and 15 present that mean scores of diabetic and hypertension patients are 10.11 (SD = 1.68) and 7.83 (SD = 2.36), respectively, and the difference between two means is 2.28. According to the findings, hypertensive patients have a poor quality of life spirituality than diabetic patients.

Quality of life factor spirituality with regard to Gender

Tables 17 and 19 explain the F value and mean score for the gender of diabetic and hypertensive patients, with the mean difference and F ratio reported to be significant F(1,200) = 7.62, p <.01 The mean value obtained by the male patient is 8.69 (SD = 2.42), while female patients have 9.25 (SD = 2.24), with a mean difference of 0.56 between the two groups. This mean difference (Table No.19 & Chart No.16) indicated that both groups have a nominal mean difference. Female patients with diabetes and hypertension have slight better spirituality as compared to male patients.

Quality of life factor spirituality with regard to Hereditary status:

The calculated F value of Hereditary status was F (1, 200) = 0.002, which was insignificant Table No. 20 and chart no.17 highlighted that the mean score of patients with hereditary status is 8.97 (SD=2.36). In contrast, a mean score of patients without hereditary status is 8.98 (SD=2.33) and the difference between mean scores was 0.01, which is negligible. One can say that hereditary status had no impact on Quality of life trait spirituality. It seems both groups of patients appear to have been similarly influenced by spirituality.

Interaction Effect

Quality of life factor spirituality with regard to Types of disease and Gender:

The study's primary goal was to determine whether diabetic male and female patients, as well as male and female hypertensive patients, have different Quality of Life factors spirituality. Table no.17 showed that F value for the interaction of Types of disease and Gender is also observed to be insignificant F (1,100) = 3.69, *p*> .05. By the same point of view Table, no.21 and chart no.18 displayed that mean scores of male and female diabetic patients are(M=10.03, SD= 1.66) and (M = 10.20, SD = 1.71) respectively, whereas the mean difference of both the group of patients is 0.17. As the mean scores of male and female hypertensive patients are (M =7.36, SD = 2.32) and (M = 8.31, SD = 2.31), respectively, the mean difference of both groups of patients is 0.95. According to the mean difference between the four groups, disease type and gender significantly impact the quality of life factor spirituality.

Quality of life factor spirituality with regard to Types of disease and Hereditary status:

F (1, 100) =.78 for Types of disease and Hereditary status, which was not significant (p>05). The mean value of diabetic patients with hereditary status is 10.20 (SD = 1.84) in table 22 and chart 19, while the mean score for diabetic patients without hereditary status is 10.03. (SD 1.68). Statistically significant mean difference is 0.17, whereas the mean of hypertension patients with hereditary status is 7.74 (SD = 2.18) and mean score of hypertension patients non-genetic status is 7.74 (SD = 2.53), the difference between two means is 0.19. It may be inferred all four groups have a comparable amount of spirituality.

Quality of life factor-spirituality with regard to Gender and Hereditary status:

It is found that the calculated value of the interaction between gender and the heredity of diabetes and hypertension is F(1,100) = 4.70, which is significant. Table no.23 and chart no.20 mean value of male patients with heredity is 8.91 (SD = 2.49), and mean of male patients without heredity is 8.48 (SD =2.33), whereas the difference of mean scores is 0.43. Hereditary status of female patients have a mean score of 9.03 (SD = 2.23), while non hereditary status of female patients have a mean score of 9.48 (SD = 2.24). The mean score difference is 0.45. The mean difference is 0.45. Almost all four groups have a significant mean difference. As a result, all four groups of patients reported varying levels of satisfaction with the quality of life factor spirituality.

Quality of life factor- spirituality with regard to Types of disease, Gender and Hereditary status:

Diabetic and hypertensive patients' F ratio for disease types, gender, and hereditary status is insignificant ($F (1, 50) = 0.002$, $p>.05$). Diabetic male patients with heredity have a mean score of 10.34 (SD =1.79), while diabetic male patients without heredity have a mean score of 9.72 (SD =1.48). The mean difference of both the group is 0.28 which was also statistically less. As seen from the Table, the mean score of hypertension male patients with heredity is 7.48 (SD =2.28) whereas mean score of hypertension male patients without hereditary status is 7.24 (SD = 2.38).The difference in average scores is 0.24, which is statistically insignificant. Female hypertension patients with heredity have a mean score of 8.00 (SD = 2.07), while female hypertension patients without heredity have a mean score of 8.62 (SD = 2.52). The mean difference is 0.62, according to the calculations. All eight groups of diabetic and hypertensive patients have similar quality of life factor Spirituality.

Table: 25

Showing ANOVA summary for the quality of life factor- Happiness

Source	Type III Sum of Squares	df	Mean Square	F	Sig. Level
Diseases (A)	82.810	1	82.810	22.672	*p*<.01
Gender (B)	92.160	1	92.160	25.232	*p*<.01
Heredity status (C)	225.000	1	225.000	61.603	*p*<.01
*Diseases * Gender* (A*B)	5.760	1	5.760	1.577	NS
*Diseases * Heredity status* (A*C)	23.040	1	23.040	6.308	*p*<.01
*Gender * Heredity status* (B*C)	7.290	1	7.290	1.996	NS
*Diseases * Gender * Heredity status* (A*B*C)	13.690	1	13.690	3.748	NS
Error	1431.760	392	3.652		
Total	40180.000	400			
Corrected Total	1881.510	399			

Levene's Test of Equality of Error Variances[a]

Dependent Variable: Q4

F	df1	df2	Sig.
8.935	7	392	.000

Tests the null hypothesis that the error variance of the dependent variable is equal across groups.

a. Design: Intercept + Diseases + Gender + HS + Diseases * Gender + Diseases * HS + Gender * HS + Diseases * Gender * HS

Table 26

Showing Mean, SD & Mean difference between patients of diabetes and hypertension for quality of life factor- Happiness.

Diseases (A)	N	Mean	SD	Mean Difference
Diabetes A1	200	10.54	1.90	1.51
Hypertension A2	200	9.03	2.32	

Figure no.22

Showing comparisons of mean scores between patients of diabetes and hypertension for quality of life factor- Happiness.

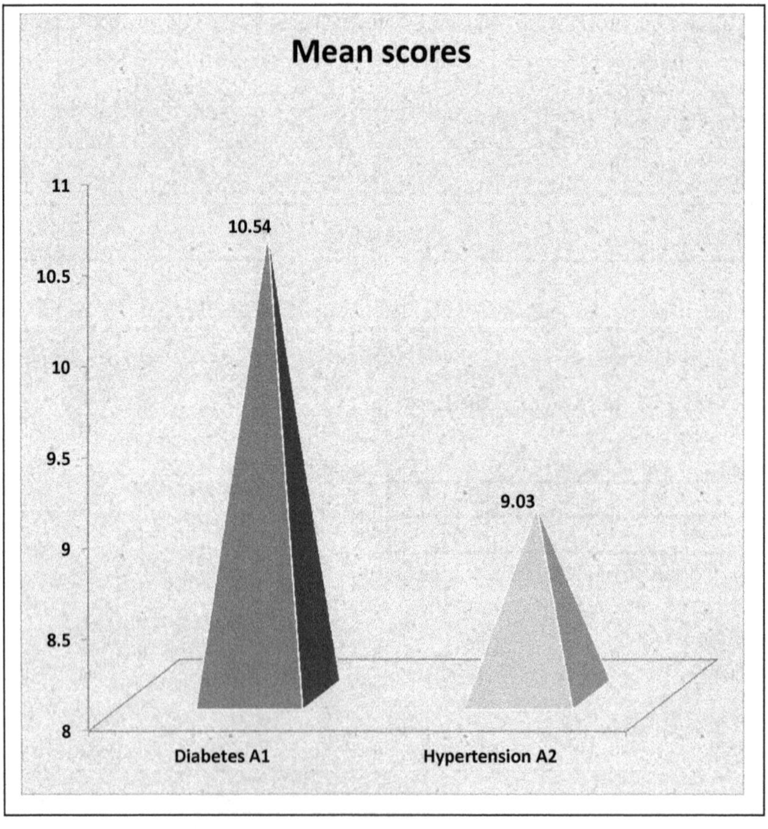

Table 27
Showing Mean, SD & Mean difference between male and female patients with diabetes and hypertension for quality of life factor- Happiness.

Gender (B)	N	Mean	SD	Mean Difference
Male B1	200	8.80	2.33	1.76
Female B2	200	10.56	1.87	

Figure no.23
Showing comparisons of mean scores between male and female patients with diabetes and hypertension for quality of life factor- Happiness.

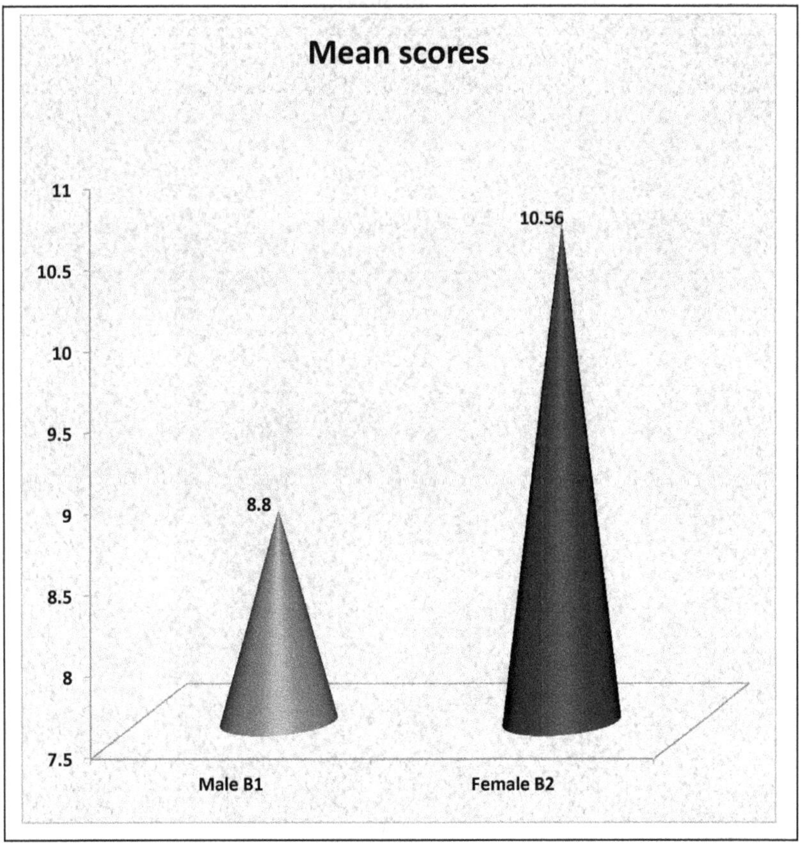

Table 28
Showing Mean, SD & Mean difference between patients with and without hereditary status for quality of life factor- Happiness.

Hereditary status (C)	N	Mean	SD	Mean Difference
Hereditary C1	200	8.83	2.41	1.7
Non-hereditary C2	200	10.53	1.58	

Figure no.24
Showing comparisons of means scores between patients with and without hereditary status for quality of life factor- Happiness.

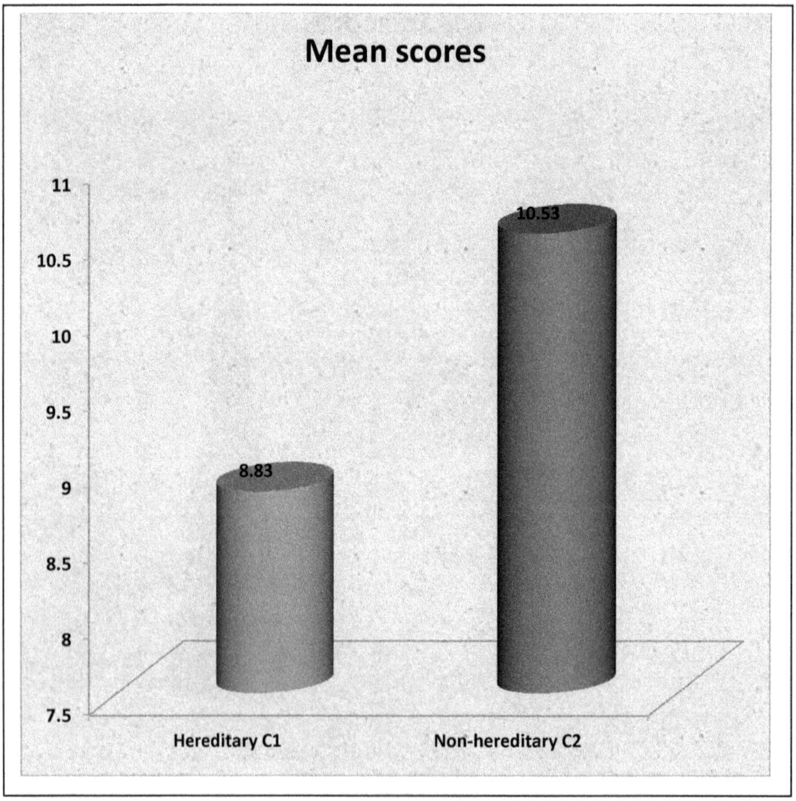

Table 29
Showing Mean, SD & Mean difference among interaction of diseases and Gender of patients with diabetes and hypertension for quality of life factor- Happiness.

Diseases (A)	Gender (B)	N	Mean	SD	Mean Difference
Diabetes A1	Male B1	100	9.88	2.04	0.72
	Female B2	100	10.60	1.68	
Hypertension A2	Male B1	100	8.73	2.47	1.2
	Female B2	100	9.93	2.00	

Figure no. 25

Showing comparisons of mean scores among interaction of diseases and Gender of patients with diabetes and hypertension for quality of life factor- Happiness.

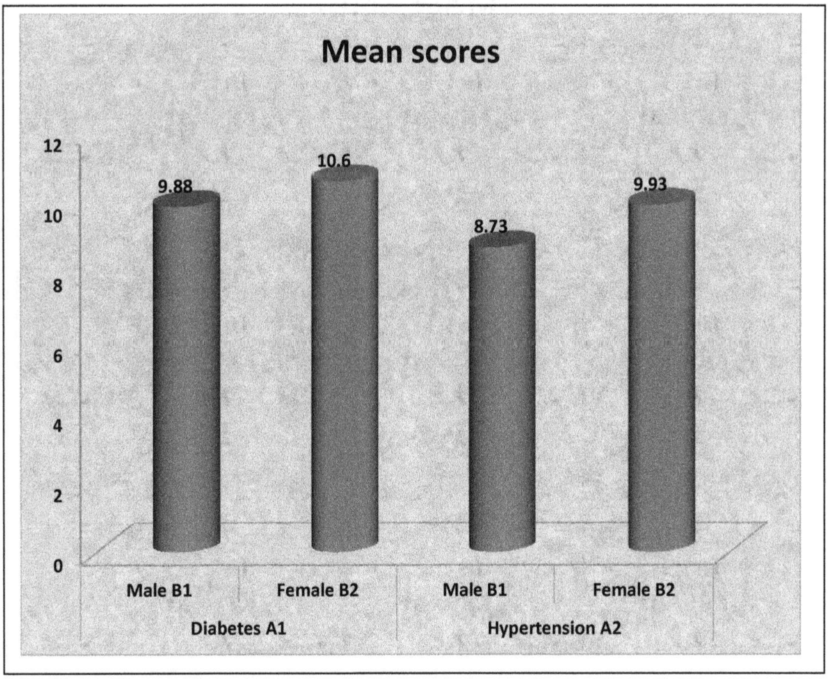

Table 30
Showing Mean, SD & Mean difference among interaction of diseases and hereditary status of patients for quality of life factor- Happiness.

Diseases (A)	Hereditary (C)	N	Mean	SD	Mean Difference
Diabetes A1	Hereditary *C1*	100	9.73	2.17	1.02
	Non- hereditary *C2*	100	10.75	1.42	
Hypertension A2	Hereditary *C1*	100	8.34	2.44	1.98
	Non- hereditary *C2*	100	10.32	1.71	

Figure no. 26
Showing comparisons of mean scores among interaction of diseases and hereditary status of patients for quality of life factor- Happiness.

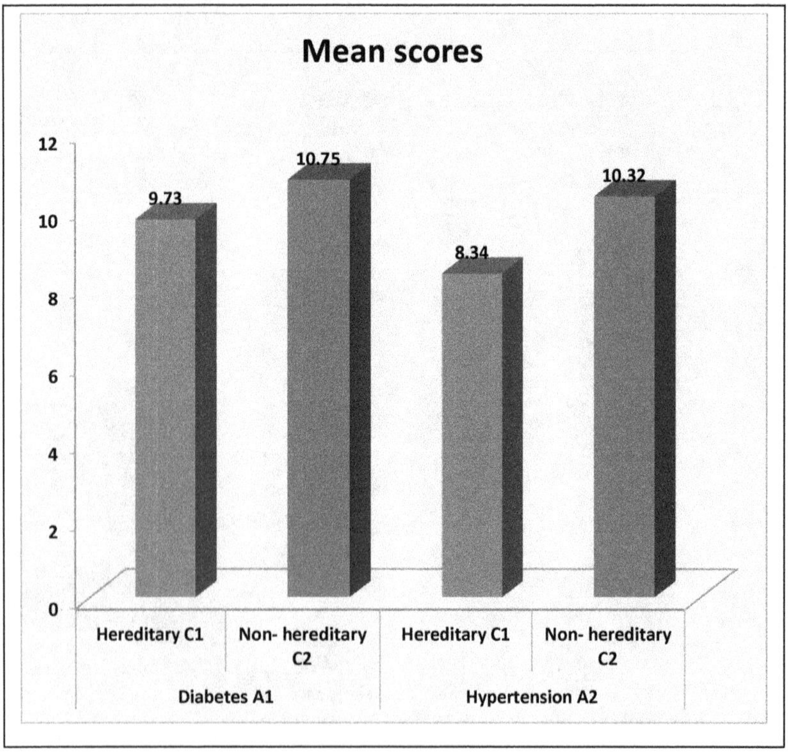

Table 31
Showing Mean, SD & Mean difference among interaction of Gender and hereditary status of patients for quality of life factor- Happiness.

Gender (B)	Hereditary status (C)	N	Mean	SD	Mean Difference
Male	Hereditary *C1*	100	8.42	2.60	1.77
	Non-hereditary *C2*	100	10.19	1.61	
Female	Hereditary *C1*	100	9.65	2.03	1.23
	Non-hereditary *C2*	100	10.88	1.47	

Figure no. 27
Showing comparisons of mean scores among interaction of Gender and hereditary status of patients for quality of life factor- Happiness.

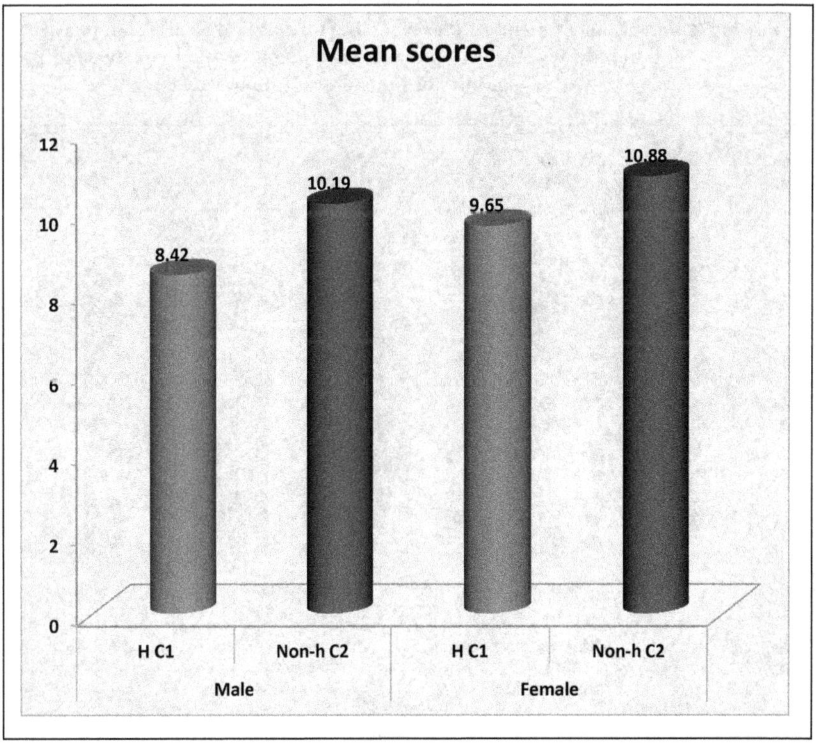

Table 32

Showing Mean, SD & Mean difference among interaction of diseases, gender and hereditary status of patients with diabetes and hypertension for quality of life factor- Happiness.

Diseases (A)	Gender (B)	Hereditary status (C)	N	Mean	SD	Mean Difference
Diabetes A1	*Male B1*	*Hereditary C1*	50	9.42	2.39	0.92
		Non- hereditary C2	50	10.34	1.50	
	Female B2	*Hereditary C1*	50	10.04	1.90	1.12
		Non- hereditary C2	50	11.16	1.21	
Hypertension A2	*Male B1*	*Hereditary C1*	50	7.42	2.43	2.62
		Non- hereditary C2	50	10.04	1.72	
	Female B2	*Hereditary C1*	50	9.26	2.10	1.34
		Non- hereditary C2	50	10.60	1.66	

Figure no. 28

Showing comparisons of mean of scores among interaction of diseases, gender and hereditary status of patients with diabetes and hypertension for quality of life factor- Happiness.

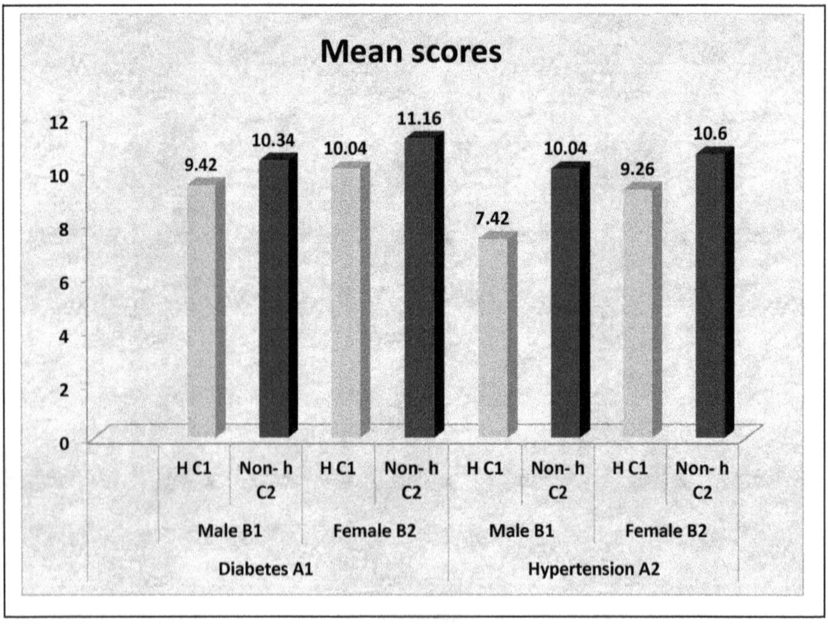

Main Effect:

Quality of life factor happiness with regard to Types of disease:

When using the F test to study the effect of the type of disease in patients with diabetes and hypertension on Quality of life factors happiness ,it is observed that the F value is significant. The F (1, 200) = 22.67, p<.01 (Table no.25) was emphasized. The mean values of diabetic and hypertension patients are 10.54 (SD = 1.90) and 9.03 (SD = 2.32), respectively; according to Tables 26 and 22, the difference between the two means is 1.51. Hypertensive patients have less happiness than diabetic patients, according to the findings.

Quality of life factor happiness with regard to Gender

The F value and mean score for diabetic and hypertensive patients' in relation to gender are shown in Tables 25, with the mean difference and F ratio reported to be significant F(1,200) = 25.23, *p*<.01. Male patients have an average value of 8.80 (SD = 2.33), while female patients have an average value of 10.56 (SD = 1.87), resulting in a mean difference of 1.76 between the two groups. This mean difference (Table No.27 & Chart No.23) denoted that both groups have a nominal mean difference. According to the above findings, it can be concluded that female patients have a higher quality of life factor happiness as compared to male patients.

Quality of life factor happiness with regard to Hereditary status:

Hereditary status has a calculated F value of F (1, 200) = 61.60, which was significant. Table No. 28 and chart No. 24 show that patients with hereditary status have a mean score of 8.83 (SD=2.41), while patients without hereditary status have a mean score of 10.53 (SD=1.58), a significant difference of mean is 1.7. Patients without heredity have better happiness in comparison to patients with heredity.

Interaction Effect

Quality of life factor happiness with regard to Types of disease and Gender:

The study's main goal was to see if diabetic male and female patients, as well as male and female hypertensive patients, have different levels of happiness, with reference to quality of life factor happiness. Table no.25 revealed that the F value for the interaction of disease types and gender is also insignificant, F (1,100) = 1.57, p>.05. Table 29 and chart 25 show that the mean scores of male and female diabetic patients are (M=9.88, SD= 2.04) and (M = 10.60, SD = 1.68), respectively, with a mean difference of 0.72 between the two groups of patients. The mean difference between male and female hypertensive patients is 1.2 because their mean scores are (M =8.73 SD=2.47) and (M=9.93 SD=2.00), respectively. This non-significant mean difference among the four groups displayed that all the four groups of patients have equal quality of life factor happiness.

Quality of life factor happiness with regard to Types of disease and Hereditary status:

Types of disease and Hereditary status had a significant F (1, 100) = 6.30 (p<.01). Table 30 and chart 26 highlight that the mean score for diabetic patients with hereditary status is 9.73 (SD = 2.17), while the mean score for diabetic patients without genetic status is 10.75. (SD=1.42). Statistically significant mean difference is 1.02, whereas the mean of hypertension patients with hereditary status is 8.34 (SD = 2.44) and the mean score of hypertension patients non-hereditary status is 10.32 (SD = 1.71), the difference between two means is 1.98. It indicates that all four groups of patients have a different level of happiness.

Quality of life factor-happiness with regard to Gender and Hereditary status:

The calculated value of the interaction between gender and diabetes and hypertension heredity status is reported to be F(1,100) = 1.99, which is non-significant. The mean value of male patients with hereditary status is 8.42 (SD = 2.60), while the mean value of male patients without hereditary status is 10.19 (SD =1.61), with a 1.77 difference in mean scores. Female patients with hereditary status have a mean score of 9.65 (SD = 2.03), while non hereditary status female patients have a mean score of 10.88 (SD = 1.47). The mean difference is 1.23. Almost all four groups have an insignificant mean difference. As a result, all four groups of patients highlighted similar levels of quality of life factor happiness.

Quality of life factor- happiness with regard to Types of disease, Gender and Hereditary status:

Diabetic and hypertensive patients' F ratios for disease types, gender, and hereditary status are insignificant (F (1, 50) = 3.74, p >.05). Diabetic male patients with heredity have a mean score of 9.42 (SD =2.39), whereas diabetic male patients without heredity have a mean score of 10.34 (SD =1.50). Between the two groups, there is a 0.92 mean difference. Again, the mean values for diabetic female patients with and without hereditary status are 10.04 (SD = 1.90) and 11.16 (SD = 1.21). The mean difference between the two groups is 1.12, which is statistically insignificant. As shown in Table, the mean score of male hypertension patients with heredity is 7.42 (SD =2.43), while the mean score of male hypertension patients without hereditary status is 10.04 (SD = 1.72). The difference in average scores is 2.62, which is statistically insignificant. Similarly, the mean score of female hypertension patients with heredity is 9.26 (SD = 2.10), while the mean score of female hypertension patients without heredity is 10.60 (SD = 1.66). The mean difference is calculated to be 1.34. The quality of life factor happiness is by and large similar in all eight groups of diabetic and hypertensive patients.

Table- 33

Showing ANOVA summary for the quality of life factor- Hopes and Wishes.

Source	Type III Sum of Squares	df	Mean Square	F	Sig. Level
Diseases (A)	.360	1	.360	.173	NS
Gender (B)	4.410	1	4.410	2.117	NS
Heredity status (C)	1.210	1	1.210	.581	NS
*Diseases * Gender* (A*B)	1.690	1	1.690	.811	NS
*Diseases * Heredity status* (A*C)	32.490	1	32.490	15.596	$p<.01$
*Gender * Heredity status* (B*C)	.160	1	.160	.077	NS
*Diseases * Gender * Heredity status* (A*B*C)	23.040	1	23.040	11.060	$p<.01$
Error	816.640	392	2.083		
Total	19924.000	400			
Corrected Total	880.000	399			

Table-34
Showing Mean, SD & Mean difference between patients of diabetes and hypertension for quality of life factor- Hopes and Wishes.

Diseases (A)	N	Mean	SD	Mean Difference
Diabetes A1	200	6.87	1.43	0.06
Hypertension A2	200	6.93	1.53	

Figure no.29
Showing comparison of mean scores between patients of diabetes and hypertension for quality of life factor- Hopes and Wishes

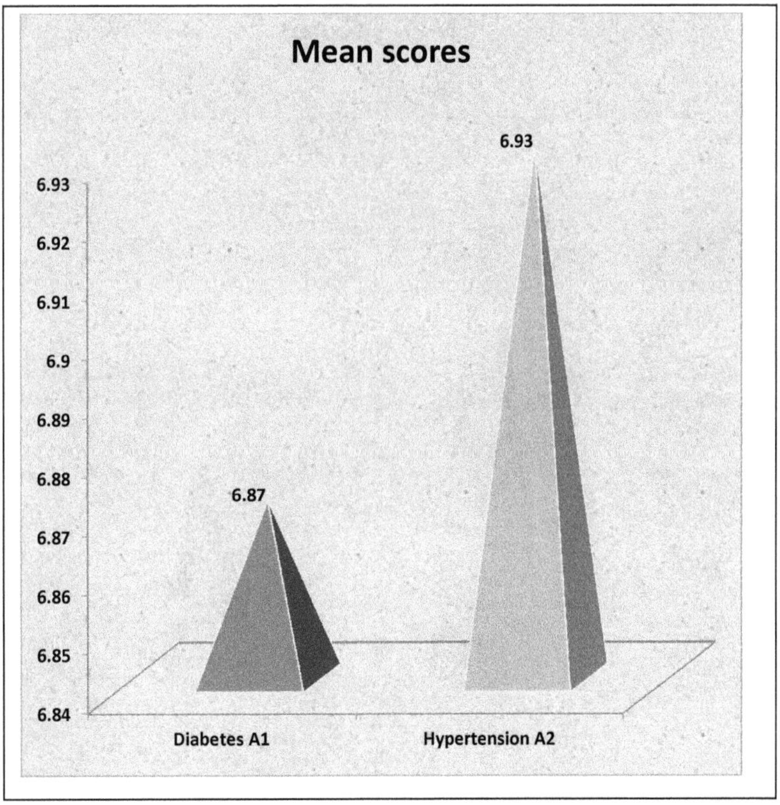

Table 35

Showing Mean, SD & Mean difference between male and female patients with diabetes and hypertension for quality of life factor- Hopes and Wishes.

Gender (B)	N	Mean	SD	Mean Difference
Male B1	200	7.00	1.63	0.21
Female B2	200	6.79	1.31	

Figure no.30

Showing comparisons of mean scores between male and female patients with diabetes and hypertension for quality of life factor- Hopes and Wishes.

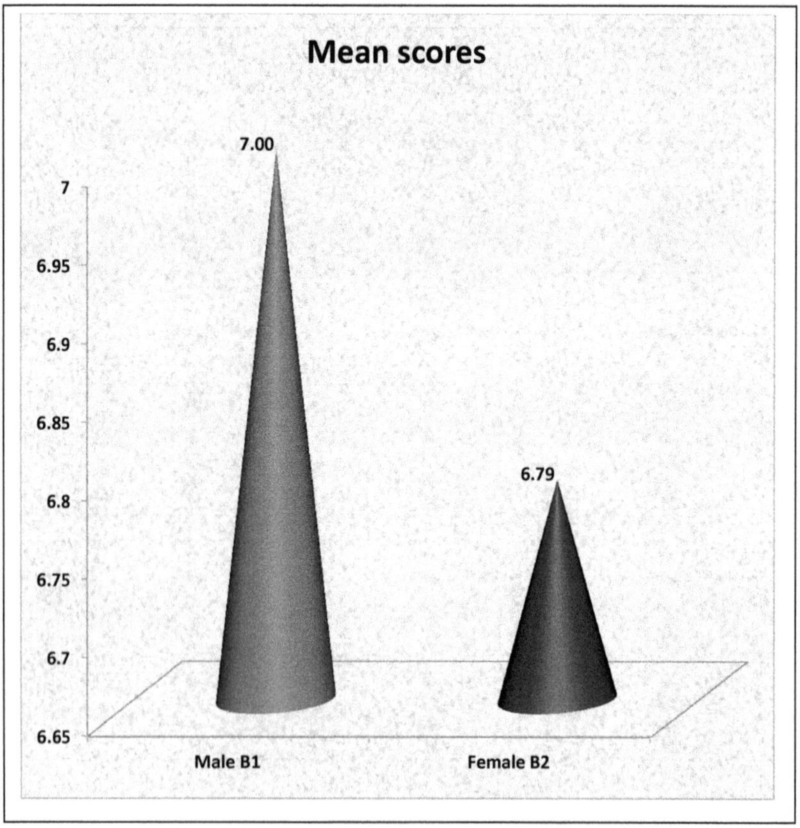

Table- 36
Showing Mean, SD & Mean difference between patients with and without hereditary status for quality of life factor- Hopes and Wishes.

Hereditary status (C)	N	Mean	SD	Mean Difference
Hereditary C1	200	6.95	1.66	0.11
Non-hereditary C2	200	6.84	1.28	

Figure no. 31
Showing composition of mean scores between patients with and without hereditary status for quality of life factor- Hopes and Wishes.

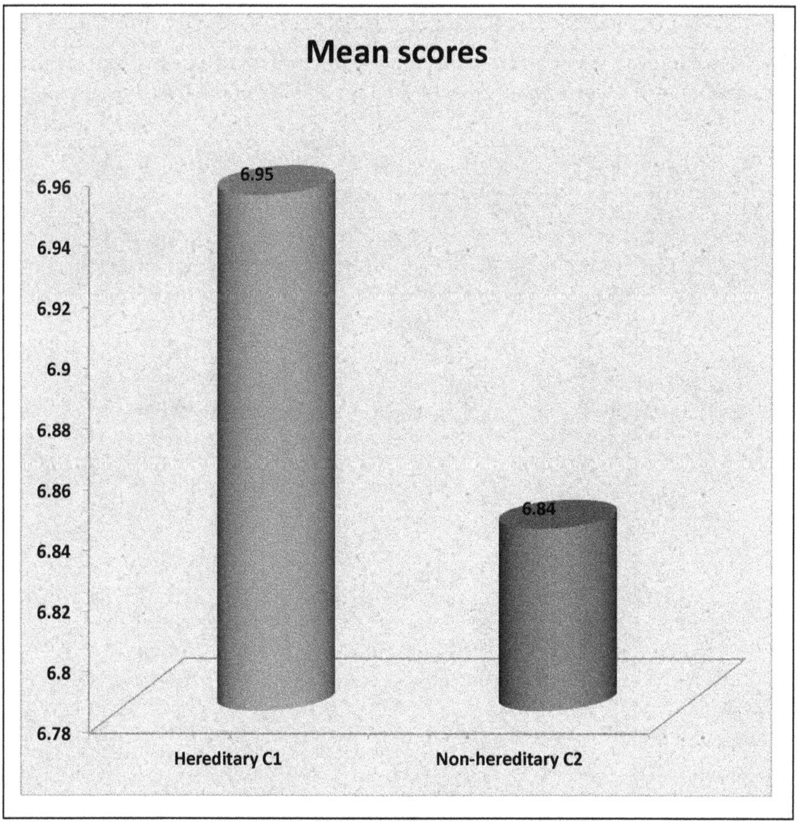

Table 37

Showing Mean, SD & Mean difference among interaction of diseases and Gender of patients with diabetes and hypertension for quality of life factor- Hopes and Wishes.

Diseases (A)	Gender (B)	N	Mean	SD	Mean Difference
Diabetes A1	Male B1	100	7.04	1.58	0.34
	Female B2	100	6.70	1.25	
Hypertension A2	Male B1	100	6.97	1.68	0.08
	Female B2	100	6.89	1.38	

Figure no. 32

Showing comparisons of mean scores among interaction of diseases and Gender of patients with diabetes and hypertension for quality of life factor- Hopes and Wishes.

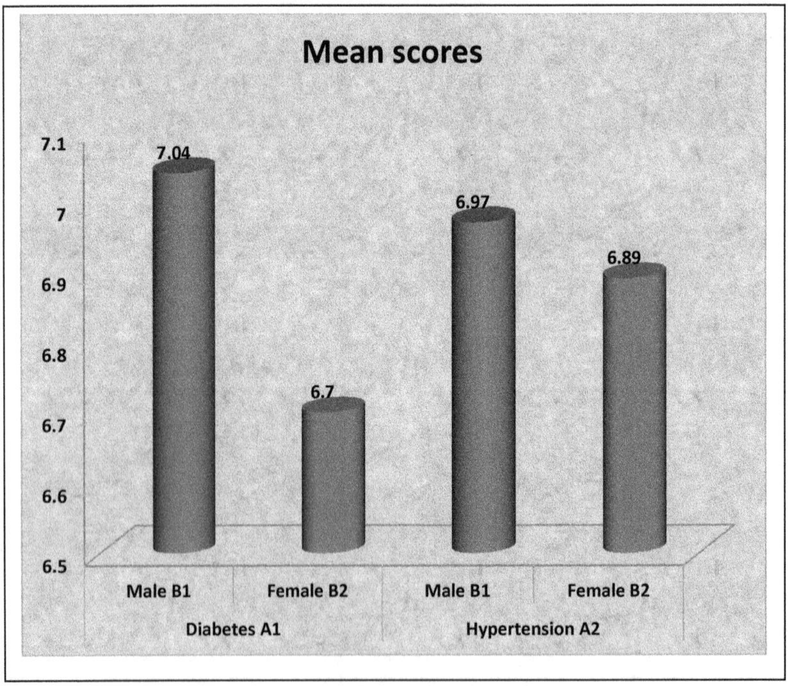

Table 38
Showing Mean, SD & Mean difference among interaction of diseases and hereditary status of patients for quality of life factor- Hopes and Wishes.

Diseases (A)	Hereditary (C)	N	Mean	SD	Mean Difference
Diabetes A1	Hereditary C1	100	7.21	1.63	0.68
	Non- hereditary C2	100	6.53	1.10	
Hypertension A2	Hereditary C1	100	6.70	1.65	0.46
	Non- hereditary C2	100	7.16	1.38	

Figure no. 33
Showing comparisons of mean scores among interaction of diseases and hereditary status of patients for quality of life factor- Hopes and Wishes.

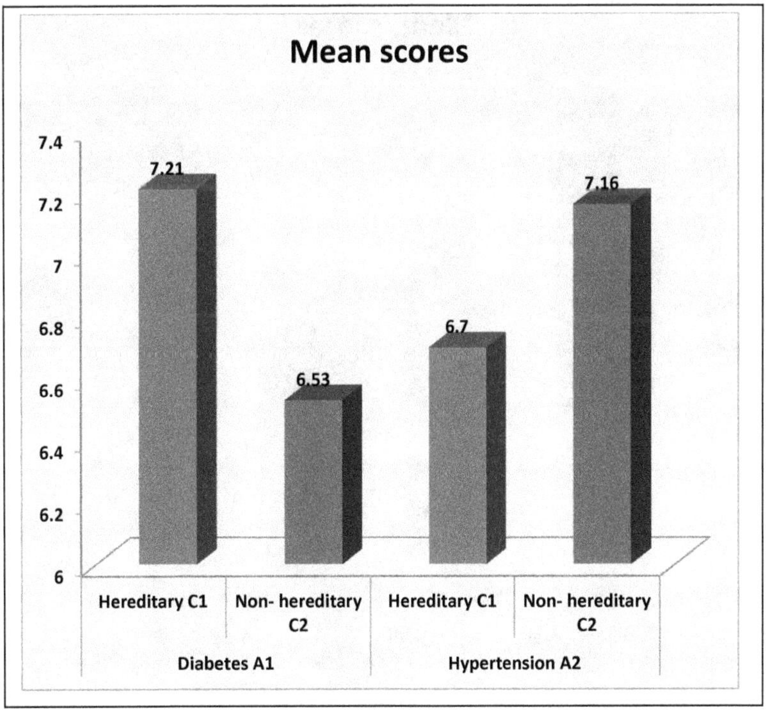

Table 39
Showing Mean, SD & Mean difference among interaction of Gender and hereditary status of patients for quality of life factor- Hopes and Wishes.

Gender (B)	Hereditary status (C)	N	Mean	SD	Mean Difference
Male	Hereditary *C1*	100	7.08	1.77	0.15
	Non-hereditary *C2*	100	6.93	1.47	
Female	Hereditary *C1*	100	6.83	1.53	0.07
	Non-hereditary *C2*	100	6.76	1.07	

Figure no. 34
Showing comparisons of mean scores among interaction of Gender and hereditary status of patients for quality of life factor- Hopes and Wishes.

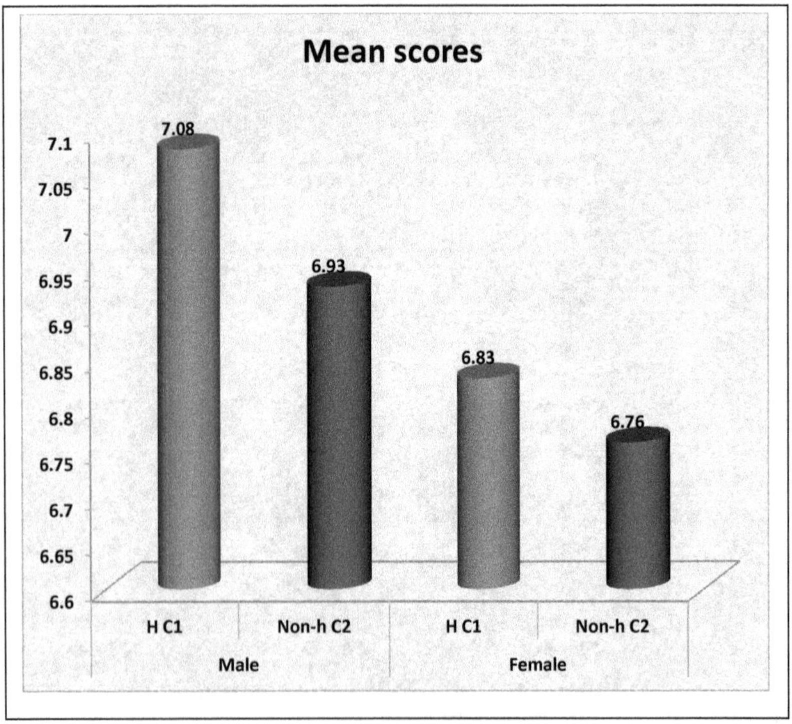

Table 40
Showing Mean, SD & Mean difference among interaction of diseases, gender and hereditary status of patients with diabetes and hypertension for quality of life factor- Hopes and Wishes.

Diseases (A)	Gender (B)	Hereditary status (C)	N	Mean	SD	Mean Difference
Diabetes A1	*Male B1*	*Hereditary C1*	50	7.64	1.69	1.2
		Non- hereditary C2	50	6.44	1.19	
	Female B2	*Hereditary C1*	50	6.78	1.46	0.16
		Non- hereditary C2	50	6.62	1.00	
Hypertension A2	*Male B1*	*Hereditary C1*	50	6.52	1.69	0.9
		Non- hereditary C2	50	7.42	1.56	
	Female B2	*Hereditary C1*	50	6.88	1.61	0.02
		Non- hereditary C2	50	6.90	1.12	

Figure no. 35
Showing comparisons of mean scores among interaction of diseases, gender and hereditary status of patients with diabetes and hypertension for quality of life factor- Hopes and Wishes.

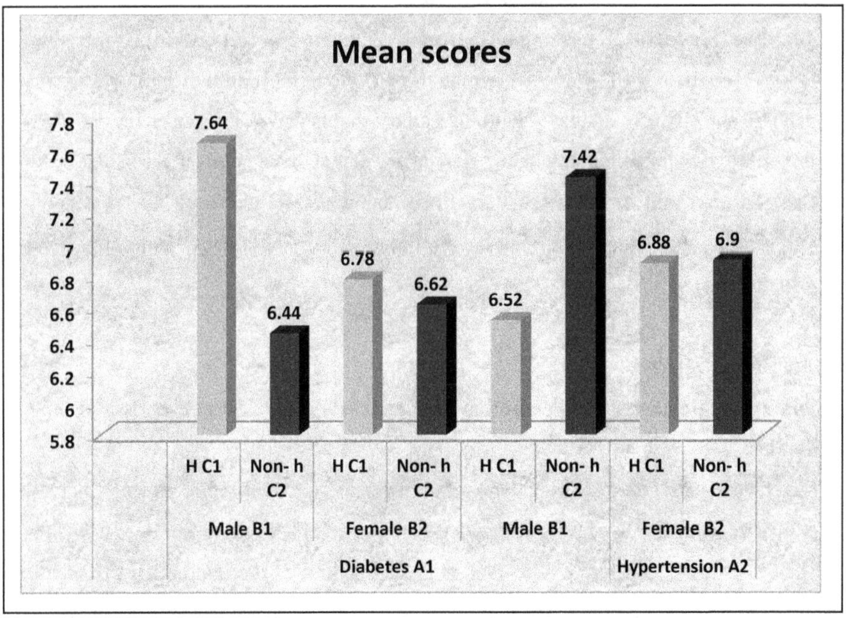

Main Effect:

Quality of life factor-Hopes and Wishes with regard to Types of disease:

To know the effect of disease type on quality of life trait hopes and wishes in patients with diabetes and hypertension, the F test was employed, it is observed insignificant (F (1, 200) = 0.17, p>.05). (Table no.33) was highlighted. The mean scores of diabetic and hypertension patients are 6.87 (SD = 1.43) and 6.93 (SD = 1.53), respectively, according to Tables 29, and the difference between the two means is 0.06. Hypertensive and diabetic patients have more or less similar hope and wish towards their life.

Quality of life factor Hopes and wishes with regard to Gender

Tables 35 and 30 show the F value and mean score for the gender of patient with diabetes and hypertension, with the mean difference and F ratio reported as non significant F(1,200) = 2.11, p>.05. The average value for male patients is 7.00 (SD = 1.63), while the average value for female patients is 6.79 (SD = 1.31), resulting in a mean difference of 0.21 between the two groups.. This mean difference (Table No.35 & Chart No.30) denoted that both groups have a nominal mean difference. According to the above findings, it may be clerified that both female and male patients have equal quality of life factor hopes and wishes.

Quality of life factor hopes and wishes with regard to Hereditary status:

The calculated F value for hereditary status was F (1, 200) = 0.58, which was insignificant (p>.05). Patients with hereditary status have a mean score of 6.95 (SD=1.66), while patients without hereditary status have a mean score of 6.84 (SD=1.28), a significant difference of 0.11 in table No. 36 and chart No.31. Patients with heredity and without heredity have more or less equal quality of life hopes and wishes.

Interaction Effect

Quality of life factor hopes and wishes with regard to Types of disease and Gender:

The study's main goal was to understand if male and female diabetic patients, as well as male and female hypertensive patients, have different levels of hopes and wishes when it came to Quality of Life factors. The F value for the interaction of disease types and gender is F (1,100) =.81, p<.05, was also insignificant in Table no.33. Table

37 and chart 32 show that the mean scores of male and female diabetic patients are (M=7.04, SD= 1.58) and (M = 6.70, SD = 1.25), respectively, with a mean difference of 0.34 between the two groups of patients. The mean difference between male and female hypertensive patients is 0.08, because their mean scores are (M =6.97 SD=1.68) and (M=6.89 SD=1.38), respectively. It concluded that the mean difference among the four groups, disease and gender, significantly impact the quality of life factor hopes and wishes.

Quality of life factor hopes and wishes with regard to Types of disease and Hereditary status:

The F (1, 100) =15.59 is observed significant ($p<.01$) for disease types and hereditary status. Table 38 and chart 33 show that diabetic patients with hereditary status have a mean score of 7.21 (SD = 1.63), while diabetic patients without hereditary status have a mean score of 6.53 (SD=1.10). While the mean score of hypertension patients with hereditary status is 6.70 (SD = 1.65) and the mean score of hypertension patients without hereditary status is 7.16 (SD = 1.38), the statistically significant mean difference is 0.68. It is clear that each of the four groups has a different level of quality of life hope and wishes.

Quality of life factor-hope and wishes with regard to Gender and Hereditary status:

The F(1,100) = 0.07, which is not significant, and calculated value of the interaction between gender and heredity. Male patients with hereditary status have a mean score of 7.08 (SD = 1.77), while male patients without hereditary status have a mean score of 6.93 (SD =1.47), a 0.15 difference in mean scores. Female patients with hereditary status have a mean score of 6.83 (SD = 1.53), while those with non-hereditary status have a mean score of 6.76 (SD = 1.07). The difference in mean value is 0.07. Almost all four groups have a by and large negligible mean difference. As a result, all four groups of patients highlighted similar score on the quality of life factor hope and wishes.

Quality of life factor- hope and wishes with regard to Types of disease, Gender and Hereditary status:

F ratios for disease types, gender, and hereditary status in diabetic and hypertensive patients are insignificant (F (1, 50) = 11.06, p>.05). The mean score for diabetic male patients with heredity is 7.64 (SD =1.69), while the mean score for diabetic male patients without heredity is 6.44 (SD =1.19). There is a 1.2 mean difference between the two groups.. For diabetic female patients with and without hereditary status, the mean values are 6.78 (SD = 1.46) and 6.62 (SD = 1.00), respectively. Between the two groups, the mean difference is 0.16, which is statistically significant. As shown in Table, the mean score of male hypertension patients with heredity is 6.52 (SD =1.69), while the mean score of male hypertension patients without hereditary status is 7.42 (SD = 1.56). The difference in average scores is 0.90, which is statistically insignificant. Female hypertension patients with heredity have a mean score of 6.88 (SD = 1.61), while female hypertension patients without heredity have a mean score of 6.90 (SD = 1.12). It is calculated that the mean difference is 0.02. In all eight groups of diabetic and hypertensive patients, the quality of life trait hope and wishes is similar.

Table: 41

Showing ANOVA summary for the quality of life factor- Stress reduction.

Source	Type III Sum of Squares	Df	Mean Square	F	Sig. Level
Diseases (A)	1.563	1	1.563	.296	NS
Gender (B)	4.623	1	4.623	.875	NS
Heredity status (C)	1.323	1	1.323	.250	NS
Diseases * *Gender* (A*B)	2.403	1	2.403	.455	NS
Diseases * *Heredity status* (A*C)	14.823	1	14.823	2.805	NS
Gender * *Heredity status* (B*C)	8.123	1	8.123	1.537	NS
Diseases * *Gender* * *Heredity status* (A*B*C)	2.403	1	2.403	.455	NS
Error	2071.420	392	5.284		
Total	23525.000	400			
Corrected Total	2106.678	399			

Levene's Test of Equality of Error Variances[a]

Dependent Variable: Q6

F	df1	df2	Sig.
.978	7	392	.446

Tests the null hypothesis that the error variance of the dependent variable is equal across groups.

a. Design: Intercept + Diseases + Gender + HS + Diseases * Gender + Diseases * HS + Gender * HS + Diseases * Gender * HS

Table 42
Showing Mean, SD & Mean difference between patients of diabetes and hypertension for quality of life factor- Stress reduction.

Diseases (A)	N	Mean	SD	Mean Difference
Diabetes A1	200	7.25	2.23	0.13
Hypertension A2	200	7.38	2.36	

Figure.36
Showing comparisons of mean scores between patients of diabetes and hypertension for quality of life factor- Stress reduction.

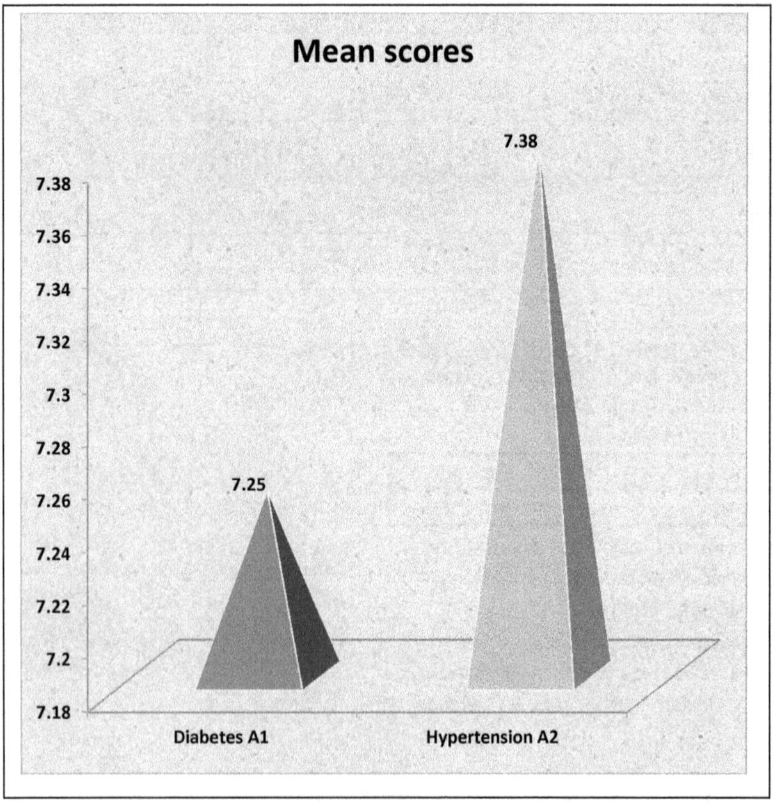

Table 43
Showing Mean, SD & Mean difference between male and female patients with diabetes and hypertension for quality of life factor- Stress reduction.

Gender (B)	N	Mean	SD	Mean Difference
Male B1	200	7.42	2.27	0.21
Female B2	200	7.21	2.32	

Figure no.37
Showing comparisons of mean scores between male and female patients with diabetes and hypertension for quality of life factor- Stress reduction.

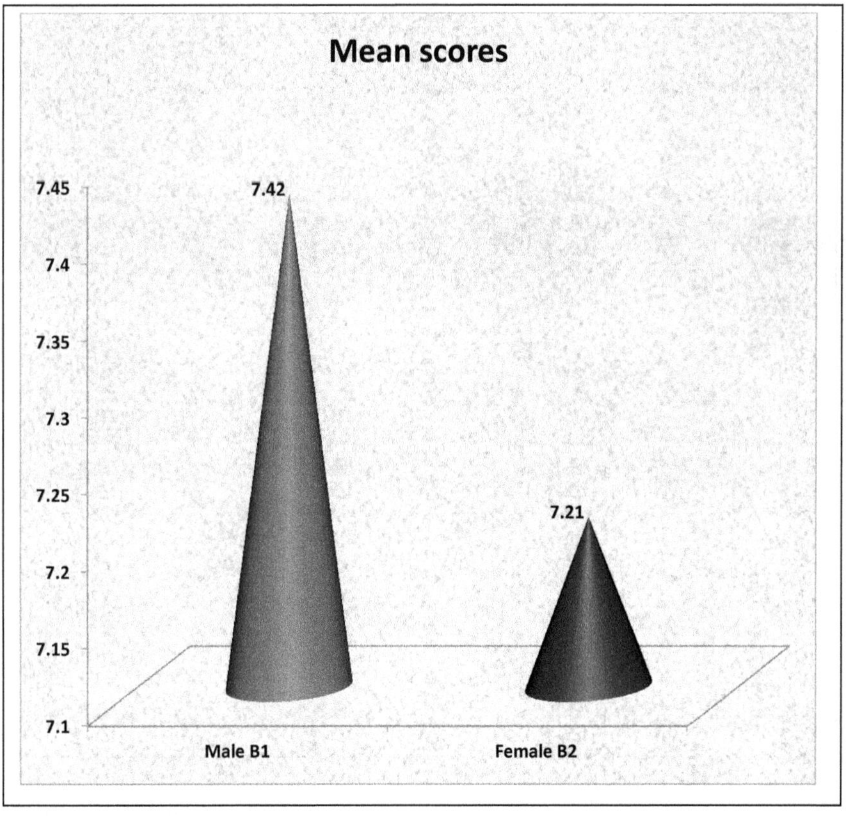

Table 44
Showing Mean, SD & Mean difference between patients with and without hereditary status for quality of life factor- Stress reduction.

Hereditary status (C)	N	Mean	SD	Mean Difference
Hereditary C1	200	7.37	2.22	0.11
Non-hereditary C2	200	7.26	2.37	

Figure no. 38
Showing comparisons of mean scores between patients with and without hereditary status for quality of life factor- Stress reduction.

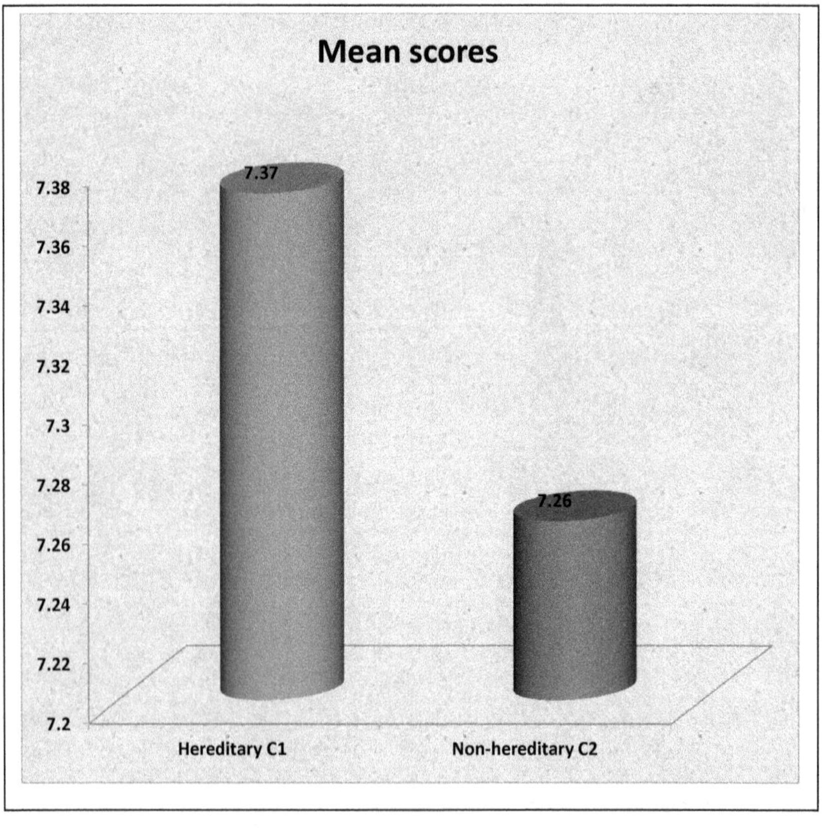

Table 45
Showing Mean, SD & Mean difference among interaction of diseases and Gender of patients with diabetes and hypertension for quality of life factor- Stress reduction.

Diseases (A)	Gender (B)	N	Mean	SD	Mean Difference
Diabetes A1	Male B1	100	7.44	2.31	0.37
	Female B2	100	7.07	2.15	
Hypertension A2	Male B1	100	7.41	2.24	0.06
	Female B2	100	7.35	2.48	

Figure no. 39
Showing comparisons of mean scores among interaction of diseases and Gender of patients with diabetes and hypertension for quality of life factor- Stress reduction.

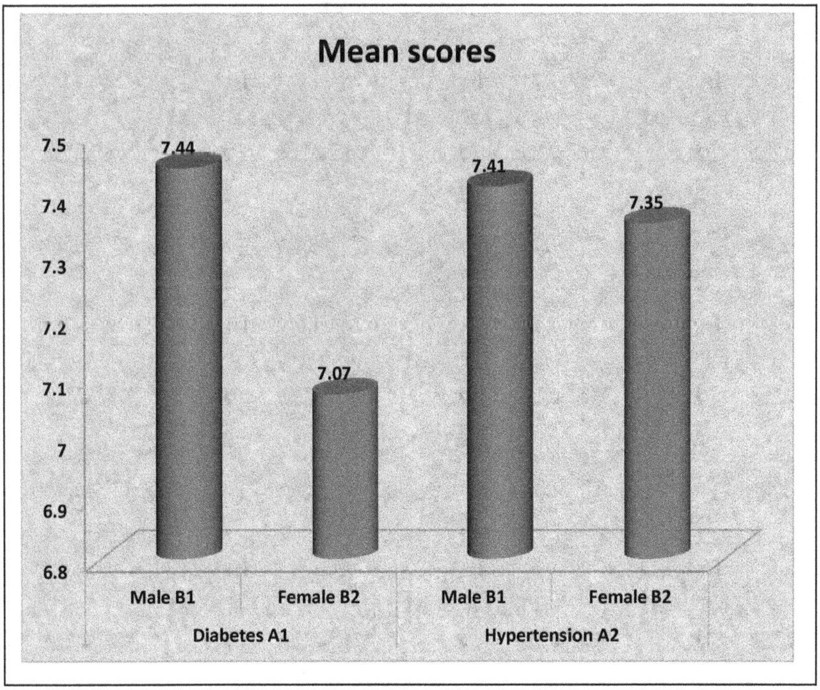

Table 46
Showing Mean, SD & Mean difference among interaction of diseases and hereditary status of patients for quality of life factor- Stress reduction.

Diseases (A)	Hereditary (C)	N	Mean	SD	Mean Difference
Diabetes A1	Hereditary *C1*	100	7.12	2.20	0.27
	Non- hereditary *C2*	100	7.39	2.26	
Hypertension A2	Hereditary *C1*	100	7.63	2.21	0.50
	Non- hereditary *C2*	100	7.13	2.48	

Figure no. 40
Showing comparisons of mean scores among interaction of diseases and hereditary status of patients for quality of life factor- Stress reduction

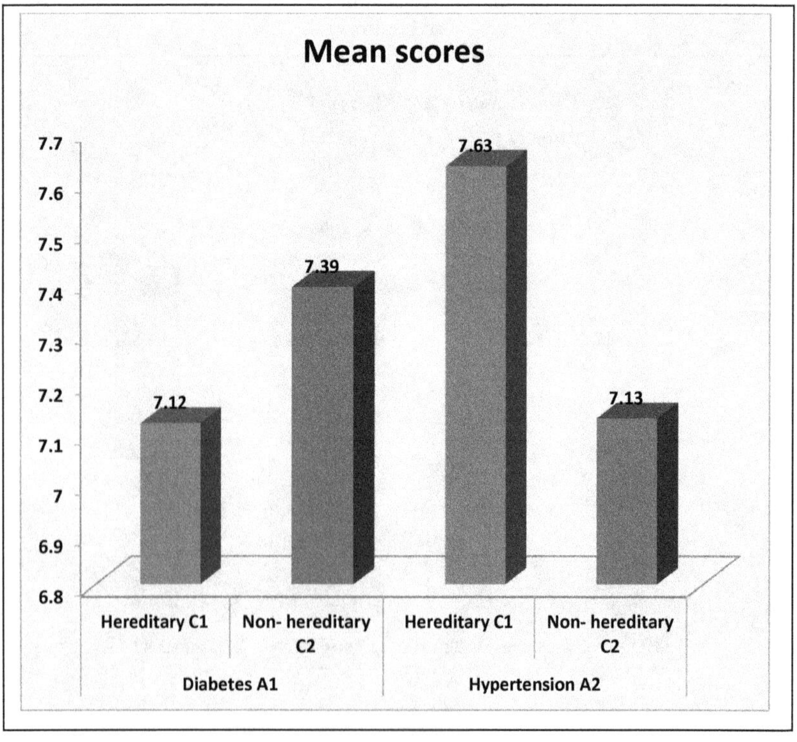

Table 47
Showing Mean, SD & Mean difference among interaction of Gender and hereditary status of patients for quality of life factor- Stress reduction.

Gender (B)	Hereditary status (C)	N	Mean	SD	Mean Difference
Male	Hereditary *C1*	100	7.34	2.16	0.17
	Non-hereditary *C2*	100	7.51	2.38	
Female	Hereditary *C1*	100	7.41	2.28	0.40
	Non-hereditary *C2*	100	7.01	2.35	

Figure no. 41
Showing comparisons of mean scores among interaction of Gender and hereditary status of patients for quality of life factor- Stress reduction.

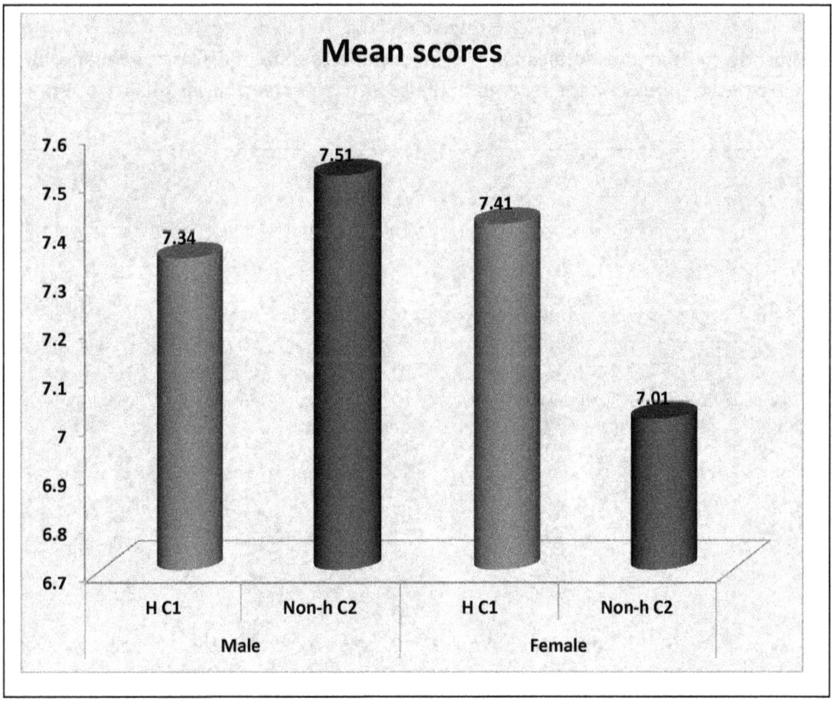

Table 48
Showing Mean, SD & Mean difference among interaction of diseases, gender and hereditary status of patients with diabetes and hypertension for quality of life factor- Stress reduction.

Diseases (A)	Gender (B)	Hereditary status (C)	N	Mean	SD	Mean Difference
Diabetes A1	*Male B1*	*Hereditary C1*	50	7.24	2.30	0.4
		Non- hereditary C2	50	7.64	2.31	
	Female B2	*Hereditary C1*	50	7.00	2.11	0.14
		Non- hereditary C2	50	7.14	2.20	
Hypertension A2	*Male B1*	*Hereditary C1*	50	7.44	2.02	0.44
		Non- hereditary C2	50	7.38	2.46	
	Female B2	*Hereditary C1*	50	7.82	2.39	1.00
		Non- hereditary C2	50	6.88	2.51	

Figure no. 42
Showing comparisons of mean scores among interaction of diseases, gender and hereditary status of patients with diabetes and hypertension for quality of life factor-Stress reduction

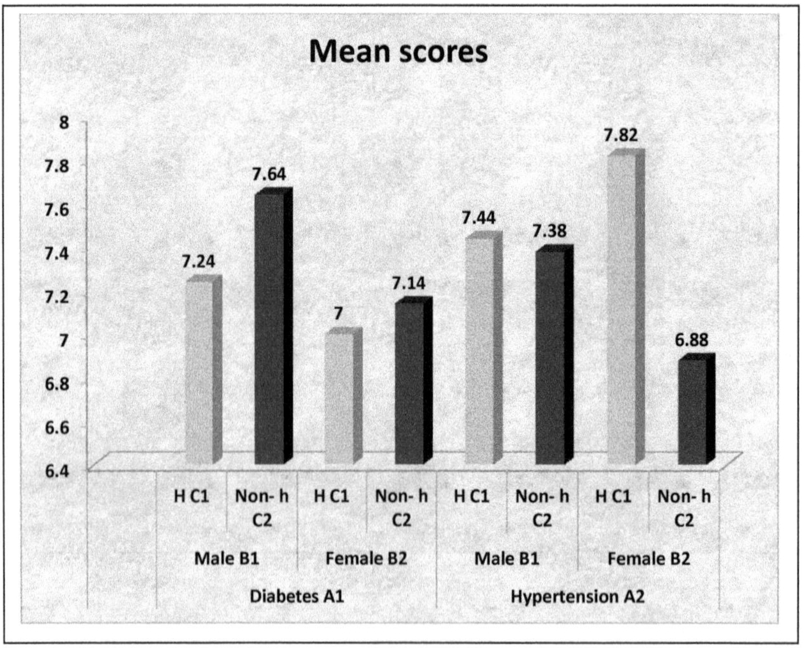

Main Effect:

Quality of life factor-stress reduction with regard to Types of disease:

The F value is exposed insignificant when the F test is used to investigate the effect of disease type on Quality of life trait stress reduction in patients with diabetes and hypertension. F (1, 200) =0.29, p >.05. Diabetic and hypertension patients have mean scores of 7.25 (SD = 2.23) and 7.38 (SD = 2.36), respectively. According to Tables 42 and 36, and the difference between the two means is 0.13. Thus, it can be said that hypertensive and diabetic patients have a similar level of stress reduction process.

Quality of life factor stress reduction with regard to Gender

The F value and mean score for diabetic and hypertensive patients are revealed in Tables 43 and 37, with the mean difference and F ratio reported as non-significant F(1,200) =.87, p>.05. Male patients have an average value of 7.42 (SD = 2.27), while female patients have an average value of 7.21 (SD = 2.32), the mean difference is 0.21 between the two groups. This mean difference (Table No.43 & Chart No.37) indicated that both groups have a nominal mean difference. The above findings showed that, that both female and male patients have equal stress reduction levels.

Quality of life factor stress reduction with regard to Hereditary status:

For hereditary status, the calculated F value was F (1, 200) = 0.25, which was insignificant. In table No. 44 and chart No.38, patients with hereditary status have a mean score of 7.37(SD=2.22), while patients without hereditary status have a mean score of 7.26(SD=2.37), a mean difference is 0.11. Patients with and without heredity have similar levels of stress reduction in terms of quality of life.

Interaction Effect

Quality of life factor stress reduction with regard to Types of disease and Gender:

The primary goal of the study was to study, if male and female diabetic patients, as well as male and female hypertensive patients, have any difference in stress reduction process. Table no.41 showed that the F value for the interaction of disease types and gender, F (1,100) =.45 p>.05, was also insignificant. Table 45 and chart 39 show that the mean scores of male and female diabetic patients are (M=7.44, SD= 2.31) and (M = 7.07, SD = 2.15) respectively, with a mean difference of 0.37 between the two groups of patients. The mean difference between male and female hypertensive patients is 0.06 because their mean scores are (M =7.41 SD=2.24) and (M=7.35 SD=2.48), respectively. The mean difference among the four groups indicated that all the groups of patients have equal quality of life factor stress reduction.

Quality of life factor stress reduction with regard to Types of disease and Hereditary status:

Disease types and hereditary status had a non-significant interaction, The F (1, 100) =2.80 is highlighted insignificant (p>.05). Diabetic patients with hereditary status have a mean score of 7.12 (SD = 2.20) in Table 46 and chart 40, whereas diabetic patients without hereditary status have a mean score of 7.39 (SD=2.26). The average difference is 0.27. While the mean score of hypertension patients with hereditary status is 7.63 (SD =2.21) and the mean score of hypertension patients without hereditary status is 7.13 (SD =2.48), the statistically insignificant mean difference is 0.50. It is clear that each of the four groups has a similar level of quality of life trait stress reduction.

Quality of life factor-stress reduction with regard to Gender and Hereditary status:

The calculated value of the interaction between gender and heredity is F(1,100) = 1.53, which is insignificant (Table no.47 and chart 41). The mean score for male patients with hereditary status is 7.34 (SD =2.16), while the mean score for male patients without hereditary status is 7.51 (SD =2.38), a 0.17 difference in mean scores. Female patients with hereditary status have a mean value of 7.41 (SD = 2.28), while those with non-hereditary status have a mean score of 7.01(SD = 2.35). The difference in mean value is 0.40. All four groups have insignificant mean differences. As a result, all four groups of patients quality of life factor stress reduction.

Quality of life factor-stress and reduction with regard to Types of disease, Gender and Hereditary status:

In diabetic and hypertensive patients, F ratios for disease types, gender, and hereditary status are insignificant (F (1, 50) =.45, p>.05). Diabetic male patients with heredity have a mean score of 7.24 (SD =2.30), while diabetic male patients without heredity have a mean score of 7.64 (SD =2.31). The mean difference between the two groups is 0.40. The mean values for diabetic female patients with and without hereditary status are 7.00 (SD = 2.11) and 7.14 (SD = 2.20), respectively. Between the two groups, the mean difference is 0.14, which is statistically insignificant. The mean score of male hypertension patients with heredity is 7.44 (SD =2.02), while the mean score of male hypertension patients without hereditary status is 7.38(SD =2.46). The difference in average scores is 0.44, which is statistically insignificant. The mean score for female hypertension patients with heredity is 7.82 (SD =2.39), while the mean score for female hypertension patients without heredity is 6.88 (SD =2.51). The mean difference is calculated to be 1.00. The quality of life trait stress reduction was similar in all eight groups of diabetic and hypertensive patients.

Table: 49

Showing ANOVA summary for the quality of life factor- Frustration, Depression/ Anxiety

Source	Type III Sum of Squares	df	Mean Square	F	Sig. Level
Diseases (A)	9.000	1	9.000	1.93	NS
Gender (B)	10.890	1	10.890	2.33	NS
Heredity status (C)	19.000	1	19.000	3.82	*NS*
Diseases * *Gender* (A*B)	9.000	1	9.000	1.93	. NS
Diseases * *Heredity status* (A*C)	34.810	1	34.810	7.47	$p<.01$
Gender * *Heredity status* (B*C)	9.890	1	9.890	1.99	NS
Diseases * *Gender* * *Heredity status* (A*B*C)	2.890	1	2.890	.621	NS
Error	1825.400	392	4.657		
Total	23020.000	400			
Corrected Total	1965.990	399			

Table- 50

Showing Mean, SD & Mean difference between patients of diabetes and hypertension for quality of life factor- Frustration, Depression/ Anxiety.

Diseases (A)	N	Mean	SD	Mean Difference
Diabetes A1	200	7.10	2.24	0.30
Hypertension A2	200	7.40	2.18	

Figure no.43
Showing comparisons of mean scores between patients of diabetes and hypertension for quality of life factor- Frustration, Depression/ Anxiety

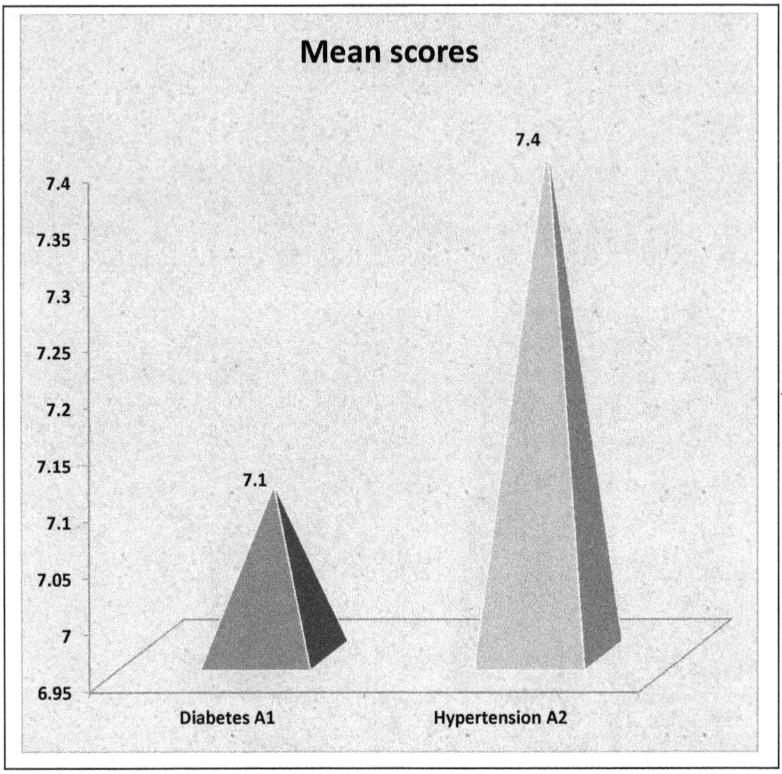

Table 51

Showing Mean, SD & Mean difference between male and female patients with diabetes and hypertension for quality of life factor- Frustration, Depression/ Anxiety

Gender (B)	N	Mean	SD	Mean Difference
Male B1	200	7.42	2.25	0.33
Female B2	200	7.09	2.17	

Figure no.44

Showing comparisons of mean scores between male and female patients with diabetes and hypertension for quality of life factor- Frustration, Depression/ Anxiety

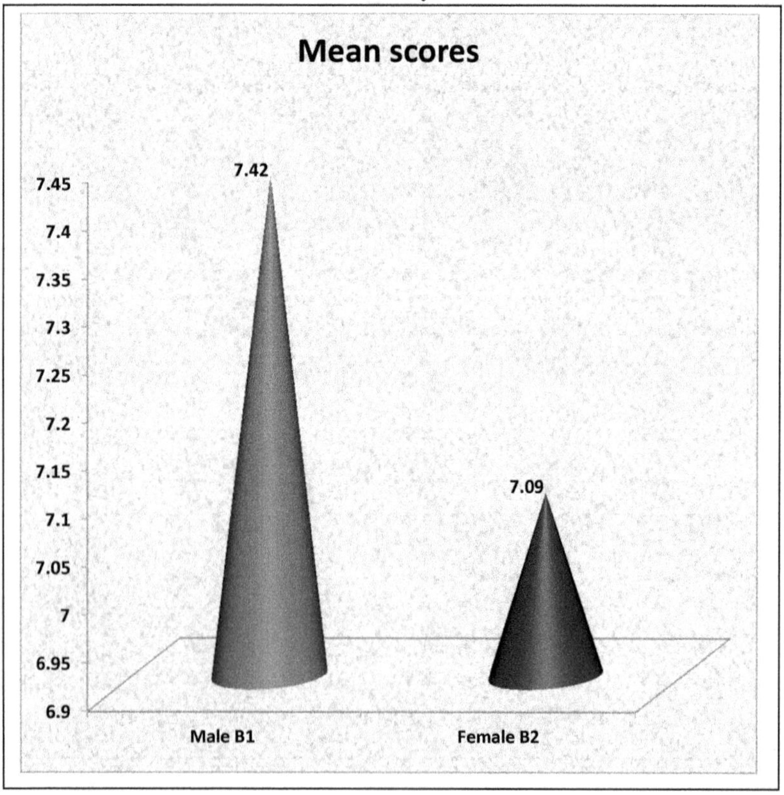

Table 52

Showing Mean, SD & Mean difference between patients with and without hereditary status for quality of life factor- Frustration, Depression/ Anxiety.

Hereditary status (C)	N	Mean	SD	Mean Difference
Hereditary C1	200	7.60	2.36	0.70
Non-hereditary C2	200	6.90	2.01	

Figure no.45
Showing comparisons of means scores between patients with and without hereditary status for quality of life factor- Frustration, Depression/ Anxiety.

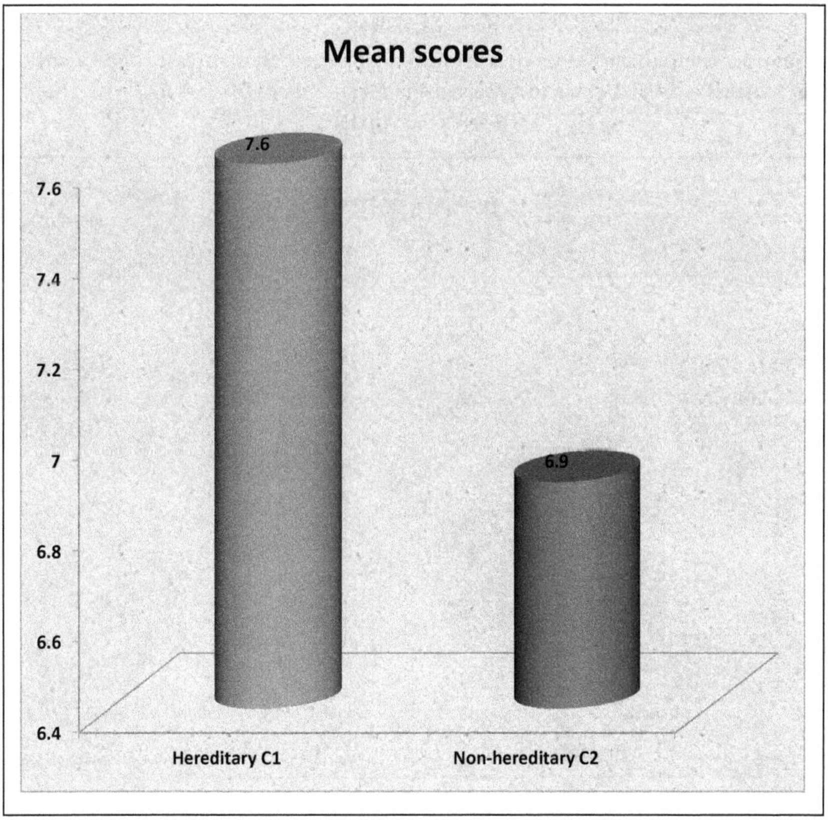

Table 53

Showing Mean, SD & Mean difference among interaction of diseases and Gender of patients with diabetes and hypertension for quality of life factor- Frustration, Depression/ Anxiety.

Diseases (A)	Gender (B)	N	Mean	SD	Mean Difference
Diabetes A1	Male B1	100	7.12	2.24	0.03
	Female B2	100	7.09	2.25	
Hypertension A2	Male B1	100	7.72	2.23	0.63
	Female B2	100	7.09	2.10	

Figure no.46
Showing comparisons of mean scores among interaction of diseases and Gender of patients with diabetes and hypertension for quality of life factor- Frustration, Depression/ Anxiety.

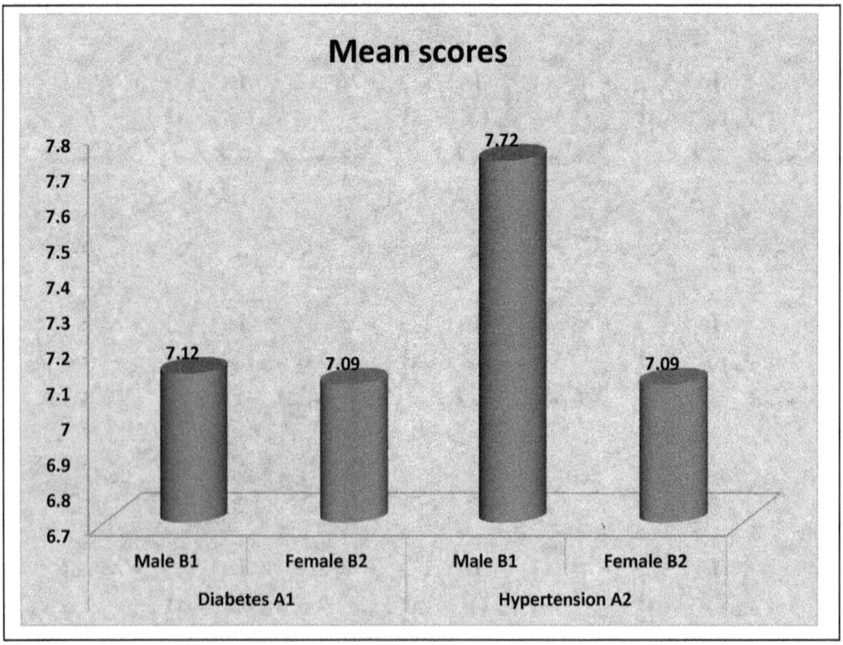

Table 54

Showing Mean, SD & Mean difference among interaction of diseases and hereditary status of patients for quality of life factor- Frustration, Depression/ Anxiety.

Diseases (A)	Hereditary (C)	N	Mean	SD	Mean Difference
Diabetes A1	Hereditary *C1*	100	7.75	2.63	1.29
	Non- hereditary *C2*	100	6.46	1.53	
Hypertension A2	Hereditary *C1*	100	7.46	2.05	0.11
	Non- hereditary *C2*	100	7.35	2.32	

Figure no. 47
Showing comparisons of mean scores among interaction of diseases and hereditary status of patients for quality of life factor- Frustration, Depression/ Anxiety.

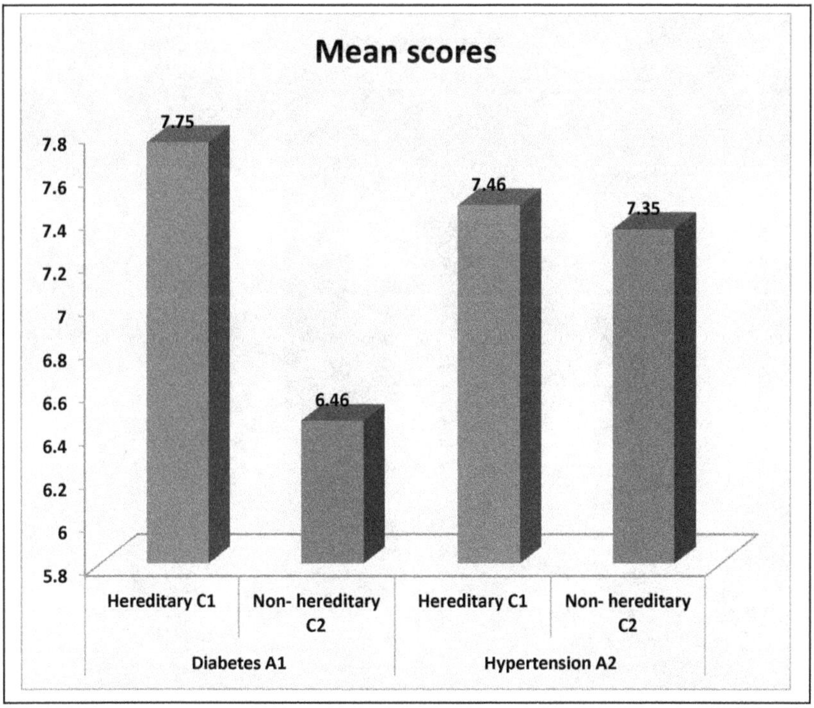

Table 55

Showing Mean, SD & Mean difference among interaction of Gender and hereditary status of patients for quality of life factor- Frustration, Depression/ Anxiety

Gender (B)	Hereditary status (C)	N	Mean	SD	Mean Difference
Male	Hereditary *C1*	100	7.52	2.23	0.20
	Non-hereditary *C2*	100	7.32	2.28	
Female	Hereditary *C1*	100	7.69	2.48	1.20
	Non-hereditary *C2*	100	6.49	1.61	

Figure no. 48

Showing comparisons of mean score among interaction of Gender and hereditary status of patients for quality of life factor- Frustration, Depression/ Anxiety.

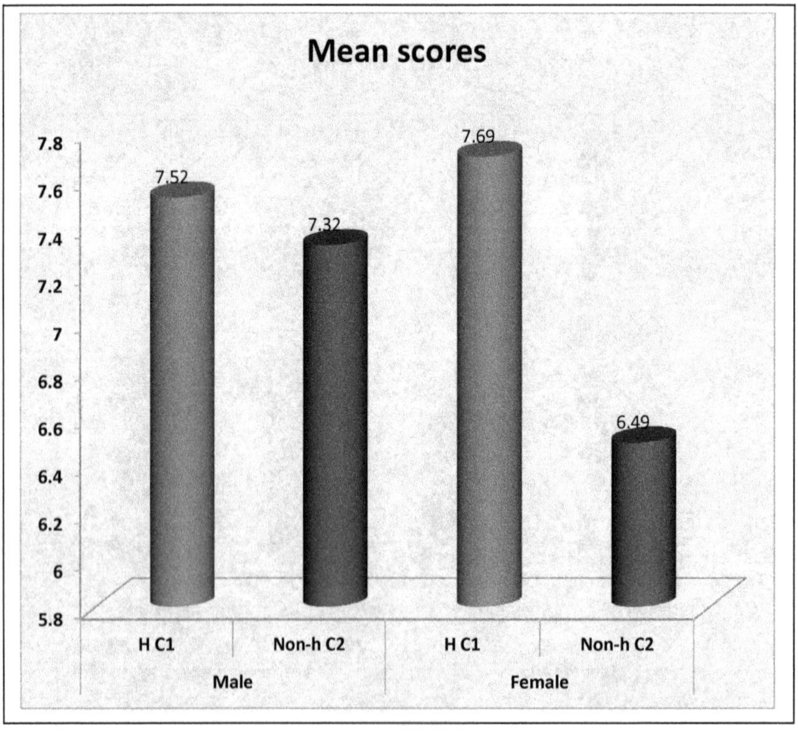

Table 56

Showing Mean, SD & Mean difference among interaction of diseases, gender and hereditary status of patients with diabetes and hypertension for quality of life factor- Frustration, Depression/ Anxiety.

Diseases (A)	Gender (B)	Hereditary status (C)	N	Mean	SD	Mean Difference
Diabetes A1	*Male B1*	*Hereditary C1*	50	7.60	2.71	0.96
		Non- hereditary C2	50	6.64	1.54	
	Female B2	*Hereditary C1*	50	7.90	2.58	1.62
		Non- hereditary C2	50	6.28	1.51	
Hypertension A2	*Male B1*	*Hereditary C1*	50	7.44	1.65	0.52
		Non- hereditary C2	50	8.00	2.68	
	Female B2	*Hereditary C1*	50	7.48	2.40	0.78
		Non- hereditary C2	50	6.70	1.69	

Figure no. 49

Showing comparisons of mean scores among interaction of diseases, gender and hereditary status of patients with diabetes and hypertension for quality of life factor- Frustration, Depression/ Anxiety.

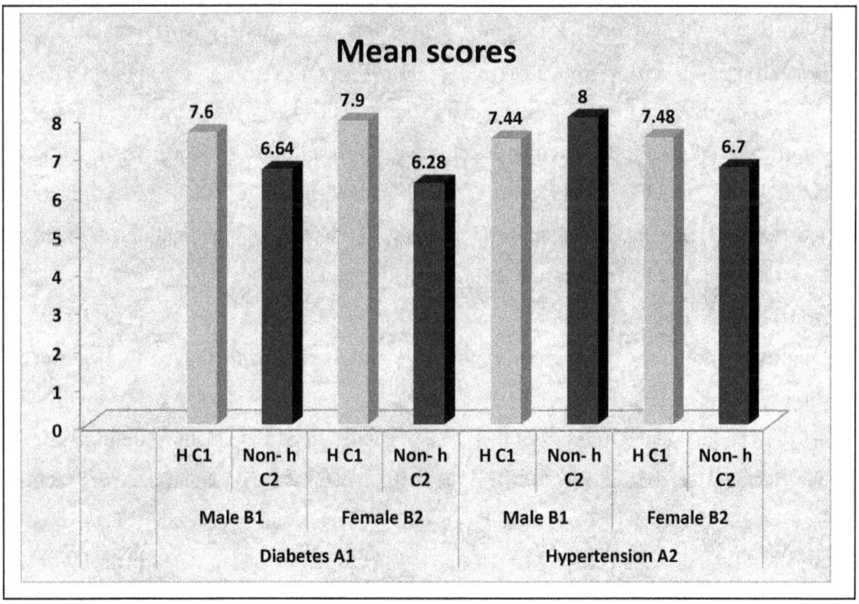

Main Effect:

Quality of life factor-frustration, depression and anxiety with regard to Types of disease:

The first main effect for types of disease was observed insignificant; the F value was displayed ($F (1, 200) = 1.93$, $p > .05$). Diabetic and hypertension patients have mean scores of 7.10 (SD =2.24) and 7.40 (SD = 2.18), respectively. Tables 42 and 36 showed the difference between the two means is 0.30. Hence, it can be assumed that hypertensive and diabetic patients have more or less similar level of frustration, depression and anxiety.

Quality of life factor frustration, depression and anxiety with regard to Gender:

The F value and mean score for male and female diabetic and hypertensive patients are shown in Tables 49 and 44; the mean difference and F ratio reported not significant $F(1,200) = 2.33$, $p > .05$. Male patients have an average value of 7.42 (SD = 2.25), while female patients have an average value of 7.09 (SD = 2.17), resulting in a mean difference of 0.33 between the two groups. This mean difference (Table No.51 & Chart No.44) denoted that both groups have a nominal mean difference. The above findings showed that both female and male patients have equal quality of life trait frustration, depression, and anxiety.

Quality of life factor frustration, depression and anxiety with regard to Hereditary status:

The obtained F value for hereditary status was $F (1, 200) = 3.82$, which was not significant. Patients with hereditary status have a mean score of 7.60 (SD=2.36) in table No. 52 and chart No.45, while patients without hereditary status have a mean score of 6.90 (SD=2.01), a mean difference is 0.70. Patients with and without heredity have different levels of frustration, depression and anxiety.

Interaction Effect

Quality of life factor frustration, depression and anxiety with regard to Types of disease and Gender:

The interaction of types of disease and gender are not interacting significantly, the F value was reported $F (1,100) = 1.93$ $p > .05$, which was non-significant. As seen in Table no.53 and chart 46 that the mean scores of male and female diabetic patients are (M=7.12, SD= 2.24) and (M = 7.09, SD = 2.25) respectively, mean difference is 0.37 between the two groups of patients. The mean difference between male and female hypertensive patients is 0.63 and their mean scores are (M =7.72 SD=2.23) and (M=7.09 SD=2.10), respectively. The mean difference among the four groups regarding disease and gender indicated that all the patients have similar feelings of frustration, depression, and anxiety.

Quality of life factor frustration, depression and anxiety with regard to Types of disease and Hereditary status:

The interaction of Types of disease and Hereditary status was demonstrated significant, the ratio is F (1, 100) = 7.47 ($p<.01$). Table 54 and chart 47 depicted that diabetes patients with hereditary status have a mean score of 7.75 (SD = 2.63), while diabetic patients without hereditary status have a mean score of 6.46 (SD=1.53). The mean difference is 1.29. While the mean score of hypertension patients with hereditary status is 7.46 (SD =2.05) and the mean score of hypertension patients without hereditary status is 7.35(SD =2.32), the mean difference is 0.11. It is evident that each of the four groups has a different level of frustration, depression, and anxiety in terms of quality of life.

Quality of life factor-frustration, depression/anxiety with regard to Gender and Hereditary status:

The calculated value of the interaction between gender and heredity is F (1,100) = 1.99, which is quite insignificant. As from the Table no.55 and chart no.48 the mean score for male patients with hereditary status is 7.52 (SD =2.23), while the mean score for male patients without hereditary status is 7.32(SD =2.28). Female patients with hereditary status have a mean value of 7.69 (SD = 2.48), while those with non-hereditary status have a mean score of 6.49 (SD = 1.61). The difference in mean value is 1.20. The mean difference in all four groups is non-significant. As a result, all four groups of patients displayed similar degrees of frustration, depression, and anxiety as a quality of life factor.

Quality of life factor-frustration, depression and anxiety with regard to Types of disease, Gender and Hereditary status:

F ratios in diabetes and hypertensive patients for the interaction disease types, gender, and hereditary status are insignificant (F (1, 50) =.62 $p>.05$). Diabetic male patients with heredity have a mean score of 7.60 (SD =2.71), while diabetic male patients without heredity have a mean score of 6.64 (SD =1.54). The mean difference between the two groups is 0.96. For diabetic female patients with and without hereditary status, the mean values are 7.90 (SD = 2.58) and 6.28 (SD = 1.51), respectively. Between the two groups, the mean difference is 1.62. The mean score of male hypertension patients with heredity is 7.44 (SD =1.65), while the mean score of male hypertension patients without hereditary status is 8.00 (SD= 2.68). The difference in average scores is 0.52, which is statistically insignificant. The mean score for female hypertension patients with heredity is 7.48 (SD =2.40), while the mean score for female hypertension patients without heredity is 6.70 (SD=1.69). The mean difference is 0.78. All eight groups of diabetic and hypertension patients have more or less similar levels of frustration, depression and anxiety.

Table: 57

Showing ANOVA summary for the quality of life factor- Adjustment

Source	Type III Sum of Squares	df	Mean Square	F	Sig. Level
Diseases **(A)**	1.440	1	1.440	.351	NS
Gender **(B)**	184.960	1	184.960	45.077	$p<.01$
Heredity status **(C)**	72.250	1	72.250	17.608	$p<.01$
Diseases * Gender **(A*B)**	.490	1	.490	.119	NS
Diseases * Heredity status **(A*C)**	3.240	1	3.240	.790	NS
Gender * Heredity status **(B*C)**	.360	1	.360	.088	NS
Diseases * Gender * Heredity status **(A*B*C)**	.810	1	.810	.197	NS
Error	1608.440	392	4.103		
Total	36134.000	400			
Corrected Total	1871.990	399			

Levene's Test of Equality of Error Variances[a]

Dependent Variable: Q8

F	df1	df2	Sig.
9.270	7	392	.000

Tests the null hypothesis that the error variance of the dependent variable is equal across groups.

a. Design: Intercept + Diseases + Gender + HS + Diseases * Gender + Diseases * HS + Gender * HS + Diseases * Gender * HS

Table 58
Showing Mean, SD & Mean difference between patients of diabetes and hypertension for quality of life factor- Adjustment.

Diseases (A)	N	Mean	SD	Mean Difference
Diabetes A1	200	9.19	2.15	0.12
Hypertension A2	200	9.31	2.18	

Figure no.50
Showing comparisons of mean scores between patients of diabetes and hypertension for quality of life factor- Adjustment.

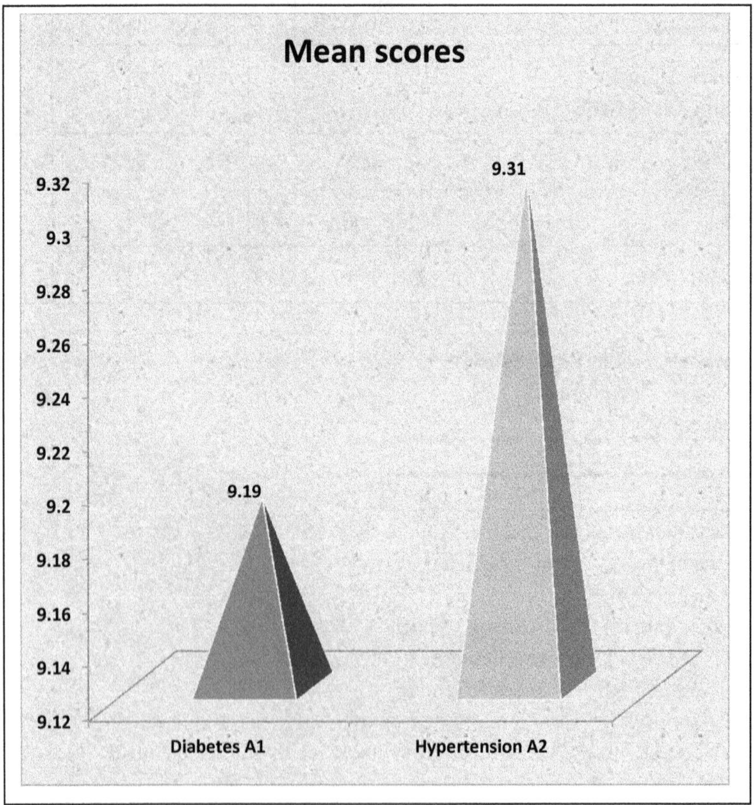

Table 59
Showing Mean, SD & Mean difference between male and female patients with diabetes and hypertension for quality of life factor- Adjustment.

Gender (B)	N	Mean	SD	Mean Difference
Male B1	200	7.57	2.27	2.36
Female B2	200	9.93	1.81	

Figure no.51
Showing comparisons of mean scores between male and female patients with diabetes and hypertension for quality of life factor- Adjustment.

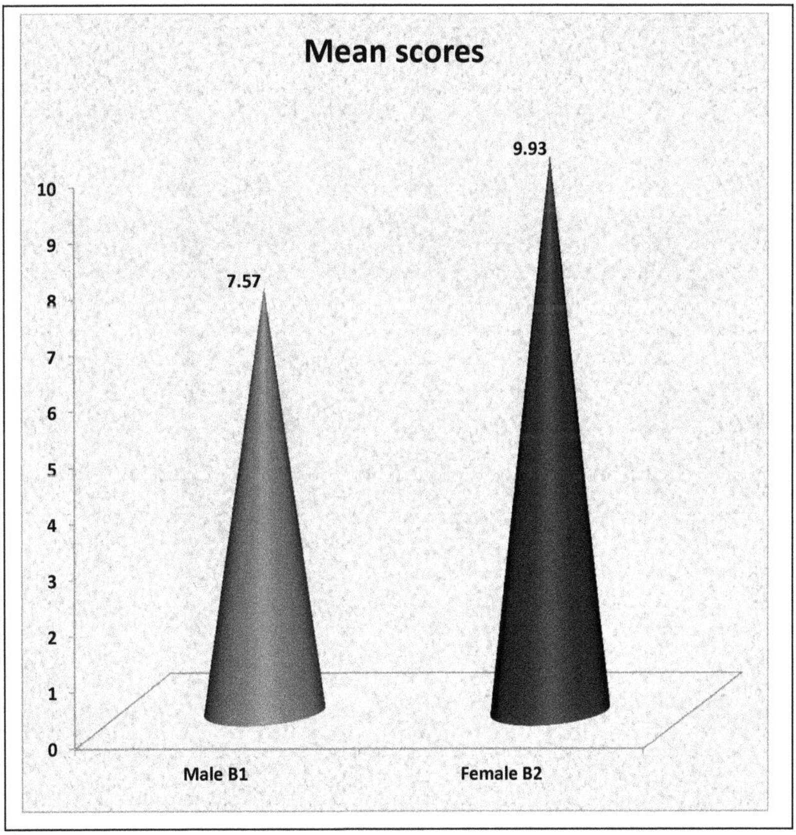

Table 60
Showing Mean, SD & Mean difference between patients with and without hereditary status for quality of life factor- Adjustment.

Hereditary status (C)	N	Mean	SD	Mean Difference
Hereditary C1	200	8.83	2.34	0.85
Non-hereditary C2	200	9.68	1.87	

Figure no. 52
Showing comparisons of mean scores between patients with and without hereditary status for quality of life factor- Adjustment.

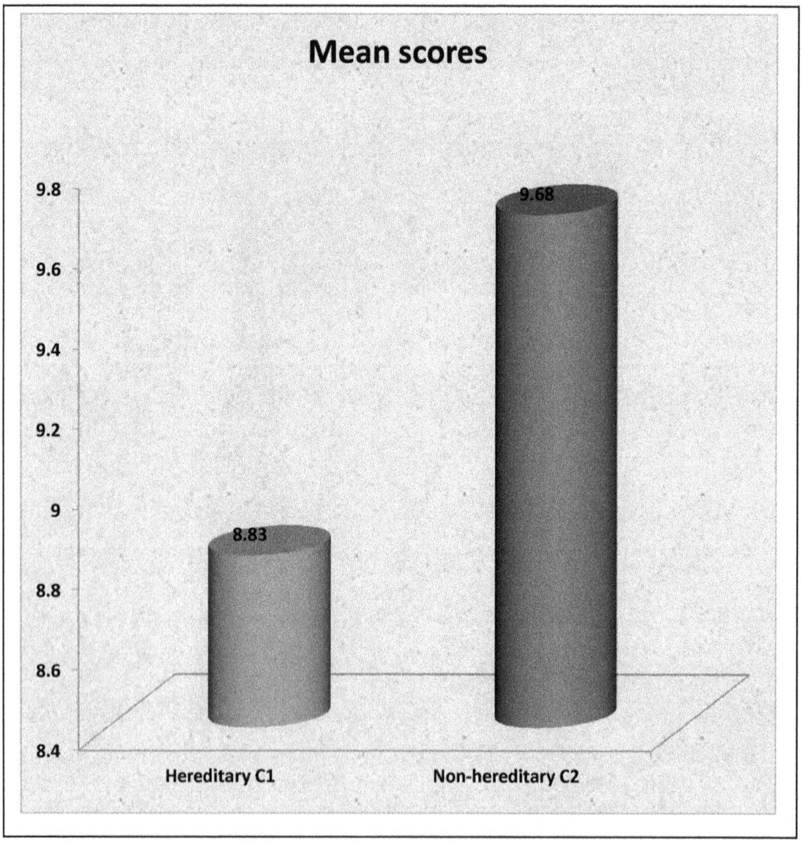

Table 61
Showing Mean, SD & Mean difference among interaction of diseases and Gender of patients with diabetes and hypertension for quality of life factor- Adjustment.

Diseases (A)	Gender (B)	N	Mean	SD	Mean Difference
Diabetes A1	**Male B1**	100	8.48	2.29	1.43
	Female B2	100	9.91	1.72	
Hypertension A2	**Male B1**	100	8.67	2.25	1.29
	Female B2	100	9.96	1.91	

Figure no. 53
Showing comparisons of mean scores among interaction of diseases and Gender of patients with diabetes and hypertension for quality of life factor- Adjustment

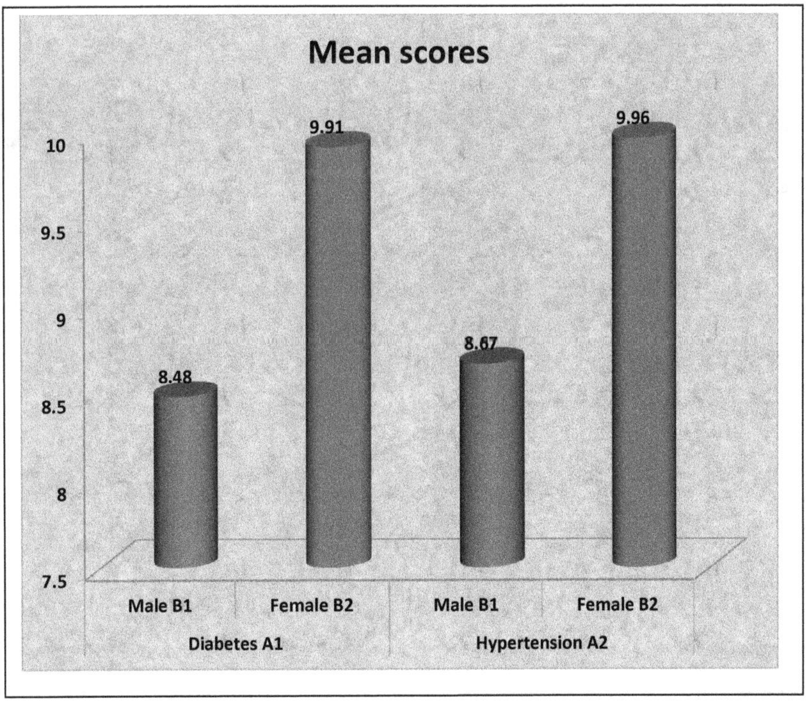

Table 62
Showing Mean, SD & Mean difference among interaction of diseases and hereditary status of patients for quality of life factor- Adjustment.

Diseases (A)	Hereditary (C)	N	Mean	SD	Mean Difference
Diabetes A1	Hereditary *C1*	100	8.86	2.33	0.67
	Non- hereditary *C2*	100	9.53	1.90	
Hypertension A2	Hereditary *C1*	100	8.80	2.37	1.03
	Non- hereditary *C2*	100	9.83	1.84	

Figure no. 54
Showing comparisons of mean scores among interaction of diseases and hereditary status of patients for quality of life factor- Adjustment.

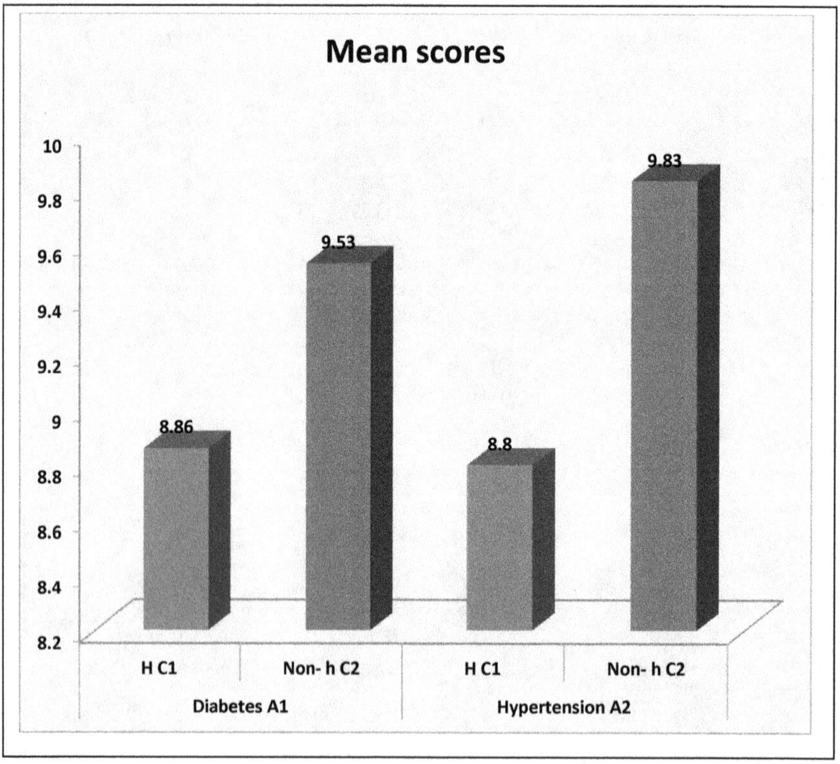

Table 63

Showing Mean, SD & Mean difference among interaction of Gender and hereditary status of patients for quality of life factor- Adjustment.

Gender (B)	Hereditary status (C)	N	Mean	SD	Mean Difference
Male	**Hereditary *C1***	100	8.12	2.23	0.91
	Non-hereditary *C2*	100	9.03	2.23	
Female	**Hereditary *C1***	100	9.54	2.25	0.79
	Non-hereditary *C2*	100	10.33	1.11	

Figure no. 55

Showing comparisons of mean scores among interaction of Gender and hereditary status of patients for quality of life factor- Adjustment.

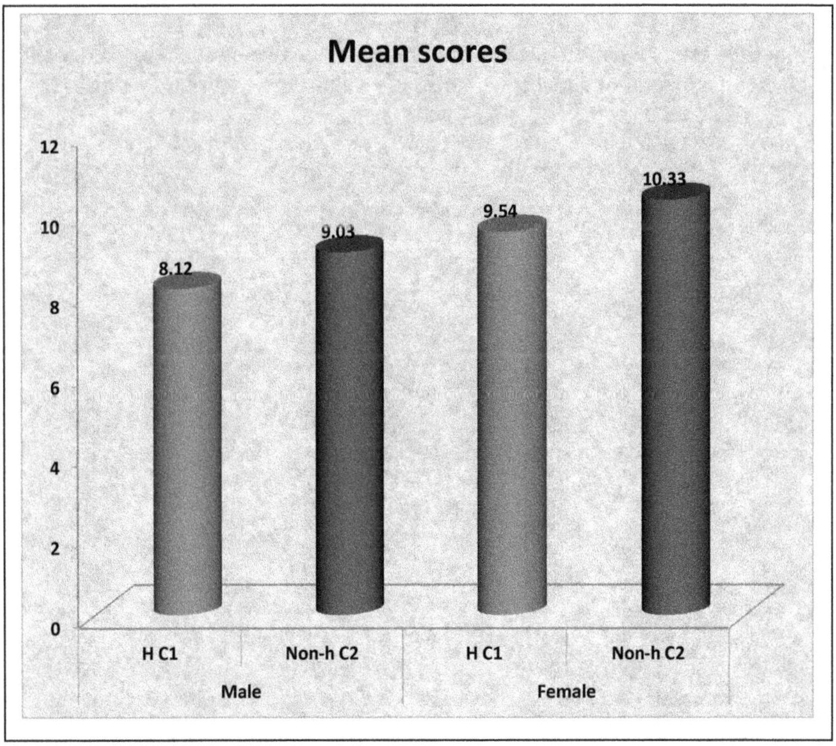

Table 64
Showing Mean, SD & Mean difference among interaction of diseases, gender and hereditary status of patients with diabetes and hypertension for quality of life factor- Adjustment.

Diseases (A)	Gender (B)	Hereditary status (C)	N	Mean	SD	Mean Difference
Diabetes A1	*Male B1*	*Hereditary C1*	50	8.16	2.29	0.64
		Non- hereditary C2	50	8.80	2.27	
	Female B2	*Hereditary C1*	50	9.56	2.16	0.7
		Non- hereditary C2	50	10.26	1.04	
Hypertension A2	*Male B1*	*Hereditary C1*	50	8.08	2.19	1.18
		Non- hereditary C2	50	9.26	2.18	
	Female B2	*Hereditary C1*	50	9.52	2.35	0.88
		Non- hereditary C2	50	10.40	1.19	

Figure no. 56
Showing comparisons of mean scores among interaction of diseases, gender and hereditary status of patients with diabetes and hypertension for quality of life factor- Adjustment

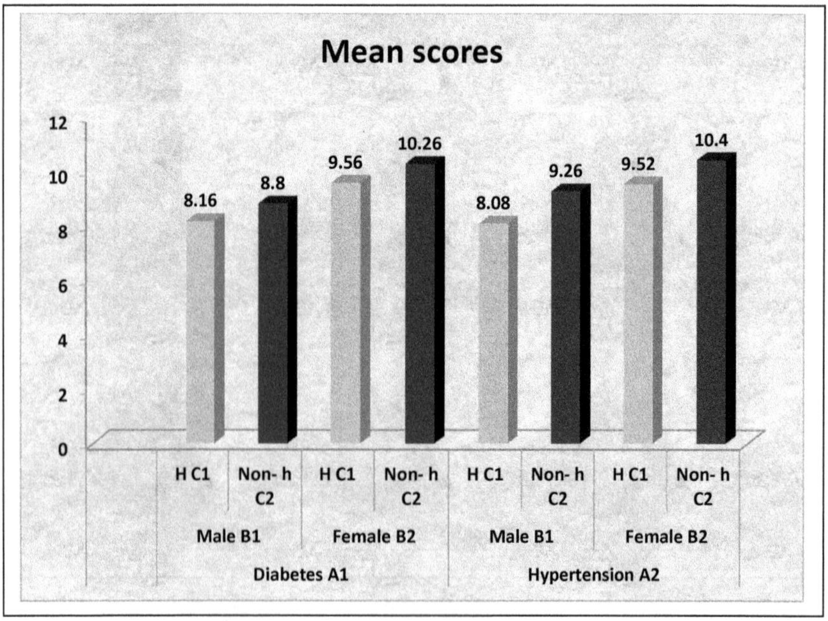

Main Effect:

Quality of life factor-Adjustment with regard to Types of disease:

The F value is insignificant when the F test was conducted to examine the impact of illness type on Quality of life trait adjustment in diabetic and hypertension patients. The F (1, 200) =.35, $p>.05$ was highlighted in (Table no.57) was insignificance. Patients with diabetes have a mean value of 9.19 (SD = 2.15), while those with hypertension have a mean value of 9.31 (SD = 2.18). The difference between the two means is 0.12, According to the above findings, hypertensive and diabetic patients have similar quality of life factor adjustments.

Quality of life factor adjustment with regard to Gender

Tables 57 and 51 show the F value and mean score for male and female patients, F ratio is observed significant F(1,200) = 45.07, $p<.01$. The mean value for male patients is 7.57 (SD = 2.27), while the mean score for female patients is 9.93 (SD = 1.81), resulting in a mean difference of 2.36. This mean difference (Table No. 59 & Chart No. 51) indicated that there was a significant mean difference between the two groups. The female patients have higher adjustment as compared to male patients.

Quality of life factor adjustment with regard to Hereditary status:

The third main effect i.e. hereditary status is displayed significant F (1, 200) = 17.60, which was significant. In table No. 60 and chart No.52, patients with hereditary status have a mean score of 8.83(SD=2.34), while patients without hereditary status have a mean score of 9.68(SD=1.87), the mean difference is 0.70. Patients without hereditary status have higher characteristics adjustment in comparison of patients with hereditary status.

Interaction Effect

Quality of life factor adjustment with regard to Types of disease and Gender:

As it can be seen from the table that interaction of types of disease and gender are not interacting with each other for the Quality of Life trait adjustment. The F value is obtained, F (1,100) = 0.11 $p>.05$, which was not significant. The mean scores of male and female diabetic patients are (M=8.48, SD= 2.29) and (M = 9.91, SD = 1.72), respectively, as shown in Table 61 and Chart 53, with a mean difference of 1.43. the mean values of male and female hypertension patients are (M =8.67 SD=2.25) and (M=9.96 SD=1.91), respectively, the mean difference between male and female hypertensive patients is 1.29. The mean difference among the four groups, as well as disease and gender, were found to have more or less similar impact on the quality of life factor adjustment.

Quality of life factor adjustment with regard to Types of disease and Hereditary status:

The types of disease and hereditary status of the patient are not interacting with each other for the quality of life domain adjustment. The F ratio is found non-significant (F (1, 100) = 0.79 $p>.05$) Diabetes patients with hereditary status have a mean score of 8.86 (SD = 2.33), while diabetic patients without hereditary status have a mean score of 9.53 (SD=1.90), with a mean difference of 0.67. Similarly, the mean score of hypertension patients with hereditary status is 8.80 (SD =2.37) and 9.83 (SD =1.84), the mean difference is 1.03. All the groups of the patients have more or less similar level of quality of life trait adjustment.

Quality of life factor-adjustment with regard to Gender and Hereditary status:

The calculated value of the interaction between gender and heredity is F (1,100) =.08, which is quite insignificant. According to Table 63 and Chart 55, the mean score for male patients with hereditary status is 8.12 (SD =2.23), while the mean score for male patients without hereditary status is 9.03 (SD =2.23), showing a 0.91 difference in mean scores. Female patients with hereditary status have a mean value of 9.54 (SD = 2.25), while those with non-hereditary status have a mean score of 10.54 (SD = 1.11). The difference in mean value is 0.79. The mean difference is insignificant and on the basis of this insignificant mean difference as a result, all four patient groups showed similar levels of quality of life factor adjustment.

Quality of life factor-adjustment with regard to Types of disease, Gender and Hereditary status:

F ratios for disease , gender, and hereditary status are insignificant in diabetic and hypertensive patients as F(1, 50) =.19 $p>.05$. Diabetic male patients with hereditary status have a mean score of 8.16 (SD =2.29), whereas diabetic male patients without hereditary status have a mean score of 8.80 (SD =2.27). The difference in mean value between the two groups is 0.64. The mean values for diabetes female patients with hereditary status is 9.56 (SD = 2.16) and for non hereditary female patients is 10.26 (SD = 1.04). The mean difference between the two groups is 0.70, which is statistically significant. Male hypertension patients with heredity have mean score of 8.08 (SD=2.19), while those without hereditary status have an mean score of 9.26 (SD =2.18). The mean difference is 1.18, which is also insignificant. Female hypertension patients with heredity have a mean score of 9.52 (SD=2.35), while those without heredity have a mean score of 10.40 (SD=1.19). The mean difference is 0.88. The quality of life trait adjustment is quite similar in all eight groups of diabetic and hypertensive patients.

Table: 65

Showing ANOVA summary for the quality of life factor- Physical well-being & Self care

Source	Type III Sum of Squares	df	Mean Square	F	Sig. Level
Diseases (A)	141.610	1	141.610	37.506	$p<.01$
Gender (B)	.160	1	.160	.042	NS
Heredity status (C)	.490	1	.490	.130	NS
*Diseases * Gender* (A*B)	.810	1	.810	.215	NS
*Diseases * Heredity status* (A*C)	12.960	1	12.960	3.433	NS
*Gender * Heredity status* (B*C)	8.410	1	8.410	2.227	NS
*Diseases * Gender * Heredity status* (A*B*C)	43.560	1	43.560	11.537	$p<.01$
Error	1480.040	392	3.776		
Total	31066.000	400			
Corrected Total	1688.040	399			

Levene's Test of Equality of Error Variances[a]

Dependent Variable: Q9

F	df1	df2	Sig.
18.460	7	392	.000

Tests the null hypothesis that the error variance of the dependent variable is equal across groups.

a. Design: Intercept + Diseases + Gender + HS + Diseases * Gender + Diseases * HS + Gender * HS + Diseases * Gender * HS

Table-66
Showing Mean, SD & Mean difference between patients of diabetes and hypertension for quality of life factor- Physical well-being &Self care.

Diseases (A)	N	Mean	SD	Mean Difference
Diabetes A1	200	9.16	1.43	2.19
Hypertension A2	200	6.97	2.39	

Figure no.57
Showing comparisons of means scores between patients of diabetes and hypertension for quality of life factor- Physical well-being & Self care.

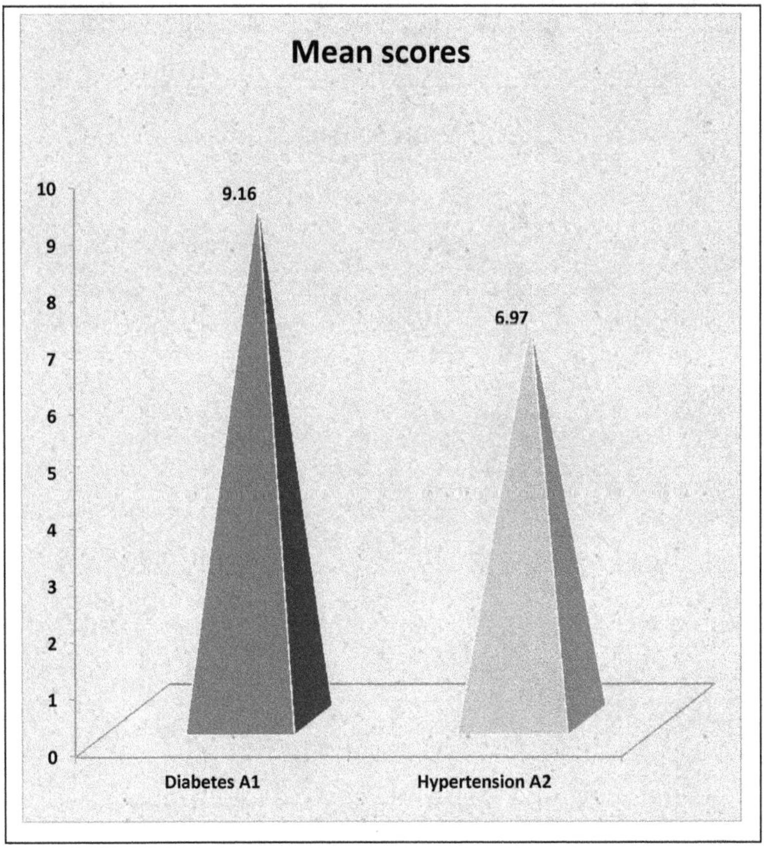

Table 67
Showing Mean, SD & Mean difference between male and female patients with diabetes and hypertension for quality of life factor- Physical well-being & Self care.

Gender (B)	N	Mean	SD	Mean Difference
Male B1	200	8.59	2.05	0.04
Female B2	200	8.55	2.06	

Figure no.58
Showing comparisons of mean scores between male and female patients with diabetes and hypertension for quality of life factor- Physical well-being & Self care.

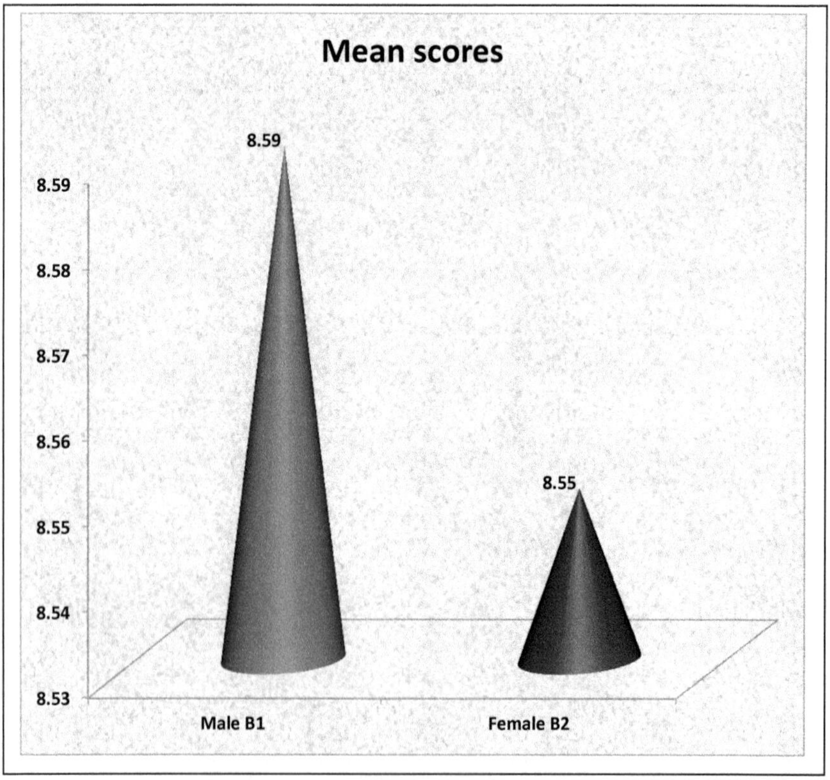

Table 68
Showing Mean, SD & Mean difference between patients with and without hereditary status for quality of life factor- Physical well-being & Self care.

Hereditary status (C)	N	Mean	SD	Mean Difference
Hereditary C1	200	8.53	2.13	0.07
Non-hereditary C2	200	8.60	1.98	

Figure no. 59
Showing comparisons of means scores between patients with and without hereditary status for quality of life factor- Physical well-being & Self care.

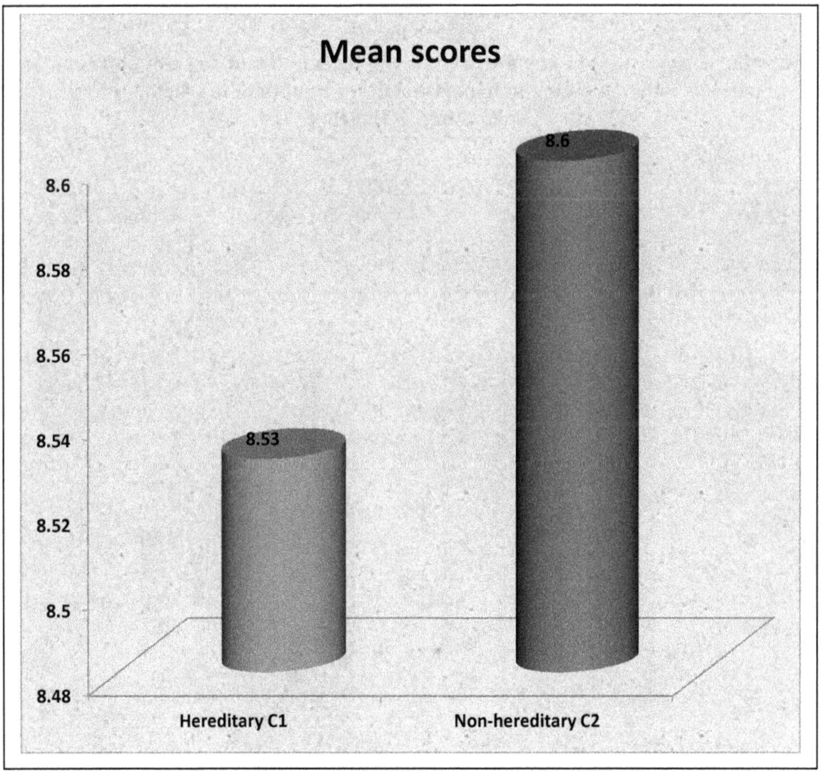

Table 69
Showing Mean, SD & Mean difference among interaction of diseases and Gender of patients with diabetes and hypertension for quality of life factor- Physical well-being & Self care.

Diseases (A)	Gender (B)	N	Mean	SD	Mean Difference
Diabetes A1	**Male B1**	100	9.14	1.44	0.05
	Female B2	100	9.19	1.43	
Hypertension A2	**Male B1**	100	8.04	2.40	0.13
	Female B2	100	7.91	2.38	

Figure no. 60
Showing comparisons of mean scores among interaction of diseases and Gender of patients with diabetes and hypertension for quality of life factor- Physical well-being & Self care.

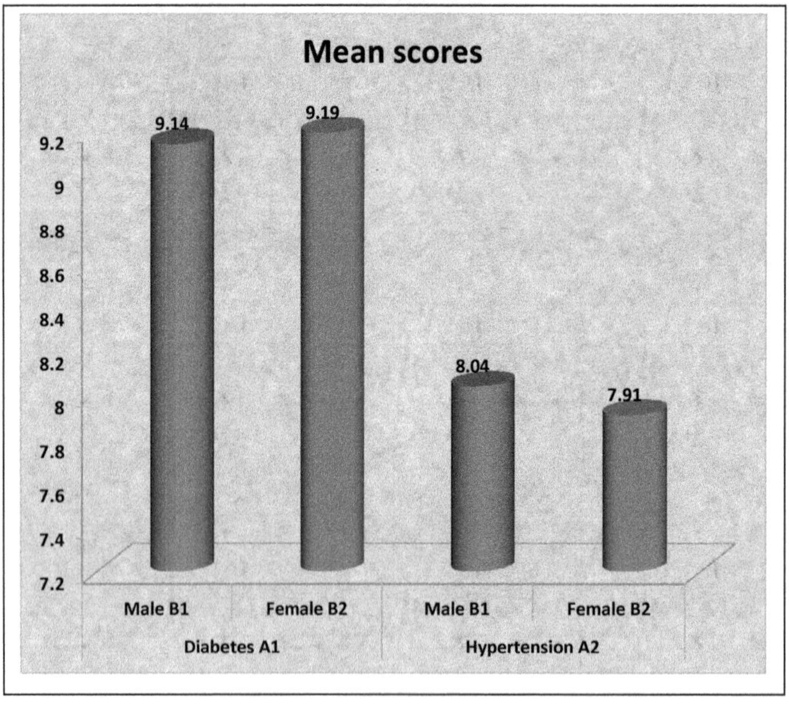

Table 70

Showing Mean, SD & Mean difference among interaction of diseases and hereditary status of patients for quality of life factor- Physical well-being & Self care.

Diseases (A)	Hereditary (C)	N	Mean	SD	Mean Difference
Diabetes A1	Hereditary *C1*	100	9.31	1.55	0.29
	Non- hereditary *C2*	100	9.02	1.29	
Hypertension A2	Hereditary *C1*	100	7.76	2.34	0.43
	Non- hereditary *C2*	100	8.19	2.42	

Figure no. 61

Showing comparisons of mean scores among interaction of diseases and hereditary status of patients for quality of life factor- Physical well-being & Self care.

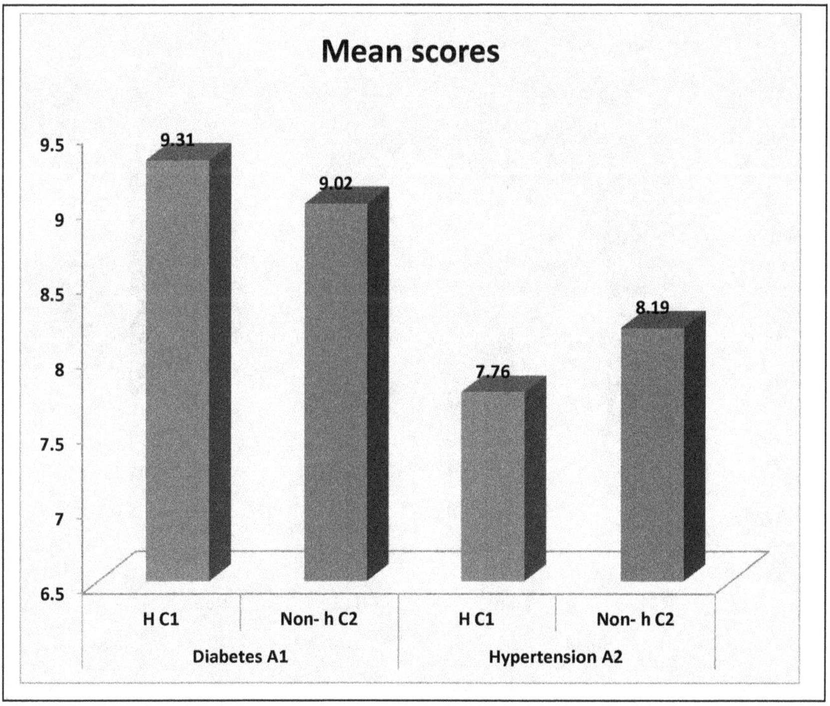

Table 71

Showing Mean, SD & Mean difference among interaction of Gender and hereditary status of patients for quality of life factor- Physical well-being & Self care.

Gender (B)	Hereditary status (C)	N	Mean	SD	Mean Difference
Male	**Hereditary *C1***	100	8.70	2.10	0.22
	Non-hereditary *C2*	100	8.48	2.00	
Female	**Hereditary *C1***	100	8.37	2.15	0.36
	Non-hereditary *C2*	100	8.73	1.95	

Figure no. 62

Showing Mean, SD & Mean difference among interaction of Gender and hereditary status of patients for quality of life factor- Physical well-being & Self care.

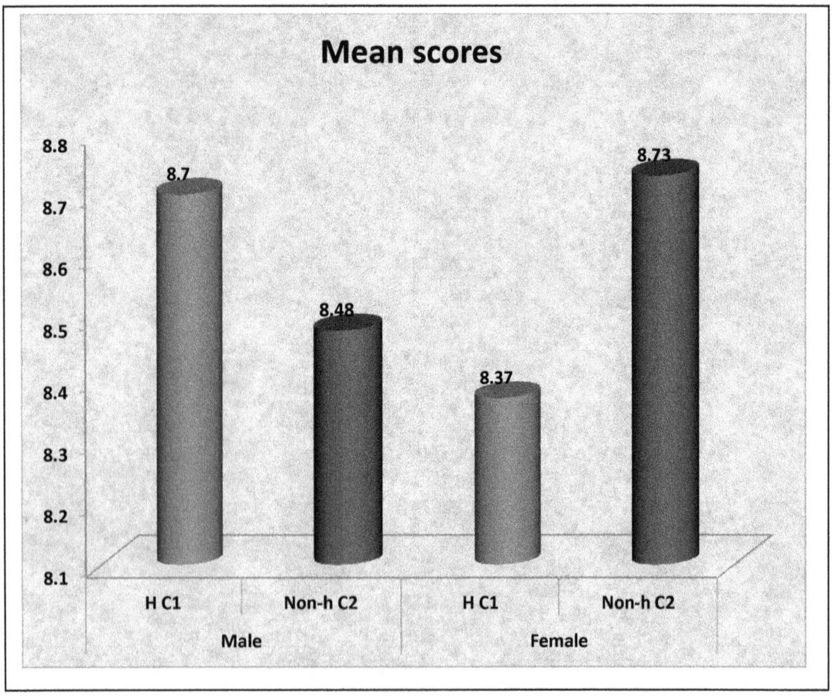

Table 72
Showing Mean, SD & Mean difference among interaction of diseases, gender and hereditary status of patients with diabetes and hypertension for quality of life factor- Physical well-being & Self care.

Diseases (A)	Gender (B)	Hereditary status (C)	N	Mean	SD	Mean Difference
Diabetes A1	*Male B1*	*Hereditary C1*	50	9.76	1.30	1.24
		Non- hereditary C2	50	8.52	1.31	
	Female B2	*Hereditary C1*	50	8.86	1.66	0.66
		Non- hereditary C2	50	9.52	1.07	
Hypertension A2	*Male B1*	*Hereditary C1*	50	7.64	2.22	0.8
		Non- hereditary C2	50	8.44	2.53	
	Female B2	*Hereditary C1*	50	7.88	2.47	0.06
		Non- hereditary C2	50	7.94	2.30	

Figure no. 63
Showing comparisons of means scores among interaction of diseases, gender and hereditary status of patients with diabetes and hypertension for quality of life factor- Physical well-being & Self care.

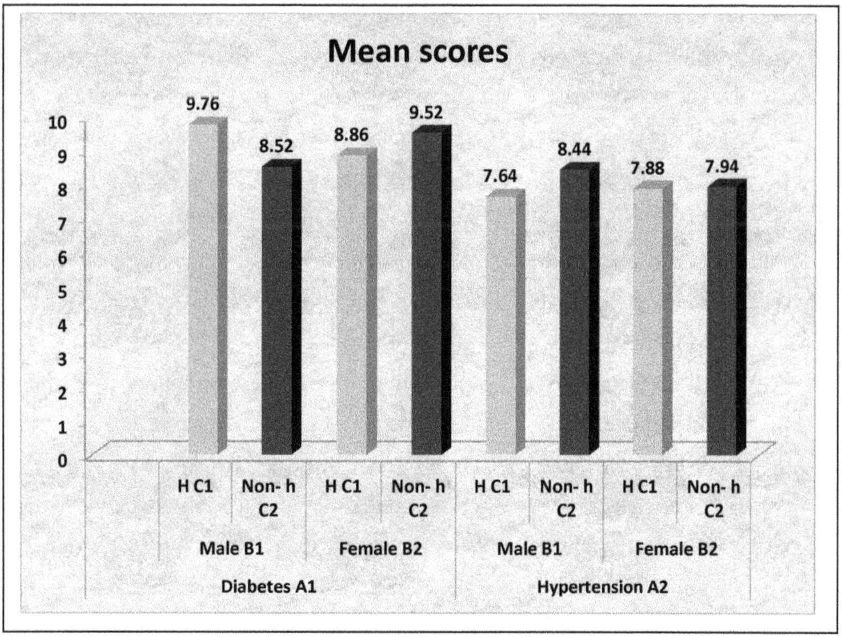

Main Effect:

Quality of life factor-physical well being & self care with regard to Types of disease:

When the F test was used to know the impact of illness type on physical well-being and self-care in diabetic and hypertensive patients, the F value was displayed significant. The significance F (1, 200) =37.50, $p<.01$ was highlighted in (Table no.65). The mean value for diabetes patients is 9.16 (SD = 1.43), while the mean value for hypertension patients is 6.97 (SD = 2.39). According to Tables 66 and 57, the difference between the two means is 2.19. Above findings showed that diabetic patients have higher physical well-being and self-care in terms of quality of life.

Quality of life factor physical well being and self care with regard to Gender

The F value and mean score for diabetic and hypertensive patients with reference to gender are shown in Tables 65 and 58. The mean difference and F ratio reported as insignificant F(1,200) =0.42, $p>.05$. Male patients have an average score of 8.59 (SD = 2.05), while female patients have an average score of 8.55 (SD = 2.06), the mean difference is 0.04 between the two groups. Hence, findings revealed that both female and male patients have equal quality of life factor physical well being and self care.

Quality of life factor physical well being and self care with regard to Hereditary status:

For hereditary status, F (1, 200) =.13 was obtained, which was not significant. Patients with hereditary status have a mean score of 8.53(SD=2.13) reported in table No. 68 and chart No. 59, while patients without hereditary status have a mean score of 8.60 (SD=1.98), and a mean difference is 0.07. Patients with hereditary and without hereditary have similar quality of life trait physical well-being and self-care.

Interaction Effect

Quality of life factor physical well being and self care with regard to Types of disease and Gender:

The first interaction effect i.e. Types of disease and Gender are not interacting with each other for physical well-being and self-care. From Table no.65, the F value for the interaction of illness types and gender was F (1,100) =.21 $p>.05$, which was insignificant. As shown in Table 69 and Chart 60, the mean scores of male and female diabetic patients are (M=9.14, SD=1.44) and (M = 9.19, SD = 1.43), respectively, with a mean difference of 0.05. The mean score of hypertensive male and female patients are (M =8.04 SD=2.40) and (M=7.91 SD=2.38), respectively. The mean difference between male and female hypertensive patients is 0.13. The mean difference between the four groups indicated that all the groups of patients have equal quality of life factor physical well-being and self-care.

Quality of life factor physical well being and self care with regard to Types of disease and Hereditary status:

The F (1, 100) = 3.43 $p>.05$ indicated that there was no significant interaction between disease and heredity status for quality of life factor physical well being and self care. The diabetic patients with hereditary status have a mean score of 9.31 (SD =1.55), while diabetic patients without hereditary status have a mean score of 9.02 (SD=1.29) and mean difference is observed 0.29, While the mean score for hereditary status with hypertensive patients is 7.76 (SD =2.34) and 8.19 (SD =2.42), the statistically non-significant mean difference is 0.43. On the basis of insignificant mean difference, one can well imagine that all the groups of patients have equal Quality of life factor physical well being and self care.

Quality of life factor-physical well being and self care with regard to Gender and Hereditary status:

The interaction between gender and heredity was calculated non-significant (F (1,100) = 2.22, $p>.0$). The mean score for male patients with hereditary status is 8.70 (SD =2.10), while the mean score for male patients without hereditary status is 8.48 (SD =2.00), indicating a 0.22 in mean difference, according to Table 71 and Chart 62. The mean score for female patients with hereditary status is 8.37 (SD = 2.15), while the mean score for non-hereditary patients is 8.73 (SD = 1.95). The mean difference is 0.36. In all four groups, the mean difference is insignificant. As a result, it can be said that all four patient groups showed similar levels of physical well-being and self-care.

Quality of life factor-physical well being and self care with regard to Types of disease, Gender and Hereditary status:

In diabetic and hypertensive patients, F ratio for disease, gender, and hereditary status is reported significant, F (1, 50) =11.53 $p<.01$. Diabetic male patients with hereditary have a mean score of 9.76 (SD =1.31), similarly, diabetic male patients without hereditary have a mean value of 8.52 (SD =1.31). The difference in mean values between the two groups is 1.24. Female diabetic patients with hereditary status have mean values of 8.86 (SD = 1.66) and non-hereditary female diabetic patients have mean values of 9.52 (SD = 1.07). Between the two groups, the mean difference is 0.66, which is statistically significant. Male patients of hereditary status with hypertension have a mean score of 7.64 (SD=2.22), while those without hereditary status have a mean score of 8.44 (SD =2.53). The mean difference is also insignificant at 0.8. The mean score for female hypertension patients with heredity is 7.88 (SD=2.47), while the mean score for those without heredity is 7.94 (SD=2.30). The mean difference is 0.06. The quality of life trait of physical well being and self care is similar in all eight groups of diabetic and hypertensive patients.

Table: 73

Showing ANOVA summary for the quality of life factor- Efficacy of myself

Source	Type III Sum of Squares	df	Mean Square	F	Sig. Level
***Diseases* (A)**	44.223	1	44.223	16.381	p<.01
***Gender* (B)**	1.823	1	1.823	.675	NS
***Heredity status* (C)**	18.922	1	18.922	7.009	p<.01
***Diseases * Gender* (A*B)**	2.723	1	2.723	1.008	NS
***Diseases * Heredity status* (A*C)**	.423	1	.423	.157	NS
***Gender * Heredity status* (B*C)**	.202	1	.202	.075	NS
***Diseases * Gender * Heredity status* (A*B*C)**	1.103	1	1.103	.408	NS
Error	1058.260	392	2.700		
Total	21051.000	400			
Corrected Total	1127.677	399			

Levene's Test of Equality of Error Variances[a]

Dependent Variable: Q10

F	df1	df2	Sig.
4.956	7	392	.000

Tests the null hypothesis that the error variance of the dependent variable is equal across groups.

a. Design: Intercept + Diseases + Gender + HS + Diseases * Gender + Diseases * HS + Gender * HS + Diseases * Gender * HS

Table74

Showing Mean, SD & Mean difference between patients of diabetes and hypertension for quality of life factor- Efficacy of myself.

Diseases (A)	N	Mean	SD	Mean Difference
Diabetes A1	200	8.39	1.79	1.57
Hypertension A2	200	6.52	1.49	

Figure no.64

Showing comparisons mean scores between patients of diabetes and hypertension for quality of life factor- Efficacy of myself.

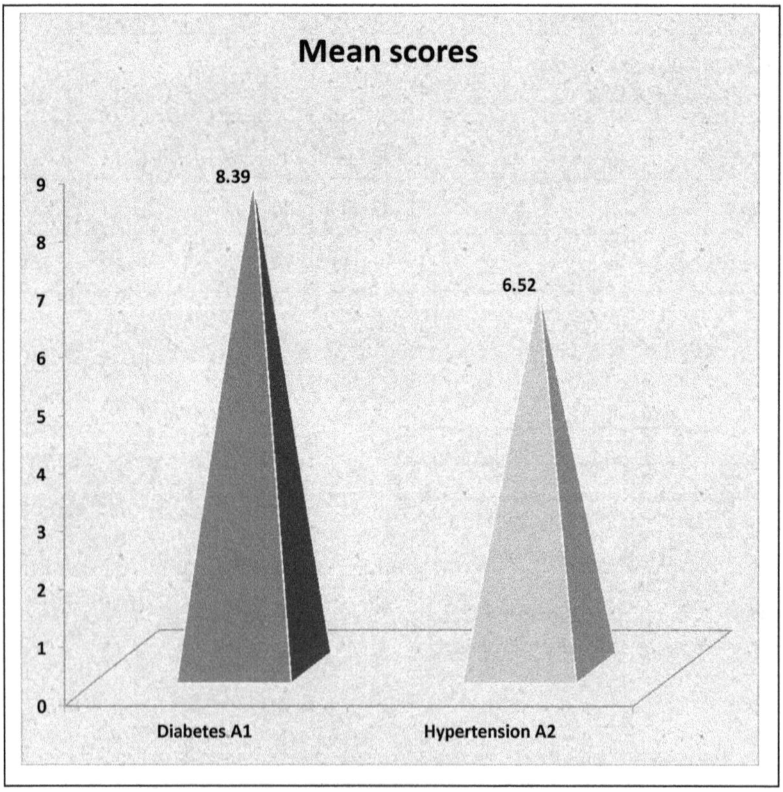

Table 75

Showing Mean, SD & Mean difference between male and female patients with diabetes and hypertension for quality of life factor- Efficacy of myself.

Gender (B)	N	Mean	SD	Mean Difference
Male B1	200	6.99	1.69	0.13
Female B2	200	7.12	1.67	

Figure no.65

Showing comparisons of mean scores between male and female patients with diabetes and hypertension for quality of life factor- Efficacy of myself.

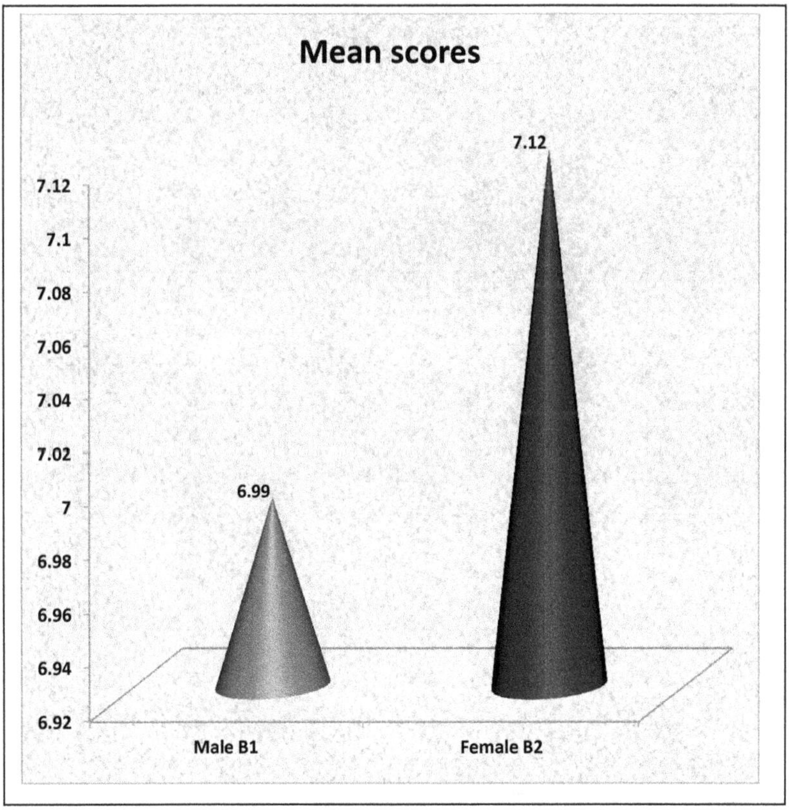

Table 76
Showing Mean, SD & Mean difference between patients with and without hereditary status for quality of life factor- Efficacy of myself.

Hereditary status (C)	N	Mean	SD	Mean Difference
Hereditary C1	200	7.27	1.93	0.43
Non-hereditary C2	200	6.84	1.35	

Figure no.66
Showing comparisons of mean scores between patients with and without hereditary status for quality of life factor- Efficacy of myself.

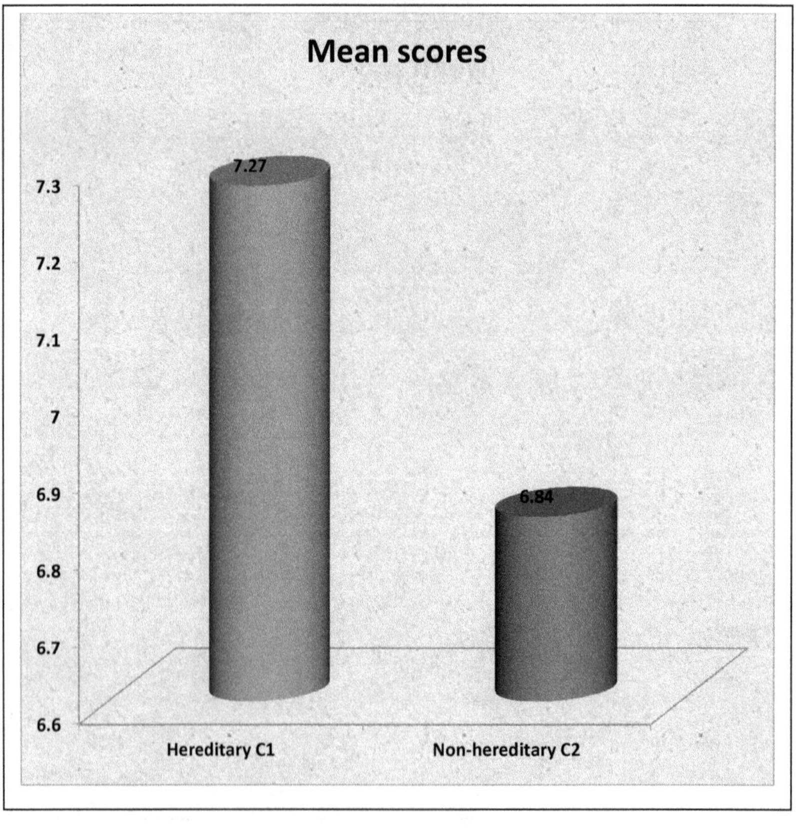

Table 77
Showing Mean, SD & Mean difference among interaction of diseases and Gender of patients with diabetes and hypertension for quality of life factor- Efficacy of myself.

Diseases (A)	Gender (B)	N	Mean	SD	Mean Difference
Diabetes A1	Male B1	100	7.24	1.80	0.30
	Female B2	100	7.54	1.77	
Hypertension A2	Male B1	100	6.74	1.54	0.03
	Female B2	100	6.71	1.45	

Figure no. 67
Showing comparisons of mean scores among interaction of diseases and Gender of patients with diabetes and hypertension for quality of life factor- Efficacy of myself.

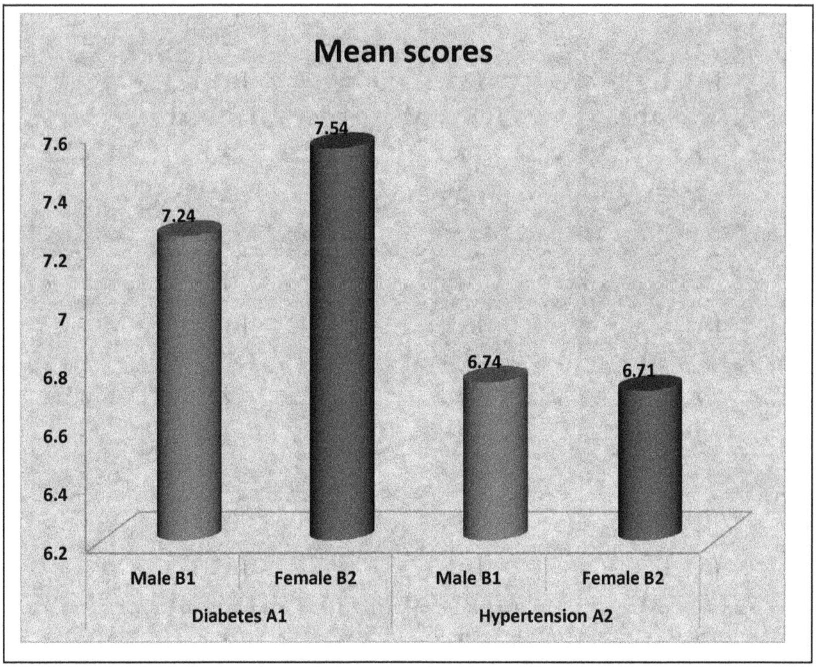

Table 78

Showing Mean, SD & Mean difference among interaction of diseases and hereditary status of patients for quality of life factor- Efficacy of myself.

***Diseases* (A)**	**Hereditary (C)**	**N**	**Mean**	**SD**	**Mean Difference**
Diabetes A1	**Hereditary *C1***	100	7.64	2.24	0.50
	Non-* hereditary *C2	100	7.14	1.13	
Hypertension A2	**Hereditary *C1***	100	6.91	1.49	0.37
	Non-* hereditary *C2	100	6.54	1.47	

Figure no. 68

Showing comparisons of mean scores among interaction of diseases and hereditary status of patients for quality of life factor- Efficacy of myself.

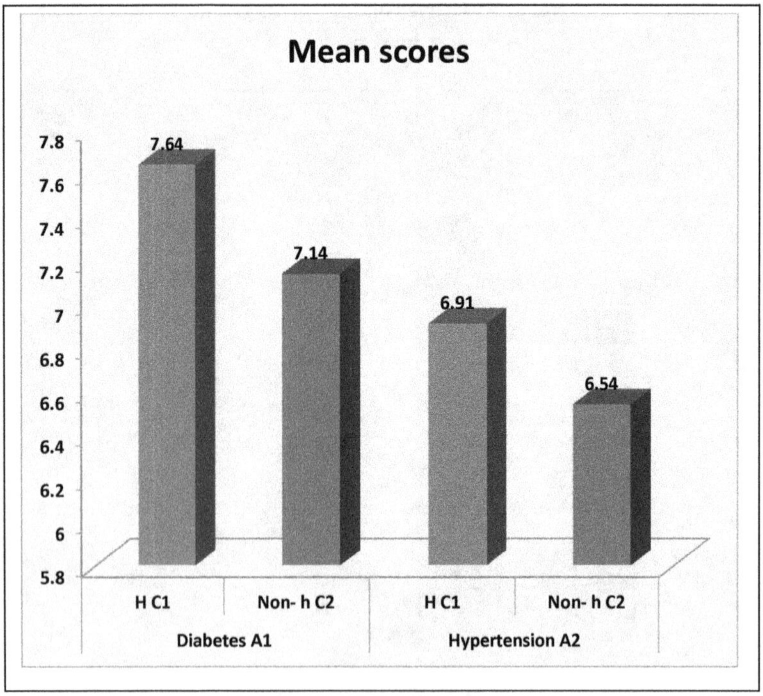

Table 79

Showing Mean, SD & Mean difference among interaction of Gender and hereditary status of patients for quality of life factor- Efficacy of myself.

Gender (B)	Hereditary status (C)	N	Mean	SD	Mean Difference
Male	Hereditary *C1*	100	7.23	1.94	0.48
	Non-hereditary *C2*	100	6.75	1.35	
Female	Hereditary *C1*	100	7.32	1.93	0.39
	Non-hereditary *C2*	100	6.93	1.34	

Figure no. 69

Showing comparisons of mean scores among interaction of Gender and hereditary status of patients for quality of life factor- Efficacy of myself.

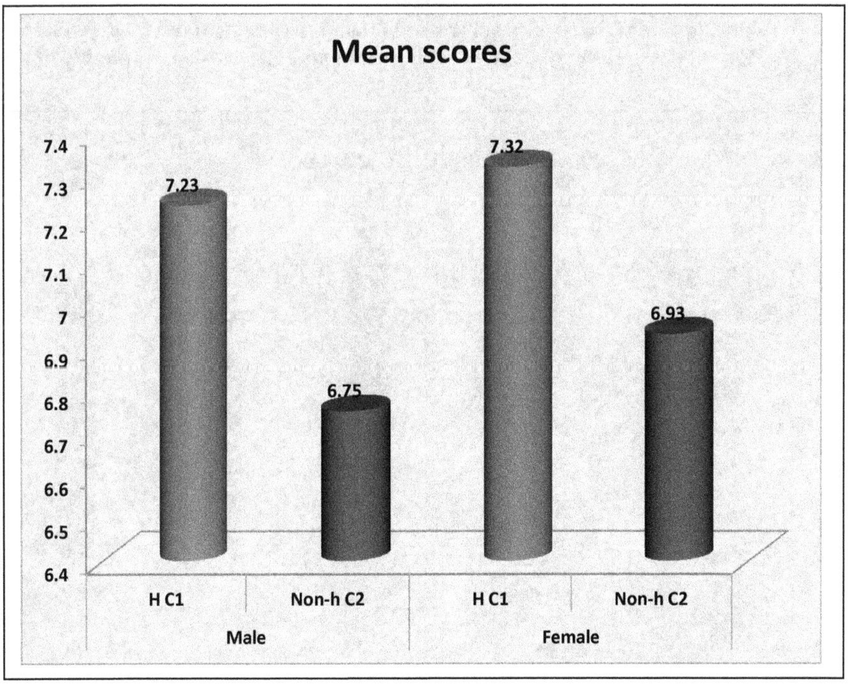

Table 80
Showing Mean, SD & Mean difference among interaction of diseases, gender and hereditary status of patients with diabetes and hypertension for quality of life factor- Efficacy of myself.

Diseases (A)	Gender (B)	Hereditary status (C)	N	Mean	SD	Mean Difference
Diabetes A1	*Male B1*	*Hereditary C1*	50	7.46	2.20	0.44
		Non- hereditary C2	50	7.02	1.26	
	Female B2	*Hereditary C1*	50	7.82	2.29	0.56
		Non- hereditary C2	50	7.26	1.73	
Hypertension A2	*Male B1*	*Hereditary C1*	50	7.00	1.64	0.52
		Non- hereditary C2	50	6.48	1.40	
	Female B2	*Hereditary C1*	50	6.82	1.33	0.22
		Non- hereditary C2	50	6.60	1.56	

Figure no. 70
Showing comparisons of mean scores among interaction of diseases, gender and hereditary status of patients with diabetes and hypertension for quality of life factor- Efficacy of myself.

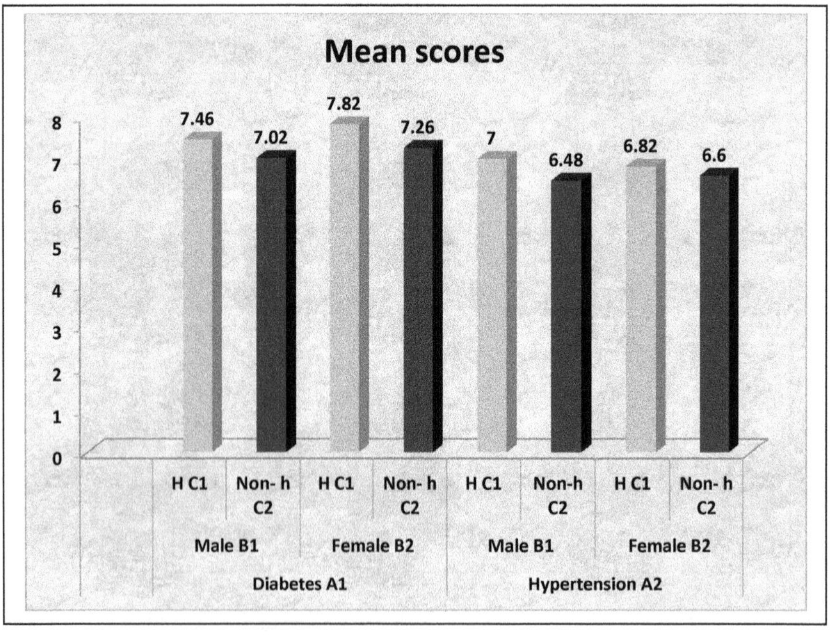

Main Effect:

Quality of life factor-efficacy of myself with regard to Types of disease:

The F value was significant when the F test was used to investigate the impact of illness type on efficacy of myself in diabetic and hypertensive patients. F (1, 200) =16.83, $p<.01$ was highlighted in (Table no.73). Patients with diabetes have mean score of 8.39 (SD = 1.79), while those with hypertension have mean score of 6.52 (SD = 1.49). The difference between the two means, according to Tables 74 and 64, is 1.57. The diabetic patients have better quality of life factors efficacy of myself, than the Hypertensive patients.

Quality of life factor efficacy of myself with regard to Gender

Tables 73 and 65 showed the F value and mean score for the gender of diabetic and hypertensive patients, the mean difference and F ratio reported as insignificant F(1,200) =0.67, p>.05. The mean score for male patients is 6.99 (SD =1.69), while the mean score for female patients is 7.12 (SD = 1.67), the mean difference is 0.13 between the two groups. According to the findings, the quality of life factor efficacy of myself is similar between male and female patients.

Quality of life factor efficacy of myself with regard to Hereditary status:

The significant F (1, 200) =7.00 was obtained for hereditary status. In table No.76 and chart No.66, patients with hereditary status have a mean score of 7.27 (SD=1.93), while patients without hereditary status have a mean score of 6.84 (SD=1.35) and a mean difference is 0.43. Patients with hereditary status have higher trait efficacy of myself in terms of quality of life.

Interaction Effect

Quality of life factor efficacy of myself with regard to Types of disease and Gender:

The primary goal of the study was to see if male and female diabetic patients, as well as male and female hypertensive patients, have different levels of efficacy of myself Quality of Life trait. The F value for the interaction between disease types and gender was highlighted F (1,100) =1.00 $p>.05$, in Table no.73, not significant. The mean scores of male and female diabetic patients are (M=7.24, SD=1.80) and (M = 7.54, SD =1.77), respectively, as shown in Table 77 and Chart 67, with a mean difference of 0.30. Male and female hypertensive patients have mean scores of (M =6.74 SD=1.54) and (M=6.71 SD=1.45), respectively. Male and female hypertensive patients have a 0.03 difference in mean. The mean difference in disease and gender among the four groups equal quality of life factor efficacy of myself.

Quality of life factor efficacy of myself with regard to Types of disease and Hereditary status:

There was insignificant relationship between disease and heredity status, as F(1, 100)=0.15, p>.05 indicated. Diabetic patients with hereditary status have a mean score of 7.64 (SD =2.24), while diabetic patients without hereditary status have a mean score of 7.14 (SD=1.13), with a mean difference of 0.50. The insignificant mean difference between hereditary status with hypertensive patient have scores of 6.91(SD =1.49) and 6.54(SD =1.47). All four groups have a similar level of quality of life factor efficacy of myself.

Quality of life factor-efficacy of myself with regard to Gender and Hereditary status:

F(1,100) =.07 was calculated as the interaction between gender and heredity, which was insignificant. According to Table 79 and Chart 69, the mean score for male patients with hereditary status is 7.23 (SD =1.94), while the mean score for male patients without hereditary status is 6.75 (SD =1.35), the mean difference is revealed 0.48. Female patients with hereditary status have a mean score of 7.32 (SD = 1.93), while non-hereditary patients have a mean score of 6.93 (SD = 1.34). The mean difference is 0.39. The mean difference is non-significant in all four groups. As a result, all four patient groups demonstrated similar levels of efficacy of myself as a quality of life factor.

Quality of life factor-efficacy of myself with regard to Types of disease, Gender and Hereditary status:

F ratios for disease, gender, and hereditary status are insignificant in diabetic and hypertensive patients, (F(1, 50) =.04 p<.01). The mean score for diabetic male patients with hereditary is 7.46 (SD =2.20), compared to 7.02 (SD =1.26) for diabetic male patients without hereditary. The difference between the two groups mean value is 0.44. Female diabetic patients with hereditary status have mean values of 7.82 (SD = 2.29) and female diabetic patients without hereditary status have mean values of 7.26 (SD = 1.73). The mean difference between the two groups is 0.56, which is statistically non-significant. Patients of hereditary status with hypertension have a mean score of 7.00 (SD=1.64), while those without hereditary status have a mean score of 6.48(SD =1.40). The mean difference is also insignificant at 0.52. The mean score for female hypertension patients with heredity is 6.82 (SD=1.33), while the mean score for those without heredity is 6.60 (SD=1.56). The mean difference is 0.22. In all eight groups of diabetic and hypertensive patients, the quality of life trait efficacy of myself is similar.

Table: 81

Showing ANOVA summary for the quality of life factor- Personal development/ Personal evolution

Source	Type III Sum of Squares	df	Mean Square	F	Sig. Level
***Diseases* (A)**	193.210	1	193.210	37.714	p<.01
***Gender* (B)**	5.290	1	5.290	1.033	NS
***Heredity status* (C)**	12.960	1	12.960	2.530	NS
***Diseases * Gender* (A*B)**	.090	1	.090	.018	NS
***Diseases * Heredity status* (A*C)**	25.000	1	25.000	4.880	p<.05
***Gender * Heredity status* (B*C)**	1.960	1	1.960	.383	NS
***Diseases * Gender * Heredity status* (A*B*C)**	1.000	1	1.000	.195	NS
Error	2008.240	392	5.123		
Total	33400.000	400			
Corrected Total	2247.750	399			

Levene's Test of Equality of Error Variances[a]

Dependent Variable: Q11

F	df1	df2	Sig.
8.414	7	392	.000

Tests the null hypothesis that the error variance of the dependent variable is equal across groups.

a. Design: Intercept + Diseases + Gender + HS + Diseases * Gender + Diseases * HS + Gender * HS + Diseases * Gender * HS

Table 82
Showing Mean, SD & Mean difference between patients of diabetes and hypertension for quality of life factor- Personal development/ Personal evolution.

Diseases (A)	N	Mean	SD	Mean Difference
Diabetes A1	200	10.52	2.00	2.39
Hypertension A2	200	8.13	2.50	

Figure no.71
Showing comparisons of mean scores between patients of diabetes and hypertension for quality of life factor- Personal development/ Personal evolution.

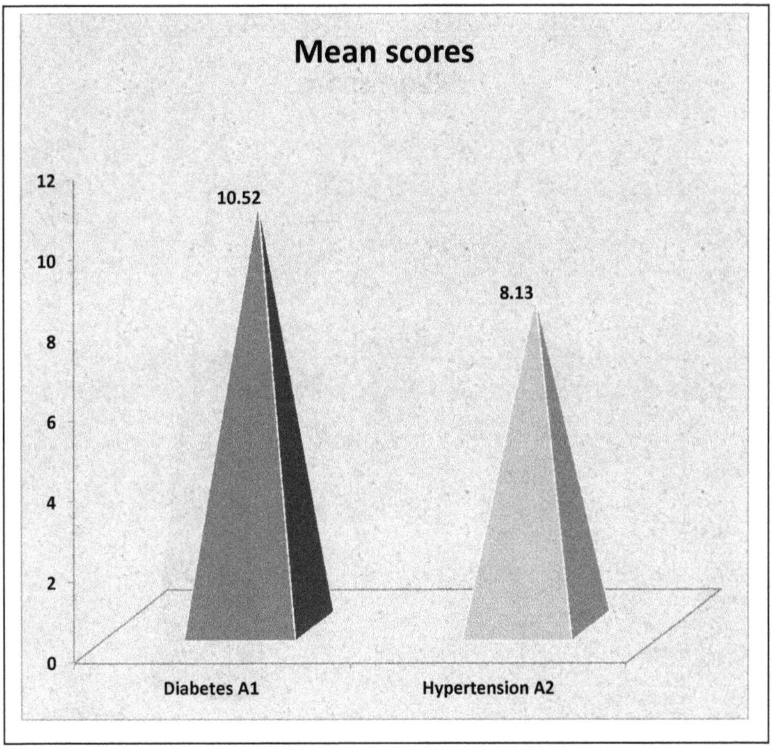

Table 83
Showing Mean, SD & Mean difference between male and female patients with diabetes and hypertension for quality of life factor- Personal development/ Personal evolution.

Gender (B)	N	Mean	SD	Mean Difference
Male B1	200	8.71	2.30	0.23
Female B2	200	8.94	2.43	

Figure no.72
Showing comparisons of mean scores between male and female patients with diabetes and hypertension for quality of life factor- Personal development/ Personal evolution.

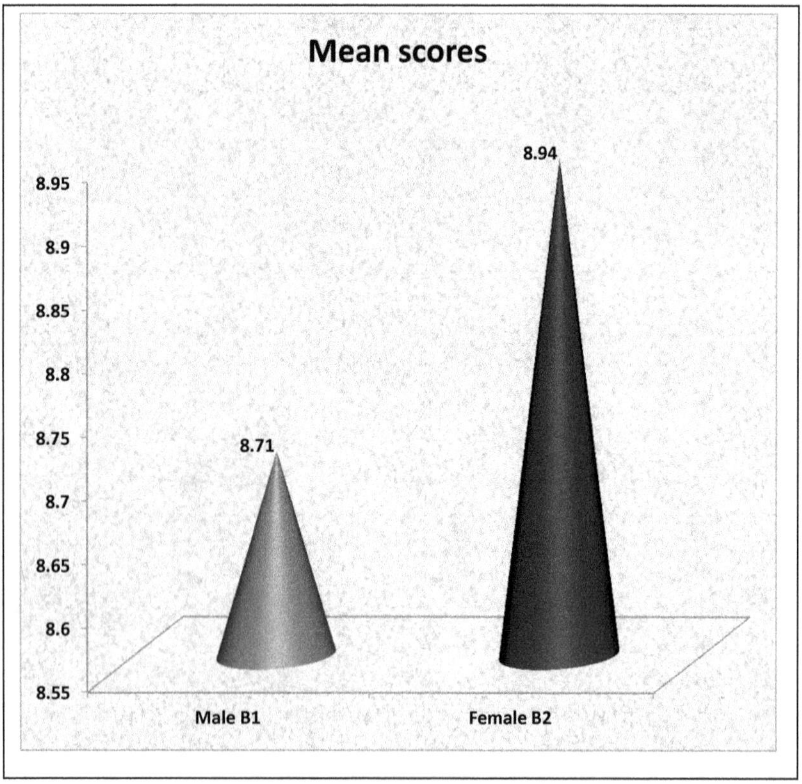

Table 84
Showing Mean, SD & Mean difference between patients with and without hereditary status for quality of life factor- Personal development/ Personal evolution.

Hereditary status (C)	N	Mean	SD	Mean Difference
Hereditary C1	200	8.64	2.70	0.36
Non-hereditary C2	200	9.00	1.97	

Figure no. 73
Showing comparisons of mean scores between patients with and without hereditary status for quality of life factor- Personal development/ Personal evolution.

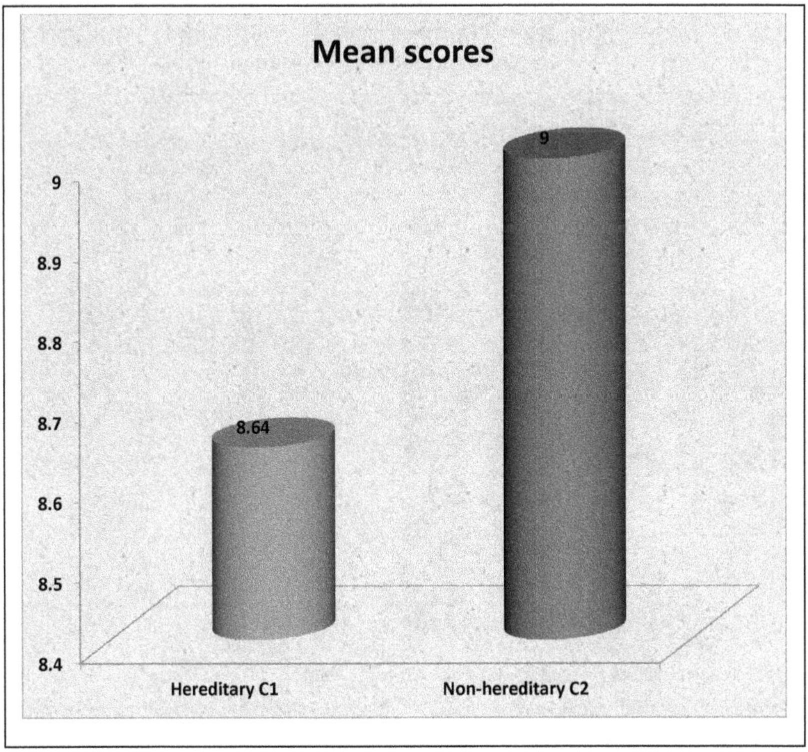

Table 85

Showing Mean, SD & Mean difference among interaction of diseases and Gender of patients with diabetes and hypertension for quality of life factor- Personal development/ Personal evolution.

Diseases (A)	Gender (B)	N	Mean	SD	Mean Difference
Diabetes A1	Male B1	100	9.39	1.99	0.26
	Female B2	100	9.65	2.02	
Hypertension A2	Male B1	100	8.03	2.40	0.20
	Female B2	100	8.23	2.61	

Figure no. 74

Showing comparisons of mean scores among interaction of diseases and Gender of patients with diabetes and hypertension for quality of life factor- Personal development/ Personal evolution.

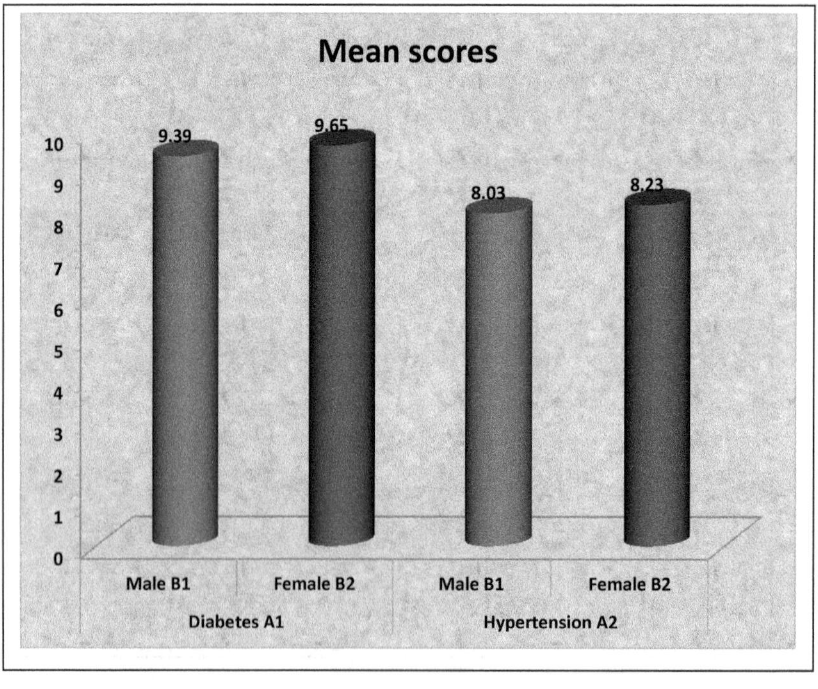

Table 86
Showing Mean, SD & Mean difference among interaction of diseases and hereditary status of patients for quality of life factor- Personal development/ Personal evolution.

Diseases (A)	Hereditary (C)	N	Mean	SD	Mean Difference
Diabetes A1	Hereditary *C1*	100	9.59	2.53	0.14
	Non- hereditary *C2*	100	9.45	1.29	
Hypertension A2	Hereditary *C1*	100	7.70	2.54	0.86
	Non- hereditary *C2*	100	8.56	2.40	

Figure no. 75
Showing comparisons of mean scores among interaction of diseases and hereditary status of patients for quality of life factor- Personal development/ Personal evolution.

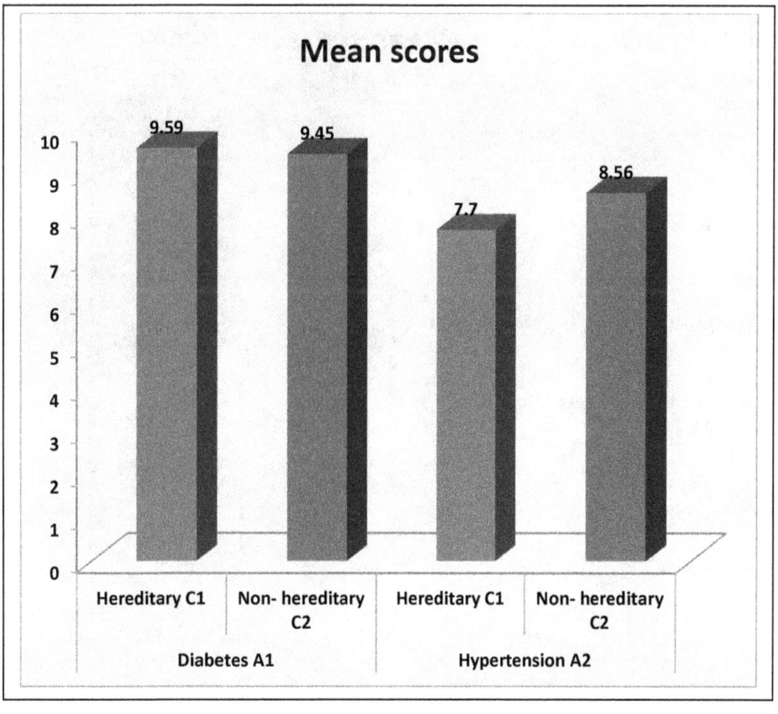

Table 87
Showing Mean, SD & Mean difference among interaction of Gender and hereditary status of patients for quality of life factor- Personal development/ Personal evolution.

Gender (B)	Hereditary status (C)	N	Mean	SD	Mean Difference
Male	Hereditary *C1*	100	8.60	2.55	0.22
	Non-hereditary *C2*	100	8.82	2.03	
Female	Hereditary *C1*	100	8.69	2.86	0.50
	Non-hereditary *C2*	100	9.19	1.90	

Figure no. 76
Showing comparisons of mean scores among interaction of Gender and hereditary status of patients for quality of life factor- Personal development/ Personal evolution.

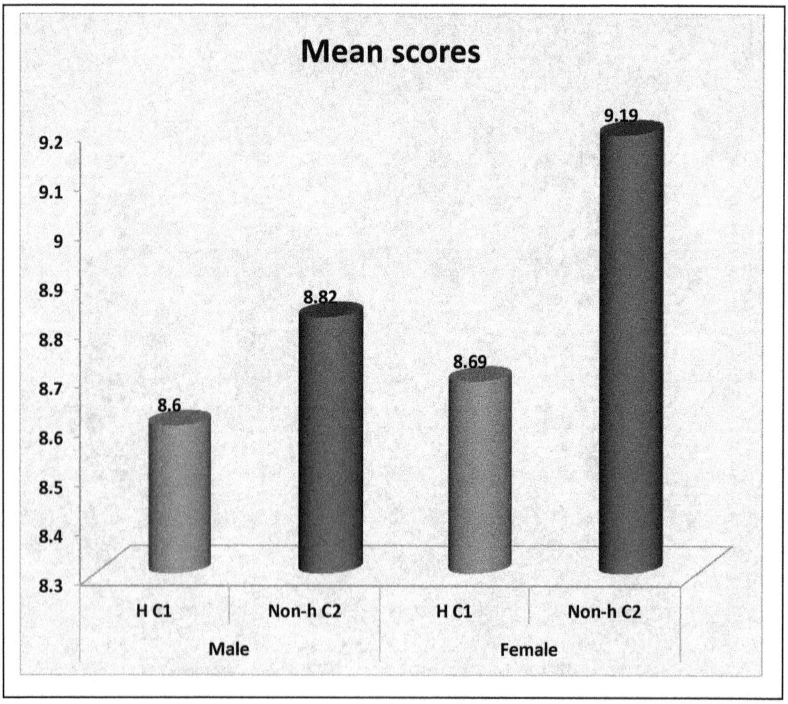

Table 88
Showing Mean, SD & Mean difference among interaction of diseases, gender and hereditary status of patients with diabetes and hypertension for quality of life factor- Personal development/ Personal evolution.

Diseases (A)	Gender (B)	Hereditary status (C)	N	Mean	SD	Mean Difference
Diabetes A1	*Male B1*	*Hereditary C1*	50	9.48	2.51	0.18
		Non- hereditary C2	50	9.30	1.29	
	Female B2	*Hereditary C1*	50	9.70	2.57	0.10
		Non- hereditary C2	50	9.60	1.29	
Hypertension A2	*Male B1*	*Hereditary C1*	50	7.72	2.29	0.62
		Non- hereditary C2	50	8.34	2.49	
	Female B2	*Hereditary C1*	50	7.68	2.80	1.10
		Non- hereditary C2	50	8.78	2.30	

Figure no. 77
Showing comparisons of mean scores among interaction of diseases, gender and hereditary status of patients with diabetes and hypertension for quality of life factor- Personal development/ Personal evolution.

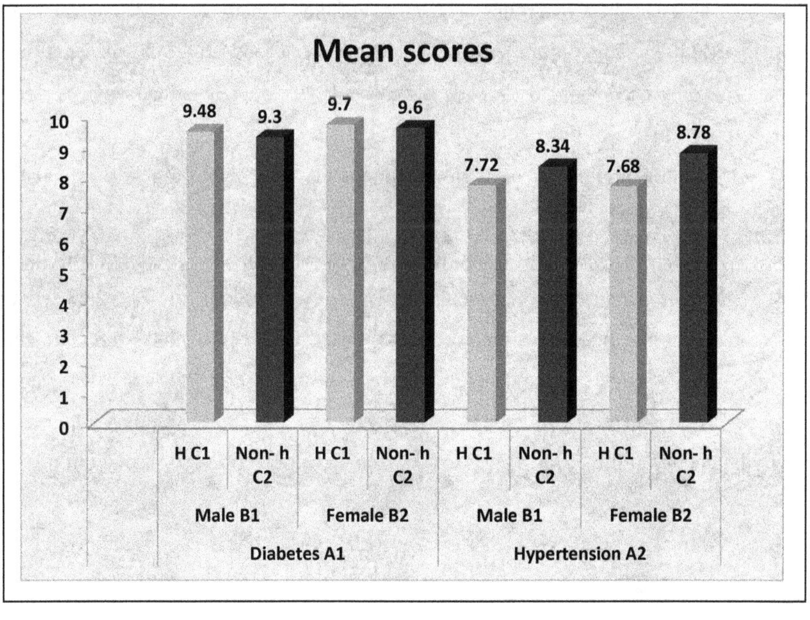

Main Effect:

Quality of life factor-personal development/personal evolution with regard to Types of disease:

When the F test was used to investigate the impact of illness type on personal development/personal evolution in diabetic and hypertensive patients, the F value was exposed significant. The significance of $F(1, 200) = 37.71$, $p < .01$ was highlighted in (Table no.82). The mean score for diabetes patients is 10.52 (SD = 2.00), while the mean value for hypertension patients is 8.13 (SD = 2.50). According to Tables 82 and 71, the difference between the two means is 2.39. On the basis of above findings it can be said that diabetic patients have greater feelings of personal development or personal evolution in comparison of patients with hypertension.

Quality of life factor personal development/personal evolution with regard to Gender

The F value and mean score for diabetic and hypertensive patients were shown in Tables 81 and 72, with the mean difference and F ratio reported as insignificant $F(1,200) = 1.03$, $p > .05$. Male patients have a mean scores of 8.71 (SD = 2.30), while female patients have a mean value of 8.94 (SD = 2.43), resulting in a mean difference of 0.23 between the two groups. The mean difference between the two groups was insignificant, as shown in the graph (Table No. 83 & Chart No. 72). Both female and male patients have more or less equal personal development or personal evolution in terms of quality of life.

Quality of life factor personal development/personal evolution with regard to Hereditary status:

Hereditary status was found to have a non significant main effect for Quality of life factor personal development or personal evolution $F(1, 2) = 2.53$, $p > .05$. Patients with heredity have a mean score of 8.64 (SD=2.70) in table No.84 and chart No.73, while patients without heredity have a mean score of 9.00 (SD=1.97) and a mean difference of 0.36. Patients with hereditary and non-hereditary status have similar quality of life traits in terms of personal development/personal evolution.

Interaction Effect

Quality of life factor personal development/personal evolution with regard to Types of disease and Gender:

The study's main goal was to determine whether male and female diabetic patients, as well as male and female hypertensive patients, have different levels of personal development or personal evolution Quality of Life trait. Table no.81 shows that the F value for the relation between disease types and gender was reported, F (1,100) =0.01 *p*>.05, was not significant. As shown in Table 85 and Chart 74, the mean scores of male and female diabetic patients are (M=9.39, SD=1.99) and (M = 9.65, SD =2.02), respectively, with a mean difference of 0.26. The mean scores for male and female hypertensive patients are (M = 8.03 SD = 2.40) and (M = 8.23 SD =2.61), respectively. The mean difference between male and female hypertensive patients is 0.20. On the basis of the above results it can be said that all the groups of patients have similar level of personal development or personal evolution.

Quality of life factor personal development/personal evolution with regard to Types of disease and hereditary status:

As F(1,100) = 4.88 *p*<.01 indicated, there was a significant interaction between disease and hereditary status of patients. Diabetic patients with hereditary status have a mean score of 9.59 (SD =2.53), while diabetic patients without hereditary status have a mean score of 9.45 (SD=1.29). The significant difference between hypertensive patients with hereditary status and hypertensive patients without hereditary status have mean scores of 7.70 (SD =2.54) and 8.56 (SD =2.40) is 0.86. Each of the four groups has a different level of personal development or personal evolution as a quality of life factor.

Quality of life factor-personal development/personal evolution with regard to Gender and Hereditary status:

The interaction between gender and heredity was calculated as F(1,100) = 0.38, which was insignificant. The mean score for male patients with hereditary status is 8.60 (SD =2.55), while the mean score for male patients without hereditary status is 8.82 (SD =2.03), showing a 0.22 mean difference, according to Table 87 and Chart 76. The mean score for female patients with hereditary status is 8.69 (S=2.86), while the mean score for non-hereditary patients is 9.19 (SD=1.90). The mean difference is

0.50. In all four groups, the mean difference is negligible. As a result, quality of life factor, all four patient groups showed similar levels of personal development or personal evolution.

Quality of life factor-personal development/personal evolution with regard to Types of disease, Gender and Hereditary status:

In diabetic and hypertensive patients, F ratios for disease, gender, and hereditary status are insignificant, with $F(1,50) = 0.19$, $p>.05$. Diabetic male patients with hereditary status have a mean score of 9.48 (SD =2.51), compared to 9.30 (SD =1.29) for diabetic male patients without hereditary. The difference in mean values between the two groups is 0.18. Female diabetes patients with hereditary status have mean values of 9.70 (SD = 2.57), while those without hereditary status have mean values of 9.60 (SD = 1.29). Between the two groups, the mean difference is 0.10, which is statistically insignificant. The mean score for patients with hereditary status and hypertension is 7.72 (SD=2.29), while the mean score for those patients without hereditary status and hypertension is 8.34 (SD =2.49). With a mean difference of 0.62, the difference is also insignificant. Female hypertension patients with hereditary status have a mean score of 7.68 (SD=2.80), while those without hereditary status have a mean score of 6.60 (SD=2.30). 1.10 is the mean difference. The quality of life trait of personal development or personal evolution is similar in all eight groups of diabetic and hypertensive patients.

Table: 89

Showing ANOVA summary for the overall quality of life

Source	Type III Sum of Squares	df	Mean Square	F	Sig. Level
Diseases (A)	7965.563	1	7965.563	110.635	$p<.01$
Gender (B)	897.003	1	897.003	12.459	$p<.01$
Heredity status (C)	657.922	1	657.922	9.138	$p<.01$
*Diseases * Gender* (A*B)	33.063	1	33.063	.459	NS
*Diseases * Heredity status* (A*C)	1432.623	1	1432.623	19.898	$p<.01$
*Gender * Heredity status* (B*C)	.722	1	.722	.010	NS
*Diseases * Gender * Heredity status* (A*B*C)	287.302	1	287.302	3.990	NS
Error	28223.500	392	71.999		
Total	3487761.000	400			
Corrected Total	39497.697	399			

Table 90

Showing Mean, SD & Mean difference between patients of diabetes and hypertension for overall quality of life.

Diseases (A)	N	Mean	SD	Mean Difference
Diabetes A1	200	97.31	7.86	8.93
Hypertension A2	200	88.38	9.82	

Figure no.78

Showing comparisons of mean scores between patients of diabetes and hypertension for overall quality of life.

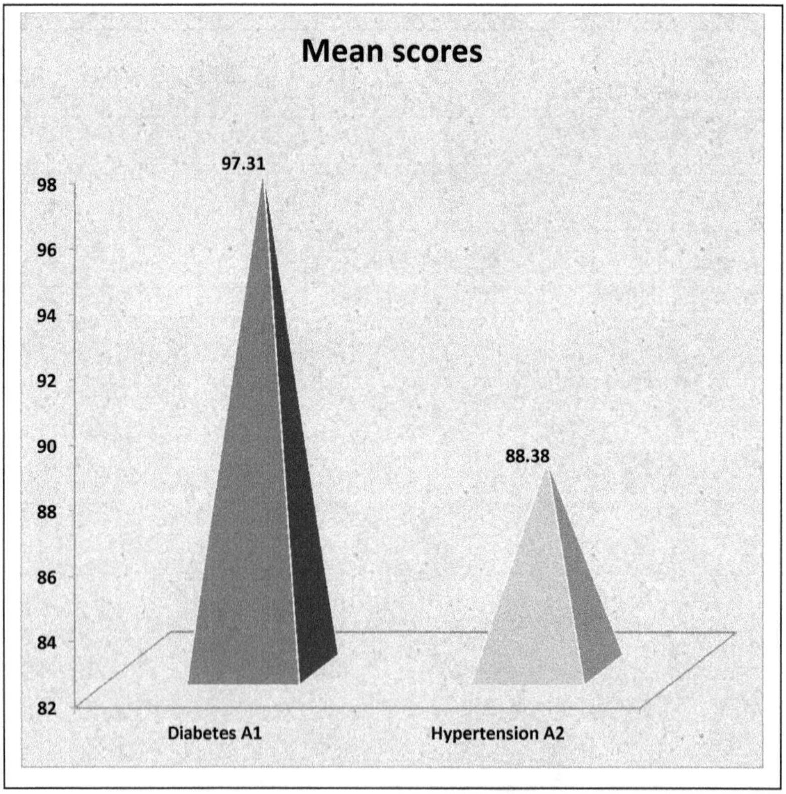

Table 91
Showing Mean, SD & Mean difference between male and female patients with diabetes and hypertension for overall quality of life factor.

Gender (B)	N	Mean	SD	Mean Difference
Male B1	200	91.35	9.93	2.99
Female B2	200	94.34	9.75	

Figure no.79
Showing comparisons of mean scores between male and female patients with diabetes and hypertension for overall quality of life factor.

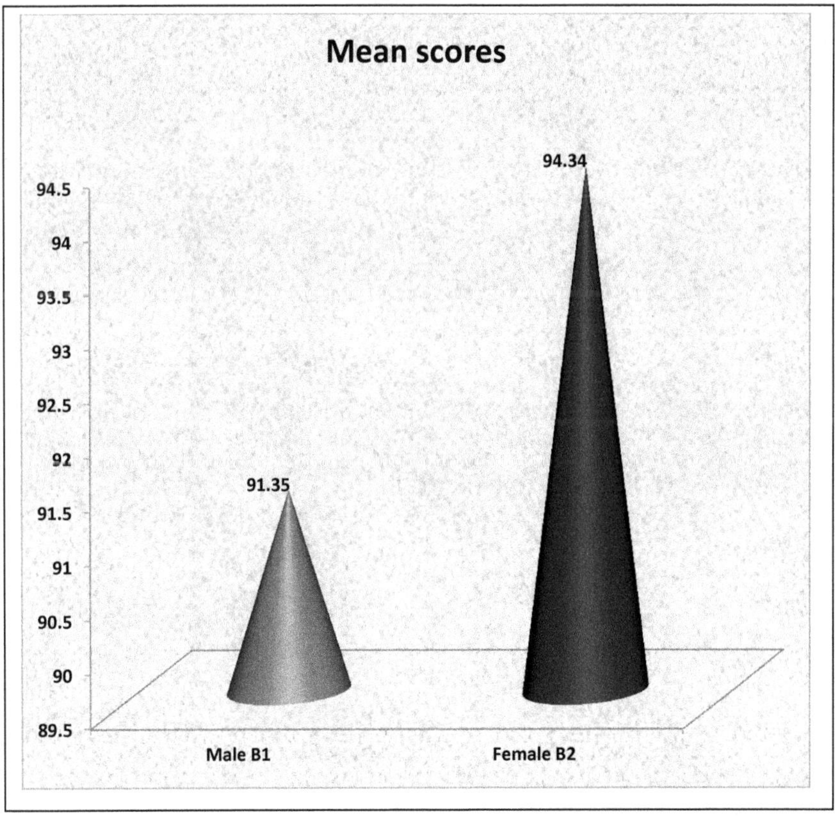

Table 92
Showing Mean, SD & Mean difference between patients with and without hereditary status for overall quality of life factor.

Hereditary status (C)	N	Mean	SD	Mean Difference
Hereditary C1	200	91.56	11.65	2.57
Non-hereditary C2	200	94.13	7.69	

Figure no.80
Showing comparisons of mean scores between patients with and without hereditary status for overall quality of life factor.

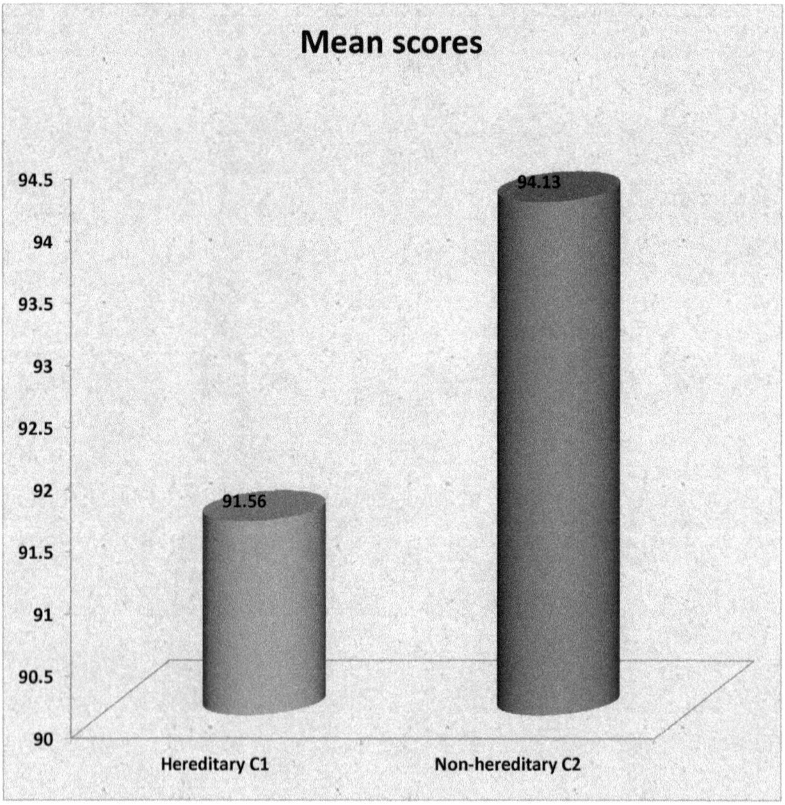

Table 93
Showing Mean, SD & Mean difference among interaction of diseases and Gender of patients with diabetes and hypertension for overall quality of life factor.

Diseases (A)	Gender (B)	N	Mean	SD	Mean Difference
Diabetes A1	**Male B1**	100	96.10	8.18	2.42
	Female B2	100	98.52	7.37	
Hypertension A2	**Male B1**	100	86.60	9.27	3.57
	Female B2	100	90.17	10.08	

Figure no. 81
Showing comparisons of mean scores among interaction of diseases and Gender of patients with diabetes and hypertension for overall quality of life factor.

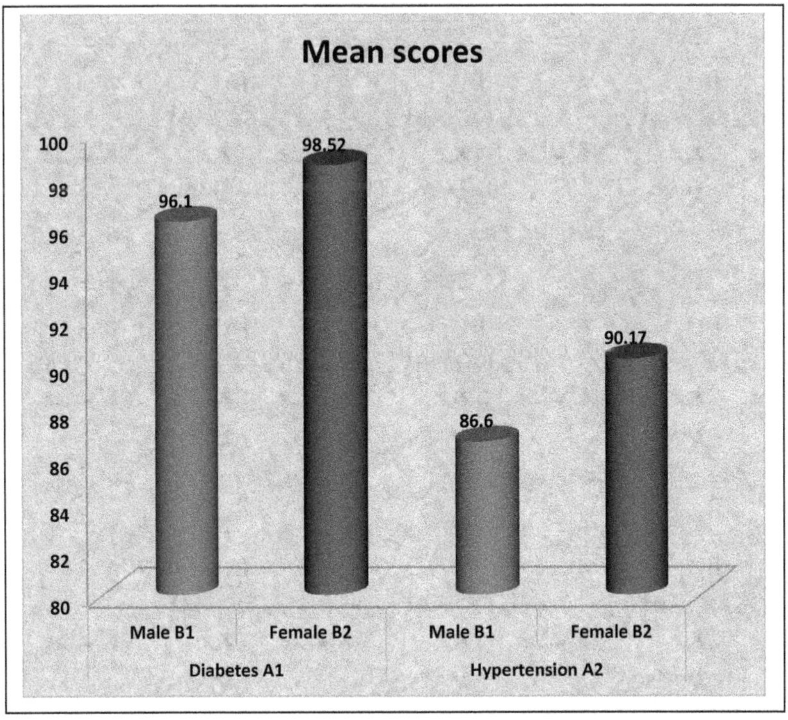

Table 94

Showing Mean, SD & Mean difference among interaction of diseases and hereditary status of patients for overall quality of life factor.

Diseases (A)	Hereditary (C)	N	Mean	SD	Mean Difference
Diabetes A1	**Hereditary *C1***	100	97.92	8.87	1.22
	Non-* hereditary *C2	100	96.70	6.69	
Hypertension A2	**Hereditary *C1***	100	85.21	10.62	6.35
	Non-* hereditary *C2	100	91.56	7.79	

Figure no. 82

Showing comparisons of mean scores among interaction of diseases and hereditary status of patients for overall quality of life factor.

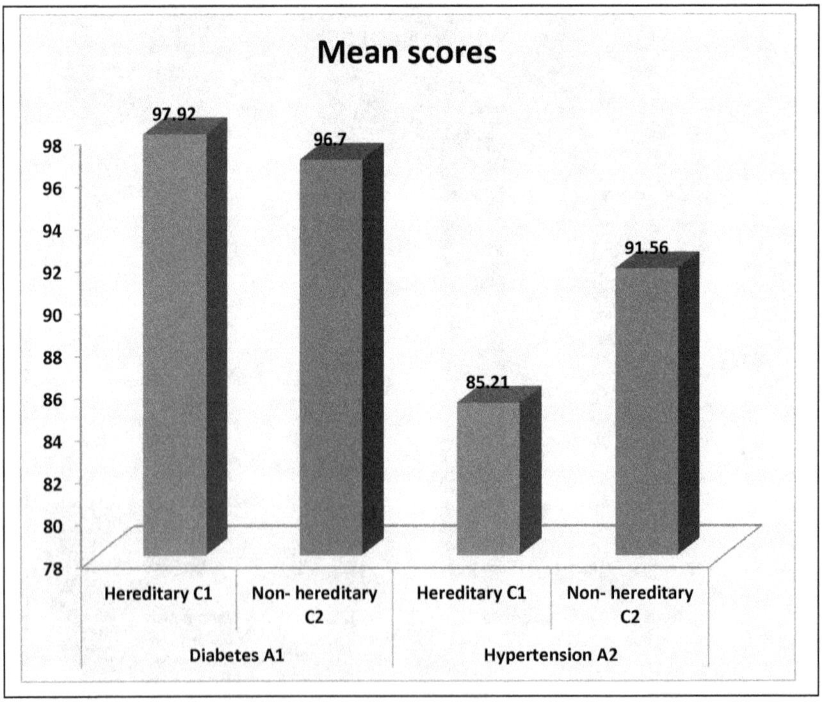

Table 95
Showing Mean, SD & Mean difference among interaction of Gender and hereditary status of patients for overall quality of life factor.

Gender (B)	Hereditary status (C)	N	Mean	SD	Mean Difference
Male	Hereditary *C1*	100	90.11	11.98	2.48
	Non-hereditary *C2*	100	92.59	7.19	
Female	Hereditary *C1*	100	93.02	11.19	2.65
	Non-hereditary *C2*	100	95.67	7.90	

Figure no. 83
Showing comparisons of mean scores among interaction of Gender and hereditary status of patients for overall quality of life factor.

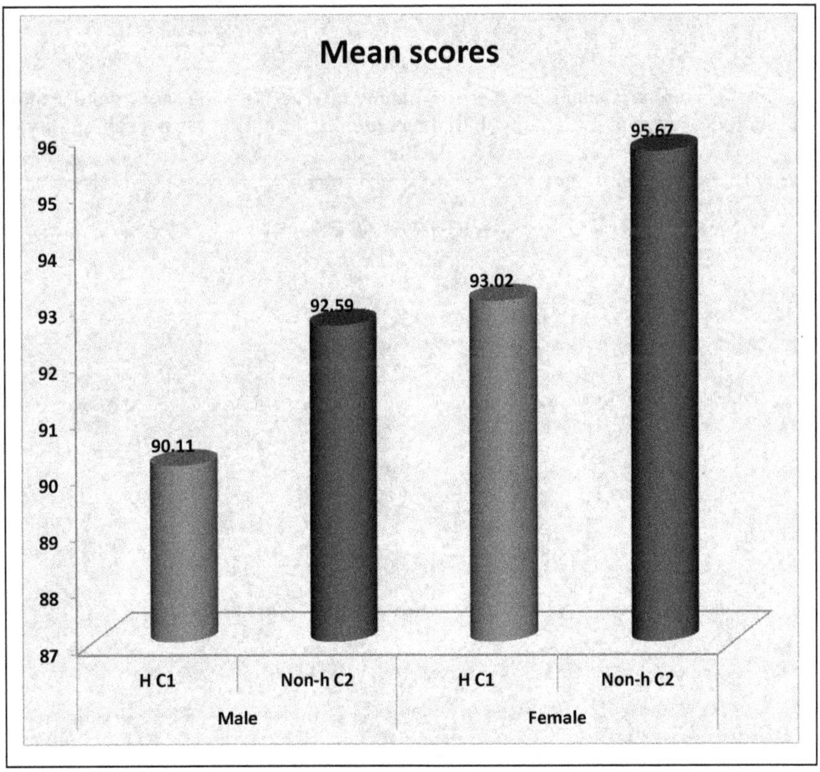

Table 96
Showing Mean, SD & Mean difference among interaction of diseases, gender and hereditary status of patients with diabetes and hypertension for overall quality of life

Diseases (A)	Gender (B)	Hereditary status (C)	N	Mean	SD	Mean Difference
Diabetes A1	*Male B1*	*Hereditary C1*	50	97.60	9.05	3.00
		Non- hereditary C2	50	94.60	6.97	
	Female B2	*Hereditary C1*	50	98.24	8.76	0.56
		Non- hereditary C2	50	98.80	5.74	
Hypertension A2	*Male B1*	*Hereditary C1*	50	82.62	9.68	7.9
		Non- hereditary C2	50	90.58	6.91	
	Female B2	*Hereditary C1*	50	87.80	10.99	4.74
		Non- hereditary C2	50	92.54	8.55	

Figure no. 84
Showing comparisons of mean scores among interaction of diseases, gender and hereditary status of patients with diabetes and hypertension for overall quality of life.

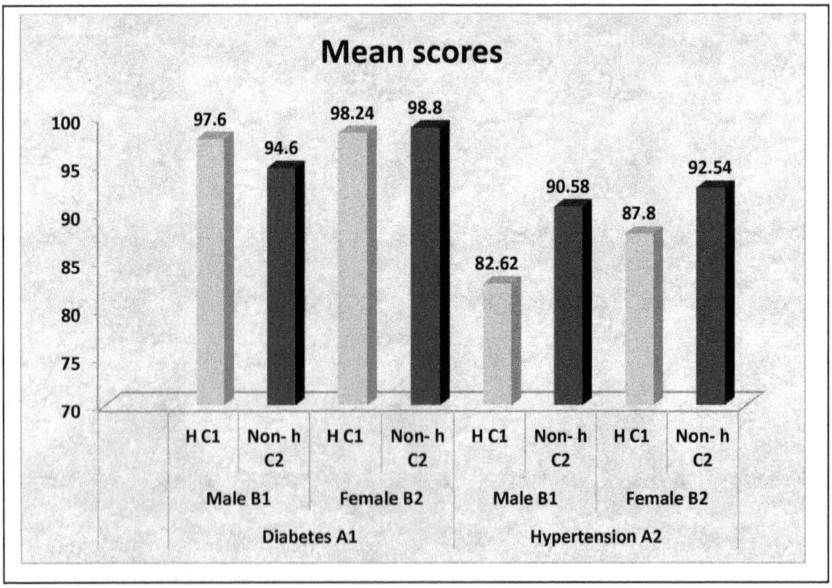

Main Effect:

Overall Quality of life with regard to Types of disease:

The F value is to be found significant, when the F test was used to examine the impact of illness type on quality of life in diabetic and hypertensive patients(F (1, 200) =110.63 p<.01), the significance of F was highlighted in (Table no.89). Patients with diabetes have a mean score of 97.31 (SD = 7.86), while those with hypertension have a mean score of 88.38 (SD = 9.82). The difference of mean value is 8.93, according to Tables 82 and chart 71. The diabetic patients have better quality of life than the patients with hypertension.

Overall Quality of life with regard to Gender

Tables 91 and 79 showed the F value and mean score for the gender of diabetic and hypertensive patients, the F ratio observed as significant F(1,200) =12.45, p<.01. The mean value for male patients is 91.35 (SD = 9.93), while the mean value for female patients is 94.34 (SD = 9.75), resulting in a mean difference of 2.99 between the two groups. The mean difference between the two groups was significant (Table No. 91 & Chart No. 79). According to the findings, female patients have better quality of life as compared to male patients.

Overall Quality of life with regard to Hereditary status:

The significance of hereditary status was discovered, the F ratio is to be reported significant F (1, 200) =9.13, p<.01. In table No.92 and chart No.80, patients with heredity have a mean score of 91.56 (SD=11.65), while patients without heredity have a mean score of 94.13 (SD=7.69) and a mean difference of 2.57. The patients with non-hereditary status have better quality of life as compared to patients with hereditary status.

Interaction Effect

Overall Quality of life with regard to Types of disease and Gender:

The study's main goal was to examine the interaction between Types of disease and Gender for overall quality of life between. The F value for the relationship between disease types and gender is exposed F (1,100) =0.45, p>.05, was not significant, as shown in Table No.89. The mean scores of male diabetic patients are (M=96.10, SD=8.18) and female diabetic patients are, (M=96.10, SD=8.18) as shown in Table 93 and Chart 81 are with a mean difference of 2.42. Male and female hypertensive patients have mean scores of (M =86.60 SD=9.27) and (M=90.17

SD=10.08), respectively. Male and female patients with hypertension have a 3.57 difference in mean scores. All the four groups of patients have more or less equal quality of life.

Overall Quality of life with regard to Types of disease and Hereditary status:

There was a significant interaction reported between disease and hereditary status of patients, the value is showed $F(1,100) = 19.89$ significant at ($p<.01$). Diabetic patients with hereditary status have a mean score of 97.92 (SD =8.87) and diabetic patients without hereditary status have a mean score of 96.70 (SD=6.69), with a mean difference of 1.22. The difference in mean scores between hypertensive patients with hereditary status and hypertensive patients without hereditary status is 6.35, with mean scores of 91.56(SD =10.62) and 91.56(SD =7.79), respectively. All the groups of patients have different level of quality of life.

Overall Quality of life factor with regard to Gender and Hereditary status:

$F(1,100) = 0.01$ was found to be an insignificant for the interaction between gender and heredity. According to Table 95 and Chart 83, the mean score for male patients with hereditary status is 90.11 (SD =11.98), while the mean score for male patients without hereditary status is 92.59 (SD =7.19), indicating a 2.48 mean difference. Female patients with hereditary status have a mean score of 93.02 (SD=11.19), while non-hereditary female patients have a mean score of 95.67 (SD=7.90). 2.65 is the mean difference. The mean difference is the more or less equal in all four groups. As a result, the quality of life factor was found similar in all four groups of patients.

Overall Quality of life factor with regard to Types of disease, Gender and Hereditary status:

F ratios for disease, gender, and hereditary status are insignificant in diabetic and hypertensive patients, with $F(1, 50) =3.99$, $p>.05$. Diabetic male patients with heredity have a mean score of 97.60 (SD =9.05), while diabetic male patients without heredity have a mean score of 94.60 (SD =6.97). The difference between the mean values of two group is 3.00. Female diabetes patients with hereditary status have mean values of 98.24 (SD = 8.76) compared to 98.80 (SD = 5.74) for those without hereditary status. The mean difference between the two groups is 0.56, which is insignificant. Patients with hereditary status and hypertension have a mean score of 82.62 (SD=9.68), while those without hereditary status and hypertension have a mean score of 90.58 (SD=6.91). The difference is also insignificant, with a mean difference of 7.9. The mean score for female hypertension patients with hereditary status is 87.80 (SD=10.99), while the mean score for those without hereditary status is 92.54 (SD=8.55). The average difference is 4.74. All eight groups of diabetic and hypertensive patients have similar quality of life traits.

Self-Efficacy

Table: 97

Showing ANOVA summary for the self-efficacy trait self -regulatory skills.

Source	**Type III Sum of Squares**	**df**	**Mean Square**	**F**	**Sig. Level**
***Diseases* (A)**	384.160	1	384.160	50.593	$p<.01$
***Gender* (B)**	42.250	1	42.250	5.564	$p<.05$
***Heredity status* (C)**	.160	1	.160	.021	NS
***Diseases * Gender* (A*B)**	11.560	1	11.560	1.522	NS
***Diseases * Heredity status* (A*C)**	.490	1	.490	.065	NS
***Gender * Heredity status* (B*C)**	.040	1	.040	.005	NS
***Diseases * Gender * Heredity status* (A*B*C)**	.810	1	.810	.107	NS
Error	2976.520	392	7.593		
Total	24412.000	400			
Corrected Total	3415.990	399			

Table 98
Showing Mean, SD & Mean difference between patients of diabetes and hypertension for self-efficacy trait self -regulatory skills.

Diseases (A)	N	Mean	SD	Mean Difference
Diabetes A1	200	8.22	3.18	1.96
Hypertension A2	200	6.26	2.25	

Figure no.85
Showing comparisons of mean scores between patients of diabetes and hypertension for self-efficacy trait self -regulatory skills.

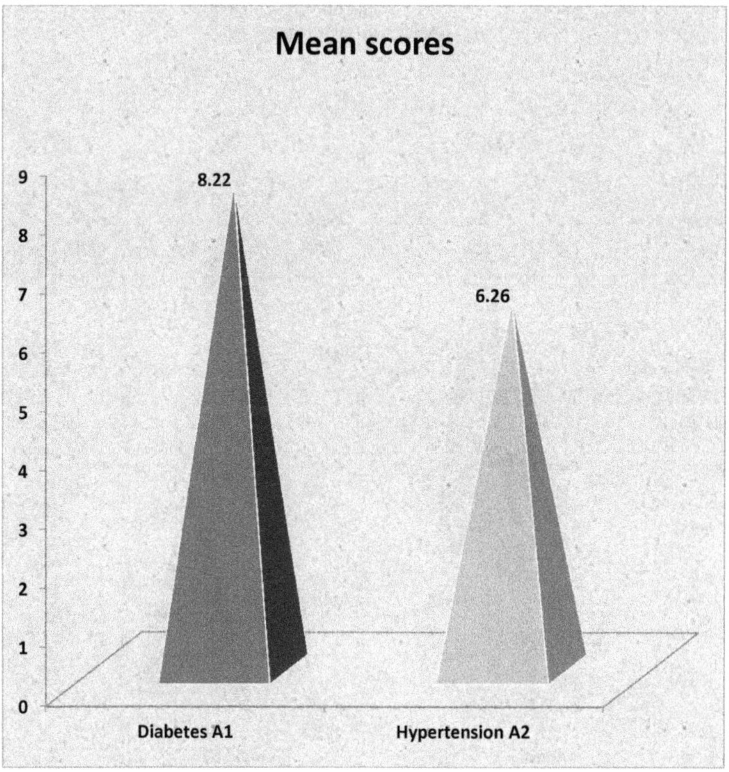

Table 99

Showing Mean, SD & Mean difference between male and female patients with diabetes and hypertension for self-efficacy trait self -regulatory skills.

Gender (B)	N	Mean	SD	Mean Difference
Male B1	200	7.57	2.91	0.65
Female B2	200	6.92	2.90	

Figure no.86

Showing comparisons of mean scores between male and female patients with diabetes and hypertension for self-efficacy trait self -regulatory skills.

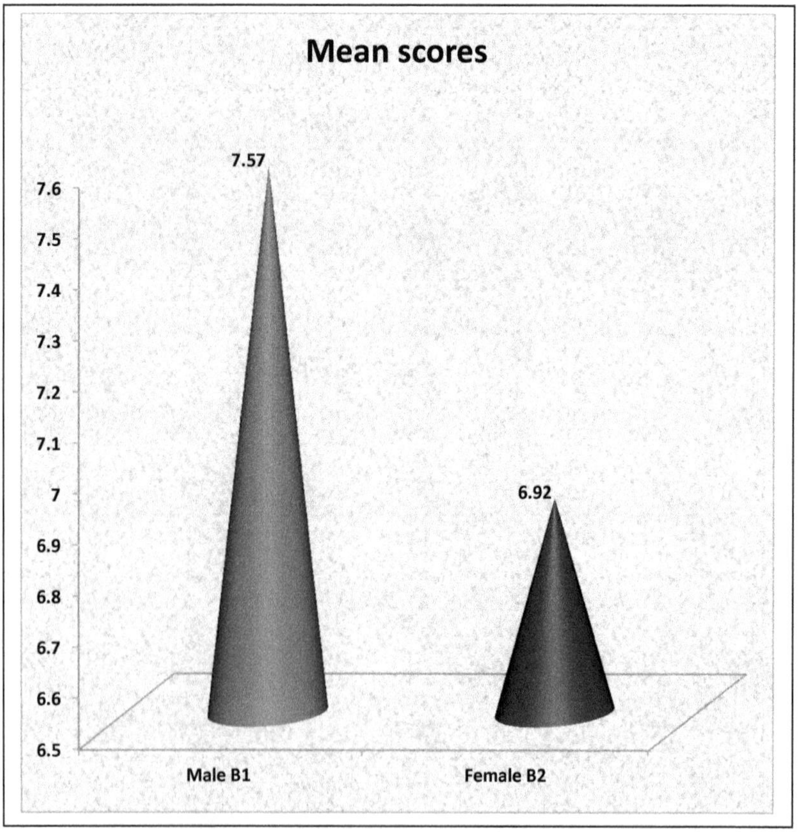

Table 100
Showing Mean, SD & Mean difference between patients with and without hereditary status for self-efficacy trait self -regulatory skills.

Hereditary status (C)	N	Mean	SD	Mean Difference
Hereditary C1	200	7.22	2.88	0.04
Non-hereditary C2	200	7.26	2.97	

Figure no. 87
Showing comparisons of mean scores between patients with and without hereditary status for self-efficacy trait self -regulatory skills.

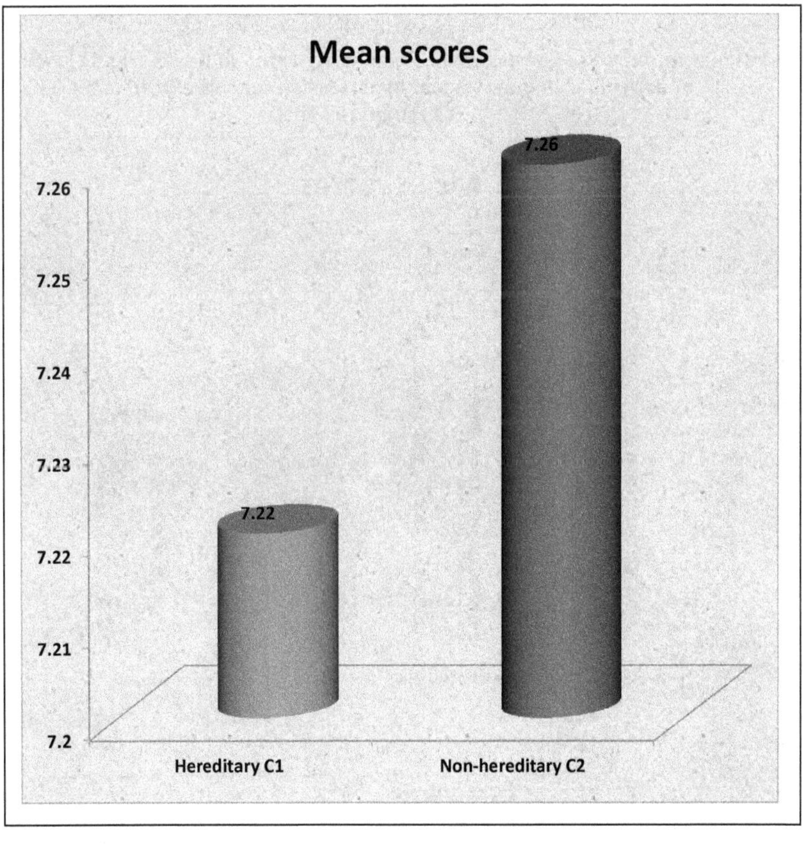

Table 101
Showing Mean, SD & Mean difference among interaction of diseases and Gender of patients with diabetes and hypertension for self-efficacy trait self - regulatory skills.

Diseases (A)	Gender (B)	N	Mean	SD	Mean Difference
Diabetes A1	Male B1	100	8.38	3.02	0.31
	Female B2	100	8.07	3.34	
Hypertension A2	Male B1	100	6.76	2.57	0.99
	Female B2	100	5.77	1.76	

Figure no. 88
Showing comparisons of mean scores among interaction of diseases and Gender of patients with diabetes and hypertension for self-efficacy trait self - regulatory skills.

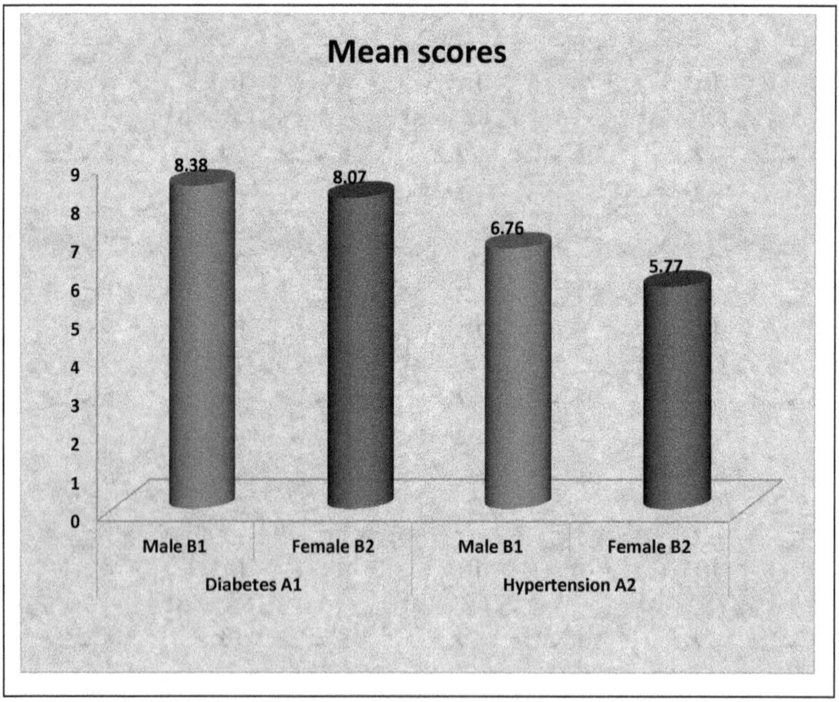

Table 102

Showing Mean, SD & Mean difference among interaction of diseases and hereditary status of patients for self-efficacy trait self -regulatory skills.

Diseases (A)	Hereditary (C)	N	Mean	SD	Mean Difference
Diabetes A1	Hereditary *C1*	100	8.24	2.91	0.03
	Non- hereditary *C2*	100	8.21	3.44	
Hypertension A2	Hereditary *C1*	100	6.21	2.47	0.11
	Non- hereditary *C2*	100	6.32	2.01	

Figure no. 89

Showing comparisons of mean scores among interaction of diseases and hereditary status of patients for self-efficacy trait self -regulatory skills.

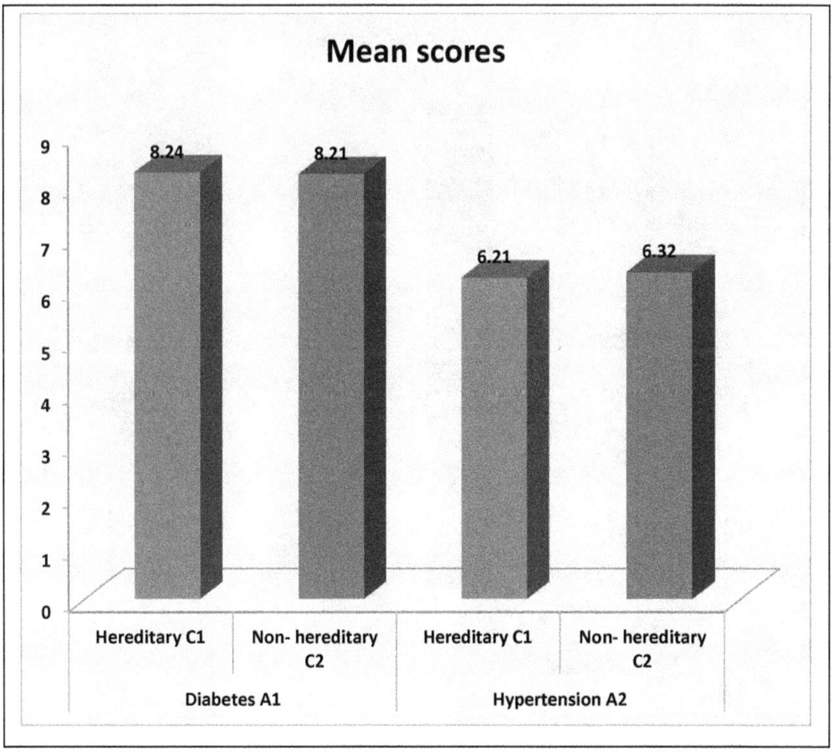

Table 103
Showing Mean, SD & Mean difference among interaction of Gender and hereditary status of patients for self-efficacy trait self -regulatory skills.

Gender (B)	Hereditary status (C)	N	Mean	SD	Mean Difference
Male	Hereditary *C1*	100	7.54	2.90	0.06
	Non-hereditary *C2*	100	7.60	2.94	
Female	Hereditary *C1*	100	6.91	2.85	0.02
	Non-hereditary *C2*	100	6.93	2.98	

Figure no. 90
Showing comparisons of mean scores among interaction of Gender and hereditary status of patients for self-efficacy trait self -regulatory skills.

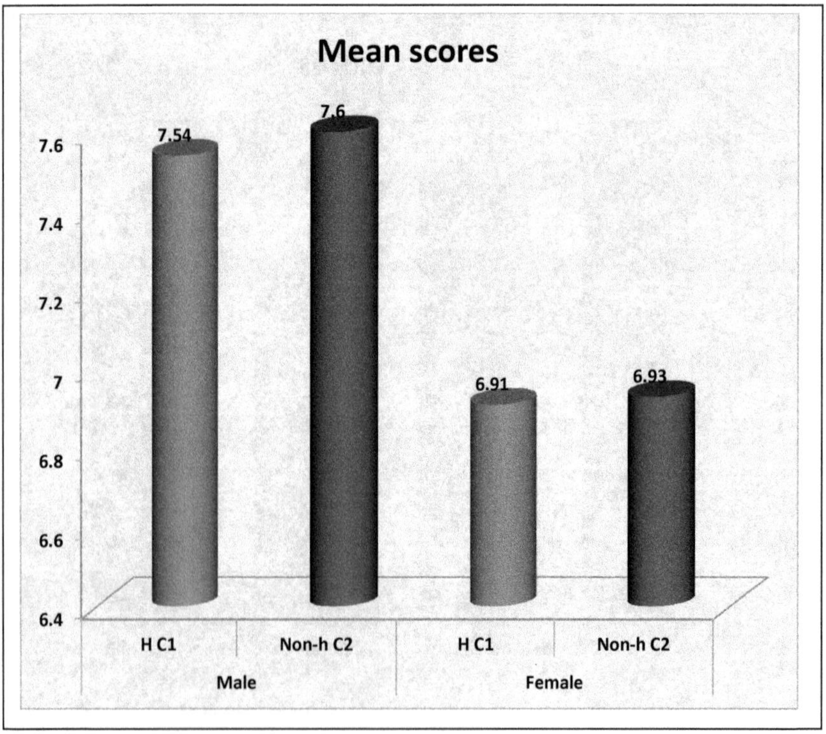

Table 104
Showing Mean, SD & Mean difference among interaction of diseases, gender and hereditary status of patients with diabetes and hypertension for self-efficacy trait self -regulatory skills.

Diseases (A)	Gender (B)	Hereditary status (C)	N	Mean	SD	Mean Difference
Diabetes A1	*Male B1*	*Hereditary C1*	50	8.34	2.66	0.08
		Non- hereditary C2	50	8.42	3.36	
	Female B2	*Hereditary C1*	50	8.14	3.16	0.14
		Non- hereditary C2	50	8.00	3.55	
Hypertension A2	*Male B1*	*Hereditary C1*	50	6.74	2.92	0.04
		Non- hereditary C2	50	6.78	2.18	
	Female B2	*Hereditary C1*	50	5.68	1.81	0.18
		Non- hereditary C2	50	5.86	1.73	

Figure no. 91
Showing comparisons of mean scores among interaction of diseases, gender and hereditary status of patients with diabetes and hypertension for self-efficacy trait self -regulatory skills.

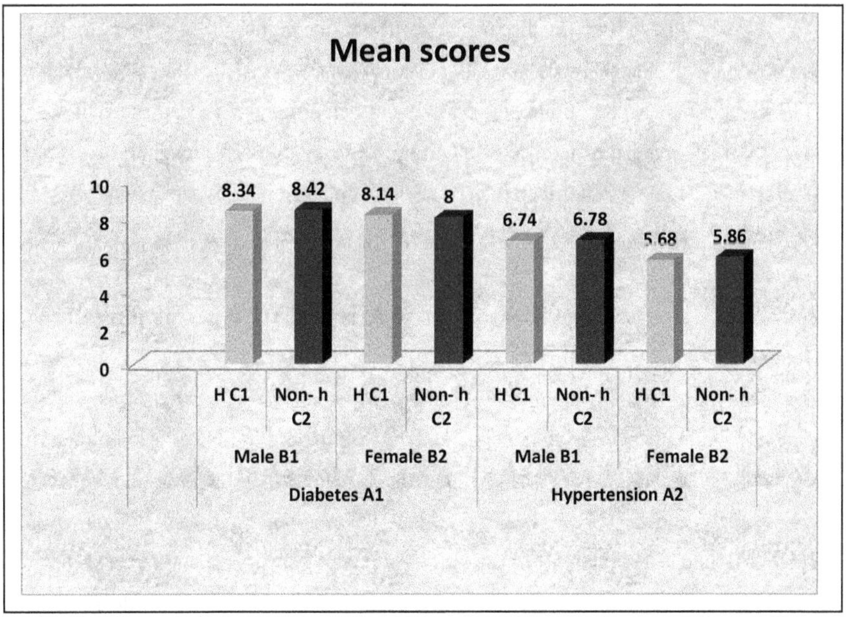

Main Effect:

Self-efficacy trait self -regulatory skills with regard to Types of disease:

When the F test was used to analyse the impact of illness type on quality of life factor in diabetic and hypertensive patients, the F value was significant. The significance of F was shown in $F (1,200) = 50.59$, $p < .01$ (Table no.97). Diabetes patients have an mean score of 8.22 (SD = 3.18), while hypertensive patients have an mean score of 6.26 (SD = 2.25). According to Table 98 and chart 85, the difference of means value is 1.96. As shown above, the diabetic patients have more Self-efficacy factor self-regulation skills as compared to hypertensive patients.

Self-efficacy trait self-regulatory skills with regard to Gender

The F value and mean score for the gender of diabetic and hypertensive patients were shown in Tables 97 and 86, with the mean difference and F ratio reported as significant $F(1,200) = 5.56$, $p < .05$. Male patients have a mean value of 7.57 (SD = 2.91), while female patients have a mean value of 6.92 (SD = 2.90), resulting in a mean difference of 0.65 between the two groups. The mean difference between the two groups was significant, as shown in (Table No. 99 & Chart No. 86). Male patients have greater characteristics of Self-efficacy trait self-regulatory skills.

Self-efficacy trait self-regulatory skills with regard to Hereditary status:

$F (1, 200) = 0.2$ was discovered to be the insignificance for the hereditary status of patients. Patients with heredity have a mean score of 7.22 (SD=2.88) in table No.100 and chart No.87, while patients without heredity have a mean score of 7.26 (SD=2.97) and a mean difference of 0.04. Self-efficacy trait self-regulatory skills are similar in hereditary and non-hereditary patients of diabetes and hypertension.

Interaction Effect

Self-efficacy trait self-regulatory skills with regard to Types of disease and Gender:

The main goal of study was to know if male and female diabetic patients, as well as male and female hypertensive patients, had any differences in Self-efficacy trait self-regulatory skills. Table No.97 shows that the F value for the relationship between disease types and gender, $F (1,100) = 1.52$ $p > .05$, was not significant. As shown in Table 101 and Chart 88, the mean scores of male diabetic patients are (M=8.38, SD=3.02) and female diabetic patients are (M=8.07, SD=3.34), with a mean difference of 0.31. The mean scores for male and female hypertensive patients are (M =6.76 SD=2.57) and (M=5.77 SD=1.76), respectively. The mean score for male and female hypertension patients differs by 0.99. The mean differences in disease and gender among the four groups had insignificant effect on the Self-efficacy trait self-regulatory skills.

Self-efficacy trait self-regulatory skills with regard to Types of disease and Hereditary status:

As F(1, 100) = 0.06, *p*>.05 showed, there was a non-significant relation between disease and hereditary status. Diabetic patients with heredity have a mean score of 8.24 (SD =2.91), while diabetic patients without heredity have a mean score of 8.12 (SD=3.44), and mean difference of a 0.03. Similarly, the mean difference between hypertensive patients with hereditary status and those without hereditary status is 0.11, with mean scores of 6.21 (SD =2.47) and 6.32 (SD =2.01), respectively. Each of the four groups has a similar Self-efficacy trait self-regulatory skills.

Self-efficacy trait self-regulatory skills with regard to Gender and Hereditary status:

Gender and heredity were found to have an insignificant interaction with F(1,100) = 0.005, *p*>05. The mean score for male patients with hereditary status is 7.54 (SD =2.90), while the mean score for male patients without hereditary status is 7.60 (SD =2.94), indicating a 0.06 mean difference, according to Table 103 and Chart 90. The mean score for female patients with hereditary status is 6.91 (SD=2.85), while the mean score for non-hereditary female patients is 6.93 (SD=2.98). The mean difference is 0.02. In all four groups, the mean difference is equal. As a result, Self-efficacy trait self-regulatory skills was reported to be similar across all four group of patients.

Self-efficacy trait self-regulatory skills with regard to Types of disease, Gender and Hereditary status:

In diabetic and hypertensive patients, F ratios for disease, gender, and hereditary status are insignificant, with F(1,50) = 0.10, *p*>.05. The mean score for diabetic male patients with hereditary status is 8.34 (SD =2.66), while the mean score for diabetic male patients without hereditary status is 8.42 (SD =3.36). The difference in mean values between the two groups is 0.08. .Mean values for female diabetic patients with hereditary status are 8.14 (SD = 3.16) compared to 8.00 (SD = 3.55) for those female diabetic patients without hereditary diabetes. The difference in mean between the two groups is 0.14, which is not statistically significant. Patients with hereditary status and hypertension have a mean score of 6.74 (SD=2.92), compared to 6.78 (SD=2.18) for those without hereditary status and hypertension. With a mean difference of 0.04, the difference is also insignificant. Female hypertension patients with hereditary status have a mean score of 5.68 (SD=1.81), while those female patients with non hereditary status have a mean score of 5.86 (SD=1.73). The difference of mean value is 0.18. Self-efficacy self-regulation skills are similar in all eight groups of diabetic and hypertensive patients.

Table: 105

Showing ANOVA summary for the self-efficacy trait self-influence.

Source	Type III Sum of Squares	df	Mean Square	F	Sig. Level
Diseases (A)	885.063	1	885.063	176.611	$p<.01$
Gender (B)	2.403	1	2.403	.479	NS
Heredity status (C)	6.503	1	6.503	1.298	NS
*Diseases * Gender* (A*B)	76.563	1	76.563	15.278	$p<.01$
*Diseases * Heredity status* (A*C)	74.563	1	74.563	15.291	$p<.01$
*Gender * Heredity status* (B*C)	.563	1	.563	.112	NS
*Diseases * Gender * Heredity status* (A*B*C)	33.063	1	33.063	6.597	$p<.05$
Error	1964.460	392	5.011		
Total	50853.000	400			
Corrected Total	3045.178	399			

Table 106
Showing Mean, SD & Mean difference between patients of diabetes and hypertension for self-efficacy trait self-influence.

Diseases (A)	N	Mean	SD	Mean Difference
Diabetes A1	200	12.42	1.59	3.18
Hypertension A2	200	9.24	2.88	

Figure no.92
Showing comparisons of mean scores between patients of diabetes and hypertension for self-efficacy trait self-influence.

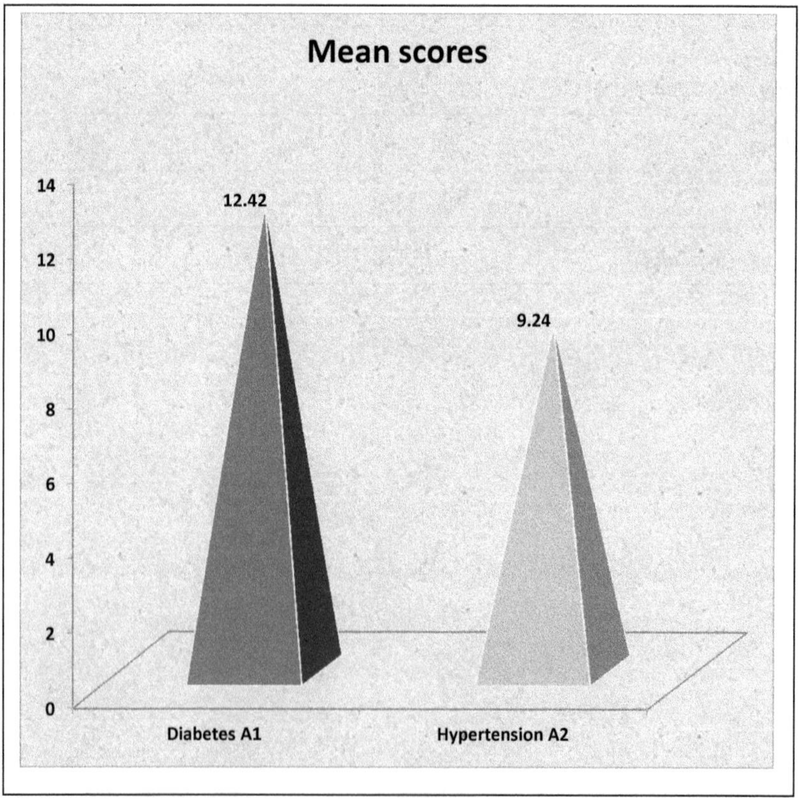

Table 107
Showing Mean, SD & Mean difference between male and female patients with diabetes and hypertension for self-efficacy trait self-influence.

Gender (B)	N	Mean	SD	Mean Difference
Male B1	200	10.85	3.01	0.16
Female B2	200	11.01	2.49	

Figure no.93
Showing comparisons of mean scores between male and female patients with diabetes and hypertension for self-efficacy trait self-influence.

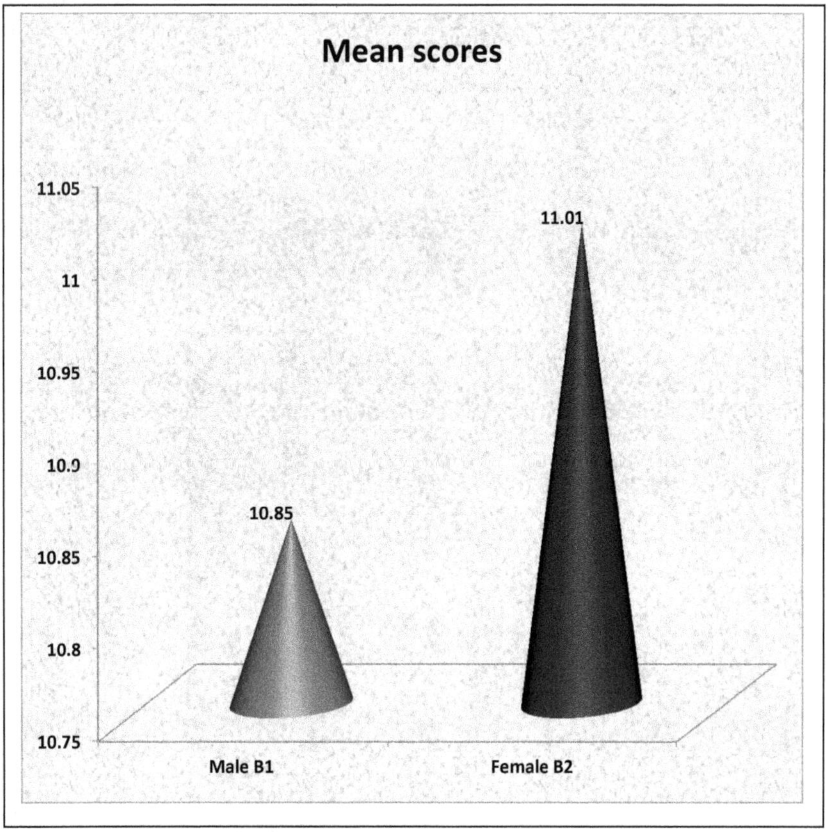

Table 108
Showing Mean, SD & Mean difference between patients with and without hereditary status for self-efficacy trait self-influence.

Hereditary status (C)	N	Mean	SD	Mean Difference
Hereditary C1	200	10.80	3.05	0.26
Non-hereditary C2	200	11.06	2.43	

Figure no. 94
Showing comparisons of mean scores between patients with and without hereditary status for self-efficacy trait self-influence.

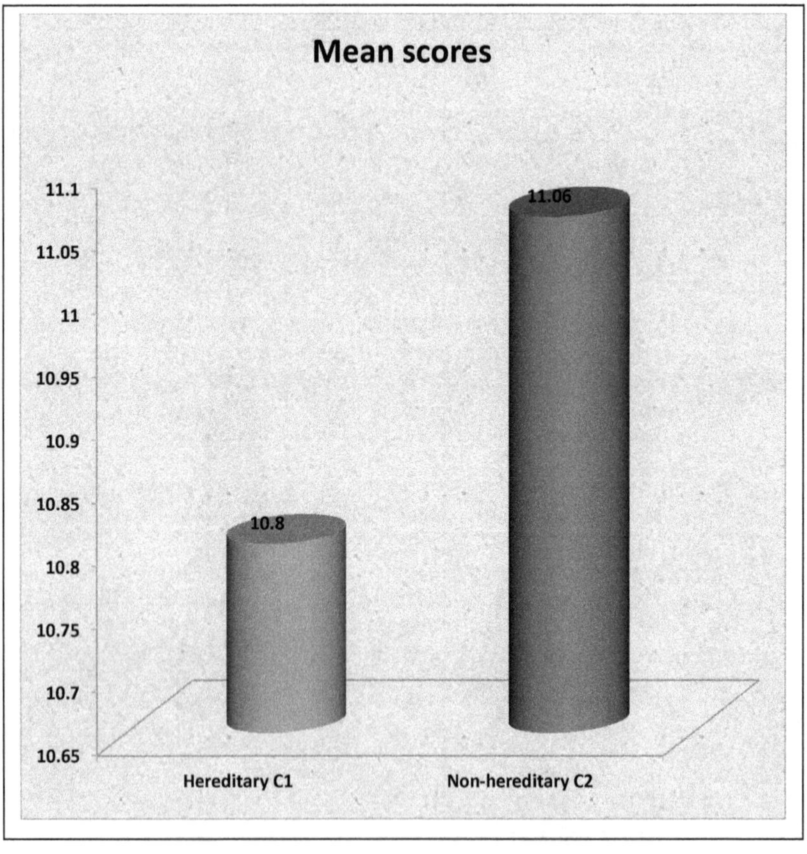

Table 109
Showing Mean, SD & Mean difference among interaction of diseases and Gender of patients with diabetes and hypertension for self-efficacy trait self-influence.

Diseases (A)	Gender (B)	N	Mean	SD	Mean Difference
Diabetes A1	Male B1	100	12.78	1.60	0.72
	Female B2	100	12.06	1.51	
Hypertension A2	Male B1	100	8.93	2.86	1.03
	Female B2	100	9.96	2.81	

Figure no. 95
Showing comparisons of mean scores among interaction of diseases and Gender of patients with diabetes and hypertension for self-efficacy trait self-influence.

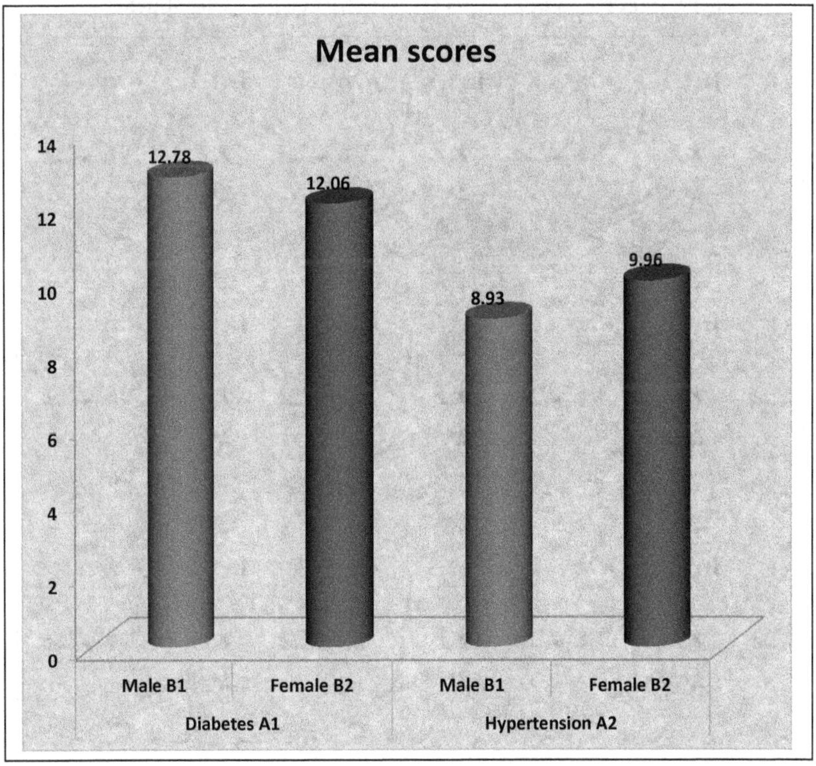

Table 110
Showing Mean, SD & Mean difference among interaction of diseases and hereditary status of patients for self-efficacy trait self-influence.

Diseases (A)	Hereditary (C)	N	Mean	SD	Mean Difference
Diabetes A1	Hereditary *C1*	100	12.73	1.39	0.62
	Non- hereditary *C2*	100	12.11	1.72	
Hypertension A2	Hereditary *C1*	100	8.88	3.05	1.13
	Non- hereditary *C2*	100	10.01	2.59	

Figure no. 96
Showing comparisons of mean scores among interaction of diseases and hereditary status of patients for self-efficacy trait self-influence.

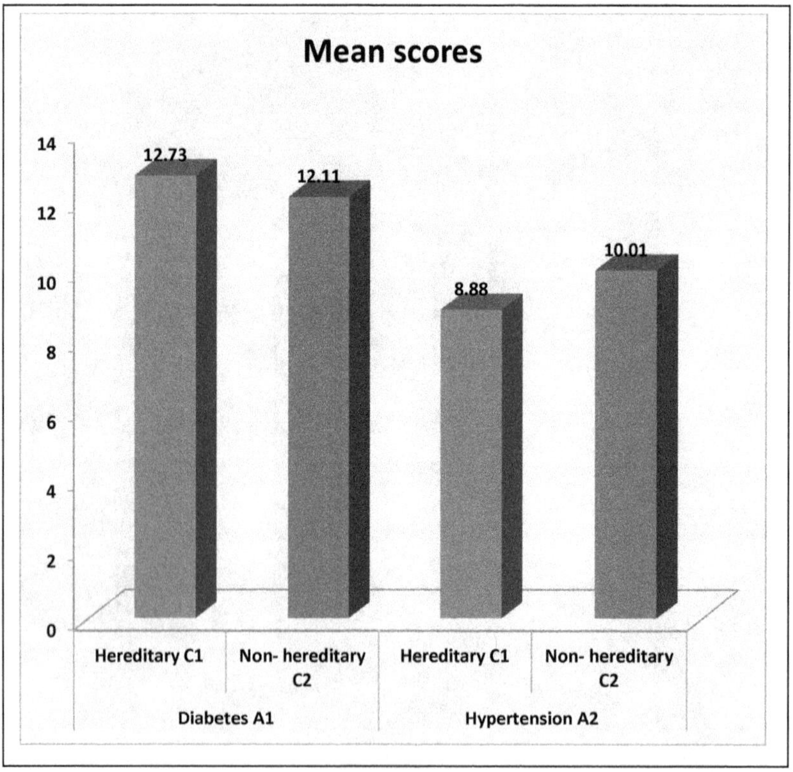

Table 111
Showing Mean, SD & Mean difference among interaction of Gender and hereditary status of patients for self-efficacy trait self-influence.

Gender (B)	Hereditary status (C)	N	Mean	SD	Mean Difference
Male	Hereditary *C1*	100	10.69	3.43	0.33
	Non-hereditary *C2*	100	11.02	2.53	
Female	Hereditary *C1*	100	10.92	2.63	0.18
	Non-hereditary *C2*	100	11.10	2.35	

Figure no. 97
Showing comparisons of mean scores among interaction of Gender and hereditary status of patients for self-efficacy trait self-influence.

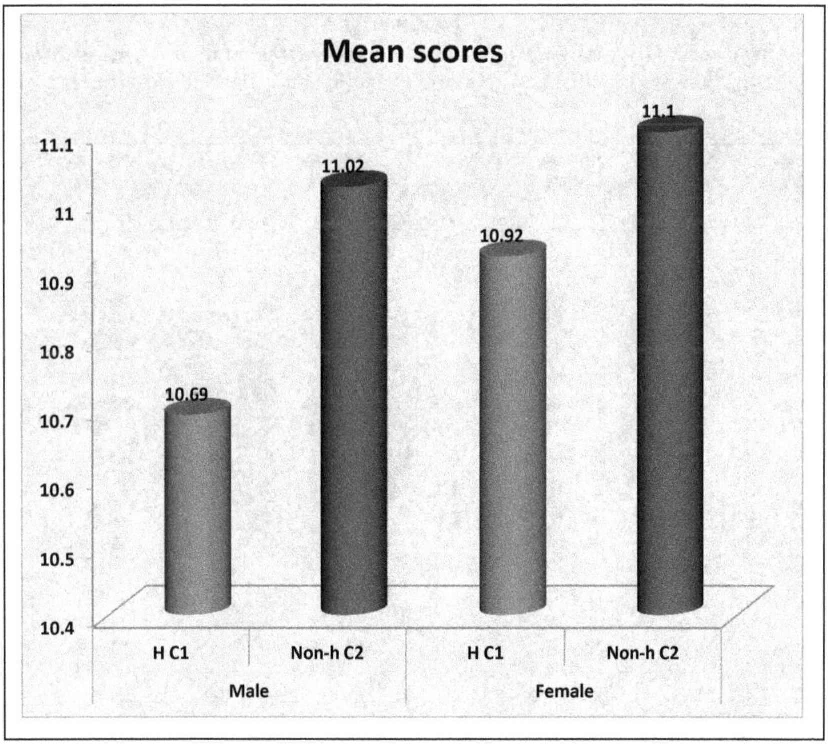

Table 112

Showing Mean, SD & Mean difference among interaction of diseases, gender and hereditary status of patients with diabetes and hypertension for self-efficacy trait self-influence.

Diseases (A)	Gender (B)	Hereditary status (C)	N	Mean	SD	Mean Difference
Diabetes A1	*Male B1*	*Hereditary C1*	50	13.34	1.00	1.12
		Non- hereditary C2	50	12.22	1.88	
	Female B2	*Hereditary C1*	50	12.12	1.47	0.12
		Non- hereditary C2	50	12.00	1.56	
Hypertension A2	*Male B1*	*Hereditary C1*	50	8.04	2.92	1.78
		Non- hereditary C2	50	9.82	2.53	
	Female B2	*Hereditary C1*	50	9.72	2.97	0.48
		Non- hereditary C2	50	10.20	2.65	

Figure no. 98

Showing comparisons of mean scores among interaction of diseases, gender and hereditary status of patients with diabetes and hypertension for self-efficacy trait self-influence.

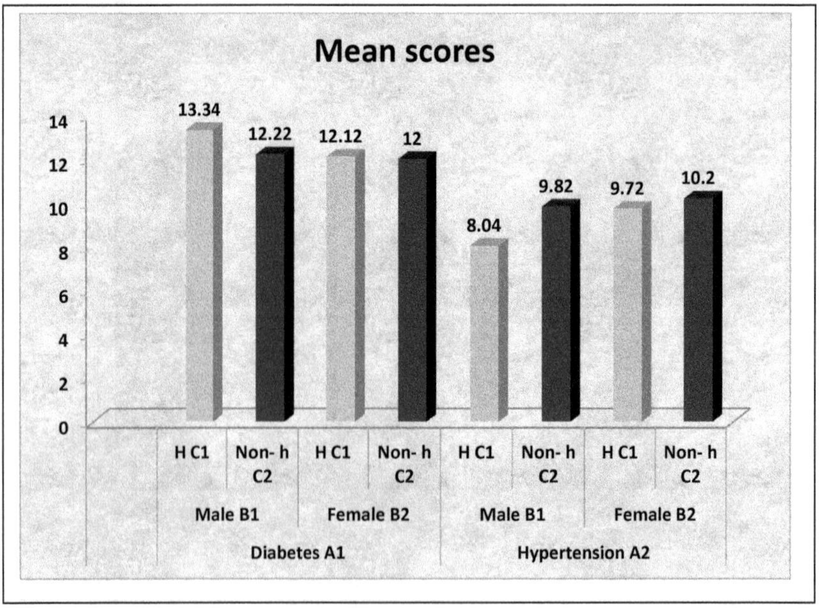

Main Effect:

Self-efficacy trait self - influence skills with regard to Types of disease:

The F value was significant when the F test was used to examine the impact of illness type on Self-efficacy trait self-influence in diabetic and hypertensive patients. $F(1,200) = 176.61$, $p < .01$ was used to show the significance of F (Table no.105). Patients with diabetes have mean score of 12.42 (SD = 1.59), while those with hypertension have an mean score of 9.24 (SD = 2.88). The difference in means value is 3.18, according to Table 106 and Chart 92. The Self-efficacy trait self-influence skills of hypertensive and diabetic patients differ, as shown above. Patients with diabetes have higher influence skills

Self-efficacy trait self-influence skills with regard to Gender

Tables 105 and 93 show the F value and mean score for gender of diabetic and hypertensive patients, with the mean difference and F ratio reported as non-significant $F(1,200) = 0.47$, $p > .05$. The mean value for male patients is 10.85 (SD = 3.01), while the mean value for female patients is 11.01 (SD = 2.49), resulting in a mean difference of 0.16 between the two groups. As shown in the graph, the mean difference between the two groups was significant (Table No.107 & Chart No.93). According to the findings, female and male patients have equal Self-efficacy trait self-influence skills.

Self-efficacy trait self-influence skills with regard to Hereditary status:

The insignificance of hereditary status was found to be $F(1, 200) = 1.29$. In table No.108 and chart No.94, patients with heredity have a mean score of 10.80 (SD=3.05), while patients without heredity have a mean score of 11.06 (SD=2.43) and a mean difference of 0.26. In both hereditary and non-hereditary patients, self-efficacy trait self-influence skills are similar.

Interaction Effect

Self-efficacy trait self-influence skills with regard to Types of disease and Gender:

The study's main goal was to check, if there were any differences in Self-efficacy trait self-influence skills between male and female diabetic patients, as well as male and female hypertensive patients. The F value for the relationship between disease types and gender, $F(1,100) = 15.27$, $p < .01$, was significant, as shown in Table No.105. Male diabetic patients have mean scores of (M=12.78, SD=1.60) and female diabetic patients have mean scores of (M=12.06, SD=1.51), with a mean difference of 0.72, as shown in Table 109 and Chart 95. Male and female hypertensive patients have mean scores of (M =8.93 SD=2.86) and (M=9.96 SD=2.81), respectively. Male and female hypertension patients have a 1.03 difference in mean score. The Self-efficacy trait self-influence skills were found different in all the groups of patients.

Self-efficacy trait self-influence skills with regard to Types of disease and Hereditary status:

As F (1,100) = 15.29, $p<.01$ showed, there was a significant interaction between disease and hereditary status. Diabetic patients with hereditary status have a mean score of 12.73 (SD =1.39), whereas diabetic patients without hereditary status have a mean score of 12.11 (SD=1.72), resulting in a 0.62 mean difference. The difference in mean value between hypertensive patients with hereditary status and those without hereditary status is 1.13, with mean scores of 8.88(SD =3.05) and 10.01(SD =2.59), respectively. Each of the four groups has different self-efficacy traits and self-influence skills.

Self-efficacy trait self-influence skills with regard to Gender and Hereditary status:

The value of F (1,100) = 0.11 revealed that gender and heredity have no significant relationship at ($p<.05$). According to Table 111 and Chart 97, the mean score for male patients with hereditary status is 10.69 (SD =3.43), while the mean score for male patients without hereditary status is 11.02 (SD =2.53), indicating a 0.33 mean difference. Female patients with hereditary status have a mean score of 10.92 (SD=2.63), while non-hereditary female patients have a mean score of 11.10 (SD=2.354). The difference of mean is 0.18. The mean difference in all four groups is the same. As a result, the Self-efficacy trait self-influence skills of all four groups of patients were observed to be similar.

Self-efficacy trait self-influence skills with regard to Types of disease, Gender and Hereditary status:

F ratio for disease, gender, and hereditary status are significant in diabetic and hypertensive patients, with $F(1, 50) = 6.59$, $p < .01$. Diabetic male patients with hereditary status have a mean score of 13.34 (SD =1.00), while diabetic male patients without hereditary status have a mean score of 12.22 (SD =1.88). The difference between the two groups' mean values is 1.12. Female diabetic patients with hereditary status have mean values of 12.12 (SD = 1.47) compared to 12.00 (SD = 1.56) for female diabetic patients without hereditary status. The difference in mean between the two groups is 0.12, which is insignificant statistically. Patients with hereditary status and hypertension have a mean score of 8.04 (SD=2.92), while those without hereditary status and hypertension have a mean score of 9.82 (SD=2.53). The difference is also insignificant, with a mean difference of 1.78. Female hypertensive Patients with hereditary status have a mean score of 9.72 (SD=2.97), while those female hypertensive patients without hereditary status have a mean score of 10.20 (SD=2.65). The mean value difference is 0.48. All eight groups of diabetic and hypertensive patients have similar self-efficacy self-influence skill.

Table: 113

Showing ANOVA summary for the self-efficacy trait self-confidence.

Source	Type III Sum of Squares	df	Mean Square	F	Sig. Level
***Diseases* (A)**	380.250	1	380.250	102.870	*p*<.01
***Gender* (B)**	13.690	1	13.690	3.704	NS
***Heredity status* (C)**	.490	1	.490	.133	NS
***Diseases * Gender* (A*B)**	.160	1	.160	.043	NS
***Diseases * Heredity status* (A*C)**	12.960	1	12.960	3.506	NS
***Gender * Heredity status* (B*C)**	1.000	1	1.000	.271	NS
***Diseases * Gender * Heredity status* (A*B*C)**	.490	1	.490	.133	NS
Error	1449.000	392	3.696		
Total	38492.000	400			
Corrected Total	1858.040	399			

Table 114

Showing Mean, SD & Mean difference between patients of diabetes and hypertension for self-efficacy trait self-confidence.

***Diseases* (A)**	**N**	**Mean**	**SD**	**Mean Difference**
Diabetes A1	200	10.54	1.44	1.95
Hypertension A2	200	8.59	2.30	

Figure no.99

Showing comparisons of mean scores between patients of diabetes and hypertension for self-efficacy trait self-confidence.

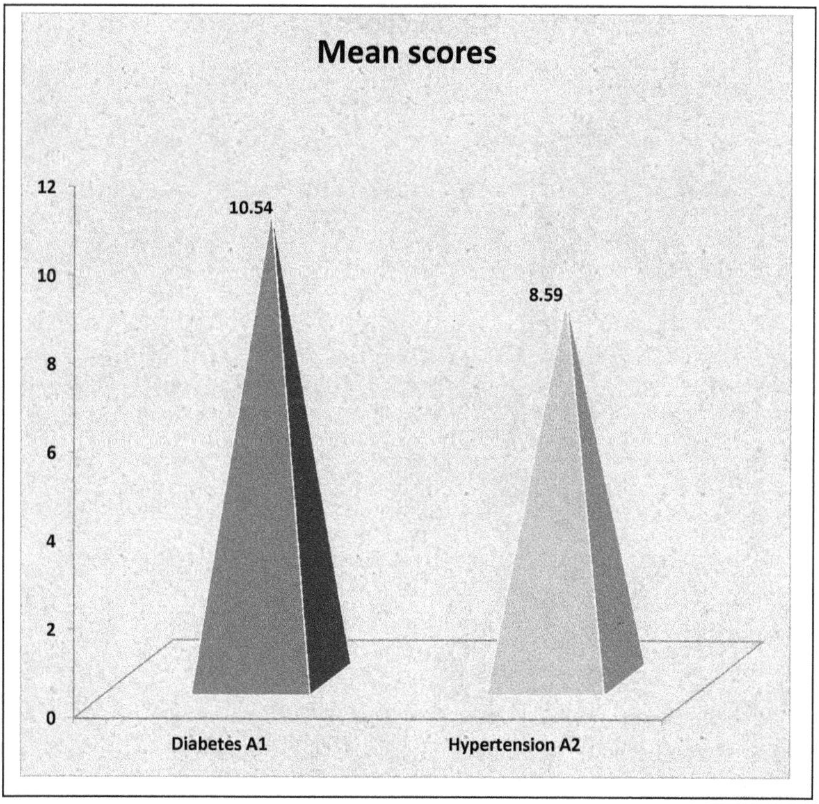

Table 115
Showing Mean, SD & Mean difference between male and female patients with diabetes and hypertension for self-efficacy trait self-confidence.

Gender (B)	N	Mean	SD	Mean Difference
Male B1	200	9.75	2.06	0.37
Female B2	200	9.38	2.23	

Figure no.100
Showing comparisons of mean scores between male and female patients with diabetes and hypertension for self-efficacy trait self-confidence.

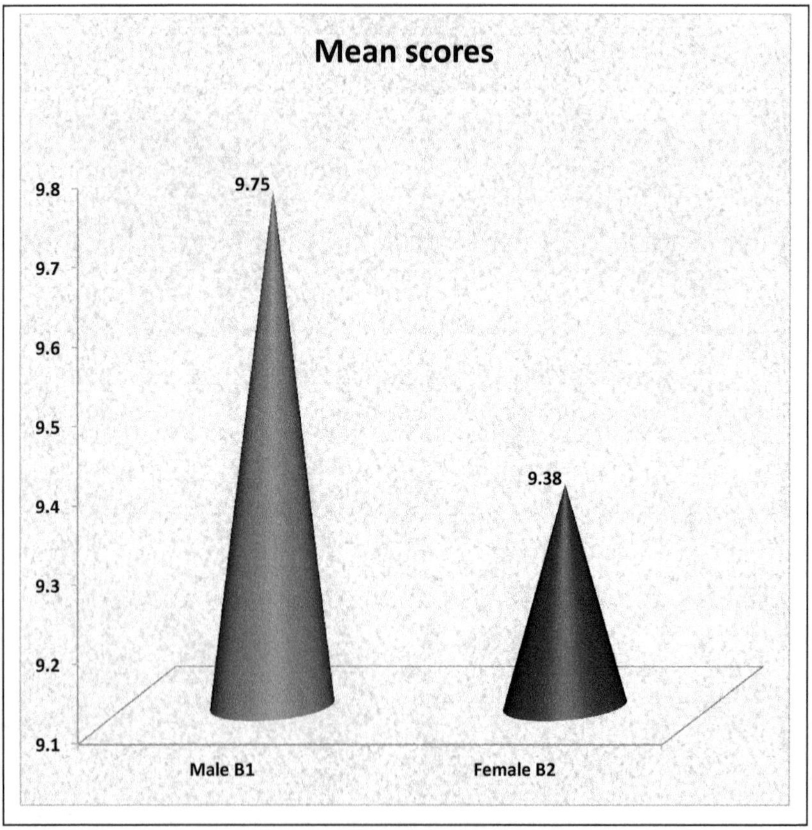

Table 116
Showing Mean, SD & Mean difference between patients with and without hereditary status for self-efficacy trait self-confidence.

Hereditary status (C)	N	Mean	SD	Mean Difference
Hereditary C1	200	9.53	2.13	0.07
Non-hereditary C2	200	9.60	2.18	

Figure no. 101
Showing comparisons of mean scores between patients with and without hereditary status for self-efficacy trait self-confidence.

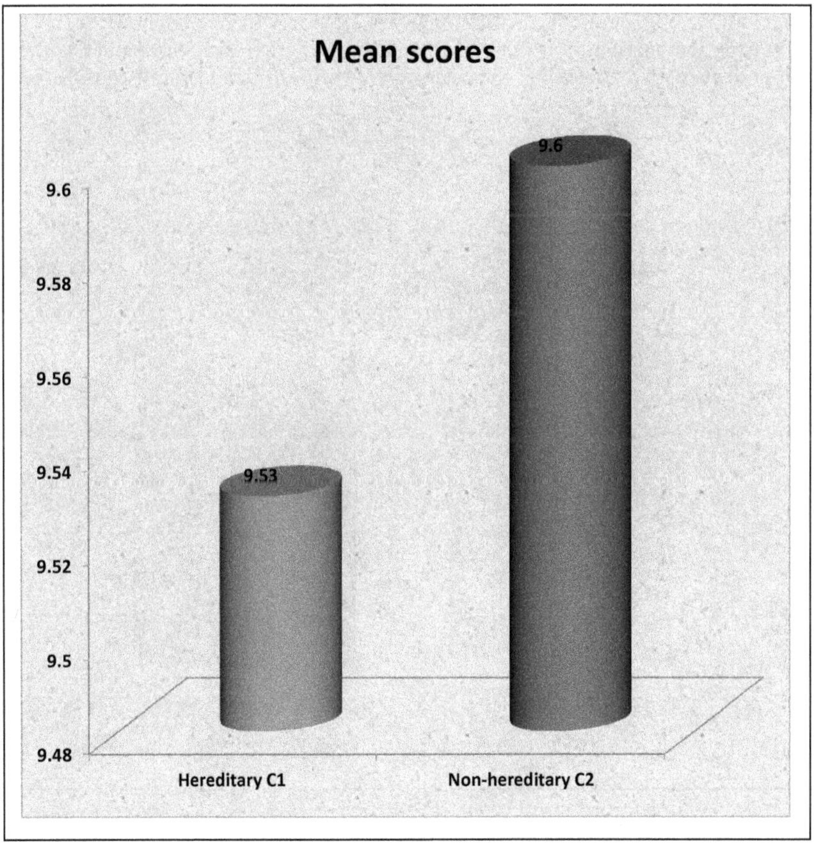

Table 117
Showing Mean, SD & Mean difference among interaction of diseases and Gender of patients with diabetes and hypertension for self-efficacy trait self-confidence.

Diseases (A)	Gender (B)	N	Mean	SD	Mean Difference
Diabetes A1	**Male B1**	100	10.75	1.35	0.41
	Female B2	100	10.34	1.51	
Hypertension A2	**Male B1**	100	8.76	2.17	0.33
	Female B2	100	8.43	2.43	

Figure no. 102
Showing comparisons of mean scores among interaction of diseases and Gender of patients with diabetes and hypertension for self-efficacy trait self-confidence.

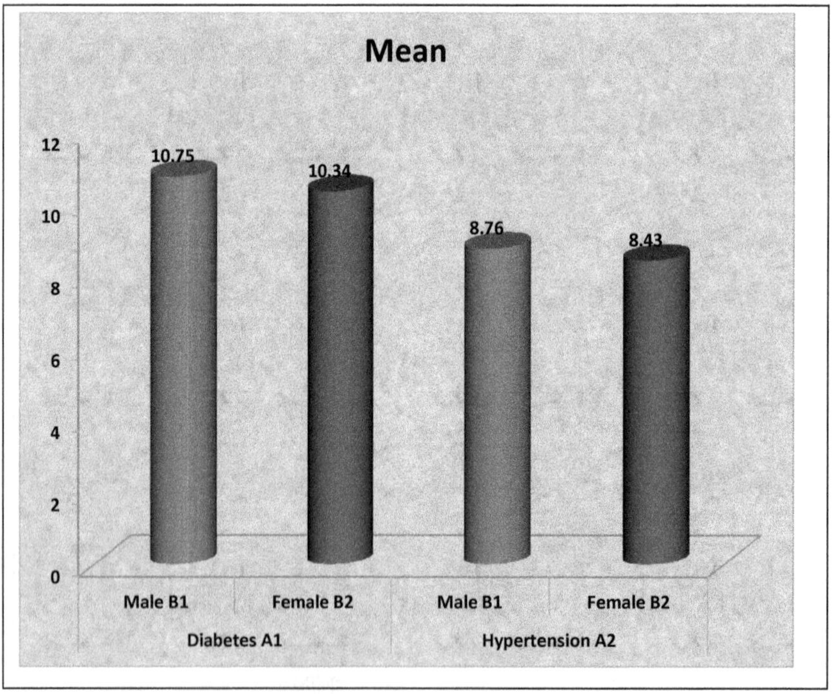

Table 118

Showing Mean, SD & Mean difference among interaction of diseases and hereditary status of patients for self-efficacy trait self-confidence.

***Diseases* (A)**	**Hereditary (C)**	**N**	**Mean**	**SD**	**Mean Difference**
Diabetes A1	**Hereditary *C1***	100	10.33	1.58	0.43
	Non-* hereditary *C2	100	10.76	1.26	
Hypertension A2	**Hereditary *C1***	100	8.74	2.30	0.29
	Non-* hereditary *C2	100	8.45	2.31	

Figure no. 103

Showing comparisons of mean scores among interaction of diseases and hereditary status of patients for self-efficacy trait self-confidence.

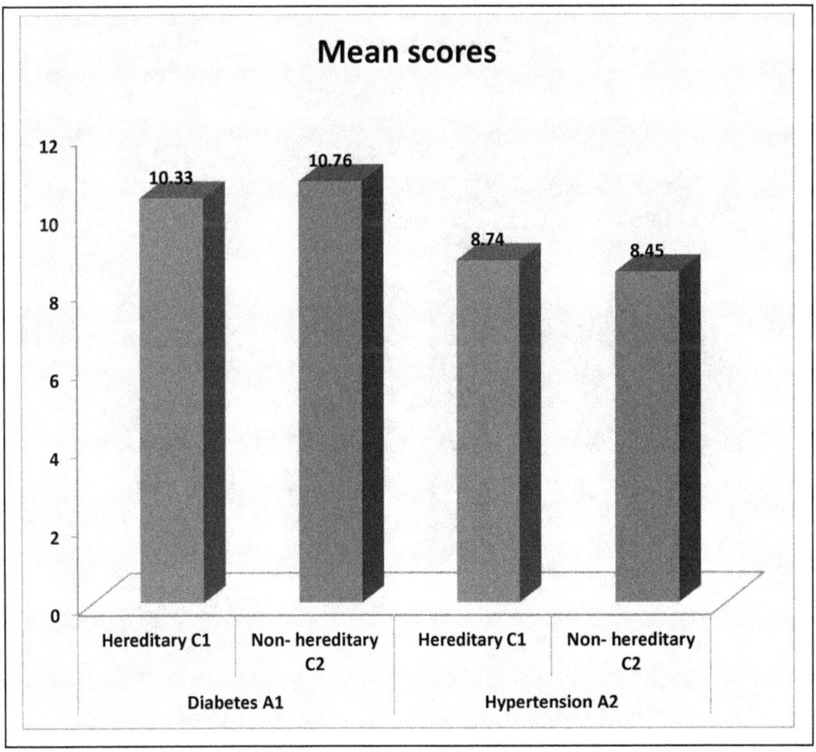

Table 119
Showing Mean, SD & Mean difference among interaction of Gender and hereditary status of patients for self-efficacy trait self-confidence.

Gender (B)	Hereditary status (C)	N	Mean	SD	Mean Difference
Male	Hereditary *C1*	100	9.67	2.00	0.17
	Non-hereditary *C2*	100	9.84	2.13	
Female	Hereditary *C1*	100	9.40	2.25	0.03
	Non-hereditary *C2*	100	9.37	2.23	

Figure no. 104
Showing comparisons of mean scores among interaction of Gender and hereditary status of patients for self-efficacy trait self-confidence.

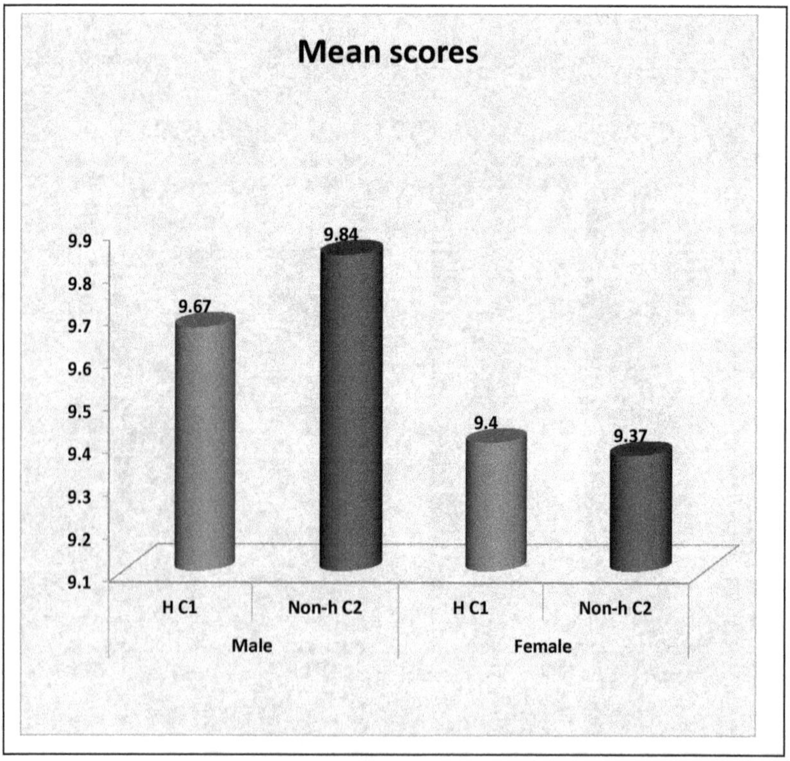

Table 120

Showing Mean, SD & Mean difference among interaction of diseases, gender and hereditary status of patients with diabetes and hypertension for self-efficacy trait self-confidence.

Diseases (A)	Gender (B)	Hereditary status (C)	N	Mean	SD	Mean Difference
Diabetes A1	*Male B1*	*Hereditary C1*	50	10.52	1.41	0.46
		Non- hereditary C2	50	10.98	1.25	
	Female B2	*Hereditary C1*	50	10.14	1.73	0.40
		Non- hereditary C2	50	10.54	1.24	
Hypertension A2	*Male B1*	*Hereditary C1*	50	8.82	2.14	0.12
		Non- hereditary C2	50	8.70	2.22	
	Female B2	*Hereditary C1*	50	8.66	2.47	0.46
		Non- hereditary C2	50	8.20	2.39	

Figure no. 105

Showing comparisons of mean scores among interaction of diseases, gender and hereditary status of patients with diabetes and hypertension for self-efficacy trait self-confidence.

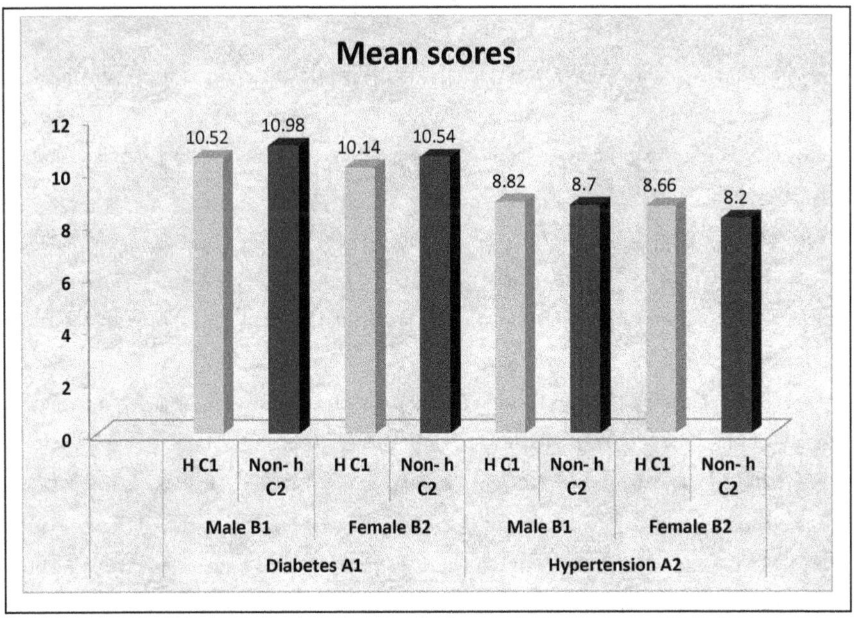

Main Effect:

Self-efficacy trait self - confidence skills with regard to Types of disease:

When the F test was used to indicate the impact of illness type on Self-efficacy trait self confidence in diabetic and hypertensive patients, the F value was reported significant F (1, 200) =102.87, $p<.01$ (Table no.105). The mean score for diabetes patients is 10.54 (SD = 1.44), while the mean score for hypertension patients is 8.59 (SD = 2.30). According to Table 114 and Chart 99, the difference in mean value is 1.95. As shown above, diabetic patients have better Self-efficacy trait self-confidence.

Self-efficacy trait self confidence with regard to Gender

The F value and mean score for male and female patients are shown in Tables 113 and 100, with the mean difference and F ratio reported as non-significant F(1,200) = 3.70, $p>.05$. Male patients have a mean value of 9.75 (SD = 2.06), while female patients have a mean value of 9.38 (SD = 2.23), and the mean difference of 0.37 between the two groups. The mean difference between the two groups was non-significant, as shown in the graph (Table No.115 & Chart No.100). Female and male patients have equal Self-efficacy factor self confidence, according to the findings.

Self-efficacy trait self confidence with regard to Hereditary status:

The F (1,200) = 0.13 was found to be the insignificant ($p>.05$) for the hereditary status. Patients with hereditary status have a mean score of 9.53 (SD=2.123) in table No.116 and chart No.101, while patients without hereditary status have a mean score of 9.60 (SD=2.18) and the mean difference is 0.07. Self-efficacy trait self-confidence is more or less similar in patients with hereditary and non-hereditary status.

Interaction Effect

Self-efficacy trait self confidence with regard to Types of disease and Gender:

Whether male and female diabetic patients, as well as male and female hypertensive patients, had any differences in Self-efficacy trait self confidence skills. Table No.113 shows that the F value for the relationship between disease types and gender, F (1,100) = 0.04, $p>.05$, was not significant. Table 117 and Chart 102 show that male diabetic patients have mean scores of (M=10.75, SD=1.35) and female diabetic patients have mean scores of (M=10.34, SD=1.51), with a mean difference of 0.41. The mean scores for male and female hypertensive patients are (M =8.76 SD=2.17) and (M=8.43 SD=2.43), respectively. The mean score for male and female hypertension patients differs by 0.33. The Self-efficacy trait self confidence was found to be similar among the four groups with regard to disease and gender.

Self-efficacy trait self confidence with regard to Types of disease and Hereditary status:

There was no significant interaction found between disease and hereditary status, as F (1, 100) =3.50, p>.05. Diabetic patients with hereditary status have a mean score of 10.33 (SD =1.58), while diabetic patients without hereditary status have a mean score of 10.76 (SD=1.26), and the mean difference of 0.43. Patients with hypertension and hereditary status have mean value of 8.74(SD=2.30) while those hypertensive patients without hereditary status have a mean score of 8.45 (SD=2.31).The mean difference between them is 0.29. Each of the four groups has by and large similar self-efficacy and self-confidence.

Self-efficacy trait self confidence with regard to Gender and Hereditary status:

Gender and heredity have no significant interaction, according to F (1,100) = 0.27, *p*>05. The mean score for male patients with hereditary status is 9.67 (SD =2.00), while the mean score for male patients without hereditary status is 9.84 (SD =2.13), indicating a 0.17 mean difference, in Table 119 and Chart 104. The mean score for female patients with hereditary status is 9.40 (SD=2.25), while the mean score for non-hereditary female patients is 9.37 (SD=2.23). The mean difference is 0.03. As a result, the Self-efficacy trait self-confidence was indicated to be equal in all four groups of patients.

Self-efficacy trait self confidence with regard to Types of disease, Gender and Hereditary status:

In diabetic and hypertensive patients, F ratios for disease, gender, and hereditary status are insignificant, with F (1, 50) =0.13, *p*>.05. The mean score for diabetic male patients with hereditary status is 10.52 (SD =1.41), while the mean score for diabetic male patients without hereditary status is 10.98 (SD =1.25). The difference in mean values between the two groups is 0.46. Female diabetic patients with hereditary status have mean values of 10.14 (SD = 1.73) compared to female diabetic patients without hereditary status have mean values of 10.54 (SD = 1.24). The mean difference between the two groups is 0.40, which is insignificant. Patients with hereditary status and hypertension have a mean score of 8.82 (SD=2.14), compared to 8.70 (SD=2.22) for those hypertensive patients without hereditary status.

With a mean difference of 0.12, which is also not significant. Female hypertensive patients with hereditary status have an mean score of 8.66 (SD=2.47), while those without hereditary status have an mean score of 8.20 (SD=2.39). The difference in mean value is 0.46. Self-efficacy self-confidence is similar among all eight groups of diabetic and hypertensive patients.

Table: 121
Showing ANOVA summary for the self-efficacy trait social achievement.

Source	Type III Sum of Squares	df	Mean Square	F	Sig. Level
***Diseases* (A)12**	176.890	1	176.890	68.53	p<.01
***Gender* (B)**	.810	1	.810	.314	NS
***Heredity status* (C)**	.360	1	.360	.139	NS
***Diseases * Gender* (A*B)**	.250	1	.250	.097	NS
***Diseases * Heredity status* (A*C)**	.160	1	.160	.062	NS
***Gender * Heredity status* (B*C)**	2.560	1	2.560	.992	NS
***Diseases * Gender * Heredity status* (A*B*C)**	1.960	1	1.960	.759	NS
Error	1011.720	392	2.581		
Total	24390.000	400			
Corrected Total	1194.710	399			

Levene's Test of Equality of Error Variances[a]

Dependent Variable: VAR00004

F	df1	df2	Sig.
2.106	7	392	.042

Tests the null hypothesis that the error variance of the dependent variable is equal across groups.

a. Design: Intercept + Diseases + Gender + HS + Diseases * Gender + Diseases * HS + Gender * HS + Diseases * Gender * HS

Table 122

Showing Mean, SD & Mean difference between patients of diabetes and hypertension for self-efficacy trait social achievement.

Diseases (A)	N	Mean	SD	Mean Difference
Diabetes A1	200	8.28	1.37	1.33
Hypertension A2	200	6.95	1.79	

Figure no.106

Showing comparisons of mean scores between patients of diabetes and hypertension for self-efficacy trait social achievement.

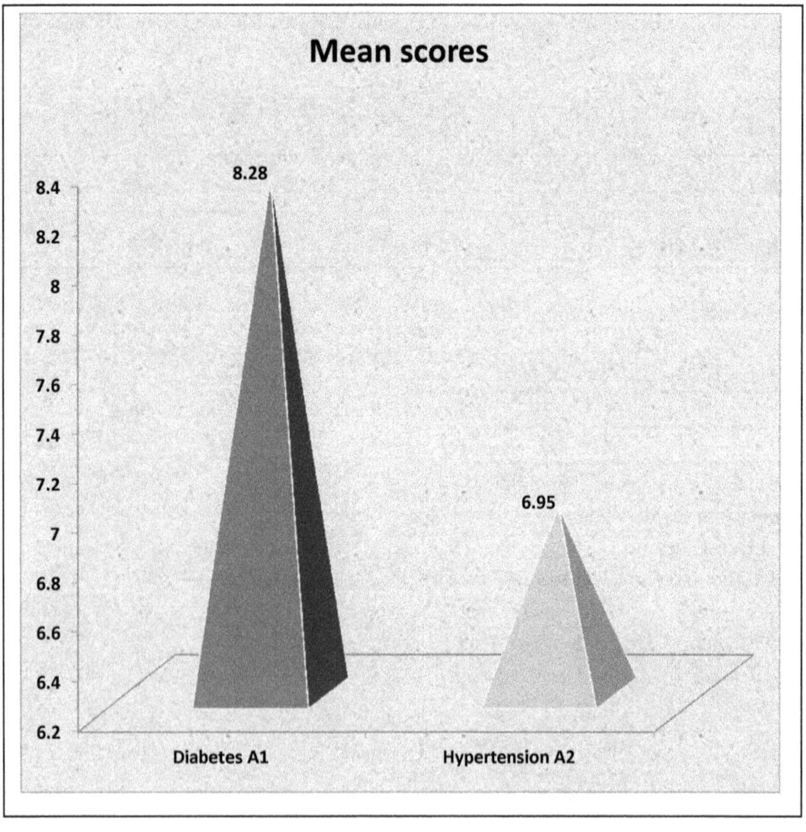

Table 123

Showing Mean, SD & Mean difference between male and female patients with diabetes and hypertension for self-efficacy trait social achievement.

Gender (B)	N	Mean	SD	Mean Difference
Male B1	200	7.57	1.72	0.09
Female B2	200	7.66	1.73	

Figure no.107

Showing comparisons of mean scores between male and female patients with diabetes and hypertension for self-efficacy trait social achievement.

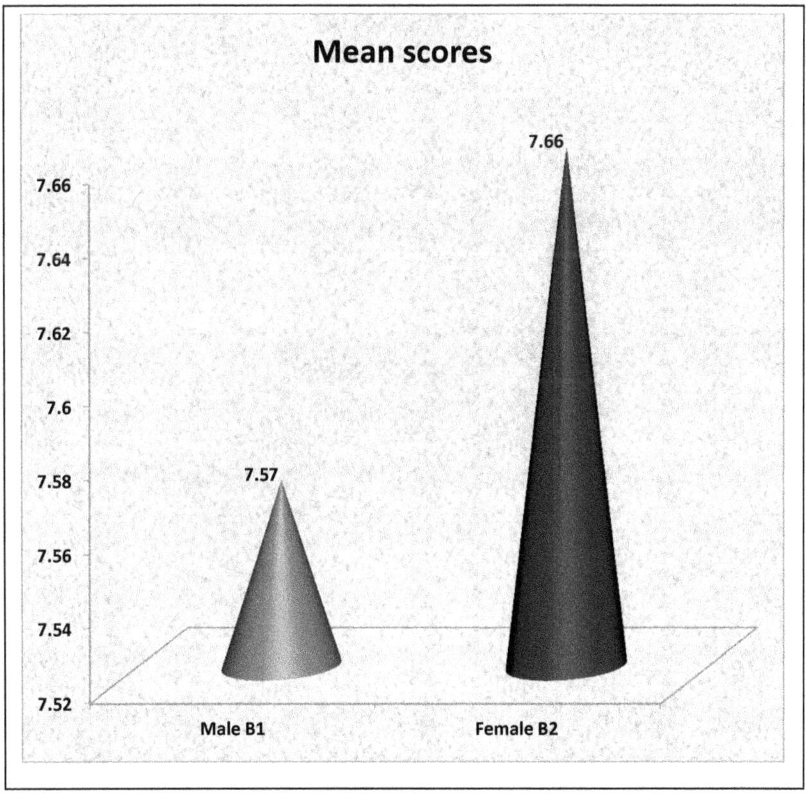

Table 124
Showing Mean, SD & Mean difference between patients with and without hereditary status for self-efficacy trait social achievement.

Hereditary status (C)	N	Mean	SD	Mean Difference
Hereditary C1	200	7.64	1.77	0.06
Non-hereditary C2	200	7.58	1.68	

Figure no. 108
Showing comparisons of mean scores between patients with and without hereditary status for self-efficacy trait social achievement.

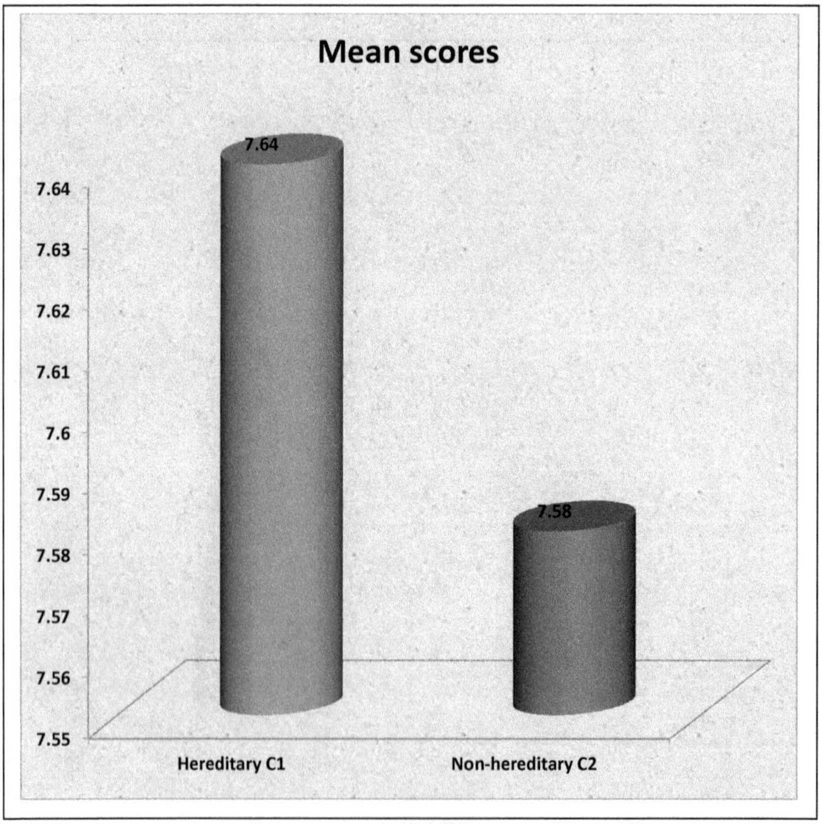

Table 125
Showing Mean, SD & Mean difference among interaction of diseases and Gender of patients with diabetes and hypertension for self-efficacy trait social achievement.

Diseases (A)	Gender (B)	N	Mean	SD	Mean Difference
Diabetes A1	**Male B1**	100	8.26	1.45	0.04
	Female B2	100	8.30	1.29	
Hypertension A2	**Male B1**	100	6.88	1.70	0.14
	Female B2	100	7.02	1.89	

Figure no. 109
Showing comparisons of mean among interaction of diseases and Gender of patients with diabetes and hypertension for self-efficacy trait social achievement.

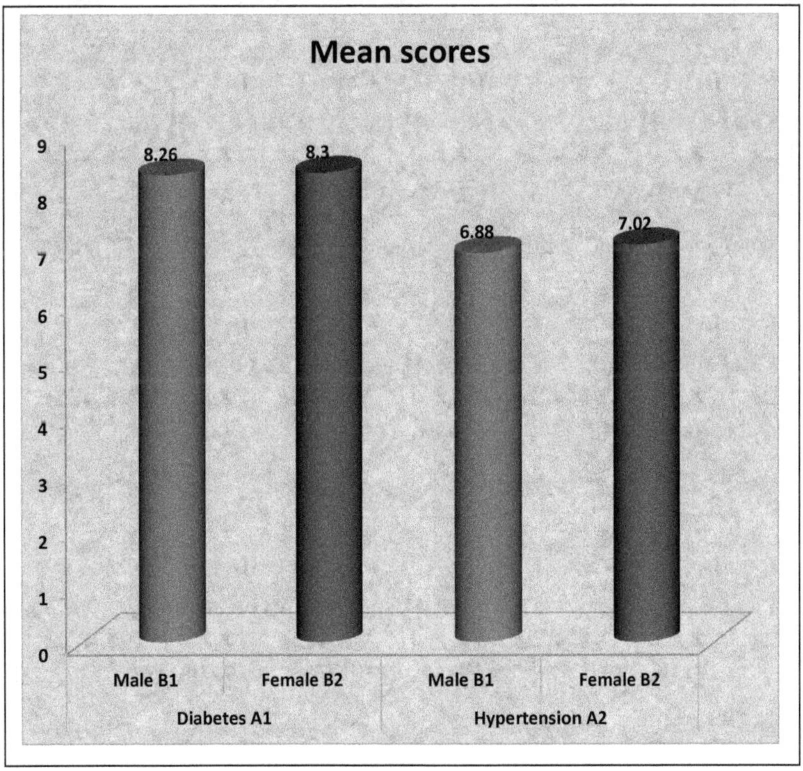

Table 126
Showing Mean, SD & Mean difference among interaction of diseases and hereditary status of patients for self-efficacy trait social achievement.

Diseases (A)	Hereditary (C)	N	Mean	SD	Mean Difference
Diabetes A1	Hereditary *C1*	100	6.96	1.86	0.02
	Non- hereditary *C2*	100	6.94	1.73	
Hypertension A2	Hereditary *C1*	100	8.33	1.38	0.10
	Non- hereditary *C2*	100	8.23	1.36	

Figure no. 110
Showing comparisons of mean scores among interaction of diseases and hereditary status of patients for self-efficacy trait social achievement.

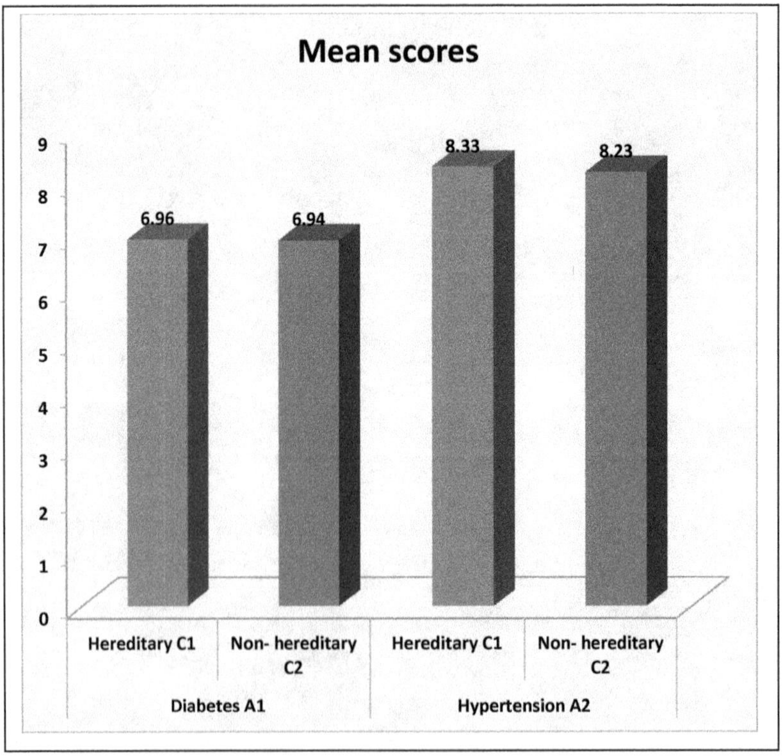

Table 127
Showing Mean, SD & Mean difference among interaction of Gender and hereditary status of patients for self-efficacy trait social achievement.

Gender (B)	Hereditary status (C)	N	Mean	SD	Mean Difference
Male	Hereditary *C1*	100	7.68	1.83	0.22
	Non-hereditary *C2*	100	7.46	1.61	
Female	Hereditary *C1*	100	7.61	1.72	0.10
	Non-hereditary *C2*	100	7.71	1.75	

Figure no. 111
Showing comparisons of mean scores among interaction of Gender and hereditary status of patients for self-efficacy trait social achievement

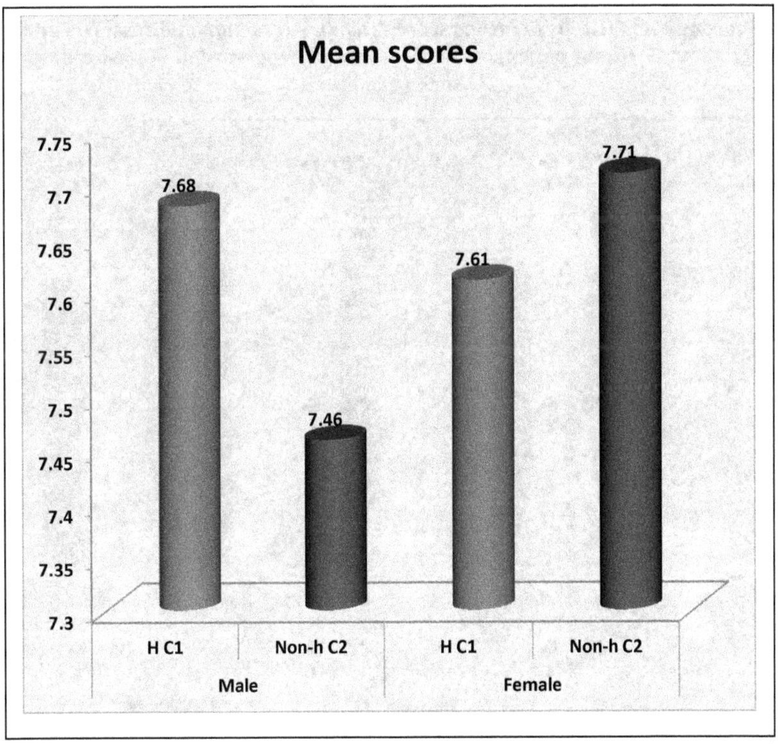

Table 128

Showing Mean, SD & Mean difference among interaction of diseases, gender and hereditary status of patients with diabetes and hypertension for self-efficacy trait social achievement.

Diseases (A)	Gender (B)	Hereditary status (C)	N	Mean	SD	Mean Difference
Diabetes A1	*Male B1*	*Hereditary C1*	50	8.46	1.50	0.40
		Non- hereditary C2	50	8.06	1.39	
	Female B2	*Hereditary C1*	50	8.20	1.26	0.20
		Non- hereditaryC2	50	8.40	1.32	
Hypertension A2	*Male B1*	*Hereditary C1*	50	6.90	1.80	0.04
		Non- hereditary C2	50	6.86	1.61	
	Female B2	*Hereditary C1*	50	7.02	1.93	0.01
		Non- hereditary C2	50	7.03	1.86	

Figure no. 112

Showing comparisons of means scores among interaction of diseases, gender and hereditary status of patients with diabetes and hypertension for self-efficacy trait social achievement.

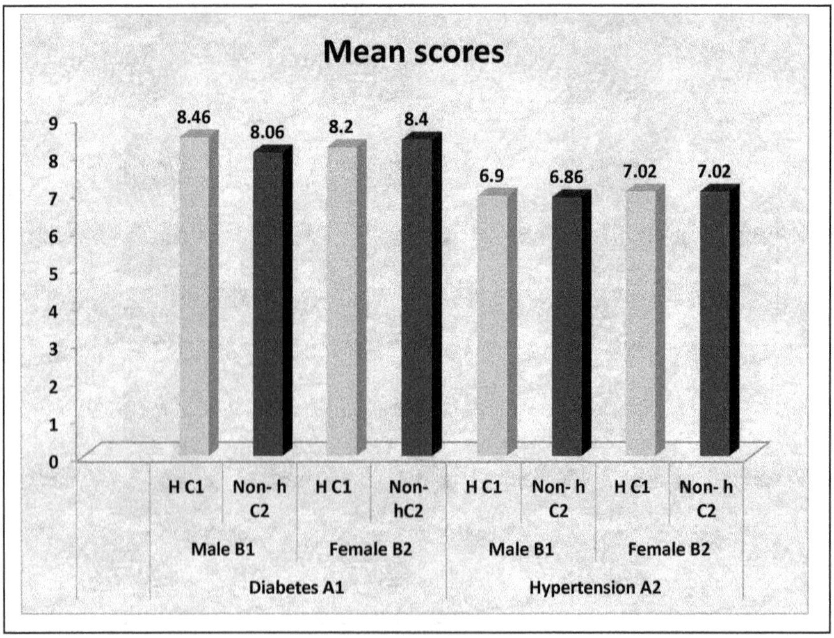

Main Effect:

Self-efficacy trait social achievement with regard to Types of disease:

The F value was significant when the F test was used to examine the effectiveness of illness type on social achievement in diabetic and hypertensive patients. F (1,200) =68.53, $p<.01$ was used to show the significance of F (Table no.121). Patients with diabetes have mean score of 8.28 (SD = 1.37), while those with hypertension have an mean score of 6.95 (SD = 1.79). The difference in means value is 1.33, according to Table 122 and Chart 106. The Self-efficacy trait social achievement of hypertensive and diabetic patients differ, as shown above. Patients with diabetes have higher social achievement self-efficacy skills.

Self-efficacy trait social achievement with regard to Gender

Tables 121 and 123 show the F value and mean score for gender of diabetic and hypertensive patients, with the mean difference and F ratio reported as non-significant F(1,200) =0.31, $p>.05$. The mean value for male patients is 7.57 (SD = 1.72), while the mean value for female patients is 7.66 (SD = 1.73), resulting in a mean difference of 0.16 between the two groups. As shown in the graph, the mean difference between the two groups was significant (Chart No.107). According to the findings, female and male patients have equal social achievement skills.

Self-efficacy trait social achievement with regard to Hereditary status:

The insignificance of hereditary status was found to be F (1, 200) =0.13. In table No.124 and chart No.108, patients with heredity have a mean score of 7.64 (SD=1.77), while patients without heredity have a mean score of 7.58 (SD=1.68) and a mean difference of 0.06. In both hereditary and non-hereditary patients, self-efficacy trait social achievement is similar.

Interaction Effect

Self-efficacy trait social achievement with regard to Types of disease and Gender:

The study's main goal was to check, if there were any differences in social achievement between male and female diabetic patients, as well as male and female hypertensive patients. The F value for the relationship between disease types and gender, F (1,100) =0.09, $p>05$, was non-significant, as shown in Table No.125. Male diabetic patients have mean scores of (M=8.26, SD=1.45) and female diabetic patients have mean scores of (M=8.30, SD=1.29), with a mean difference of 0.04, as shown in

Table 125and Chart 109. Male and female hypertensive patients have mean scores of (M =6.88 SD=1.70) and (M=7.02 SD=1.89), respectively. Male and female hypertension patients have a 0.14 difference in mean score. The social achievement skills were found equal in all the groups of patients.

Self-efficacy trait social achievement with regard to Types of disease and Hereditary status:

As F (1,100) = 0.09, *p*>.05 showed, there was a insignificant interaction between disease and hereditary status. Diabetic patients with hereditary status have a mean score of 6.96 (SD =1.86), whereas diabetic patients without hereditary status have a mean score of 6.94 (SD=1.73), resulting in a 0.02 mean difference. The difference in mean value between hypertensive patients with hereditary status and those without hereditary status is 0.10, with mean scores of 8.33 (SD =1.38) and 8.23(SD =1.36), respectively. Each of the four groups has similar self-efficacy traits social achievement.

Self-efficacy trait social achievement with regard to Gender and Hereditary status:

The value of F (1,100) = 0.99 revealed that gender and heredity have no significant relationship at (*p*<.05). According to Table 127 and Chart 111, the mean score for male patients with hereditary status is 7.68 (SD =1.83), while the mean score for male patients without hereditary status is 7.46 (SD =1.61), indicating a 0.22 mean difference. Female patients with hereditary status have a mean score of 7.61 (SD=1.72), while non-hereditary female patients have a mean score of 7.71 (SD=1.75). The difference of mean is 0.10. The mean difference in all four groups is the same. As a result, the Self-efficacy trait social achievement skills of all four groups of patients were observed to be similar.

Self-efficacy trait social achievement with regard to Types of disease, Gender and Hereditary status:

F ratio for disease, gender, and hereditary status are significant in diabetic and hypertensive patients, with F (1, 50) =0.75, *p*>05. Diabetic male patients with hereditary status have a mean score of 8.46 (SD =1.50), while diabetic male patients without hereditary status have a mean score of 8.06 (SD =1.39). The difference between the two groups' mean values is 0.40. Female diabetic patients with hereditary status have mean values of 8.20 (SD = 1.26) compared to 8.40 (SD = 1.32) for female diabetic patients without hereditary status. The difference in mean between the two groups is 0.20, which is insignificant statistically. Patients with hereditary status and hypertension have a mean score of 6.90 (SD=1.80), while those without hereditary status and hypertension have a mean score of 6.86 (SD=1.61). The difference is also insignificant, with a mean difference of 0.04. Female hypertensive Patients with hereditary status have a mean score of 7.02 (SD=1.93), while those female hypertensive patients without hereditary status have a mean score of 7.03 (SD=1.86). The mean value difference is 0.01. All eight groups of diabetic and hypertensive patients have similar self-efficacy social achievement skills.

Table: 129

Showing ANOVA summary for the self-efficacy trait self.

Source	Type III Sum of Squares	df	Mean Square	F	Sig. Level
***Diseases* (A)**	786.803	1	786.803	156.462	$p<.01$
***Gender* (B)**	7.562	1	7.562	1.504	NS
***Heredity status* (C)**	18.062	1	18.062	3.592	NS
***Diseases * Gender* (A*B)**	49.703	1	49.703	9.884	$p<.01$
***Diseases * Heredity status* (A*C)**	.013	1	.003	.003	NS
***Gender * Heredity status* (B*C)**	23.522	1	23.522	4.678	$p<.05$
***Diseases * Gender * Heredity status* (A*B*C)**	.023	1	.023	.004	NS
Error	1971.260	392	5.029		
Total	51147.000	400			
Corrected Total	2856.937	399			

Levene's Test of Equality of Error Variances[a]

Dependent Variable: VAR00005

F	df1	df2	Sig.
14.954	7	392	.000

Tests the null hypothesis that the error variance of the dependent variable is equal across groups.

a. Design: Intercept + Diseases + Gender + HS + Diseases * Gender + Diseases * HS + Gender * HS + Diseases * Gender * HS

Table 130
Showing Mean, SD & Mean difference between patients of diabetes and hypertension for self-efficacy trait self.

Diseases (A)	N	Mean	SD	Mean Difference
Diabetes A1	200	12.39	1.58	2.81
Hypertension A2	200	9.58	2.80	

Figure no.113
Showing comparisons of mean scores between patients of diabetes and hypertension for self-efficacy trait self.

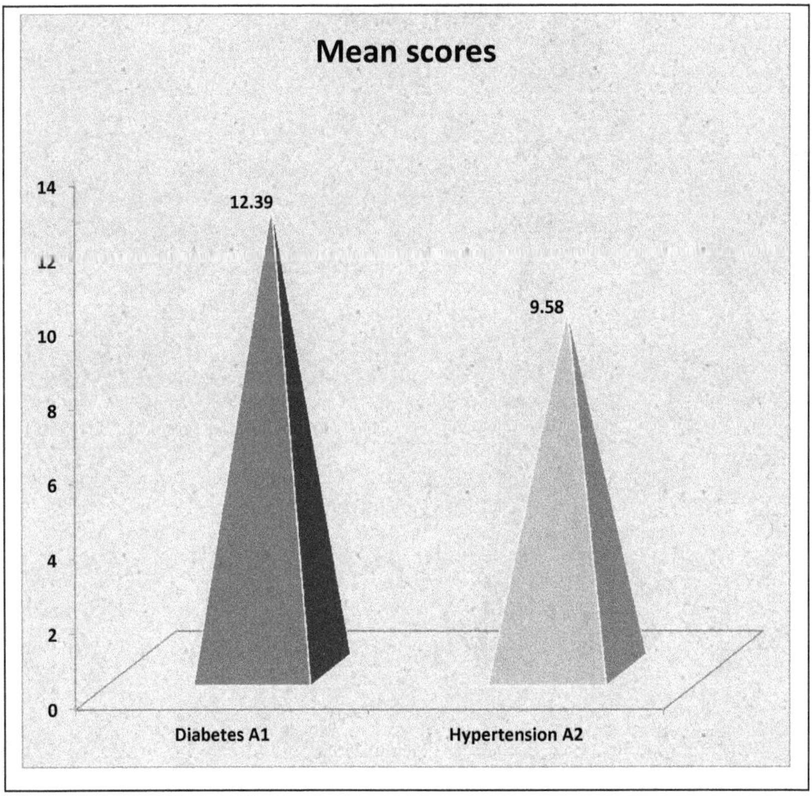

Table 131
Showing Mean, SD & Mean difference between male and female patients with diabetes and hypertension for self-efficacy trait self.

Gender (B)	N	Mean	SD	Mean Difference
Male B1	200	11.12	2.81	0.27
Female B2	200	10.85	2.52	

Figure no.114
Showing comparisons of mean scores between male and female patients with diabetes and hypertension for self-efficacy trait self.

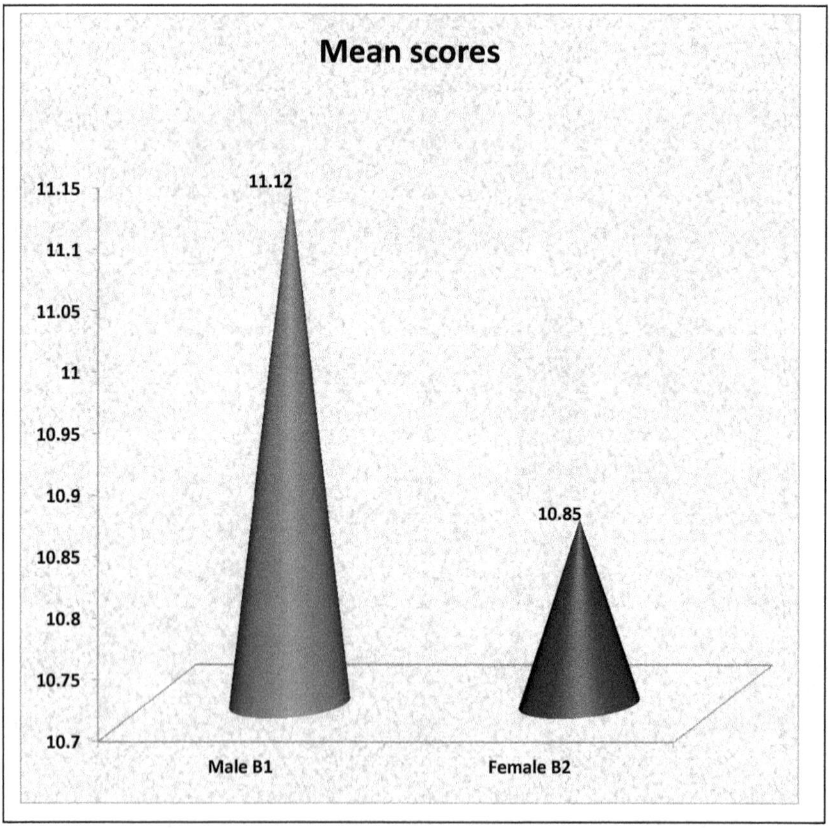

Table 132
Showing Mean, SD & Mean difference between patients with and without hereditary status for self-efficacy trait self.

Hereditary status (C)	N	Mean	SD	Mean Difference
Hereditary C1	200	11.20	2.76	0.43
Non-hereditary C2	200	10.77	2.57	

Figure no. 115
Showing comparisons of mean scores between patients with and without hereditary status for self-efficacy trait self.

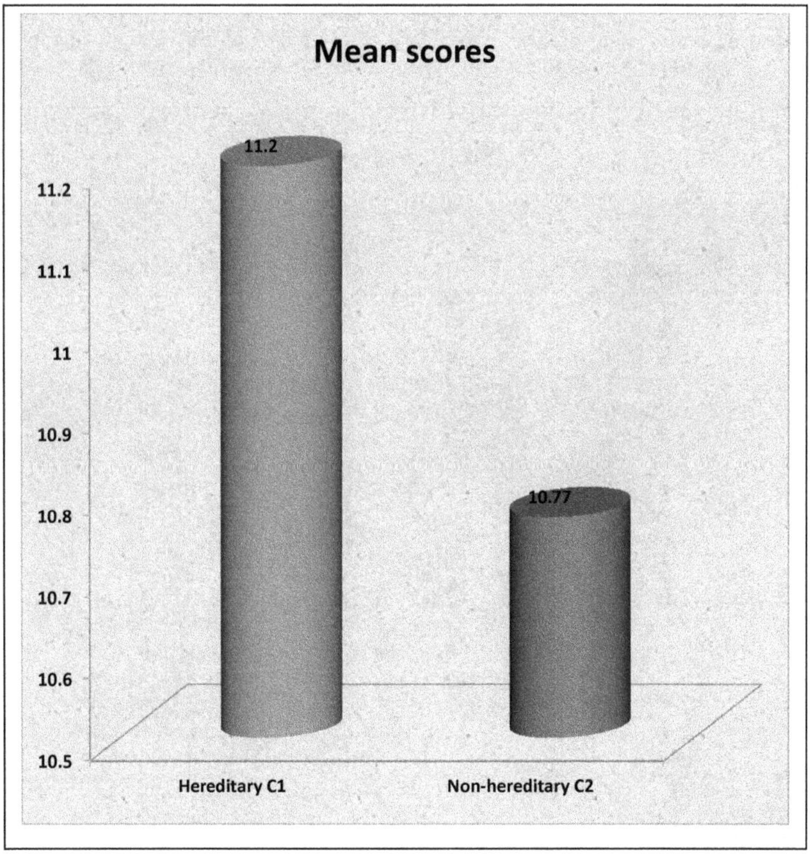

Table 133
Showing Mean, SD & Mean difference among interaction of diseases and Gender of patients with diabetes and hypertension for self-efficacy trait self.

Diseases (A)	Gender (B)	N	Mean	SD	Mean Difference
Diabetes A1	**Male B1**	100	12.88	1.63	0.98
	Female B2	100	11.90	1.37	
Hypertension A2	**Male B1**	100	9.37	2.66	0.43
	Female B2	100	9.80	2.94	

Figure no. 116
Showing comparisons of mean scores among interaction of diseases and Gender of patients with diabetes and hypertension for self-efficacy trait self.

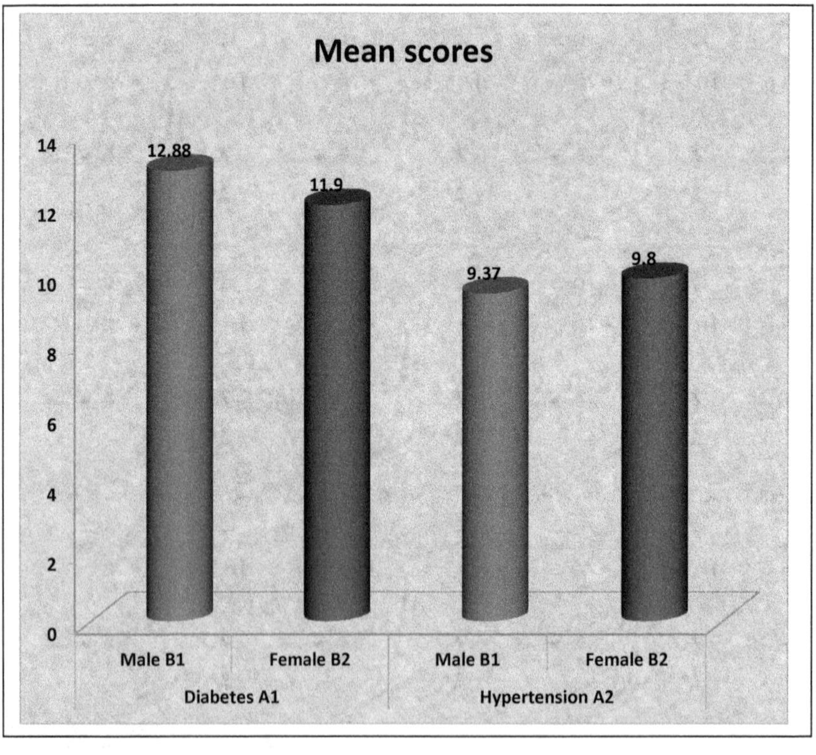

Table 134
Showing Mean, SD & Mean difference among interaction of diseases and hereditary status of patients for self-efficacy trait self.

Diseases (A)	Hereditary (C)	N	Mean	SD	Mean Difference
Diabetes A1	Hereditary *C1*	100	12.60	1.61	0.42
	Non- hereditary *C2*	100	12.18	1.53	
Hypertension A2	Hereditary *C1*	100	9.80	2.96	0.43
	Non- hereditary *C2*	100	9.37	2.64	

Figure no. 117
Showing comparisons of mean scores among interaction of diseases and hereditary status of patients for self-efficacy trait self.

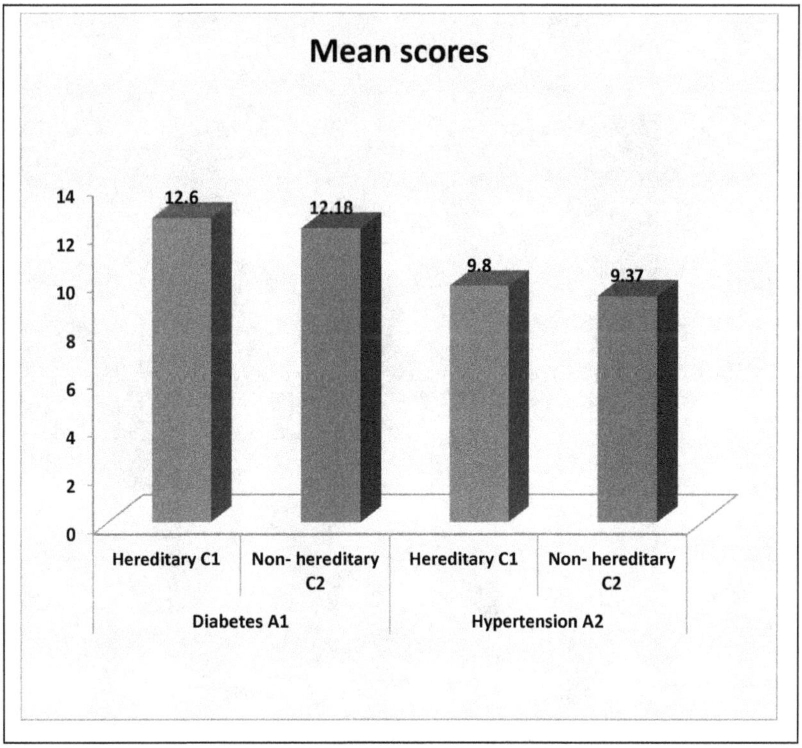

Table 135

Showing Mean, SD & Mean difference among interaction of Gender and hereditary status of patients for self-efficacy trait self.

Gender (B)	Hereditary status (C)	N	Mean	SD	Mean Difference
Male	Hereditary *C1*	100	11.58	2.84	0.91
	Non-hereditary *C2*	100	10.67	2.73	
Female	Hereditary *C1*	100	10.82	2.63	0.06
	Non-hereditary *C2*	100	10.88	2.41	

Figure no. 118

Showing comparisons of mean scores among interaction of Gender and hereditary status of patients for self-efficacy trait self.

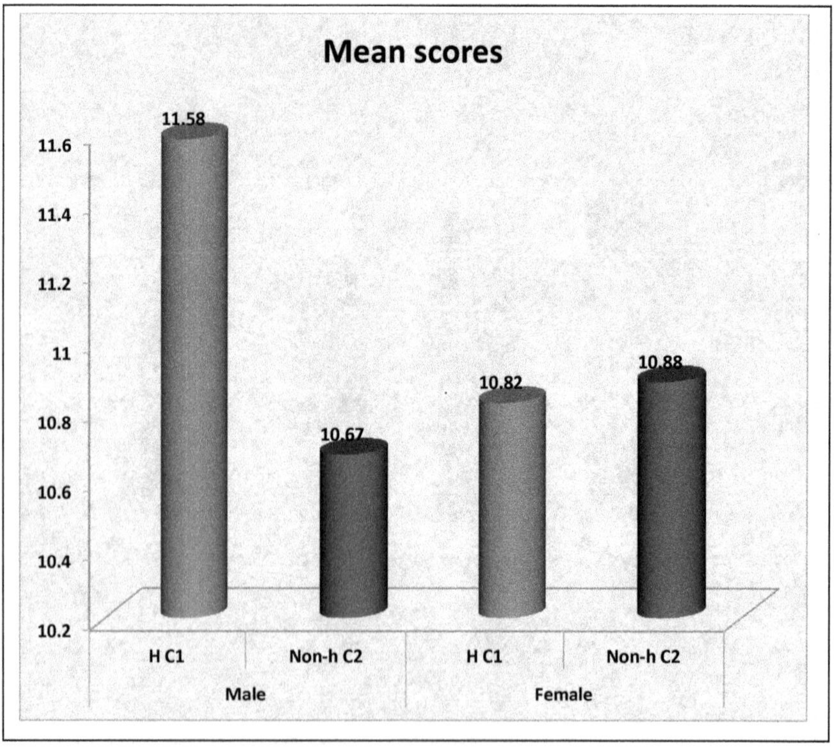

Table 136

Showing Mean, SD & Mean difference among interaction of diseases, gender and hereditary status of patients with diabetes and hypertension for self-efficacy trait self.

Diseases (A)	Gender (B)	Hereditary status (C)	N	Mean	SD	Mean Difference
Diabetes A1	*Male B1*	*Hereditary C1*	50	13.34	1.25	0.92
		Non- hereditary C2	50	12.42	1.84	
	Female B2	*Hereditary C1*	50	11.86	1.60	0.08
		Non- hereditary C2	50	11.94	1.11	
Hypertension A2	*Male B1*	*Hereditary C1*	50	9.82	2.90	0.9
		Non- hereditary C2	50	8.92	2.33	
	Female B2	*Hereditary C1*	50	9.78	3.04	0.04
		Non- hereditary C2	50	9.82	2.87	

Figure no. 119

Showing comparisons of mean scores among interaction of diseases, gender and hereditary status of patients with diabetes and hypertension for self-efficacy trait self.

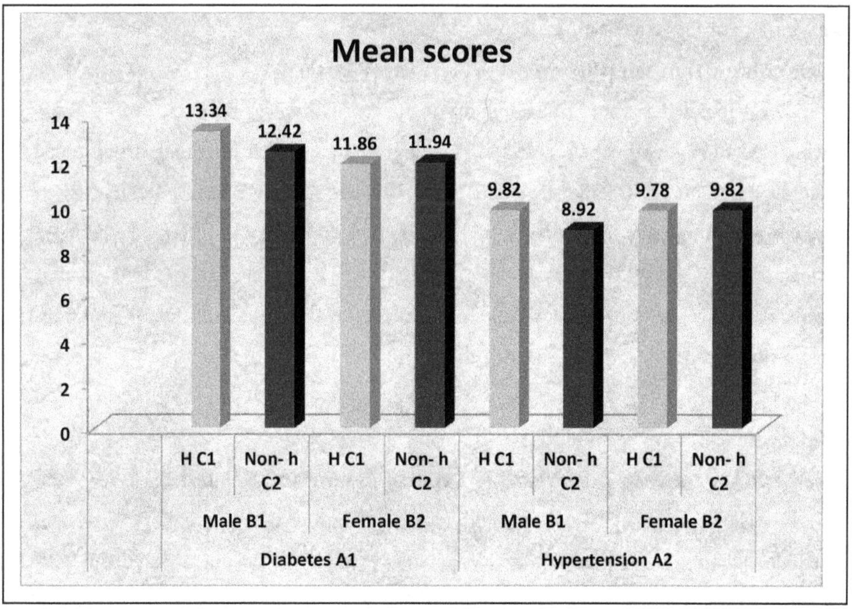

Main Effect:

Self-efficacy trait self with regard to Types of disease:

When the F test was employed to check the effect of Types of disease on Self-efficacy trait self among diabetic and hypertension patients than significant F value was reported. The F value was highlighted F (1, 200) = 156.46, $p<.01$(Table no.129) which was significant. Table no.130 and 113 displayed that mean scores of diabetic and hypertension patients are 12.39 (SD = 1.58) and 9.58 (SD = 2.80) respectively and the difference between two means is 2.81. On the basis of above results, it can be said that diabetic patients have greater Self-efficacy trait self than patients with hypertension

Self-efficacy trait self with regard to Gender:

Table no.129 & 131 indicated F value and mean score for the Gender of patients with diabetes and hypertension in which the mean difference and F ratio is reported insignificant F(1,200) = 1.50, p >.05. Mean score obtained by male patients is 11.12 (SD = 2.81) and for female patients is 10.85 (SD = 2.52), whereas the mean difference of both the group is 0.27. This mean difference (Table No131. & Chart No.114) suggested that there is a negligible mean difference among both the groups. It can be concluded that both male and female patients with diabetes and hypertension have more or less equal Self-efficacy trait self.

Self-efficacy trait self with regard to Hereditary status:

Calculated F value of Hereditary status was found to be F (1, 200) = 3.59, which was not significant. Table No. 132 and chart no. 115 highlighted that mean score of patients with hereditary status is 11.20 (SD=2.76), whereas a mean score of patients without hereditary status is 10.77 (SD=2.57) and the difference between mean scores was 0.43 which was unnoticeable. It was concluded that hereditary status had no impact on Self-efficacy trait self. Patients with or without hereditary status have similar life Self-efficacy factor self.

Interaction Effect

Self-efficacy trait self with regard to Types of disease and Gender:

The main objective of the study was to examine whether diabetic male and female patients and male and female patients with hypertension differed on Self-efficacy trait self. Table no.129 displayed that F value for interaction of Types of disease and Gender is also observed to be significant F (1,100) = 9.88, $p < .01$. By the same point of view Table no. 133 and chart no. 116 displayed that mean scores of male and female diabetic patients are (M=12.88, SD= 1.63) and (M = 11.90, SD = 1.37) respectively, whereas the mean difference of both the group of patients is 0.98. As again mean scores of male and female patients with hypertension are (M =9.37, SD = 2.66) and (M = 9.80, SD = 2.94), the mean difference of both the group of the patients is 0.43. Mean difference between all four groups highlighted that Types of disease and Gender have significant interaction on Self-efficacy trait self. All the groups of participants have different level of self.

Self-efficacy trait self with regard to Types of disease and Hereditary status:

The F ratio for Types of disease and Hereditary status is F (1,100) = 0.003, which was insignificant ($p > .05$). Table no. 134 and chart no. 117 depicted mean score of diabetic patients with hereditary status is 12.60 (SD = 1.61) and mean score for diabetic patients without hereditary status is 12.18 (SD = 1.53). Statistically significant mean difference is 0.42, whereas the mean of hypertension patients with hereditary status is 9.80 (SD = 2.96) and mean score of hypertension patients without hereditary status is 9.37 (SD = 2.64), the difference between two means is 0.43. It can be concluded that all four groups have a more or less equal level of Self-efficacy trait self.

Self-efficacy trait self with regard to Gender and Hereditary status:

The calculated value for interaction between Gender and Hereditary status of diabetic and hypertension is found to be F (1, 100) = 4.67 which was significant at .05. As seen from the Table no.135 and chart no.118 mean score of male patients with heredity is 11.58 (SD = 2.84) and mean of male patients without heredity is 10.67 (SD =2.73), whereas the difference of mean scores is 0.91. As again mean score of female patients with heredity is 10.82 (SD = 2.63) and mean score of female patients without heredity is 10.88 (SD = 2.41). The difference in mean score is 0.06. Almost all four groups have a little bit mean difference. Thus it can be concluded that all four groups of patients have reported slight different Self-efficacy trait self.

Self-efficacy trait self with regard to Types of disease, Gender and Hereditary status:

F ratio for Types of disease, Gender and Hereditary status of the patients of diabetes and hypertension is to be reported insignificant F (1, 50) = 0.004, $p > .05$. The mean score of diabetic male patients with heredity and non-heredity are 13.34 (SD =1.25) and 12.42 (SD =1.84) respectively. The mean difference between both groups is 0.92. As again mean value of diabetic female patients with and without hereditary status are 11.86 (SD = 1.60) &11.94 (SD = 1.11). The mean difference of both the group is 0.08 which was also statistically less. As seen from Table, mean score of hypertension male patients with heredity is 9.82 (SD =2.90) whereas mean score of hypertension male patients without hereditary status is 8.92 (SD = 2.33). The difference between the mean score is 0.9, which is also statistically not significant. In the same way, the mean score of hypertension female patients with heredity is 9.78 (SD = 3.04) and mean score of hypertension female patients with non-heredity is 9.82 (SD = 2.87). The mean difference is found at 0.04. All the eight groups of the patients of diabetes and hypertension are more or less equal to Self-efficacy trait self.

Table: 137

Showing ANOVA summary for the self-efficacy trait self-evaluation.

Source	Type III Sum of Squares	df	Mean Square	F	Sig. Level
Diseases (A)	.023	1	.023	.011	NS
Gender (B)	3.802	1	3.802	1.863	NS
Heredity status (C)	2.103	1	2.103	1.030	NS
*Diseases * Gender* (A*B)	6.003	1	6.003	2.940	NS
*Diseases * Heredity status* (A*C)	15.603	1	15.603	7.643	$p<.01$
*Gender * Heredity status* (B*C)	2.723	1	2.723	1.334	NS
*Diseases * Gender * Heredity status* (A*B*C)	.202	1	.202	.099	NS
Error	800.220	392	2.041		
Total	36495.000	400			
Corrected Total	830.677	399			

Levene's Test of Equality of Error Variances[a]

Dependent Variable: VAR00006

F	df1	df2	Sig.
2.175	7	392	.036

Tests the null hypothesis that the error variance of the dependent variable is equal across groups.

a. Design: Intercept + Diseases + Gender + HS + Diseases * Gender + Diseases * HS + Gender * HS + Diseases * Gender * HS

Table 138

Showing Mean, SD & Mean difference between patients of diabetes and hypertension for self-efficacy trait self-evaluation.

Diseases (A)	N	Mean	SD	Mean Difference
Diabetes A1	200	9.45	1.28	0.02
Hypertension A2	200	9.43	1.59	

Figure no.120

Showing comparisons of mean scores between patients of diabetes and hypertension for self-efficacy trait self-evaluation.

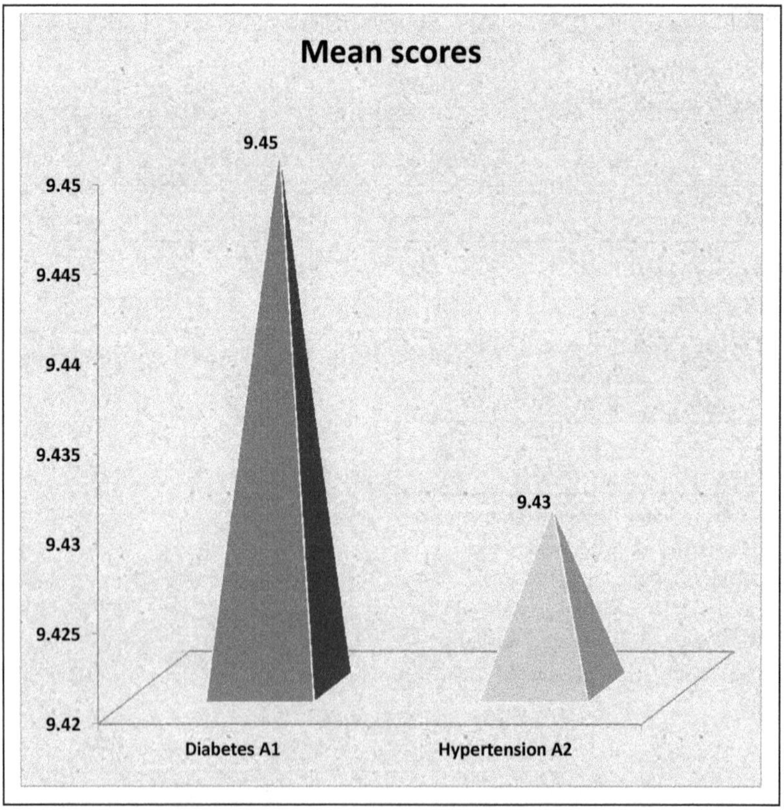

Table 139
Showing Mean, SD & Mean difference between male and female patients with diabetes and hypertension for self-efficacy trait self-evaluation.

Gender (B)	N	Mean	SD	Mean Difference
Male B1	200	9.54	1.45	0.20
Female B2	200	9.34	1.42	

Figure no.121
Showing comparisons of mean scores between male and female patients with diabetes and hypertension for self-efficacy trait self-evaluation.

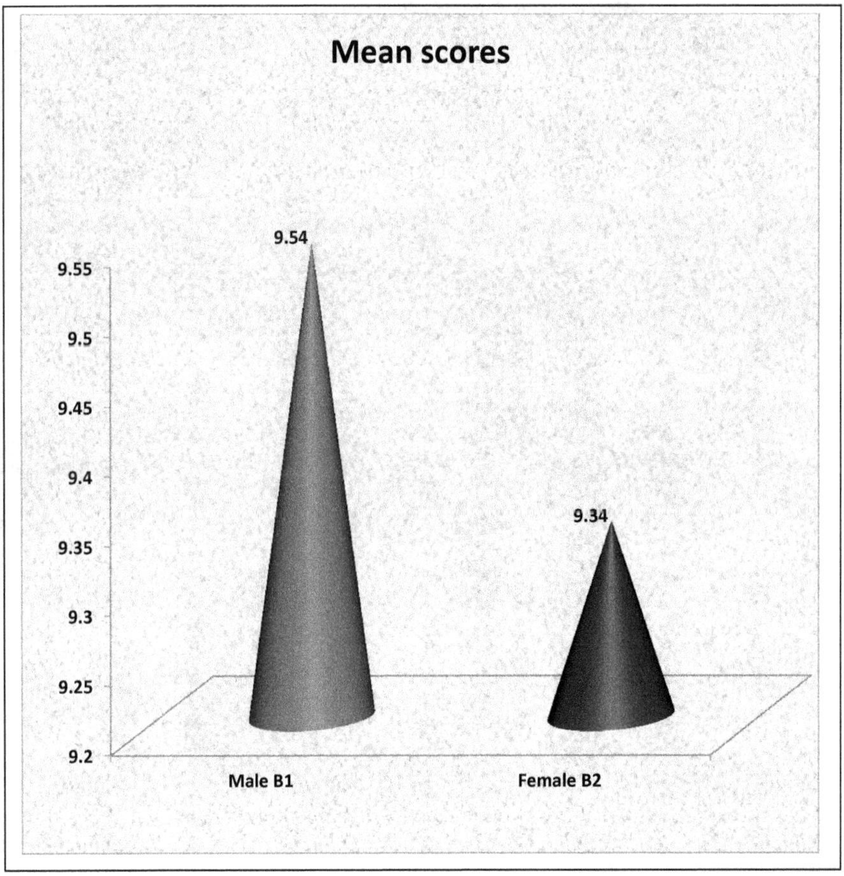

Table 140
Showing Mean, SD & Mean difference between patients with and without hereditary status for self-efficacy trait self-evaluation.

Hereditary status (C)	N	Mean	SD	Mean Difference
Hereditary C1	200	9.51	1.44	0.14
Non-hereditary C2	200	9.37	1.44	

Figure no. 122
Showing comparisons of mean scores between patients with and without hereditary status for self-efficacy trait self-evaluation.

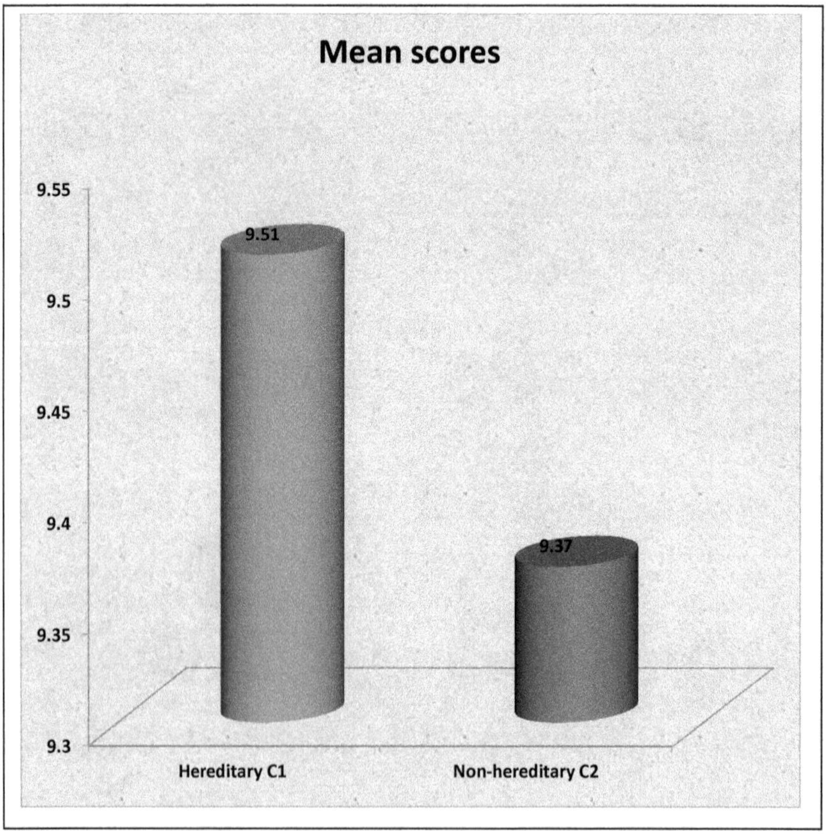

Table 141
Showing Mean, SD & Mean difference among interaction of diseases and Gender of patients with diabetes and hypertension for self-efficacy trait self-evaluation.

Diseases (A)	Gender (B)	N	Mean	SD	Mean Difference
Diabetes A1	**Male B1**	100	9.67	1.25	0.44
	Female B2	100	9.23	1.27	
Hypertension A2	**Male B1**	100	9.41	1.63	0.05
	Female B2	100	9.46	1.55	

Figure no. 123
Showing comparisons of mean scores among interaction of diseases and Gender of patients with diabetes and hypertension for self-efficacy trait self-evaluation.

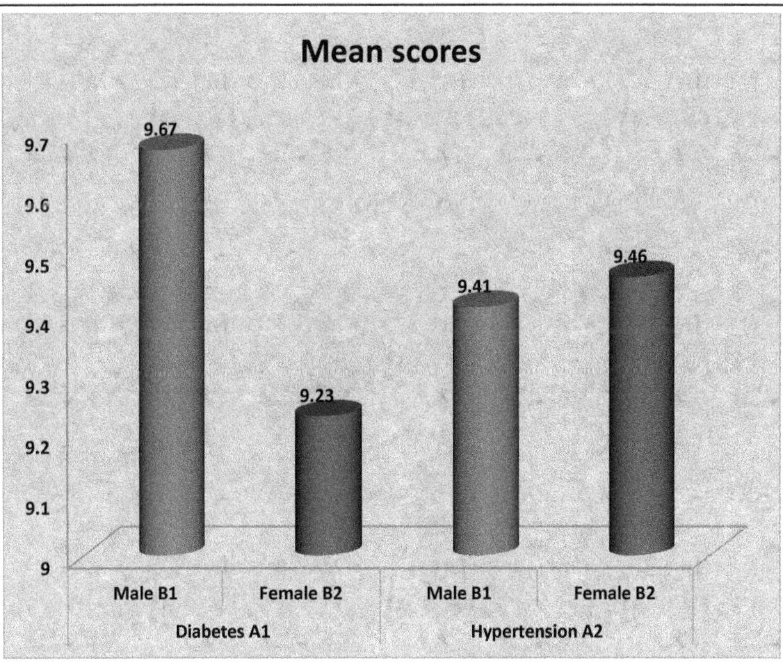

Table 142
Showing Mean, SD & Mean difference among interaction of diseases and hereditary status of patients for self-efficacy trait self-evaluation.

Diseases (A)	Hereditary (C)	N	Mean	SD	Mean Difference
Diabetes A1	Hereditary *C1*	100	9.72	1.20	0.54
	Non- hereditary *C2*	100	9.18	1.30	
Hypertension A2	Hereditary *C1*	100	9.31	1.62	0.25
	Non- hereditary *C2*	100	9.56	1.55	

Figure no. 124
Showing comparisons of mean scores among interaction of diseases and hereditary status of patients for self-efficacy trait self-evaluation

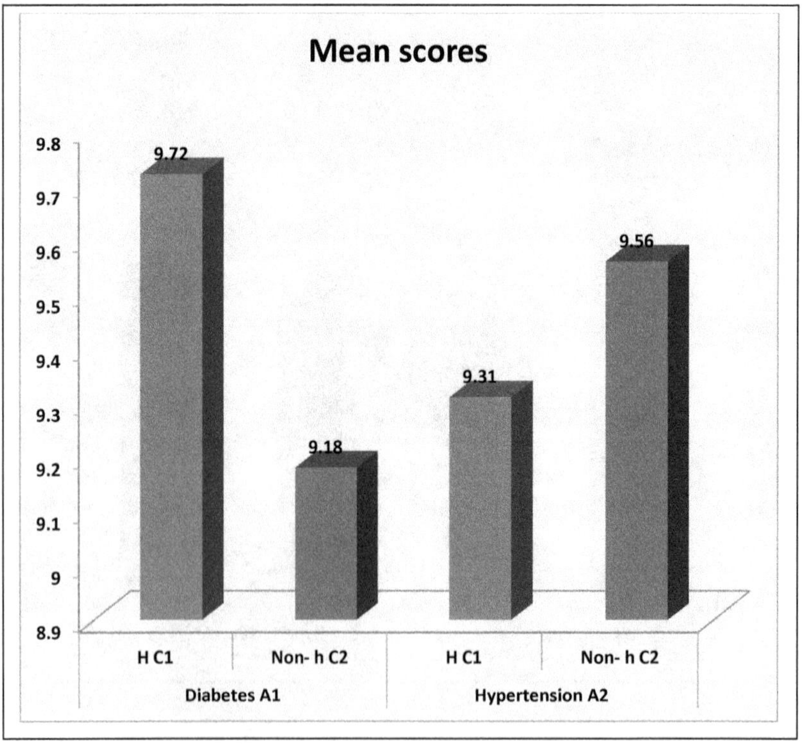

Table 143

Showing Mean, SD & Mean difference among interaction of Gender and hereditary status of patients for self-efficacy trait self-evaluation.

Gender (B)	Hereditary status (C)	N	Mean	SD	Mean Difference
Male	**Hereditary *C1***	100	9.53	1.54	0.02
	Non-hereditary *C2*	100	9.55	1.37	
Female	**Hereditary *C1***	100	9.50	1.33	0.31
	Non-hereditary *C2*	100	9.19	1.49	

Figure no. 125

Showing comparisons of mean scores among interaction of Gender and hereditary status of patients for self-efficacy trait self-evaluation.

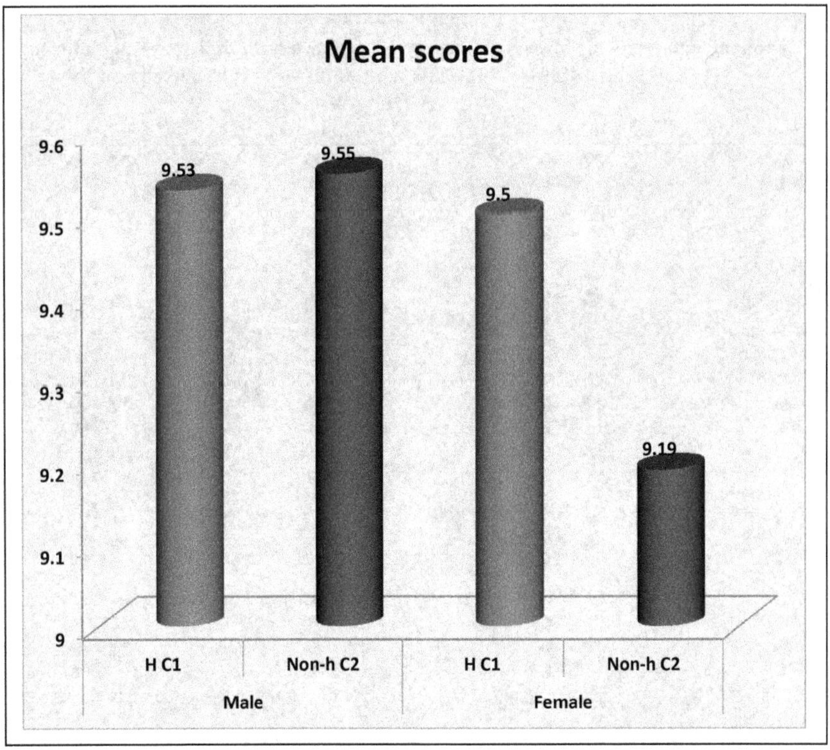

Table 144

Showing Mean, SD & Mean difference among interaction of diseases, gender and hereditary status of patients with diabetes and hypertension for self-efficacy trait self-evaluation.

Diseases (A)	Gender (B)	Hereditary status (C)	N	Mean	SD	Mean Difference
Diabetes A1	*Male B1*	*Hereditary C1*	50	9.88	1.31	0.42
		Non- hereditary C2	50	9.46	1.16	
	Female B2	*Hereditary C1*	50	9.56	1.07	0.66
		Non- hereditary C2	50	8.90	1.38	
Hypertension A2	*Male B1*	*Hereditary C1*	50	9.18	1.68	0.46
		Non- hereditary C2	50	9.64	1.56	
	Female B2	*Hereditary C1*	50	9.44	1.56	0.04
		Non- hereditary C2	50	9.48	1.55	

Figure no. 126

Showing comparisons of mean scores among interaction of diseases, gender and hereditary status of patients with diabetes and hypertension for self-efficacy trait self-evaluation.

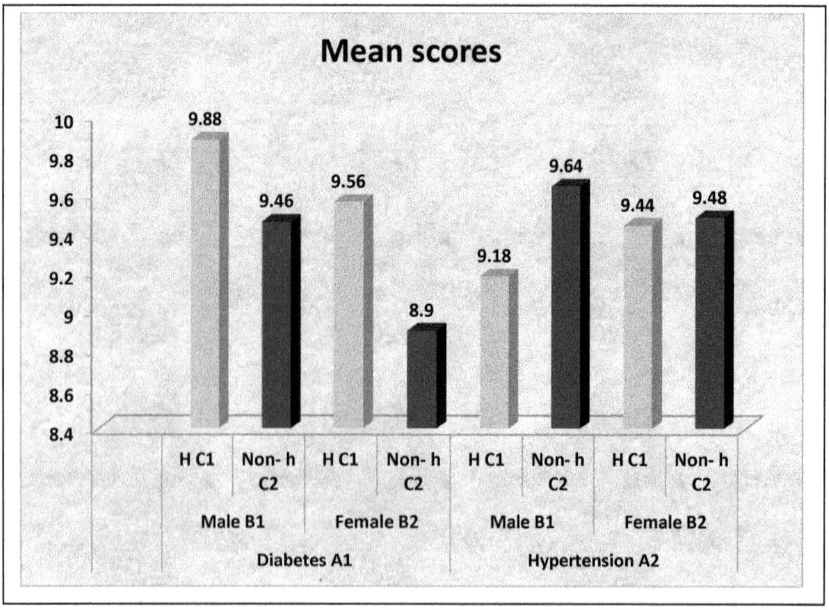

Main Effect:

Self-efficacy trait self evaluation with regard to Types of disease:

An insignificant F value was found when the F test was used to study the influence of Self-efficacy trait self evaluation in diabetic and hypertension patients. The significance of the F value F (1,200) = 0.01, *p*>.05 (Table no.137) was highlighted. Table no.138 and 120 present that mean scores of diabetic and hypertension patients are 9.45 (SD = 1.28) and 9.43 (SD = 1.59) respectively and the difference between two means is 0.02. According to the findings diabetic and hypertensive patients have more or less similar Self-efficacy trait self evaluation.

Self-efficacy trait self evaluation with regard to Gender:

Tables 137 and 121 show the F value and mean score for the gender of diabetic and hypertensive patients, with the mean difference and F ratio reported to be not significant F (1,200) = 1.86, *p* >.05 The mean value obtained by male patient is 9.54 (SD = 1.45), while female patients have 9.34 (SD = 1.42), with a mean difference of 0.20 between the two groups. This mean difference (Table No.139 & Chart No.121) indicated that both groups have a nominal mean difference. It can be concluded that both male and female patients with diabetes and hypertension have similar on Self-efficacy trait self evaluation.

Self-efficacy trait self evaluation with regard to Hereditary status:

The calculated F value of Hereditary status was F (1, 200) = 1.03, which was insignificant Table No. 140 and chart no. 122 highlighted that mean score of patients with hereditary status is 9.51 (SD=1.44), whereas a mean score of patients without hereditary status is 9.37 (SD=1.44) and the difference between mean scores was 0.14 which is negligible. It was concluded that hereditary status had no impact on Self-efficacy trait self evaluation .It seems both groups of patients appear to have been similarly influenced by self evaluation.

Interaction Effect

Self-efficacy trait self evaluation with regard to Types of disease and Gender:

The primary goal of the study was to determine whether diabetic male and female patients, as well as male and female hypertensive patients, have different Self-efficacy factor self evaluation. Table no.137 showed that F value for interaction of

Types of disease and Gender is also observed to be insignificant F (1,100) = 2.94, *p*> .05. By the same point of view Table no.141 and chart no.123 displayed that mean scores of male and female diabetic patients are(M=9.67,SD= 1.25) and (M = 9.23, SD = 1.27) respectively, whereas the mean difference of both the group of patients is 0.44. As the mean scores of male and female hypertensive patients are (M =9.41, SD = 1.63) and (M = 9.46, SD = 1.55), respectively, the mean difference of both groups of patients is 0.05. According to the mean difference between the four groups, one can well imagine that all the groups of patients have more or less equal self evaluation.

Self-efficacy trait self evaluation with regard to Types of disease and Hereditary status:

F (1,100) =7.64 for Types of disease and Hereditary status, which was significant at (*p*<.01). The mean value of diabetic patients with hereditary status is 9.72 (SD = 1.20) in table 142 and chart 124, while the mean score for diabetic patients without hereditary status is 9.18 (SD=1.30).Statistically significant mean difference is 0.54, whereas the mean of hypertension patients with hereditary status is 9.31 (SD = 1.62) and mean score of hypertension patients non hereditary status is 9.56 (SD = 1.55), the difference between two means is 1.57. It can be concluded that all four groups have a different level of Self-efficacy trait self evaluation.

Self-efficacy trait self evaluation with regard to Gender and Hereditary status:

The calculated value of the interaction between gender and diabetes and hypertension heredity is found to be F(1,100)=1.33, which is non-significant. The mean value of male patients with hereditary status is 9.53 (SD = 1.54), while the mean value of male patients without hereditary status is 9.55 (SD =1.37), with a 0.02 difference in mean scores .Hereditary status of female patients have a mean score of 9.50 (SD = 1.33), while non hereditary status of female patients have a mean score of 9.19 (SD = 1.49). The mean value difference is 0.31. Almost all four groups have a insignificant mean difference. As a result, all four groups of patients highlighted similar levels of Self-efficacy trait self evaluation .

Self-efficacy trait self evaluation with regard to Types of disease, Gender and Hereditary status:

Diabetic and hypertensive patients' F ratios for disease types, gender, and hereditary status are insignificant ($F (1, 50) = 0.09$, $p>.05$). Diabetic male patients with heredity have a mean score of 9.88 (SD =1.31), whereas diabetic male patients without heredity have a mean score of 9.46 (SD =1.16). Between the two groups, there is a 0.42 mean difference. Again, the mean value for diabetic female patients with and without hereditary status is 9.56 (SD = 1.07) and 8.90 (SD = 1.38) respectively. The mean difference between the two groups is 0.66, which is statistically significant. As shown in Table, the mean score of male hypertension patients with heredity is 9.18 (SD =1.68), while the mean score of male hypertension patients without hereditary status is 9.64 (SD = 1.56)..The difference in average scores is 0.46, which is statistically insignificant. Similarly, the mean score of female hypertension patients with heredity is 9.44 (SD = 1.56), while the mean score of female hypertension patients without heredity is 9.48 (SD = 1.55). The mean difference is calculated to be 0.04.The Self-efficacy trait self evaluation is by and large similar in all eight groups of diabetic and hypertensive patients.

Table: 145

Showing ANOVA summary for the self-efficacy trait self-esteem.

Source	Type III Sum of Squares	df	Mean Square	F	Sig. Level
***Diseases* (A)**	132.250	1	132.250	33.266	$p<.01$
***Gender* (B)**	14.010	1	14.010	3.543	NS
***Heredity status* (C)**	12.960	1	12.960	3.260	NS
***Diseases * Gender* (A*B)**	42.250	1	42.250	10.628	$p<.01$
***Diseases * Heredity status* (A*C)**	139.240	1	139.240	35.024	$p<.01$
***Gender * Heredity status* (B*C)**	7.840	1	7.840	1.972	NS
***Diseases * Gender * Heredity status* (A*B*C)**	2.560	1	2.560	.644	NS
Error	1558.400	392	3.976		
Total	12062.000	400			
Corrected Total	1921.510	399			

Levene's Test of Equality of Error Variances[a]

Dependent Variable: VAR00007

F	df1	df2	Sig.
5.721	7	392	.000

Tests the null hypothesis that the error variance of the dependent variable is equal across groups.

a. Design: Intercept + Diseases + Gender + HS + Diseases * Gender + Diseases * HS + Gender * HS + Diseases * Gender * HS

Table 146
Showing Mean, SD & Mean difference between patients of diabetes and hypertension for self-efficacy trait self-esteem.

Diseases (A)	N	Mean	SD	Mean Difference
Diabetes A1	200	5.61	2.43	1.15
Hypertension A2	200	4.46	1.75	

Figure no.127
Showing comparisons of mean scores between patients of diabetes and hypertension for self-efficacy trait self-esteem.

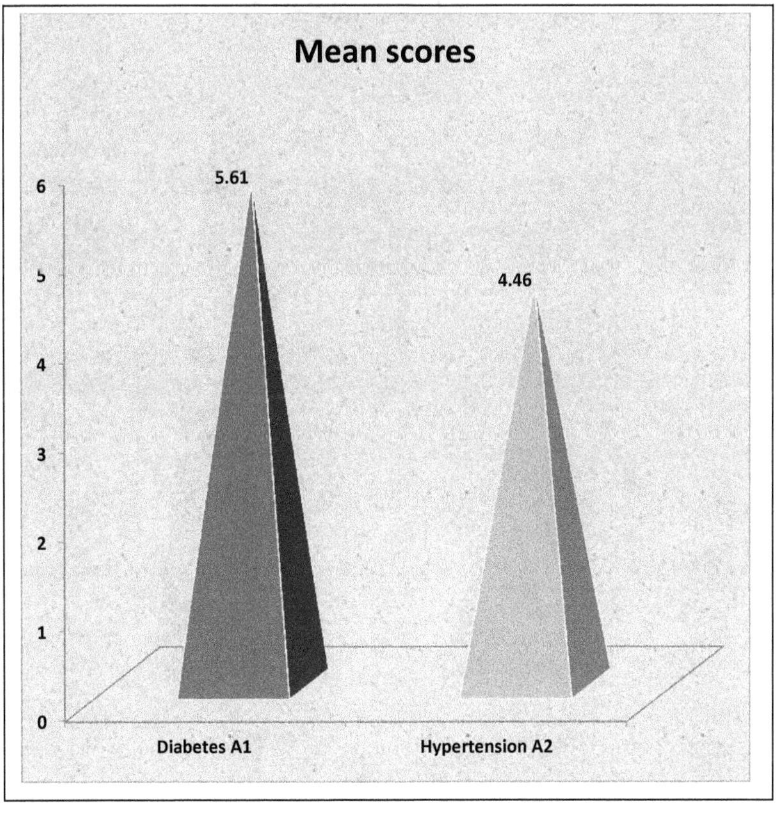

Table 147
Showing Mean, SD & Mean difference between male and female patients with diabetes and hypertension for self-efficacy trait self-esteem.

Gender (B)	N	Mean	SD	Mean Difference
Male B1	200	4.78	1.99	0.51
Female B2	200	5.29	2.35	

Figure no.128
Showing comparisons of mean scores between male and female patients with diabetes and hypertension for self-efficacy trait self-esteem.

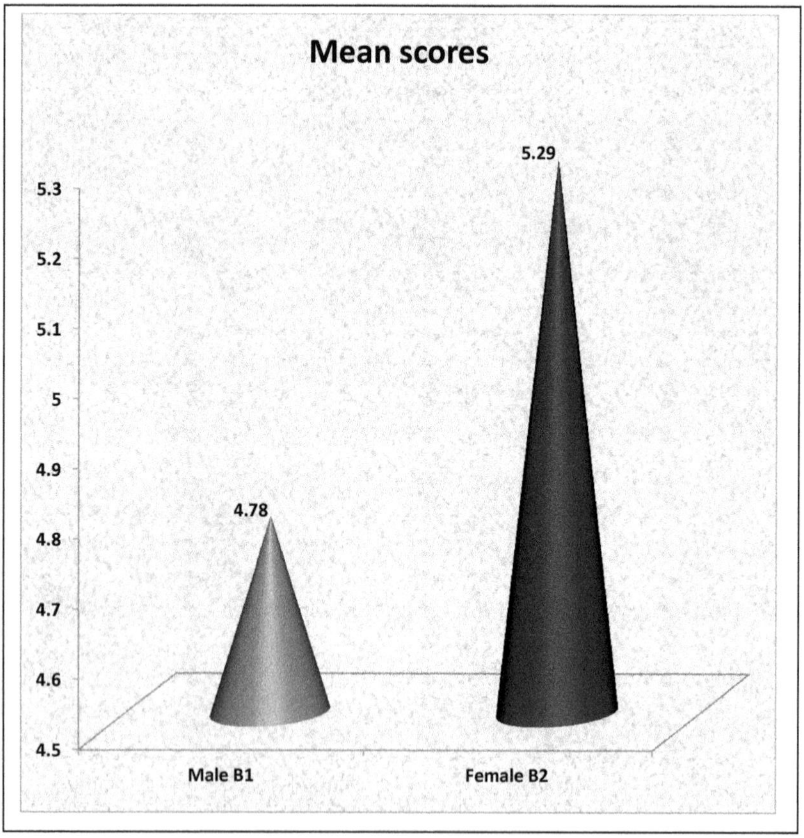

Table 148

Showing Mean, SD & Mean difference between patients with and without hereditary status for self-efficacy trait self-esteem.

Hereditary status (C)	N	Mean	SD	Mean Difference
Hereditary C1	200	4.85	1.89	0.36
Non-hereditary C2	200	5.21	2.44	

Figure no. 129

Showing comparisons of mean scores between patients with and without hereditary status for self-efficacy trait self-esteem.

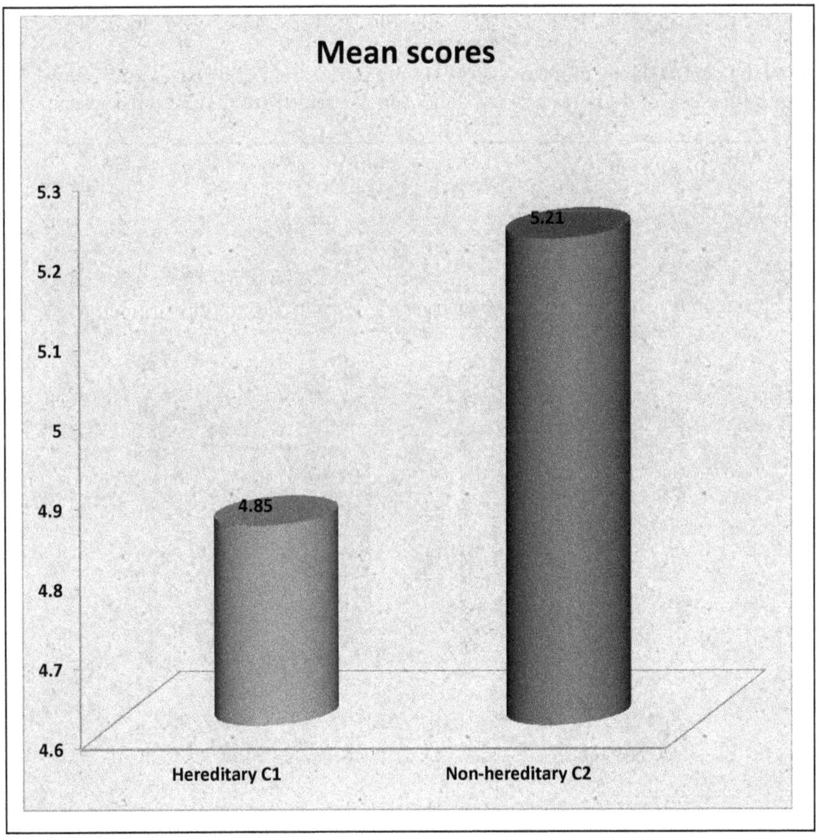

Table 149
Showing Mean, SD & Mean difference among interaction of diseases and Gender of patients with diabetes and hypertension for self-efficacy trait self-esteem.

Diseases (A)	Gender (B)	N	Mean	SD	Mean Difference
Diabetes A1	Male B1	100	5.03	2.21	1.16
	Female B2	100	6.19	2.51	
Hypertension A2	Male B1	100	4.53	1.72	0.14
	Female B2	100	4.39	1.78	

Figure no. 130
Showing comparisons of mean scores among interaction of diseases and Gender of patients with diabetes and hypertension for self-efficacy trait self-esteem.

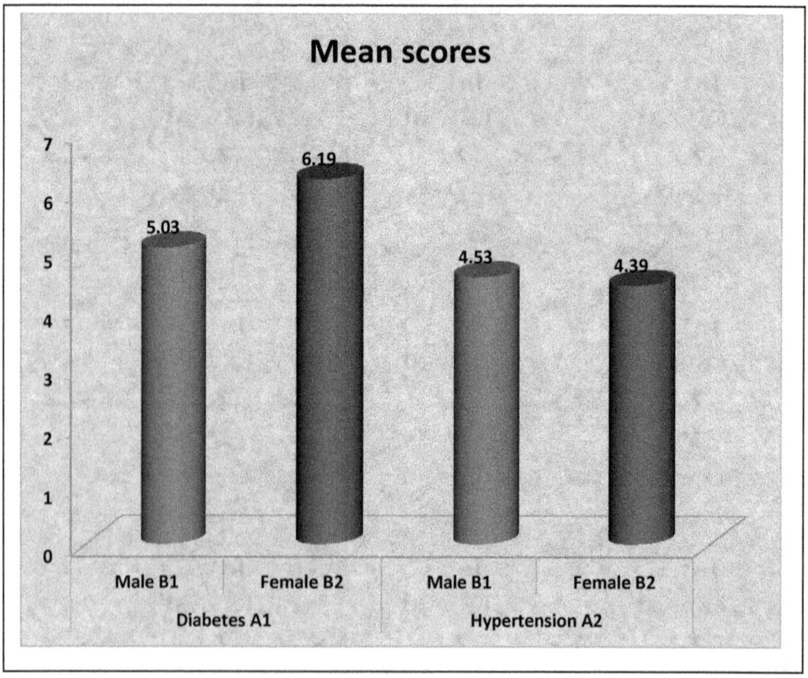

Table 150
Showing Mean, SD & Mean difference among interaction of diseases and hereditary status of patients for self-efficacy trait self-esteem.

Diseases (A)	Hereditary (C)	N	Mean	SD	Mean Difference
Diabetes A1	Hereditary *C1*	100	4.84	2.01	1.54
	Non- hereditary *C2*	100	6.38	2.57	
Hypertension A2	Hereditary *C1*	100	4.87	1.77	0.82
	Non- hereditary *C2*	100	4.05	1.62	

Figure no. 131
Showing comparisons of mean scores among interaction of diseases and hereditary status of patients for self-efficacy trait self-esteem.

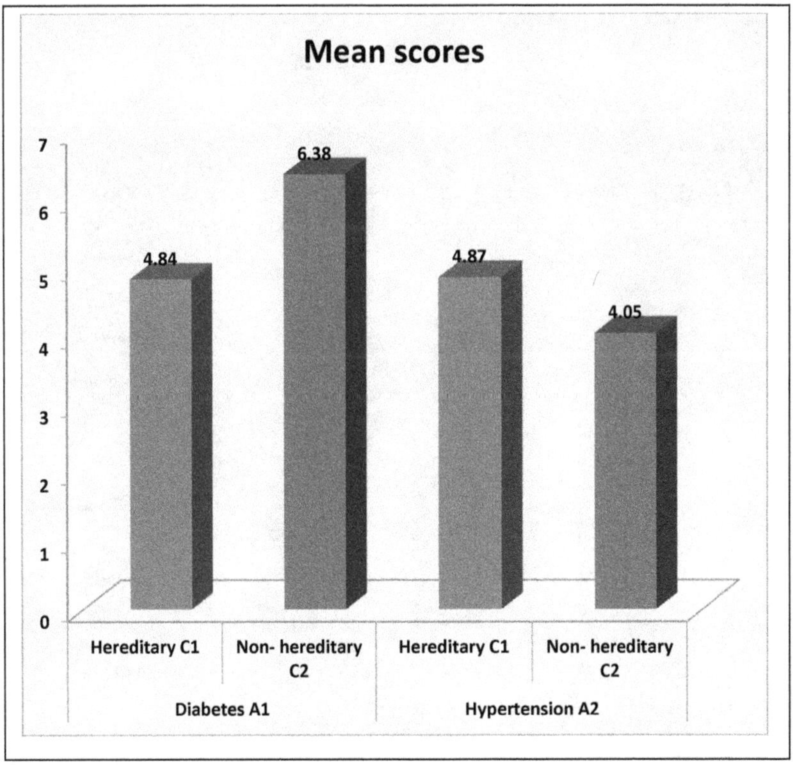

Table-151
Showing Mean, SD & Mean difference among interaction of Gender and hereditary status of patients for self-efficacy trait self-esteem.

Gender (B)	Hereditary status (C)	N	Mean	SD	Mean Difference
Male	Hereditary *C1*	100	4.74	1.83	0.08
	Non-hereditary *C2*	100	4.82	2.15	
Female	Hereditary *C1*	100	4.97	1.96	0.64
	Non-hereditary *C2*	100	5.61	2.66	

Figure no. 132
Showing comparisons of mean scores among interaction of Gender and hereditary status of patients for self-efficacy trait self-esteem.

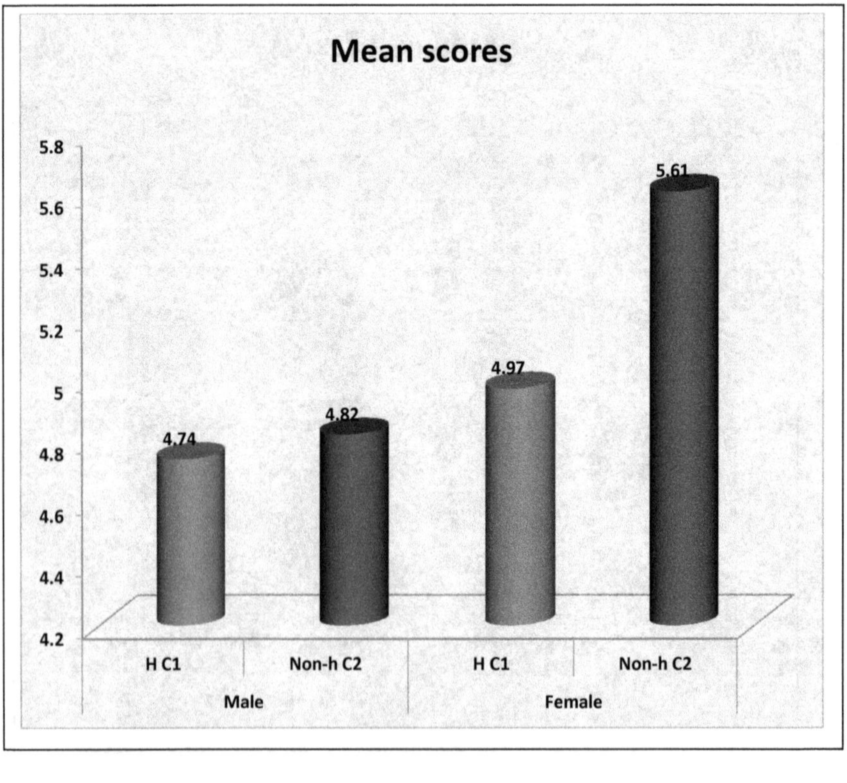

Table 152
Showing Mean, SD & Mean difference among interaction of diseases, gender and hereditary status of patients with diabetes and hypertension for self-efficacy trait self-esteem.

Diseases (A)	Gender (B)	Hereditary status (C)	N	Mean	SD	Mean Difference
Diabetes A1	*Male B1*	*Hereditary C1*	50	4.48	1.82	1.10
		Non- hereditary C2	50	5.58	2.45	
	Female B2	*Hereditary C1*	50	5.20	2.15	1.98
		Non- hereditary C2	50	7.18	2.47	
Hypertension A2	*Male B1*	*Hereditary C1*	50	5.00	1.82	0.94
		Non- hereditary C2	50	4.06	1.47	
	Female B2	*Hereditary C1*	50	4.74	1.73	0.70
		Non- hereditary C2	50	4.04	1.78	

Figure no. 133
Showing comparisons of mean scores among interaction of diseases, gender and hereditary status of patients with diabetes and hypertension for self-efficacy trait self-esteem.

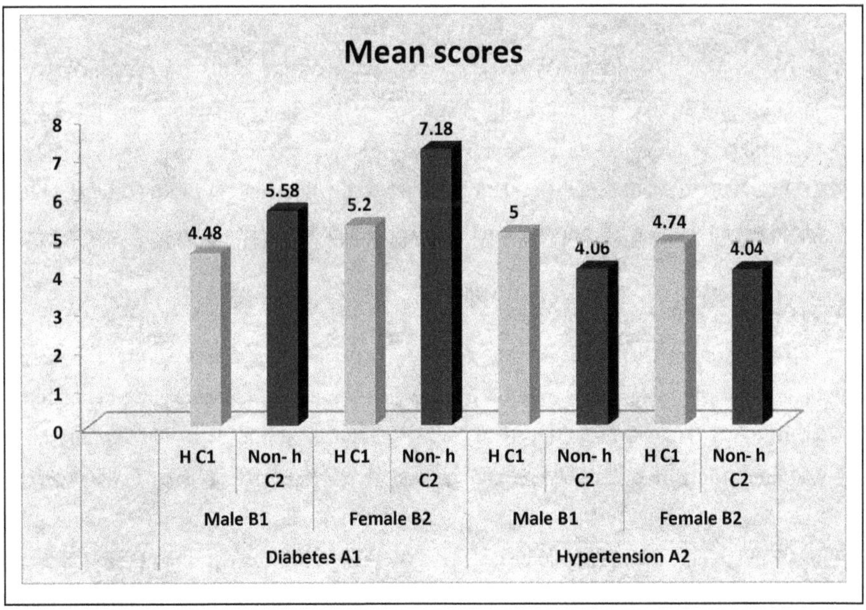

Main Effect:

Self-efficacy trait self esteem with regard to Types of disease:

When the F test is used to investigate the effect of disease type on Self-efficacy trait self esteem in patients with diabetes and hypertension, the F value is indicated to be significant. The F (1,200) = 33.26, $p<.01$. (Table no.145) was highlighted. The mean scores of diabetic and hypertension patients are 5.61 (SD = 2.43) and 4.46 (SD = 1.75), respectively, according to Tables 146 and chart 127, and the difference between the two means is 1.15. Diabetic patients have higher self esteem as compared to patients with hypertension.

Self-efficacy trait self esteem with regard to Gender

Tables 145 and 128 show the F value and mean score for patient with diabetes and hypertension, with the mean difference and F ratio reported as non significant F(1,200) = 3.54, $p>.05$. The mean value for male patients is 4.78 (SD = 1.99), while the mean value for female patients is 5.29 (SD = 2.35), resulting in a mean difference of 0.51 between the two groups. This mean difference (Table No.147 & Chart No. 128) denoted that both groups have a nominal mean difference. According to the above findings, it can be concluded that both female and male patients have equal Self-efficacy trait self esteem.

Self-efficacy trait self esteem with regard to Hereditary status:

The calculated F value for hereditary status was F (1, 200) = 3.26, which was insignificant at .05. Patients with hereditary status have a mean score of 4.85 (SD=1.89), while patients without hereditary status have a mean score of 5.21 (SD=2.44), a mean difference of 0.36 in table No. 148 and chart No.129. Patients with heredity and without heredity have more or less equal Self-efficacy trait self esteem.

Interaction Effect

Self-efficacy trait self esteem with regard to Types of disease and Gender:

As seen from table that types of disease and gender of patients are interacting significantly, have different levels of Self-efficacy trait self esteem. The F value for the interaction of disease types and gender, (F (1,100) =10.62, $p<.01$), was also significant in Table no.145. Table 149 and chart 130 show that the mean scores of male and female diabetic patients are (M=5.03, SD= 2.21) and (M = 6.19, SD = 2.51) respectively, with a mean difference of 1.16 between the two groups of patients. The mean difference between male and female hypertensive patients is 0.14, because their mean scores are (M =4.53 SD=1.72) and (M=4.39 SD=1.78), respectively. It concluded that all the four groups of patients have a different level of self esteem.

Self-efficacy trait self esteem with regard to Types of disease and hereditary status:

The significant interaction was reported for disease and hereditary status F (1,100) =35.02, *p*<.01. Table 150 and chart 131 show that diabetic patients with hereditary status have a mean score of 4.84 (SD = 2.01), while diabetic patients without hereditary status have a mean score of 6.38 (SD=2.57).The mean difference is 1.54. While the mean score of hypertension patients with hereditary status is 4.87 (SD = 1.77) and the mean score of hypertension patients without hereditary status is 4.05 (SD = 1.62), the statistically significant mean difference is 0.82. It is clear that each of the four groups has a different level of Self-efficacy trait self esteem.

Self-efficacy trait self esteem with regard to Gender and Hereditary status:

The F (1,100) = 1.97, which is not significant at *p*>.05, is the calculated value of the interaction between gender and heredity of patients. Male patients with hereditary status have a mean score of 4.74 (SD = 1.83), while male patients without hereditary status have a mean score of 4.82 (SD =2.15), a 0.08 difference in mean scores. Female patients with hereditary status have a mean score of 4.97 (SD = 1.96), while those with non-hereditary status have a mean score of 5.61 (SD = 2.66). The difference in mean value is 0.64. Almost all four groups have a by and large similar level of the Self-efficacy trait self esteem.

Self-efficacy trait self esteem with regard to Types of disease, Gender and Hereditary status:

F ratios for the interaction of disease types, gender, and hereditary status in diabetic and hypertensive patients are insignificant (F (1,50) = 0.64, *p*>.05). The mean score for diabetic male patients with heredity is 4.48 (SD =1.82), while the mean score for diabetic male patients without heredity is 5.58 (SD =2.45). There is a 1.10 mean difference between the two groups. For diabetic female patients with and without hereditary status, the mean values are 5.20 (SD = 2.15) and 7.18 (SD = 2.47), respectively. Between the two groups, the mean difference is 1.98, which is statistically insignificant. As shown in Table 152 and chart 133, the mean score of male hypertension patients with heredity is 5.00 (SD =1.82), while the mean score of male hypertension patients without hereditary status is 4.06 (SD = 1.47). The difference in average scores is 0.94, which is statistically insignificant. Female hypertension patients with heredity have a mean score of 4.74 (SD = 1.73), while female hypertension patients without heredity have a mean score of 4.04 (SD = 1.78). It is calculated that the mean difference is 0.70. In all eight groups of diabetic and hypertensive patients, the Self-efficacy trait self esteem is similar.

Table: 153

Showing ANOVA summary for the self-efficacy trait self-cognition.

Source	Type III Sum of Squares	df	Mean Square	F	Sig. Level
Diseases (A)	704.902	1	704.902	105.269	$p<.01$
Gender (B)	2.102	1	2.102	.314	NS
Heredity status (C)	74.822	1	74.822	11.174	$p<.01$
*Diseases * Gender* (A*B)	36.603	1	36.603	5.466	$p<.05$
*Diseases * Heredity status* (A*C)	8.122	1	8.122	1.213	NS
*Gender * Heredity status* (B*C)	4.623	1	4.623	.690	NS
*Diseases * Gender * Heredity status* (A*B*C)	2.723	1	2.723	.407	NS
Error	2624.900	392	6.696		
Total	43279.000	400			
Corrected Total	3458.797	399			

Table 154
Showing Mean, SD & Mean difference between patients of diabetes and hypertension for self-efficacy trait self-cognition.

Diseases (A)	N	Mean	SD	Mean Difference
Diabetes A1	200	11.30	1.73	2.65
Hypertension A2	200	8.65	3.29	

Figure no.134
Showing comparisons of mean scores between patients of diabetes and hypertension for self-efficacy trait self-cognition.

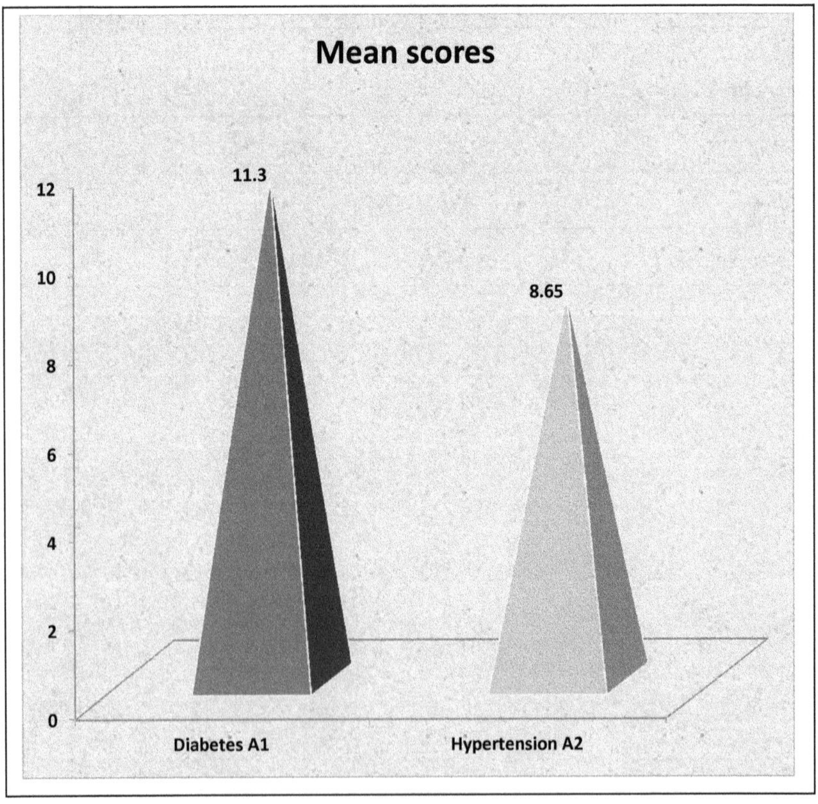

Table 155
Showing Mean, SD & Mean difference between male and female patients with diabetes and hypertension for self-efficacy trait self-cognition.

Gender (B)	N	Mean	SD	Mean Difference
Male B1	200	10.05	3.15	0.15
Female B2	200	9.90	2.72	

Figure no.135
Showing comparisons of mean scores between male and female patients with diabetes and hypertension for self-efficacy trait self-cognition.

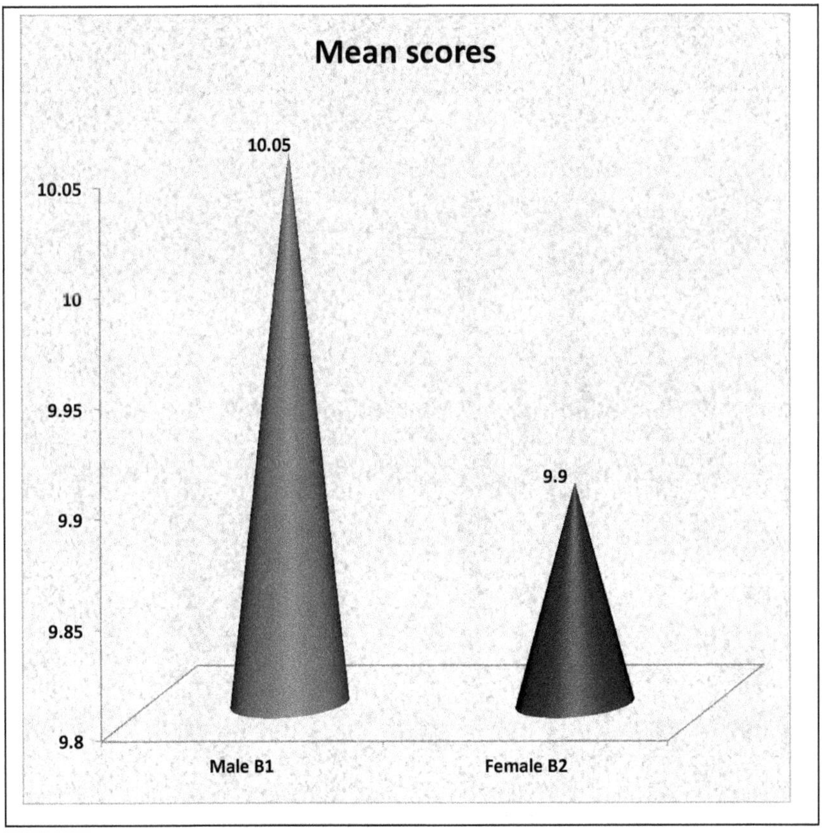

Table 156
Showing Mean, SD & Mean difference between patients with and without hereditary status for self-efficacy trait self-cognition.

Hereditary status (C)	N	Mean	SD	Mean Difference
Hereditary C1	200	10.41	3.06	0.87
Non-hereditary C2	200	9.54	2.76	

Figure no. 136
Showing comparisons of mean scores between patients with and without hereditary status for self-efficacy trait self-cognition.

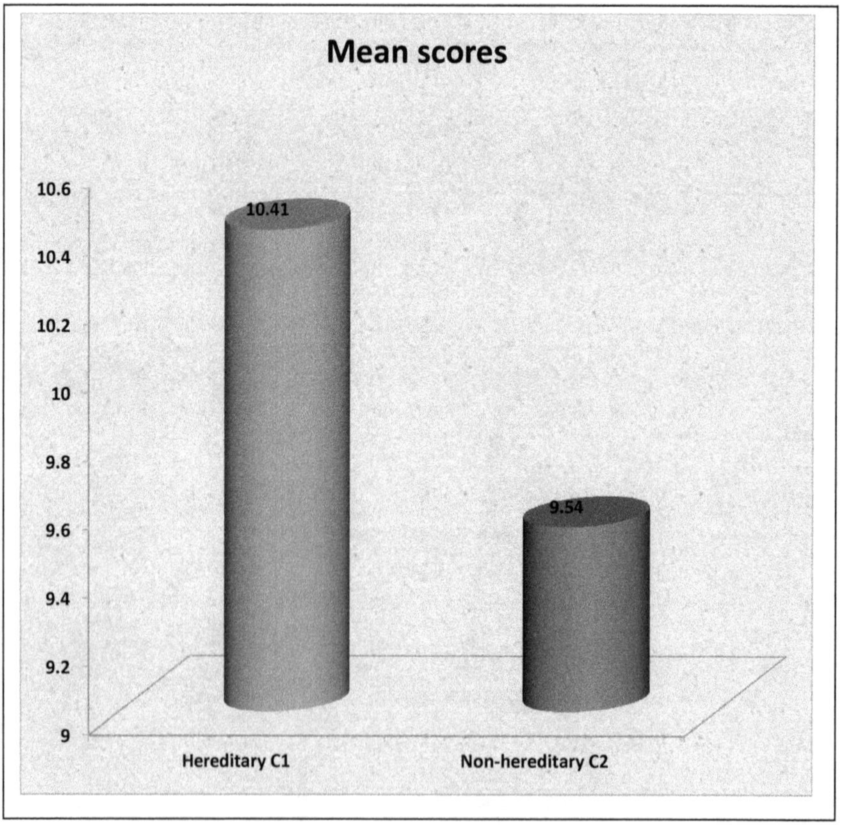

Table 157
Showing Mean, SD & Mean difference among interaction of diseases and Gender of patients with diabetes and hypertension for self-efficacy trait self-cognition.

Diseases (A)	Gender (B)	N	Mean	SD	Mean Difference
Diabetes A1	Male B1	100	11.68	1.86	0.75
	Female B2	100	10.93	1.50	
Hypertension A2	Male B1	100	8.42	3.33	0.46
	Female B2	100	8.88	3.24	

Figure no. 137
Showing comparisons of mean scores among interaction of diseases and Gender of patients with diabetes and hypertension for self-efficacy trait self-cognition.

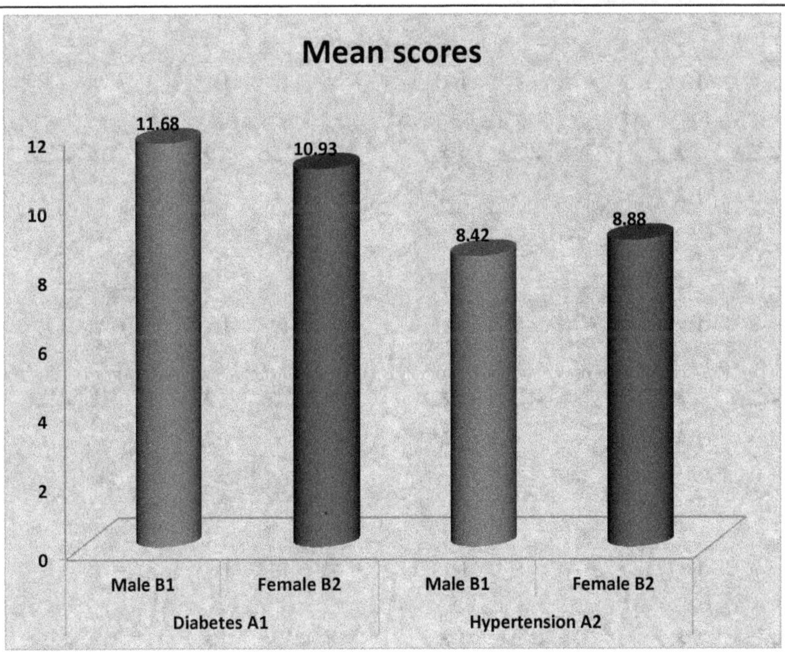

Table 158
Showing Mean, SD & Mean difference among interaction of diseases and hereditary status of patients for self-efficacy trait self-cognition.

Diseases (A)	Hereditary (C)	N	Mean	SD	Mean Difference
Diabetes A1	Hereditary *C1*	100	11.88	1.67	1.15
	Non- hereditary *C2*	100	10.73	1.60	
Hypertension A2	Hereditary *C1*	100	8.94	3.41	0.58
	Non- hereditary *C2*	100	8.36	3.15	

Figure no. 138
Showing comparisons of means cores among interaction of diseases and hereditary status of patients for self-efficacy trait self-cognition.

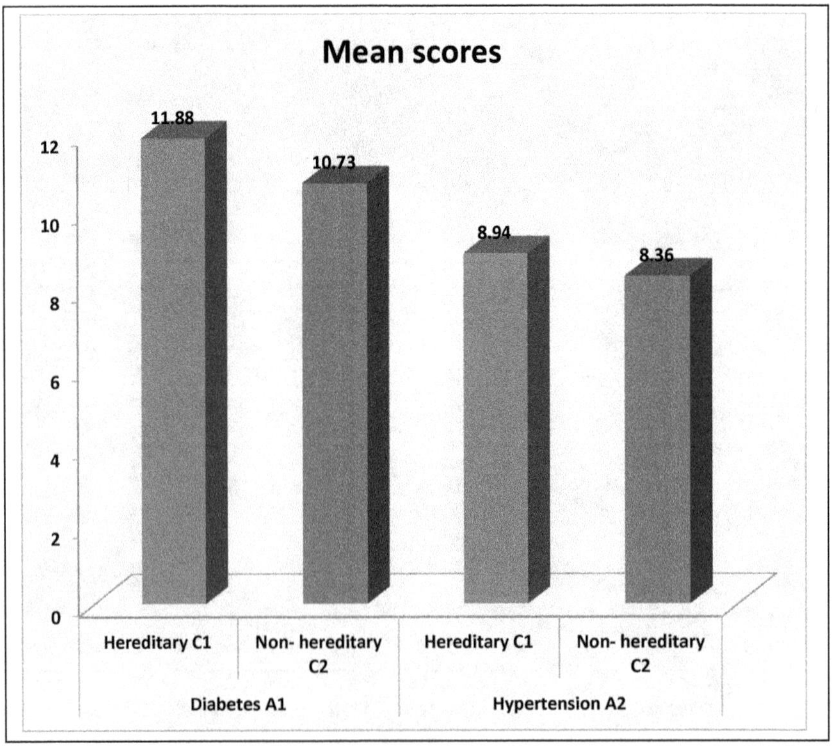

Table 159
Showing Mean, SD & Mean difference among interaction of Gender and hereditary status of patients for self-efficacy trait self-cognition.

Gender (B)	Hereditary status (C)	N	Mean	SD	Mean Difference
Male	Hereditary *C1*	100	10.59	3.18	1.08
	Non-hereditary *C2*	100	9.51	3.04	
Female	Hereditary *C1*	100	10.23	2.93	0.65
	Non-hereditary *C2*	100	9.58	2.46	

Figure no. 139
Showing comparisons of mean scores among interaction of Gender and hereditary status of patients for self-efficacy trait self-cognition.

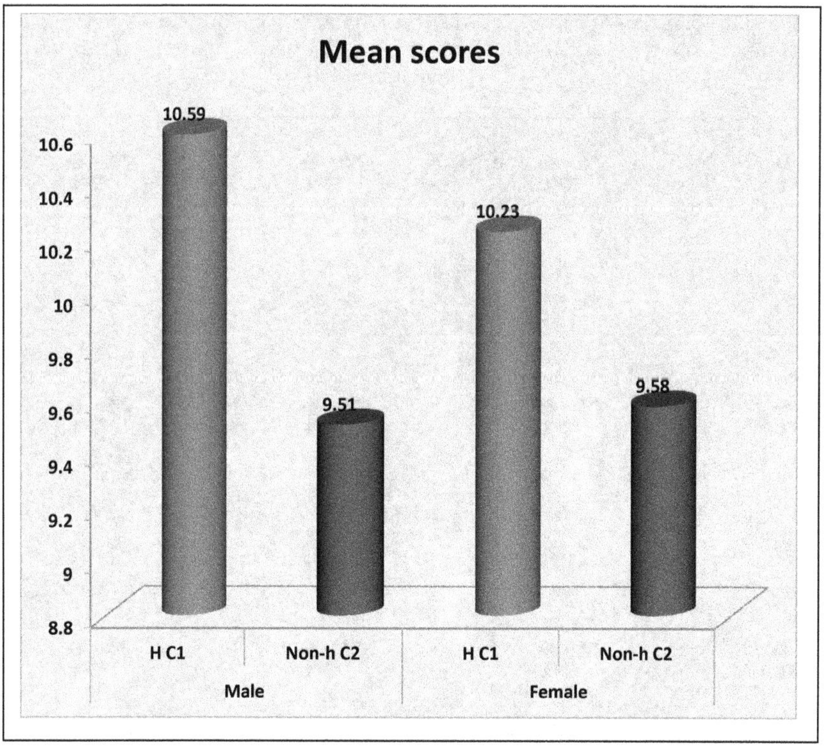

Table 160
Showing Mean, SD & Mean difference among interaction of diseases, gender and hereditary status of patients with diabetes and hypertension for self-efficacy trait self-cognition.

Diseases (A)	Gender (B)	Hereditary status (C)	N	Mean	SD	Mean Difference
Diabetes A1	*Male B1*	*Hereditary C1*	50	12.28	1.72	1.2
		Non- hereditary C2	50	11.08	1.82	
	Female B2	*Hereditary C1*	50	11.48	1.54	1.1
		Non- hereditary C2	50	10.38	1.25	
Hypertension A2	*Male B1*	*Hereditary C1*	50	8.90	3.42	0.96
		Non- hereditary C2	50	7.94	3.20	
	Female B2	*Hereditary C1*	50	8.98	3.44	0.20
		Non- hereditary C2	50	8.78	3.06	

Figure no. 140
Showing comparisons of mean scores among interaction of diseases, gender and hereditary status of patients with diabetes and hypertension for self-efficacy trait self-cognition.

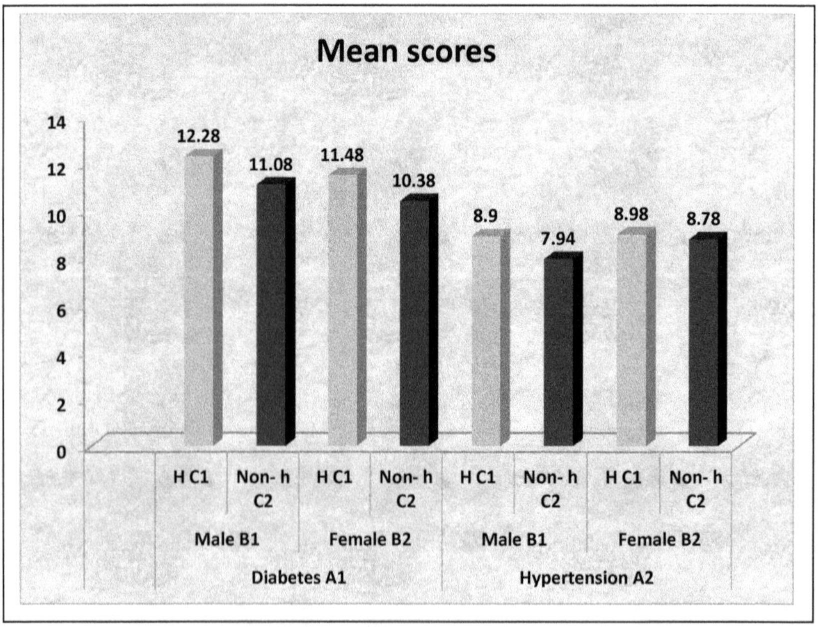

Main Effect:

Self-efficacy trait self-cognition with regard to Types of disease:

A significant F value was exposed when the F test was used to study the influence of disease like diabetic and hypertension on Self-efficacy trait self-cognition. (F (1,200) = 105.16, *p*<.01). Table no.154 and 134 present that mean scores of diabetic and hypertension patients are 11.30 (SD = 1.73) and 8.65 (SD = 3.29) respectively and the difference between two means is 2.65. According to the findings diabetic patients have higher Self-efficacy trait self cognition than hypertensive patients.

Self-efficacy trait self cognition with regard to Gender:

Tables 153 and 134 show the F value and mean score for the gender of diabetic and hypertensive patients, with the mean difference and F ratio reported to be non-significant F(1,200) = .31, *p*>.05. The mean value obtained by male patient is 10.05 (SD = 3.15), while female patients have 9.90 (SD = 2.72), with a mean difference of 0.15 between the two groups. This mean difference (Table No.155 & Chart No.135) indicated that both groups have a nominal mean difference. It can be concluded that both male and female patients with diabetes and hypertension have equal Self-efficacy trait self cognition.

Self-efficacy trait self-cognition with regard to Hereditary status:

The calculated F value of Hereditary status was F (1, 200) = 11.17, which was significant at .01. Table No. 56 and chart no. 136 highlighted that mean score of patients with hereditary status is 10.41 (SD=3.06), whereas a mean score of patients without hereditary status is 9.37 (SD=2.76) and the difference between mean scores was 0.87 which is negligible. It was concluded that hereditary status had slight impact on Self-efficacy trait self-cognition.

Interaction Effect

Self-efficacy trait self-cognition with regard to Types of disease and Gender:

The primary goal of the study was to determine whether disease type and gender of patients are interacting or not, on Self-efficacy factor self cognition. Table no.153 showed that F value for interaction of Types of disease and Gender is also observed to be significant F (1,100) = 5.46, *p*< .05. By the same point of view Table no.157 and chart no.137 displayed that mean scores of male and female diabetic patients are

(M=11.68,SD= 1.86) and (M = 10.93, SD = 1.50) respectively, whereas the mean difference of both the group of patients is 0.75. As the mean scores of male and female hypertensive patients are (M =8.42, SD = 3.33) and (M = 8.88, SD = 3.24), respectively, the mean difference of both groups of patients is 0.46. According to the mean difference between the four groups, all the groups of patients have different opinion towards Self-efficacy trait self cognition.

Self-efficacy trait self cognition with regard to Types of disease and Hereditary status:

The F (1,100) =1.21 for Types of disease and Hereditary status, which was non-significant (p>.05). The mean value of diabetic patients with hereditary status is 11.88 (SD = 1.67) in table 158 and chart 138, while the mean score for diabetic patients without hereditary status is 10.73(SD =1.60). The mean difference is 1.15, whereas the mean of hypertension patients with hereditary status is 8.94 (SD = 3.41) and mean score of hypertension patients non hereditary status is 8.36 (SD = 3.15), the difference between two means is 0.58. It can be concluded that all four groups have a similar level of Self-efficacy trait self cognition.

Self-efficacy trait self cognition with regard to Gender and Hereditary status:

The calculated value of the interaction between gender and heredity is found to be F(1,100) = 0.69, which is non-significant. The mean value of male patients with hereditary status is 10.59 (SD = 3.18), while the mean value of male patients without hereditary status is 9.51 (SD =3.04), with a 1.08 difference in mean scores .Hereditary status of female patients have a mean score of 10.23 (SD = 2.93), while non hereditary status of female patients have a mean score of 9.58 (SD = 2.46). The mean value difference is 0.65. Almost all four groups have an insignificant mean difference. As a result, all four groups of patients highlighted similar levels of Self-efficacy trait self cognition.

Self-efficacy trait self cognition with regard to Types of disease, Gender and Hereditary status:

Diabetic and hypertensive patients' F ratios for disease types, gender, and hereditary status are insignificant (F (1,50) = 0.40, p>.05). Diabetic male patients with heredity have a mean score of 12.28 (SD =1.72), whereas diabetic male patients without heredity have a mean score of 11.08 (SD =1.82). Between the two groups, there is a 1.2 mean difference. Again, the mean value for diabetic female patients with and without hereditary status is 11.48 (SD = 1.54) and 10.38 (SD = 1.25) respectively. The mean difference between the two groups is 1.1. As shown in Table 160 and chart 140, the mean score of male hypertension patients with heredity is 8.90 (SD =3.42), while the mean score of male hypertension patients without hereditary status is 7.94 (SD = 3.20)..The difference in average scores is 0.96, which is statistically insignificant. Similarly, the mean score of female hypertension patients with heredity is 8.98 (SD = 3.44), while the mean score of female hypertension patients without heredity is 8.78 (SD = 3.06). The mean difference is calculated to be 0.20. The Self-efficacy trait self cognition is by and large similar in all eight groups of diabetic and hypertensive patients.

Suicidal Tendency

Table: 161

Showing ANOVA summary for the suicidal tendency factor Personality characteristics.

Source	Type III Sum of Squares	df	Mean Square	F	Sig. Level
Diseases (A)	7752.803	1	7752.803	130.983	$p<.01$
Gender (B)	26.523	1	26.523	.448	NS
Heredity status (C)	126.563	1	126.563	2.138	NS
Diseases * *Gender* (A*B)	13.323	1	13.323	.225	NS
Diseases * *Heredity status* (A*C)	430.563	1	430.563	7.274	$p<.01$
Gender * *Heredity status* (B*C)	140.423	1	140.423	2.372	NS
Diseases * *Gender* * *Heredity status* (A*B*C)	5.522	1	5.522	.093	NS
Error	23202.220	392	59.189		
Total	230837.000	400			
Corrected Total	31697.938	399			

Levene's Test of Equality of Error Variances[a]

Dependent Variable: ST1

F	df1	df2	Sig.
19.122	7	392	.000

Tests the null hypothesis that the error variance of the dependent variable is equal across groups.

a. Design: Intercept + Diseases + Gender + HS + Diseases * Gender + Diseases * HS + Gender * HS + Diseases * Gender * HS

Table 162
Showing Mean, SD & Mean difference between patients of diabetes and hypertension for suicidal tendency factor Personality characteristics.

Diseases (A)	N	Mean	SD	Mean Difference
Diabetes A1	200	17.91	4.74	8.80
Hypertension A2	200	26.71	9.88	

Figure no.141
Showing comparisons of mean scores between patients of diabetes and hypertension for suicidal tendency factor Personality characteristics.

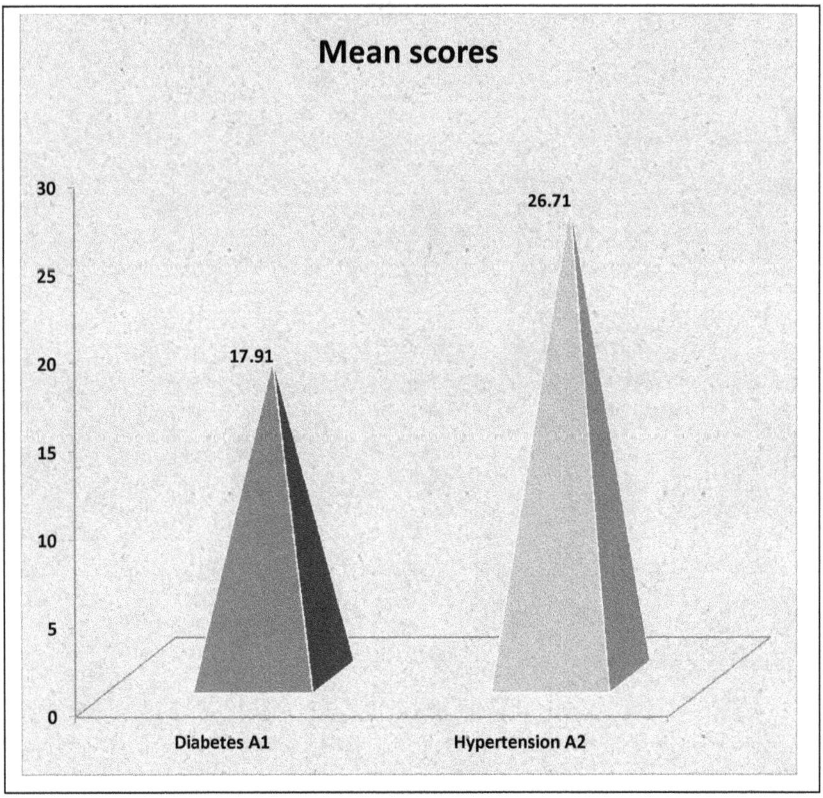

Table 163
Showing Mean, SD & Mean difference between male and female patients with diabetes and hypertension for suicidal tendency factor Personality characteristics.

Gender (B)	N	Mean	SD	Mean Difference
Male B1	200	22.57	8.56	0.52
Female B2	200	22.05	9.26	

Figure no.142
Showing comparisons of mean scores between male and female patients with diabetes and hypertension for suicidal tendency factor Personality characteristics.

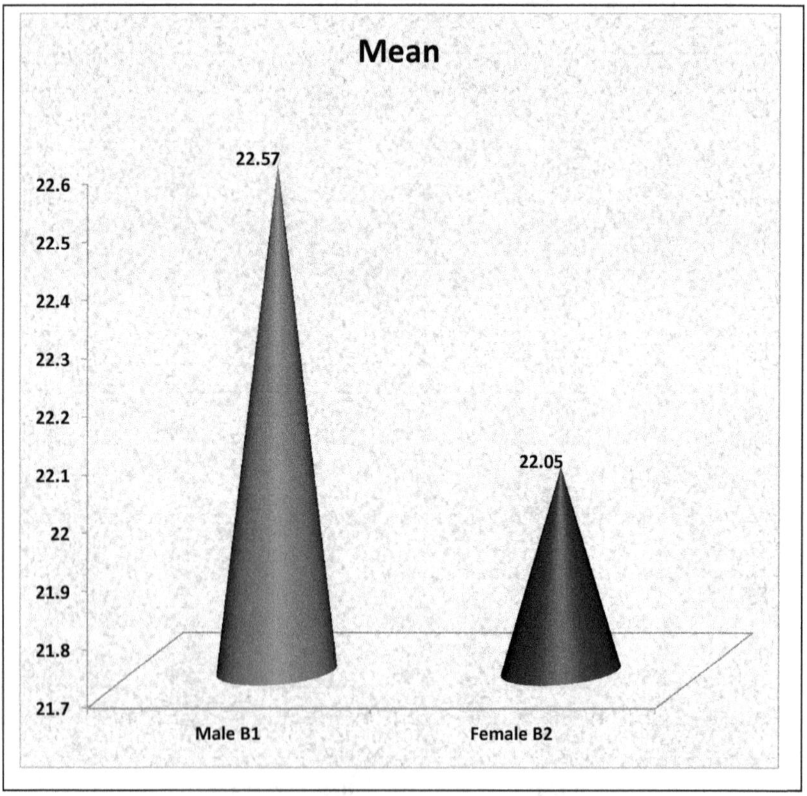

Table 164
Showing Mean, SD & Mean difference between patients with and without hereditary status for suicidal tendency factor Personality characteristics.

Hereditary status (C)	N	Mean	SD	Mean Difference
Hereditary C1	200	21.75	9.65	1.12
Non-hereditary C2	200	22.87	8.08	

Figure no. 143
Showing comparisons of mean scores between patients with and without hereditary status for suicidal tendency factor Personality characteristics.

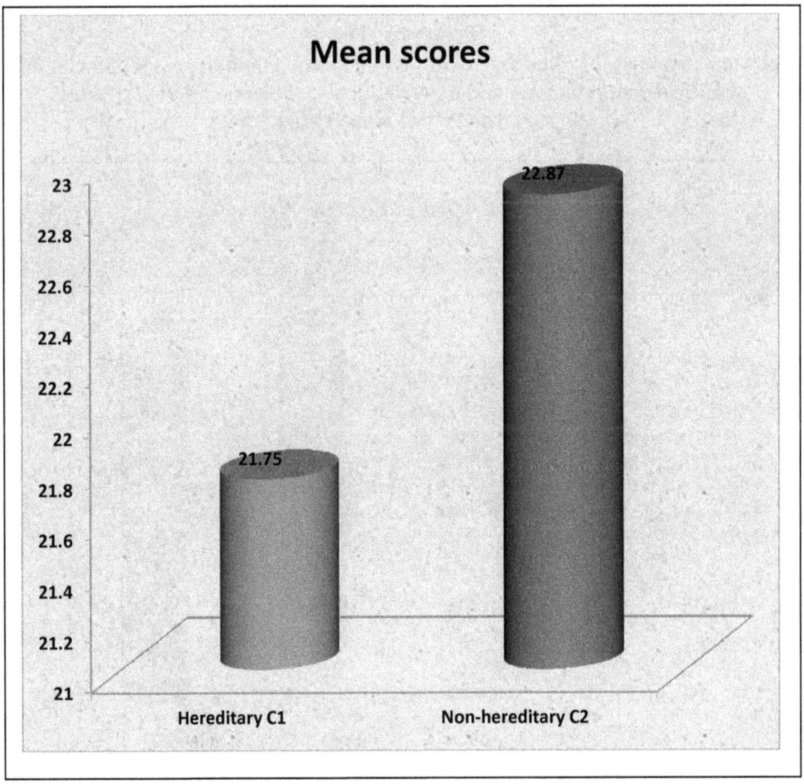

Table 165
Showing Mean, SD & Mean difference among interaction of diseases and Gender of patients with diabetes and hypertension for suicidal tendency factor Personality characteristics.

Diseases (A)	Gender (B)	N	Mean	SD	Mean Difference
Diabetes A1	Male B1	100	18.35	4.47	0.88
	Female B2	100	17.47	4.98	
Hypertension A2	Male B1	100	26.79	9.55	0.15
	Female B2	100	26.64	10.25	

Figure no. 144
Showing comparisons of mean scores among interaction of diseases and Gender of patients with diabetes and hypertension for suicidal tendency factor Personality characteristics.

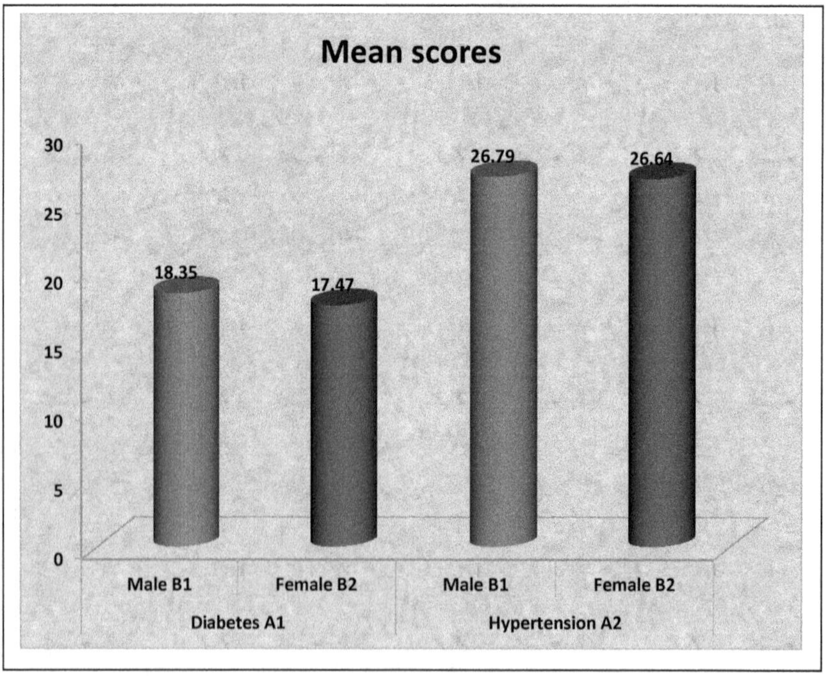

Table 166
Showing Mean, SD & Mean difference among interaction of diseases and hereditary status of patients for suicidal tendency factor Personality characteristics.

Diseases (A)	Hereditary (C)	N	Mean	SD	Mean Difference
Diabetes A1	Hereditary *C1*	100	16.31	3.97	3.2
	Non- hereditary *C2*	100	19.51	4.93	
Hypertension A2	Hereditary *C1*	100	27.19	10.57	0.95
	Non- hereditary *C2*	100	26.24	9.17	

Figure no. 145
Showing comparisons of mean scores among interaction of diseases and hereditary status of patients for suicidal tendency factor Personality characteristics.

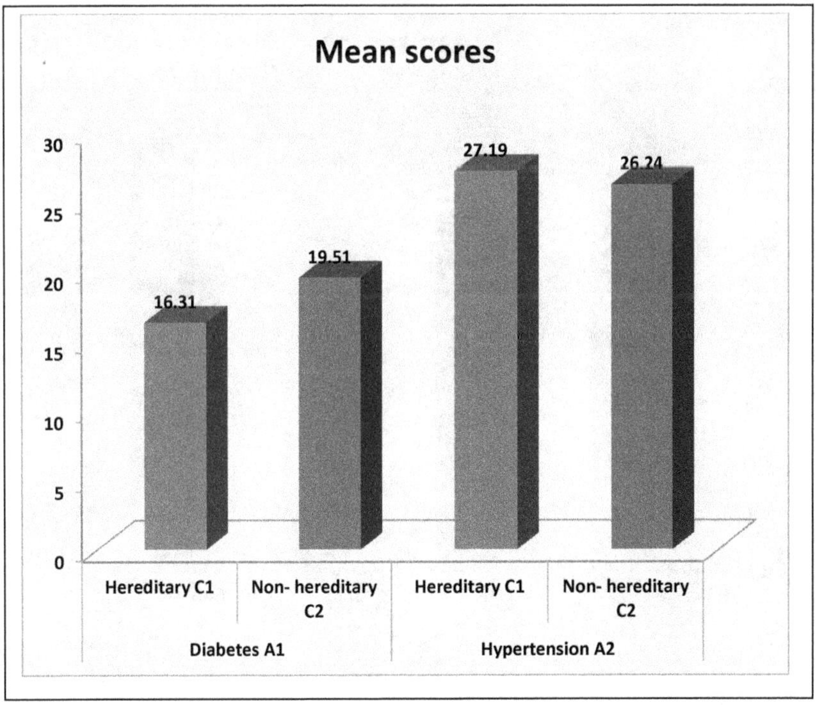

Table 167
Showing Mean, SD & Mean difference among interaction of Gender and hereditary status of patients for suicidal tendency factor Personality characteristics.

Gender (B)	Hereditary status (C)	N	Mean	SD	Mean Difference
Male	Hereditary *C1*	100	22.60	9.13	0.06
	Non-hereditary *C2*	100	22.54	7.99	
Female	Hereditary *C1*	100	20.90	10.13	2.31
	Non-hereditary *C2*	100	23.21	8.19	

Figure no. 146
Showing comparisons of mean scores among interaction of Gender and hereditary status of patients for suicidal tendency factor Personality characteristics.

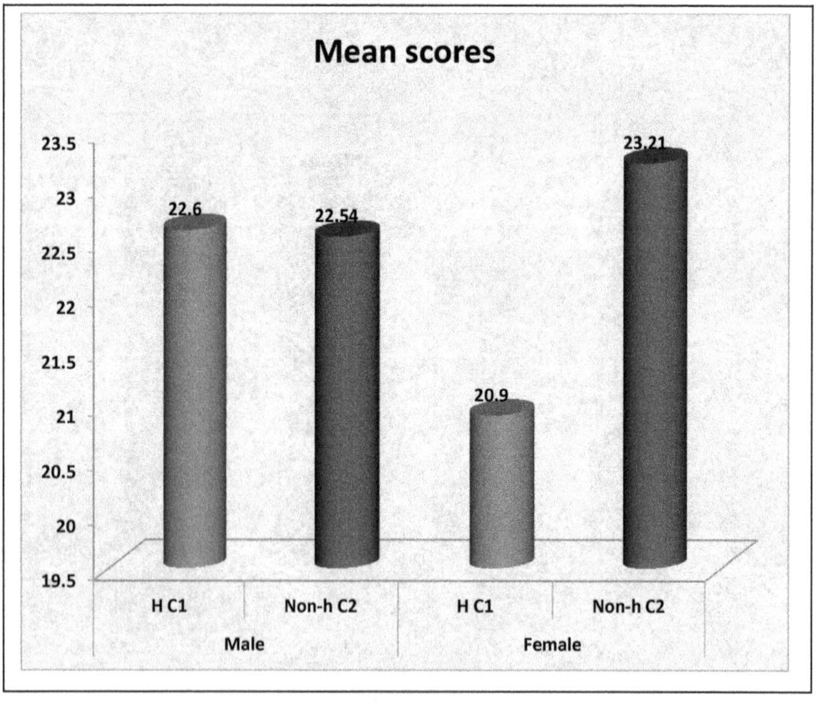

Table 168

Showing Mean, SD & Mean difference among interaction of diseases, gender and hereditary status of patients with diabetes and hypertension for suicidal tendency factor Personality characteristics.

Diseases (A)	Gender (B)	Hereditary status (C)	N	Mean	SD	Mean Difference
Diabetes A1	*Male B1*	*Hereditary C1*	50	17.46	4.16	1.78
		Non- hereditary C2	50	19.24	4.63	
	Female B2	*Hereditary C1*	50	15.16	3.44	4.62
		Non- hereditary C2	50	19.78	5.24	
Hypertension A2	*Male B1*	*Hereditary C1*	50	27.74	9.85	1.90
		Non- hereditary C2	50	25.84	9.25	
	Female B2	*Hereditary C1*	50	26.64	11.32	00
		Non- hereditary C2	50	26.64	9.18	

Figure no. 147

Showing comparisons of mean scores among interaction of diseases, gender and hereditary status of patients with diabetes and hypertension for suicidal tendency factor Personality characteristics.

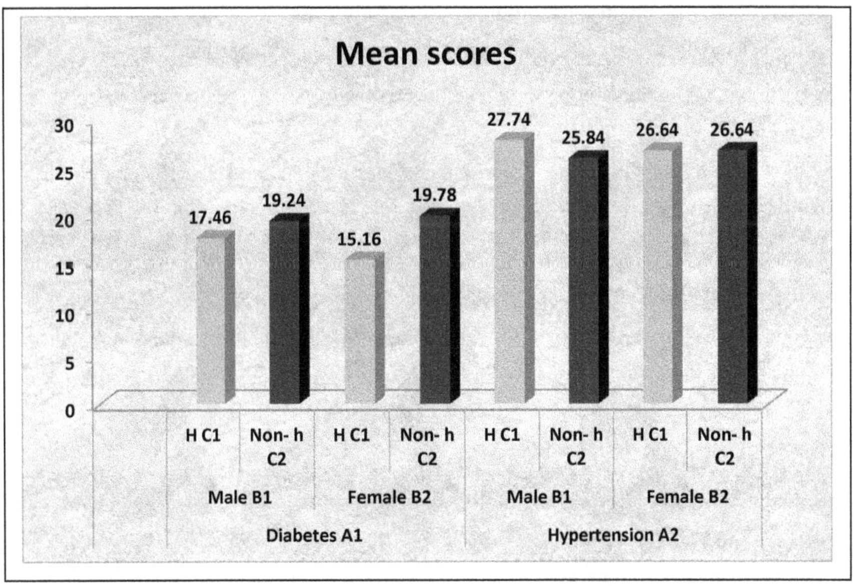

Main Effect:

Suicidal tendency factor Personality characteristics with regard to Types of disease:

The first main effect was reported significant among the diabetes and hypertension for suicidal tendency factor personality characteristics. The significance of F (1, 200) = 130.98, $p<.01$. (Table no. 161) was underlined. According to Tables 162 and table 141, diabetes and hypertension patients have mean scores of 17.91 (SD = 4.74) and 26.71 (SD = 9.88), respectively, with an 8.80 difference between them. According to the findings, hypertensive patients have more suicidal tendency factor personality characteristics than diabetic patients.

Suicidal tendency factor personality characteristics with regard to Gender

The F value and mean score for the gender of patients with diabetes and hypertension are shown in Tables 161 and 142, with the mean difference and F ratio reported as non-significant F(1,200) = 0.44, $p >.05$. Male patients have a mean value of 22.57 (SD = 8.56), while female patients have a mean value of 22.05 (SD = 9.26), resulting in a mean difference of 0.52 between the two groups. This mean difference (Table No.163 & Chart No. 142) indicated that there is a nominal mean difference between the two groups. According to the above findings, both female and male patients have the similar suicidal tendency factor personality characteristics.

Suicidal tendency factor personality characteristics with regard to Hereditary status:

Hereditary status have a calculated value of F (1, 200) = 2.13 for the third main effect hereditary status which was insignificant at $p>.05$. In table No. 164 and chart No.143, patients with hereditary status have a mean score of 21.75 (SD=9.65), while patients without hereditary status have a mean score of 22.87 (SD=8.08), a significant mean difference of 1.12. Patients with heredity status and without heredity status have more or less equal suicidal tendency factor personality characteristics.

Interaction Effect

Suicidal tendency factor Personality characteristics with regard to Types of disease and Gender:

As seen from table that interaction of disease and gender was not highlighted significant for personal characteristics of patients. Table no.161 showed that the F value for the interaction of disease types and gender, F (1,100) =0.22, *p*>.05. The mean scores of male and female diabetic patients are (M=18.35, SD= 4.47) and (M = 17.47, SD = 4.98) respectively, with a mean difference of 0.88 between the two groups of patients, as shown in table 165 and chart 144. Because their mean scores are (M =26.79 SD=9.55) and (M=26.64 SD=10.25), respectively, the mean difference between male and female hypertensive patients is 0.15. It was observed that the mean difference among the four groups, of patients have similar suicidal tendency trait personality characteristics.

Suicidal tendency factor personality characteristics with regard to Types of disease and Hereditary status:

Disease types and hereditary status had a significant interaction F (1,100) =7.27, (p<.01). Diabetic patients with hereditary status have a mean score of 16.31 (SD = 3.97), while diabetic patients without hereditary status have a mean score of 19.51 (SD=4.93), as shown in table 166 and chart 145. The mean difference is 3.2. The mean score of hypertension patients with hereditary status is 27.19 (SD = 10.57), and the mean score of hypertension patients without hereditary status is 26.27 (SD = 9.17), with a statistically significant mean difference of 0.95. Each of the four groups has different level of suicidal tendency factor personality characteristics.

Suicidal tendency factor personality characteristics with regard to Gender and Hereditary status:

The calculated value of the interaction between gender and heredity is depicted non-significant F(1,100) = 2.37, *p*>.05.The mean score for male patients with hereditary status is 22.60 (SD = 9.13), while the mean score for male patients without hereditary status is 22.54 (SD =7.99), and 0.06 is their difference in mean scores. Female hereditary patients have a mean score of 20.90 (SD = 10.13), while non-hereditary patients have a mean score of 23.21 (SD = 8.19). The mean value difference is 2.31. Almost all four groups have the negligible mean difference. As a result, all four groups of patients had similar levels of the suicidal personality characteristics.

Suicidal tendency factor Personality characteristics with regard to Types of disease, Gender and Hereditary status:

In diabetic and hypertensive patients, F ratio for disease types, gender, and hereditary status is insignificant (F (1,50) = 0.93, *p*>.05). Diabetic male patients with heredity have a mean score of 17.46 (SD =4.16), while diabetic male patients without heredity have a mean score of 19.24 (SD =4.63). The mean difference between the two groups is 1.78. The mean values for diabetic female patients with and without hereditary status are 15.16 (SD = 3.44) and 19.78 (SD = 5.24), respectively. The mean difference between the two groups is 4.62, which is statistically significant. The mean score of male hypertension patients with heredity is 27.74 (SD = 9.85), as shown in Table 168 and chart 147, while the mean score of male hypertension patients without hereditary status is 25.84 (SD = 9.25). The mean score difference is 1.90, which is statistically insignificant. Female hypertension patients with hereditary status have a mean score of 26.64 (SD = 11.32), whereas female hypertension patients without hereditary status have a mean score of 26.64 (SD = 9.18). The mean difference is calculated to be 0.70. Suicidal tendency factor personality characteristics have by and large similar effect on all eight groups of diabetic and hypertensive patients.

Table: 169

Showing ANOVA summary for the suicidal tendency factor Emotional disturbance.

Source	Type III Sum of Squares	df	Mean Square	F	Sig. Level
***Diseases* (A)**	6146.560	1	6146.560	134.578	p<.01
***Gender* (B)**	457.960	1	457.960	10.027	p<.01
***Heredity status* (C)**	125.440	1	125.440	2.746	NS
***Diseases * Gender* (A*B)**	595.360	1	595.360	13.035	p<.01
***Diseases * Heredity status* (A*C)**	57.760	1	57.760	1.265	NS
***Gender * Heredity status* (B*C)**	.160	1	.160	.004	NS
***Diseases * Gender * Heredity status* (A*B*C)**	4.840	1	4.840	.106	NS
Error	17903.760	392	45.673		
Total	245816.000	400			
Corrected Total	25291.840	399			

Levene's Test of Equality of Error Variances[a]

Dependent Variable: ST2

F	df1	df2	Sig.
25.141	7	392	.000

Tests the null hypothesis that the error variance of the dependent variable is equal across groups.

a. Design: Intercept + Diseases + Gender + HS + Diseases * Gender + Diseases * HS + Gender * HS + Diseases * Gender * HS

Table 170
Showing Mean, SD & Mean difference between patients of diabetes and hypertension for suicidal tendency factor Emotional disturbance.

Diseases (A)	N	Mean	SD	Mean Difference
Diabetes A1	200	19.56	4.10	7.84
Hypertension A2	200	27.40	8.90	

Figure no.148
Showing comparisons of mean scores between patients of diabetes and hypertension for suicidal tendency factor Emotional disturbance.

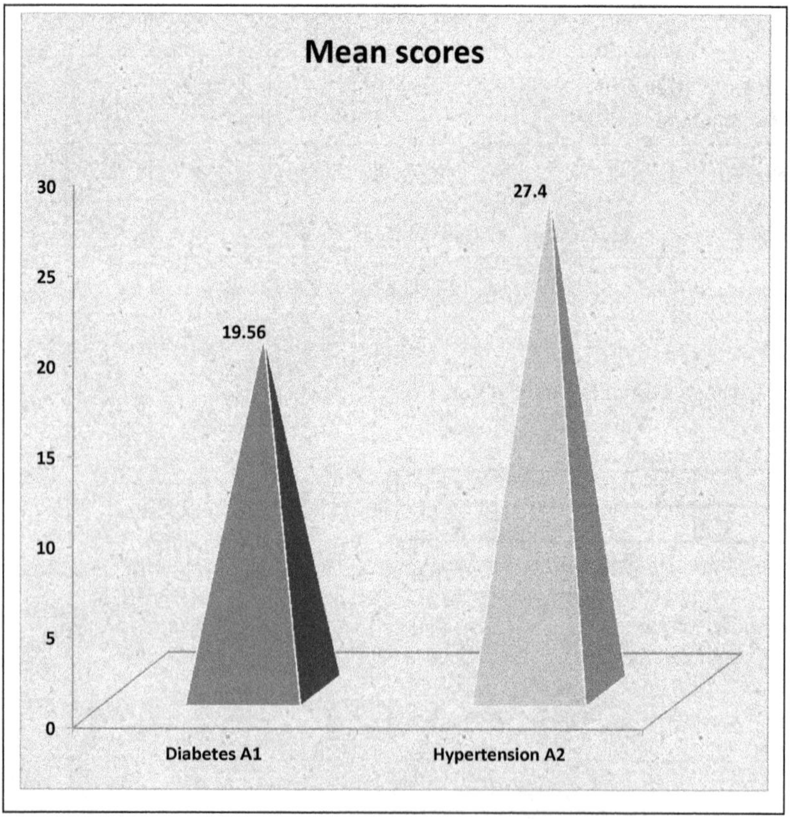

Table 171
Showing Mean, SD & Mean difference between male and female patients with diabetes and hypertension for suicidal tendency factor Emotional disturbance.

Gender (B)	N	Mean	SD	Mean Difference
Male B1	200	22.41	7.14	2.14
Female B2	200	24.55	8.58	

Figure no.149
Showing comparisons of mean scores between male and female patients with diabetes and hypertension for suicidal tendency factor Emotional disturbance.

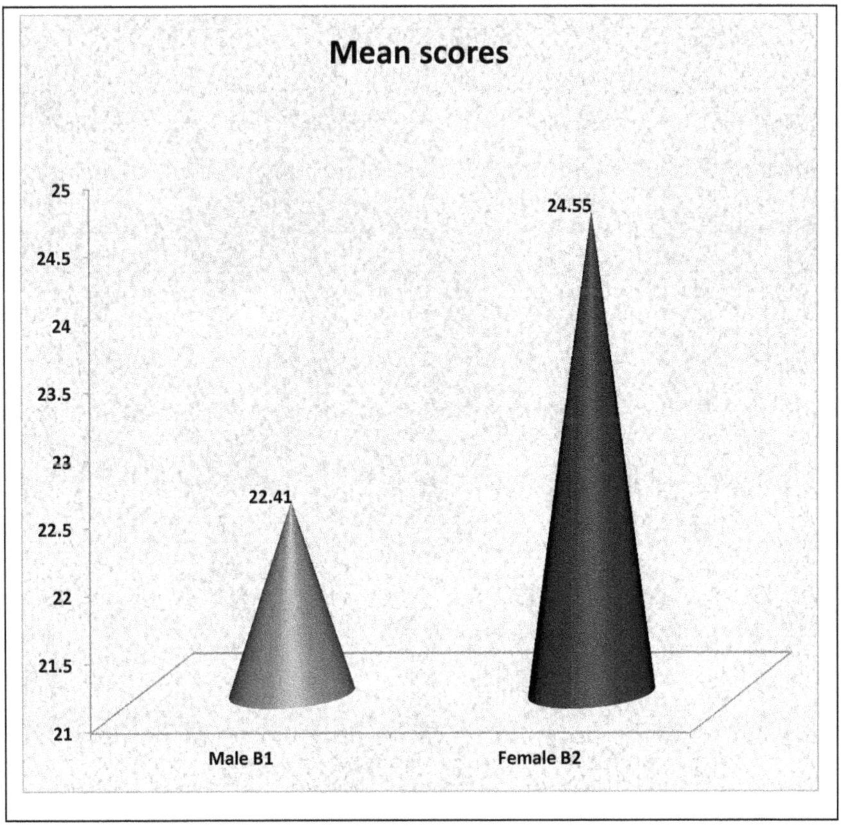

Table 172
Showing Mean, SD & Mean difference between patients with and without hereditary status for suicidal tendency factor Emotional disturbance.

Hereditary status (C)	N	Mean	SD	Mean Difference
Hereditary C1	200	22.92	8.04	1.12
Non-hereditary C2	200	24.04	7.85	

Figure no. 150
Showing comparisons of mean scores between patients with and without hereditary status for suicidal tendency factor Emotional disturbance.

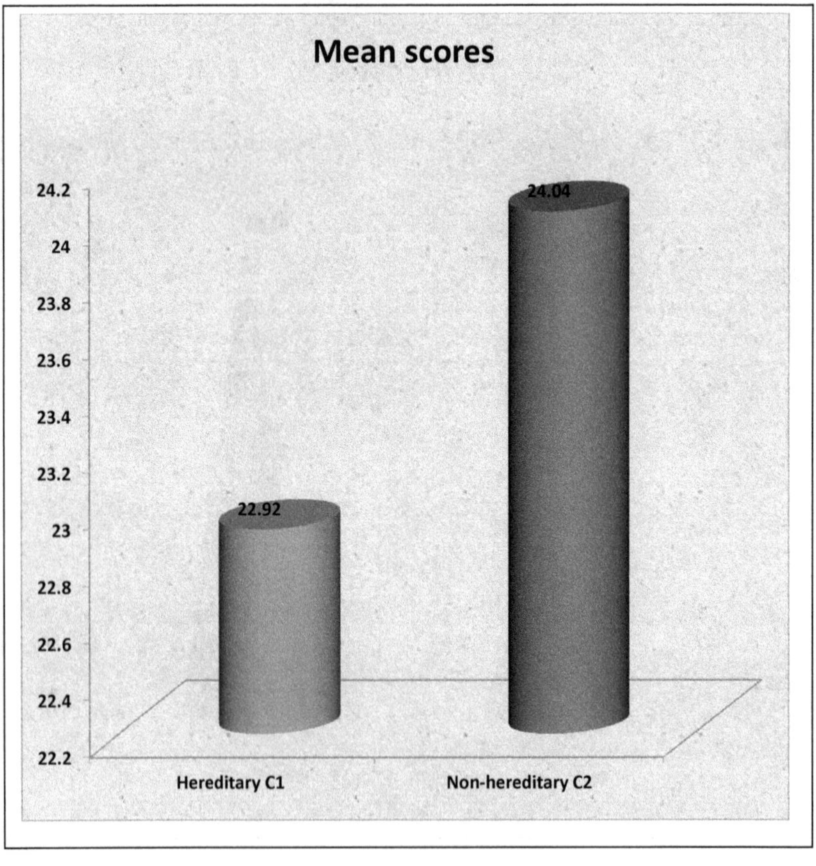

Table 173
Showing Mean, SD & Mean difference among interaction of diseases and Gender of patients with diabetes and hypertension for suicidal tendency factor Emotional disturbance.

Diseases (A)	Gender (B)	N	Mean	SD	Mean Difference
Diabetes A1	**Male B1**	100	19.71	4.03	0.30
	Female B2	100	19.41	4.19	
Hypertension A2	**Male B1**	100	25.11	8.45	4.58
	Female B2	100	29.69	8.79	

Figure no. 151
Showing comparisons of mean scores among interaction of diseases and Gender of patients with diabetes and hypertension for suicidal tendency factor Emotional disturbance.

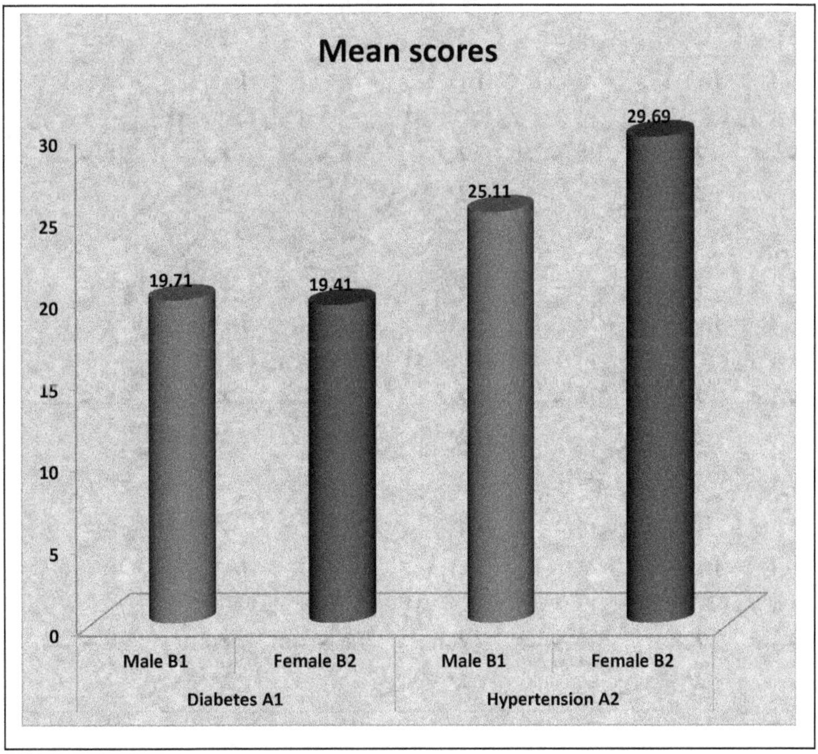

Table 174
Showing Mean, SD & Mean difference among interaction of diseases and hereditary status of patients for suicidal tendency factor Emotional disturbance.

Diseases (A)	Hereditary (C)	N	Mean	SD	Mean Difference
Diabetes A1	Hereditary *C1*	100	18.62	3.70	1.88
	Non- hereditary *C2*	100	20.50	4.29	
Hypertension A2	Hereditary *C1*	100	27.22	8.89	0.36
	Non- hereditary *C2*	100	27.58	8.95	

Figure no. 152
Showing comparisons of mean scores among interaction of diseases and hereditary status of patients for suicidal tendency factor Emotional disturbance.

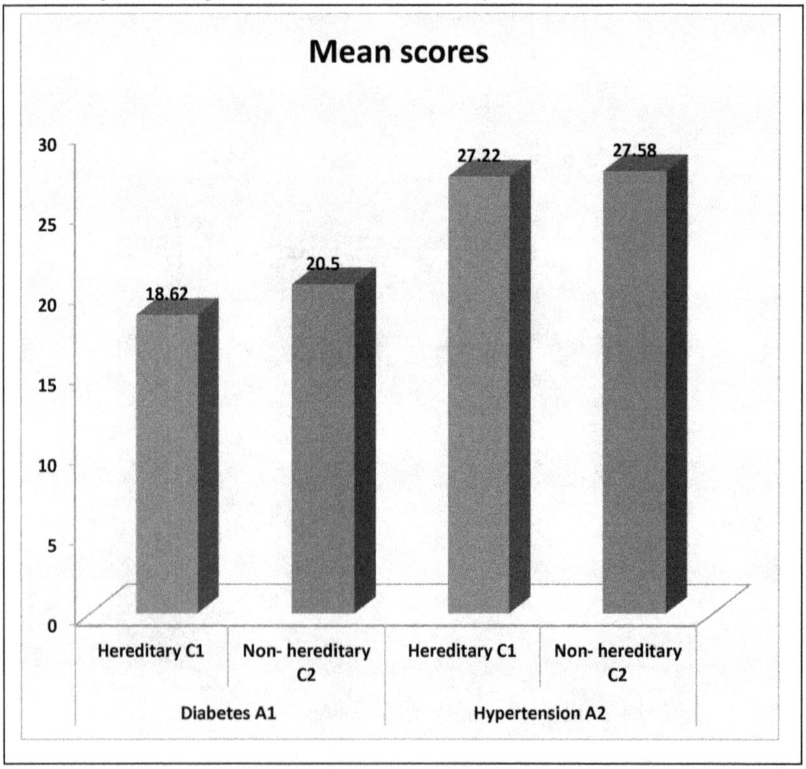

Table 175
Showing Mean, SD & Mean difference among interaction of Gender and hereditary status of patients for suicidal tendency factor Emotional disturbance.

Gender (B)	Hereditary status (C)	N	Mean	SD	Mean Difference
Male	Hereditary *C1*	100	21.87	7.39	1.1
	Non-hereditary *C2*	100	22.95	6.87	
Female	Hereditary *C1*	100	23.97	8.55	1.16
	Non-hereditary *C2*	100	25.13	8.62	

Figure no. 153
Showing comparisons of mean scores among interaction of Gender and hereditary status of patients for suicidal tendency factor Emotional disturbance.

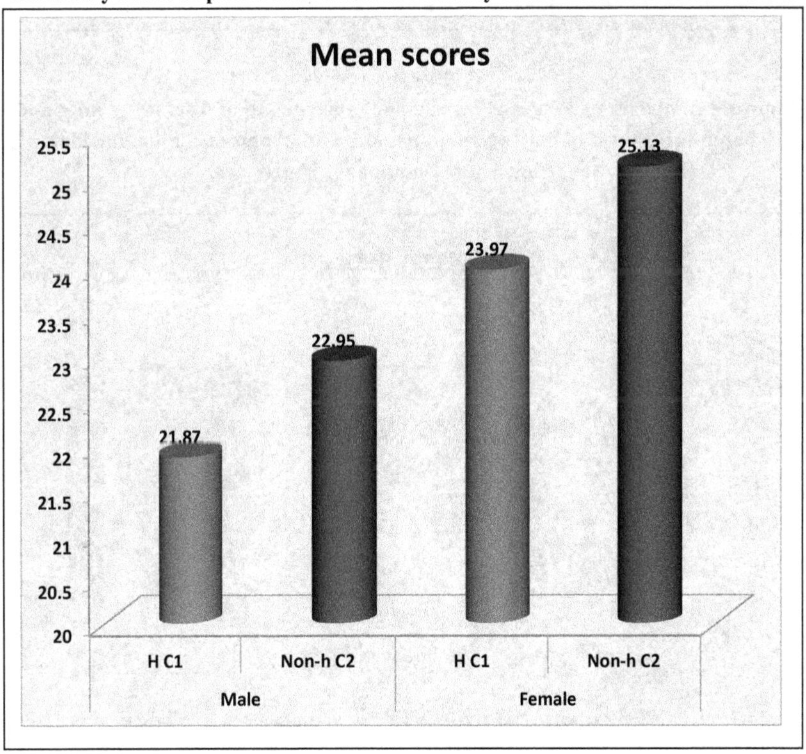

Table 176
Showing Mean, SD & Mean difference among interaction of diseases, gender and hereditary status of patients with diabetes and hypertension for suicidal tendency factor Emotional disturbance.

Diseases (A)	Gender (B)	Hereditary status (C)	N	Mean	SD	Mean Difference
Diabetes A1	*Male B1*	*Hereditary C1*	50	18.68	4.20	2.06
		Non- hereditary C2	50	20.74	3.60	
	Female B2	*Hereditary C1*	50	18.56	3.15	1.70
		Non- hereditary C2	50	20.26	4.91	
Hypertension A2	*Male B1*	*Hereditary C1*	50	25.06	8.49	0.10
		Non- hereditary C2	50	25.16	8.50	
	Female B2	*Hereditary C1*	50	29.38	8.84	0.62
		Non- hereditary C2	50	30.00	8.81	

Figure no. 154
Showing comparisons of mean scores among interaction of diseases, gender and hereditary status of patients with diabetes and hypertension for suicidal tendency factor Emotional disturbance.

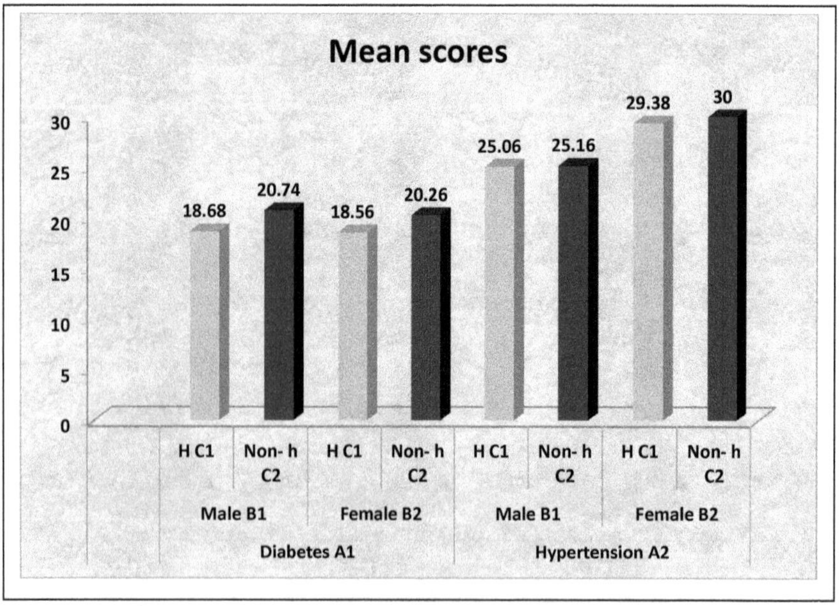

Main Effect:

Suicidal tendency factor Emotional disturbance with regard to Types of disease:

When the F test is used to investigate the effect of disease type on suicidal tendency factor emotional disturbance in diabetic and hypertensive patients, the F value is significant F(1, 200) =134.57, *p*>.01. The mean scores for diabetic and hypertension patients are 19.56 (SD = 4.10) and 27.40 (SD = 8.90), respectively. The difference between the two means is 7.84, according to Tables 170 and Chart 148. Hypertensive patients were more emotionally disturbed in terms of suicidal tendency.

Suicidal tendency factor emotional disturbance with regard to Gender:

Tables 169 and 149 displays the F value and mean score for gender of diabetic and hypertensive patients, with the mean difference and F ratio reported as significant F(1,200) =10.02, *p*<.01. The mean value for male patients is 22.41 (SD = 7.14), while the average value for female patients is 24.55 (SD = 8.58), resulting in a mean difference of 2.14 between the two groups. This mean difference (Table No.171 & Chart No. 149) indicated that there is a significant mean difference between the two groups. According to the findings, both female have more emotional disturbance.

Suicidal tendency factor emotional disturbance with regard to Hereditary status:

The calculated F value for hereditary status was F (1, 200) =2.74, which was insignificant at *p*>.05. Patients with hereditary status have a mean score of 22.92(SD=8.04) in Table No. 172 and chart No.150, while patients without hereditary status have a mean score of 24.04(SD=7.85), and their mean difference of 1.12. Suicidal tendency factor emotional disturbance is similar in patients with and without heredity.

Interaction Effect

Suicidal tendency factor Emotional disturbance with regard to Types of disease and Gender:

The study's main goal was to observe if male and female diabetic patients, as well as male and female hypertensive patients, have different levels of suicidal tendency factor emotional disturbance. The F value for the interaction of disease types and gender, F (1,100) =13.03 *p*<.01, was also significant, as shown in Table no.169. Table

173 and chart 151 show that the mean scores of male and female diabetic patients are (M=19.71, SD= 4.03) and (M = 19.41, SD = 4.19) respectively, with a mean difference of 0.30 between the two groups of patients. Because their mean scores are (M =25.11 SD=8.45) and (M=29.69 SD=8.79), respectively, the mean difference between male and female hypertensive patients is 4.58. The mean differences between the four groups, of patients have more or less equal on the suicidal tendency factor emotional disturbance.

Suicidal tendency factor emotional disturbance with regard to Types of disease and Hereditary status:

It can be seen from table F (1,100) =1.26 showed a non-significant (p>.05) interaction between disease types and hereditary status. Table 174 and chart 152 show that diabetic patients with hereditary status have a mean score of 18.62 (SD = 3.70), while diabetic patients without hereditary status have a mean score of 20.50 (SD=4.29). 1.88 is the average difference. The mean difference between the mean scores of hypertension patients with hereditary status (27.22 (SD =8.89) and hypertension patients without hereditary status (27.58 (SD =8.95) is 0.36. It is clear that each of the four groups has a suicidal tendency factor emotional disturbance level that is largely similar.

Suicidal tendency factor Emotional disturbance with regard to Gender and Hereditary status:

The interaction between gender and heredity has a calculated value of F(1,100)=0.004, which is insignificant at .05. The mean score for male patients with hereditary status is 21.87 (SD =7.39), while the mean score for male patients without hereditary status is 22.95 (SD =6.87), a difference in mean scores is 1.1, as shown in Table 175 and Chart 153. The mean score for female patients with hereditary status is 23.97 (SD = 8.55), while the mean score for non-hereditary patients is 25.13 (SD = 8.62). The mean value difference is 1.16. In all four groups, the mean difference is roughly the same. As a result, the suicidal tendency factor emotional disturbance was similar in all four groups of patients.

Suicidal tendency factor emotional disturbance with regard to Types of disease, Gender and Hereditary status:

F ratios in diabetes and hypertensive patients for disease types, gender, and hereditary status are insignificant ($F(1, 50) = 0.10$, $p > .05$). Diabetic male patients with heredity have a mean score of 18.68(SD =4.20), while diabetic male patients without heredity have a mean score of 20.74(SD =3.60). The mean difference between the two groups is 2.06. For diabetic female patients with and without hereditary status, the mean values are 18.56 (SD = 3.15) and 20.26 (SD = 4.91), respectively. Between the two groups, the mean difference is 1.70, which is statistically insignificant. The mean score of male hypertension patients with heredity is 25.06(SD =8.49), while the mean score of male hypertension patients without hereditary status is 25.06(SD =8.49). The difference in average scores is 0.10, which is insignificant. The mean score for female hypertension patients with heredity is 29.38 (SD =8.84), while the mean score for female hypertension patients without heredity is 30.00 (SD=8.81). The mean difference is 0.62. All eight groups of diabetic and hypertension patients have approximately similar levels of suicidal tendency factor emotional disturbance.

Table: 177

Showing ANOVA summary for the suicidal tendency factor Conflictive thoughts.

Source	Type III Sum of Squares	df	Mean Square	F	Sig. Level
***Diseases* (A)**	2410.810	1	2410.810	74.097	p<.01
***Gender* (B)**	453.690	1	453.690	13.944	p<.01
***Heredity status* (C)**	127.690	1	127.690	3.925	NS
***Diseases * Gender* (A*B)**	1204.090	1	1204.090	37.008	p<.01
***Diseases * Heredity status* (A*C)**	835.210	1	835.210	25.670	p<.01
***Gender * Heredity status* (B*C)**	102.010	1	102.010	3.135	NS
***Diseases * Gender * Heredity status* (A*B*C)**	110.610	1	110.610	3.352	NS
Error	12754.080	392	32.536		
Total	146982.000	400			
Corrected Total	18029.190	399			

Levene's Test of Equality of Error Variances[a]

Dependent Variable: ST3

F	df1	df2	Sig.
10.454	7	392	.000

Tests the null hypothesis that the error variance of the dependent variable is equal across groups.

a. Design: Intercept + Diseases + Gender + HS + Diseases * Gender + Diseases * HS + Gender * HS + Diseases * Gender * HS

Table 178
Showing Mean, SD & Mean difference between patients of diabetes and hypertension for suicidal tendency factor Conflictive thoughts.

***Diseases* (A)**	**N**	**Mean**	**SD**	**Mean Difference**
Diabetes A1	200	15.50	3.51	4.91
Hypertension A2	200	20.41	8.13	

Figure no.155
Showing comparisons of mean scores between patients of diabetes and hypertension for suicidal tendency factor Conflictive thoughts.

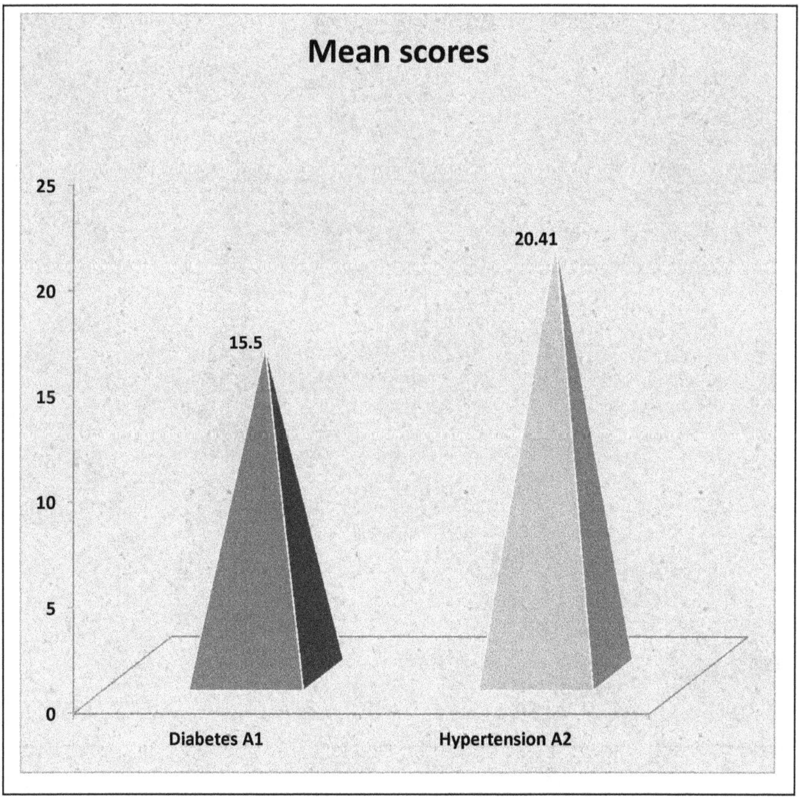

Table 179
Showing Mean, SD & Mean difference between male and female patients with diabetes and hypertension for suicidal tendency factor Conflictive thoughts.

Gender (B)	N	Mean	SD	Mean Difference
Male B1	200	16.89	4.26	2.13
Female B2	200	19.02	8.37	

Figure no.156
Showing comparisons of mean scores between male and female patients with diabetes and hypertension for suicidal tendency factor Conflictive thoughts.

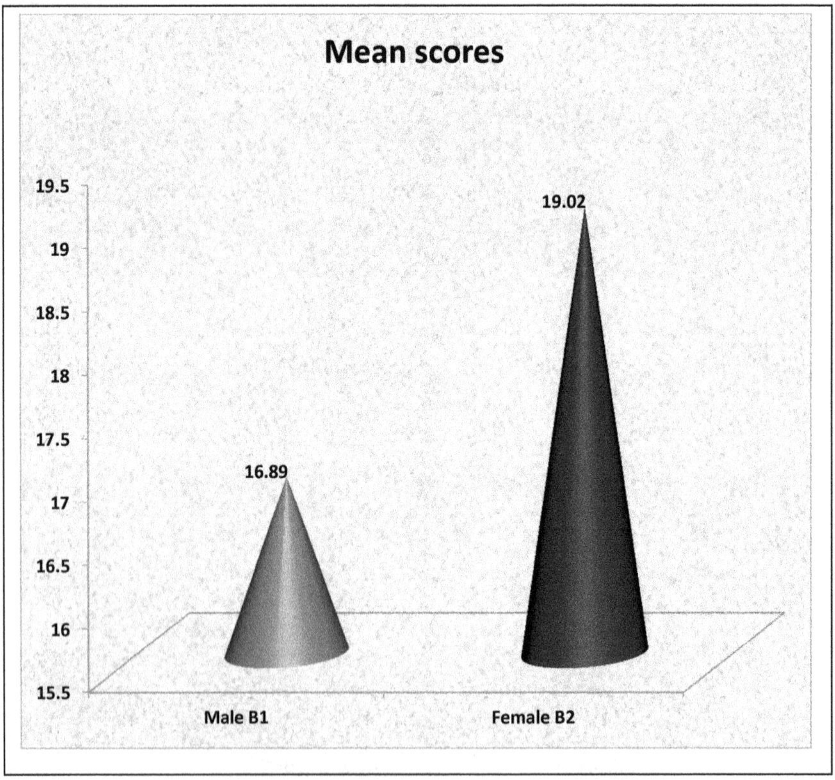

Table 180
Showing Mean, SD & Mean difference between patients with and without hereditary status for suicidal tendency factor Conflictive thoughts.

Hereditary status (C)	N	Mean	SD	Mean Difference
Hereditary C1	200	18.52	8.09	1.13
Non-hereditary C2	200	17.39	4.94	

Figure no. 157
Showing comparisons of mean scores between patients with and without hereditary status for suicidal tendency factor Conflictive thoughts.

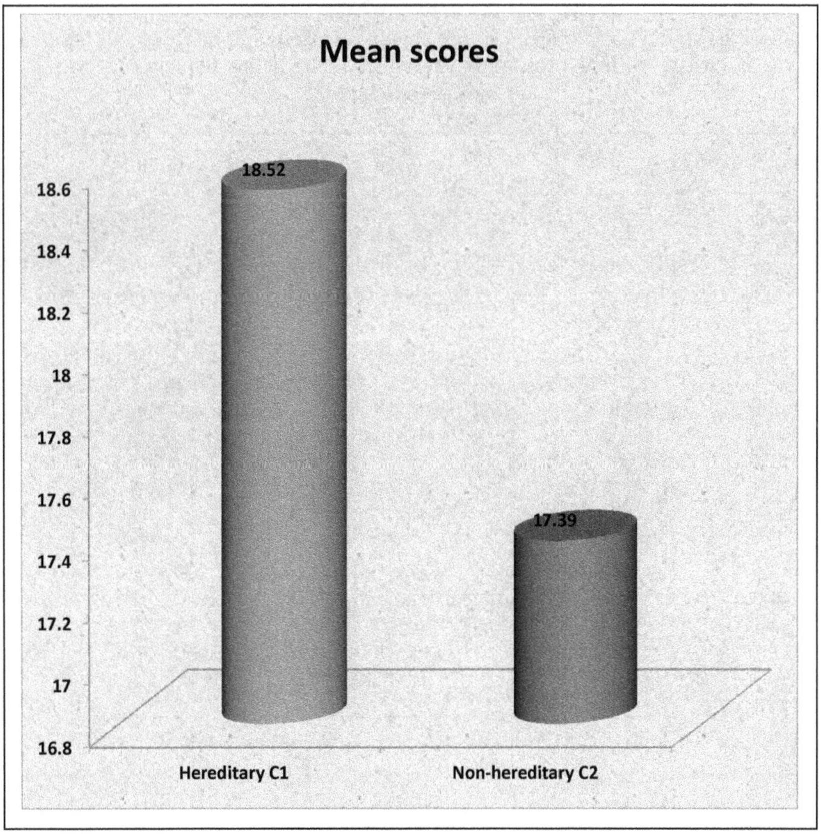

Table 181
Showing Mean, SD & Mean difference among interaction of diseases and Gender of patients with diabetes and hypertension for suicidal tendency factor Conflictive thoughts.

Diseases (A)	Gender (B)	N	Mean	SD	Mean Difference
Diabetes A1	Male B1	100	16.17	3.15	1.34
	Female B2	100	14.83	3.72	
Hypertension A2	Male B1	100	17.61	5.05	5.6
	Female B2	100	23.21	7.56	

Figure no. 158
Showing comparisons of mean scores among interaction of diseases and Gender of patients with diabetes and hypertension for suicidal tendency factor Conflictive thoughts.

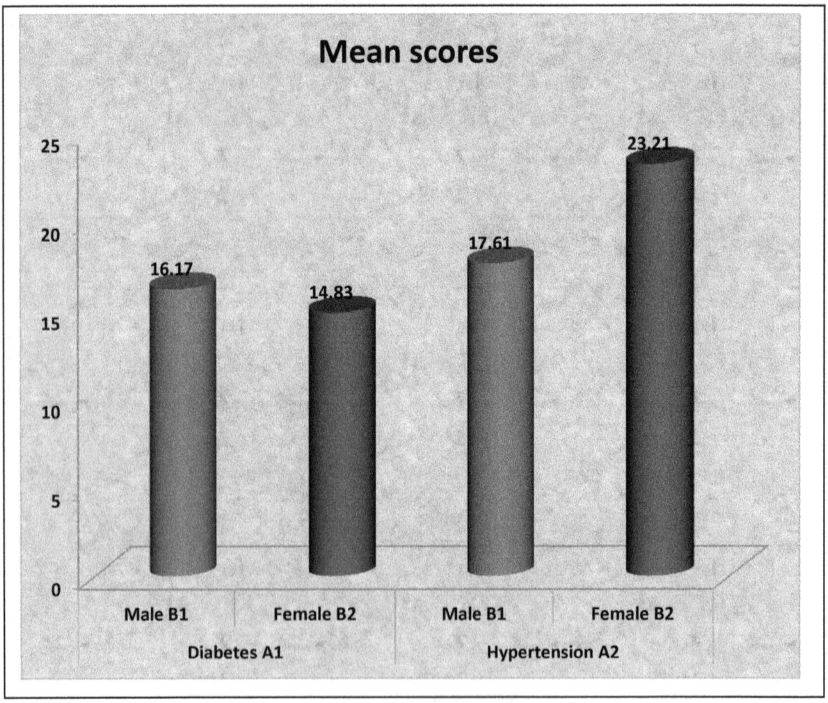

Table 182
Showing Mean, SD & Mean difference among interaction of diseases and hereditary status of patients for suicidal tendency factor Conflictive thoughts.

Diseases (A)	Hereditary (C)	N	Mean	SD	Mean Difference
Diabetes A1	Hereditary *C1*	100	14.62	3.43	1.76
	Non- hereditary *C2*	100	16.38	3.37	
Hypertension A2	Hereditary *C1*	100	22.42	7.44	4.02
	Non- hereditary *C2*	100	18.40	5.97	

Figure no. 159
Showing comparisons of mean scores among interaction of diseases and hereditary status of patients for suicidal tendency factor Conflictive thoughts.

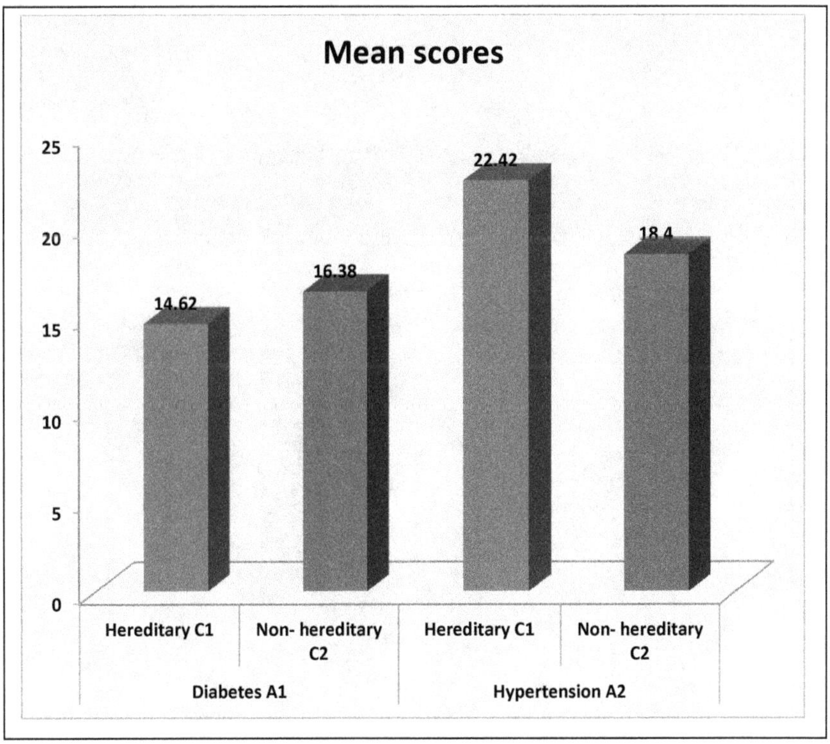

Table 183
Showing Mean, SD & Mean difference among interaction of Gender and hereditary status of patients for suicidal tendency factor Conflictive thoughts.

Gender (B)	Hereditary status (C)	N	Mean	SD	Mean Difference
Male	Hereditary *C1*	100	16.95	5.27	0.12
	Non-hereditary *C2*	100	16.83	2.95	
Female	Hereditary *C1*	100	20.09	8.94	2.14
	Non-hereditary *C2*	100	17.95	6.30	

Figure no. 160
Showing comparisons of mean scores among interaction of Gender and hereditary status of patients for suicidal tendency factor Conflictive thoughts.

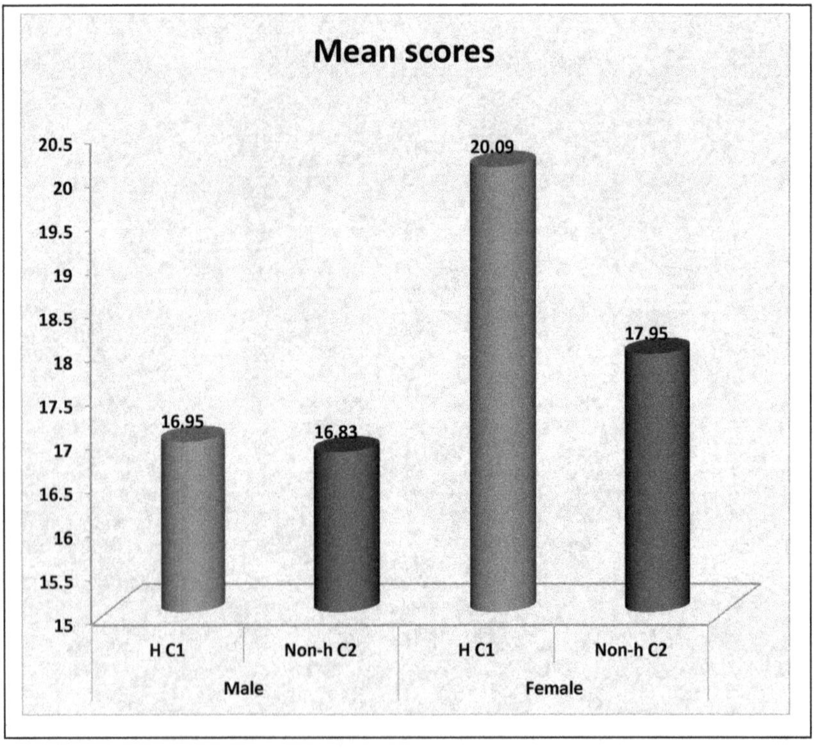

Table 184
Showing Mean, SD & Mean difference among interaction of diseases, gender and hereditary status of patients with diabetes and hypertension for suicidal tendency factor Conflictive thoughts.

Diseases (A)	Gender (B)	Hereditary status (C)	N	Mean	SD	Mean Difference
Diabetes A1	*Male B1*	*Hereditary C1*	50	15.38	3.04	1.58
		Non- hereditary C2	50	16.96	3.09	
	Female B2	*Hereditary C1*	50	13.86	3.65	1.94
		Non- hereditary C2	50	15.80	3.57	
Hypertension A2	*Male B1*	*Hereditary C1*	50	18.52	6.47	1.82
		Non- hereditary C2	50	16.70	2.83	
	Female B2	*Hereditary C1*	50	26.32	9.35	6.22
		Non- hereditary C2	50	20.10	7.62	

Figure no. 161
Showing comparisons of mean scores among interaction of diseases, gender and hereditary status of patients with diabetes and hypertension for suicidal tendency factor Conflictive thoughts.

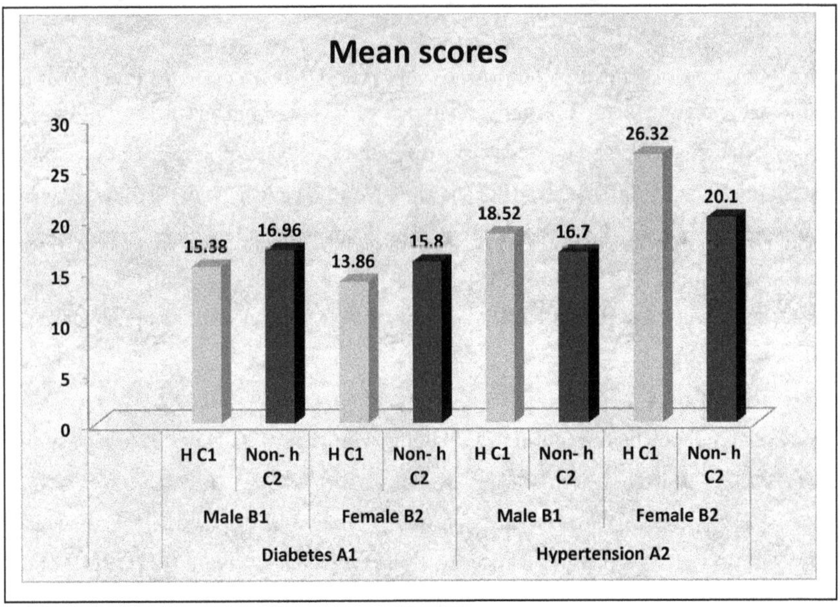

Main Effect:

Suicidal tendency factor Conflictive thoughts with regard to Types of disease:

The first main effect, i.e. types of disease was reported significant for suicidal tendency factor emotional disturbance in diabetic and hypertensive patients F(1, 200) =74.09, p >.01 (Table no.177). The patients with diabetes have a mean score of 15.50 (SD = 3.51), while those with hypertension have a mean score of 20.41 (SD = 8.13). According to Table 178 and Chart 155, the difference between the two means is 4.91. On the basis of above findings, hypertensive patients have higher suicidal tendency factor conflictive thoughts than the patients with diabetes.

Suicidal tendency factor conflictive thoughts with regard to Gender:

The F value and mean score for the gender of diabetic and hypertensive patients are shown in Tables 177 and 156, the mean difference and F ratio reported as significant F(1,200) =13.94, p<.01. Male patients have a mean value of 16.89 (SD = 4.26), while female patients have a mean value of 19.02 (SD = 8.37), resulting in a mean difference of 2.13 between the two groups. This mean difference (Table No.180 & Chart No. 156) exposed that the two groups have a significant mean difference. Female patients have higher traits of suicidal tendency factors conflictive thoughts in comparison of and male patients.

Suicidal tendency factor conflictive thoughts with regard to Hereditary status:

Hereditary status have a calculated F value of F (1, 200) = 3.92, which was insignificant at .05. In Table No. 180 and chart No.157, patients with hereditary status have a mean score of 18.52 (SD=8.09), while patients without hereditary status have a mean score of 17.39 (SD=4.94), with a mean difference of 1.13. Patients with and without heredity have similar levels of suicidal tendency factor conflictive thoughts.

Interaction Effect

Suicidal tendency factor conflictive thoughts with regard to Types of disease and Gender:

The primary goal of the research was to observe if male and female diabetic patients, as well as male and female hypertensive patients, have different levels of suicidal tendency factor conflictive thoughts. Table no.177 highlighted that the F value for the interaction of disease types and gender, F (1,100) =37.00 $p<.01$, was also significant. The mean scores of male and female diabetic patients are (M=16.17, SD= 3.15) and (M = 14.83, SD = 3.72), respectively, as shown in table 181 and chart 158, with a mean difference of 1.34 between the two groups of patients. Male and female hypertensive patients have mean scores of (M =17.61 SD=5.05) and (M=23.31 SD=7.56), respectively. Male and female hypertensive patients have a mean difference of 5.6. The suicidal tendency factor conflictive thoughts were found to be significantly differed among the four groups of patients.

Suicidal tendency factor conflictive thoughts with regard to Types of disease and Hereditary status:

There was a significant interaction between disease types and hereditary status of patients, the F (1, 100) =25.67, value was observed significant at .01. Diabetic patients with hereditary status have a mean score of 14.62 (SD = 3.43), while diabetic patients without hereditary status have a mean score of 16.38 (SD=3.37), as shown in table 182 and chart 159. The mean difference is 1.76. The mean difference between hypertensive patients with hereditary status 22.42 (SD =7.44) and hypertensive patients without hereditary status is 18.40 (SD =5.97). The difference between mean is 4.02, which is statistically significant. Each of the four groups clearly has a different thinking pattern towards conflicting thoughts.

Suicidal tendency factor conflictive thoughts with regard to Gender and Hereditary status:

The ANOVA value is the calculated for the interaction between gender and heredity (F(1,100) = 3.14), which is insignificant at .05. Table 183 and Chart 160 show that the mean score for male patients with hereditary status is 16.95 (SD =5.27), while the mean score for male patients without hereditary status is 16.83 (SD =2.95), and a mean difference of 0.12. Female patients with hereditary status have a mean score of 20.09 (SD = 8.94), while non-hereditary patients have a mean score of 17.95 (SD = 6.30). The difference in mean value is 2.14. The mean difference is by and large the same in all four groups. As a result, in all four groups of patients, the suicidal tendency factor conflictive thoughts were similar.

Suicidal tendency factor conflictive thoughts with regard to Types of disease, Gender and Hereditary status:

Ratio of F for disease types, gender, and hereditary status in diabetic and hypertensive patients are insignificant ($F(1, 50) = 3.35$, $p > .05$). The mean score for diabetic male patients with heredity is 15.38 (SD = 3.04), while the mean score for diabetic male patients without heredity is 16.96 (SD = 3.09). 1.58 is the mean difference between the two groups. The mean values for diabetic female patients with and without hereditary status are respectively 13.86(SD = 3.65) and 15.80(SD = 3.57). The mean difference between the two groups is 1.94, which is statistically insignificant. Male hypertensive patients with heredity have a mean score of 18.52 (SD =6.74), while male hypertensive patients without hereditary status have a mean score of 16.70 (SD =2.83). The mean difference is 1.82, which is not statistically significant. Female hypertension patients with hereditary have a mean score of 26.32 (SD =9.35), while those female patients without hereditary status have a mean score of 20.10 (SD=7.62). 6.22 is the average difference. The levels of suicidal tendency factor conflictive thoughts are almost similar among all eight groups of diabetic and hypertension patients.

Table: 185

Showing ANOVA summary for the suicidal tendency factor Self- harm tendency.

Source	Type III Sum of Squares	df	Mean Square	F	Sig. Level
Diseases **(A)**	2209.000	1	2209.000	66.806	p<.01
Gender **(B)**	73.960	1	73.960	2.237	.000
Heredity status **(C)**	10.240	1	10.240	.310	NS
Diseases * Gender **(A*B)**	882.090	1	882.090	26.677	p<.01
Diseases * Heredity status **(A*C)**	610.090	1	610.090	18.451	p<.01
Gender * Heredity status **(B*C)**	102.010	1	102.010	3.085	NS
Diseases * Gender * Heredity status **(A*B*C)**	51.840	1	51.840	1.568	NS
Error	12961.880	392	33.066		
Total	167678.000	400			
Corrected Total	16901.110	399			

Levene's Test of Equality of Error Variances[a]

Dependent Variable: ST4

F	df1	df2	Sig.
9.222	7	392	.000

Tests the null hypothesis that the error variance of the dependent variable is equal across groups.

a. Design: Intercept + Diseases + Gender + HS + Diseases * Gender + Diseases * HS + Gender * HS + Diseases * Gender * HS

Table 186
Showing Mean, SD & Mean difference between patients of diabetes and hypertension for suicidal tendency factor Self- harm tendency.

Diseases (A)	N	Mean	SD	Mean Difference
Diabetes A1	200	17.06	3.79	4.7
Hypertension A2	200	21.76	7.70	

Figure no.162
Showing comparisons of mean scores between patients of diabetes and hypertension for suicidal tendency factor Self- harm tendency.

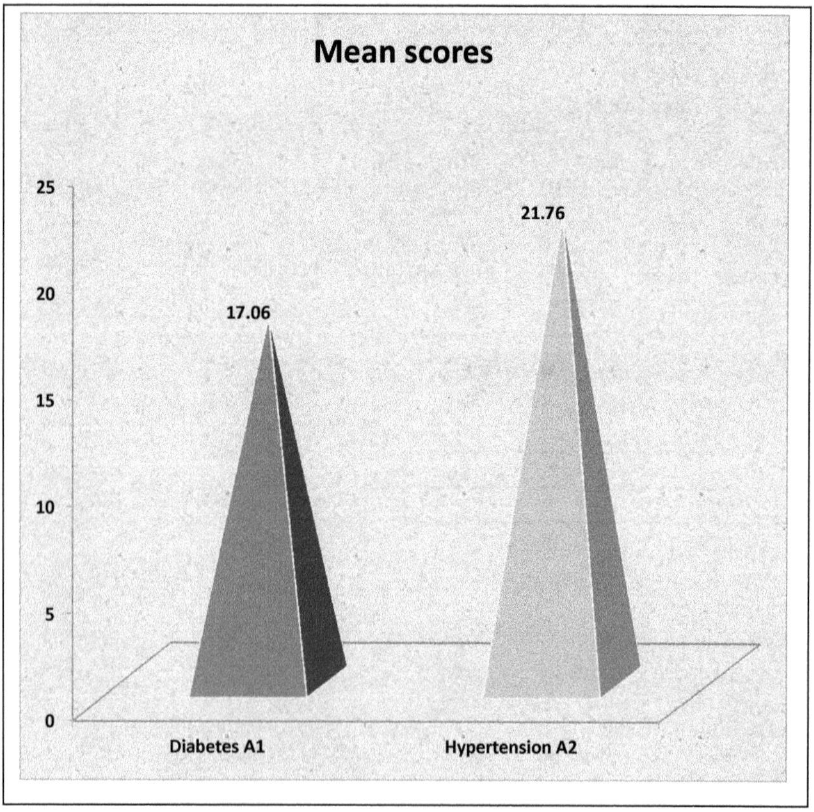

Table 187
Showing Mean, SD & Mean difference between male and female patients with diabetes and hypertension for suicidal tendency factor Self- harm tendency.

Gender (B)	N	Mean	SD	Mean Difference
Male B1	200	18.98	4.52	0.86
Female B2	200	19.84	8.00	

Figure no.163
Showing comparisons of mean scores between male and female patients with diabetes and hypertension for suicidal tendency factor Self- harm tendency.

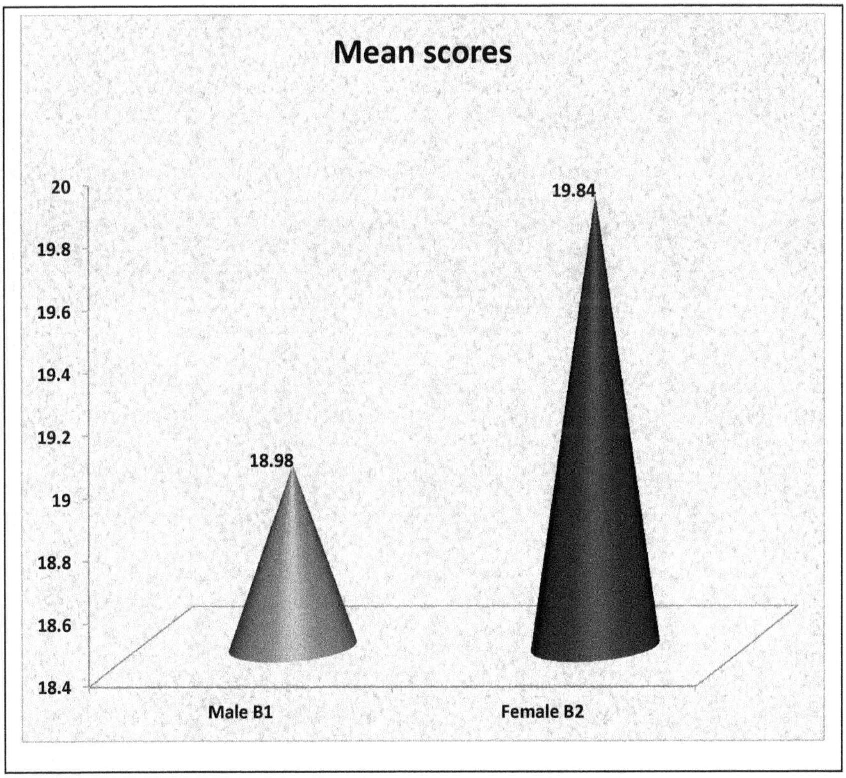

Table 188
Showing Mean, SD & Mean difference between patients with and without hereditary status for suicidal tendency factor Self- harm tendency.

Hereditary status (C)	N	Mean	SD	Mean Difference
Hereditary C1	200	19.57	7.49	0.32
Non-hereditary C2	200	19.25	5.35	

Figure no. 164
Showing comparisons of mean scores between patients with and without hereditary status for suicidal tendency factor Self- harm tendency.

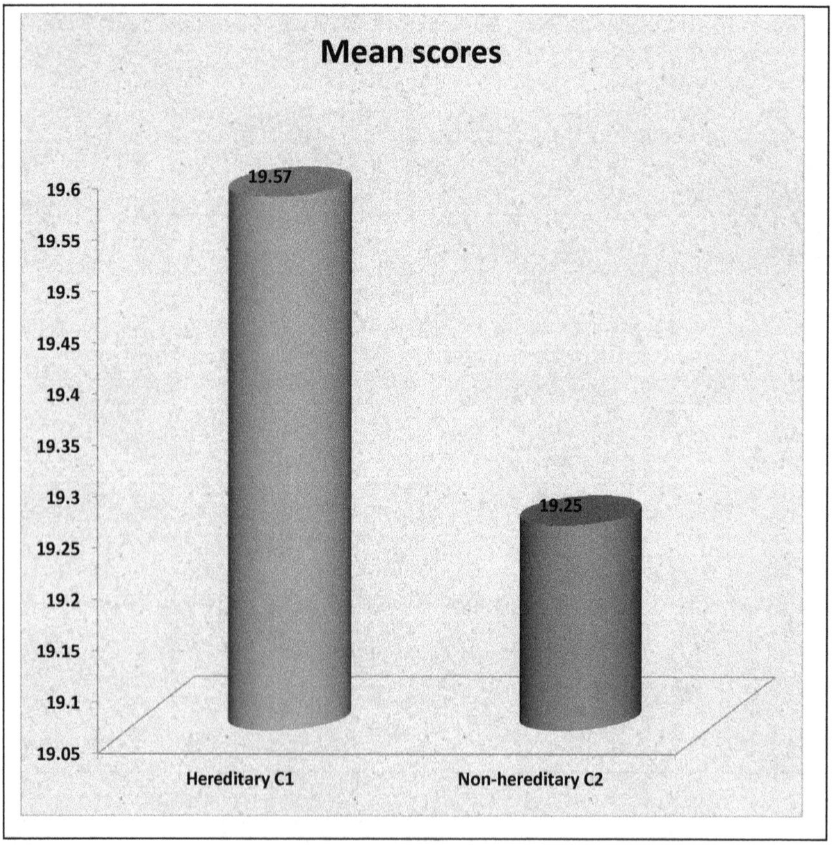

Table 189
Showing Mean, SD & Mean difference among interaction of diseases and Gender of patients with diabetes and hypertension for suicidal tendency factor Self-harm tendency.

Diseases (A)	Gender (B)	N	Mean	SD	Mean Difference
Diabetes A1	**Male B1**	100	18.12	3.79	2.11
	Female B2	100	16.01	3.51	
Hypertension A2	**Male B1**	100	19.85	5.02	3.83
	Female B2	100	23.68	9.31	

Figure no. 165
Showing comparisons of mean scores among interaction of diseases and Gender of patients with diabetes and hypertension for suicidal tendency factor Self-harm tendency.

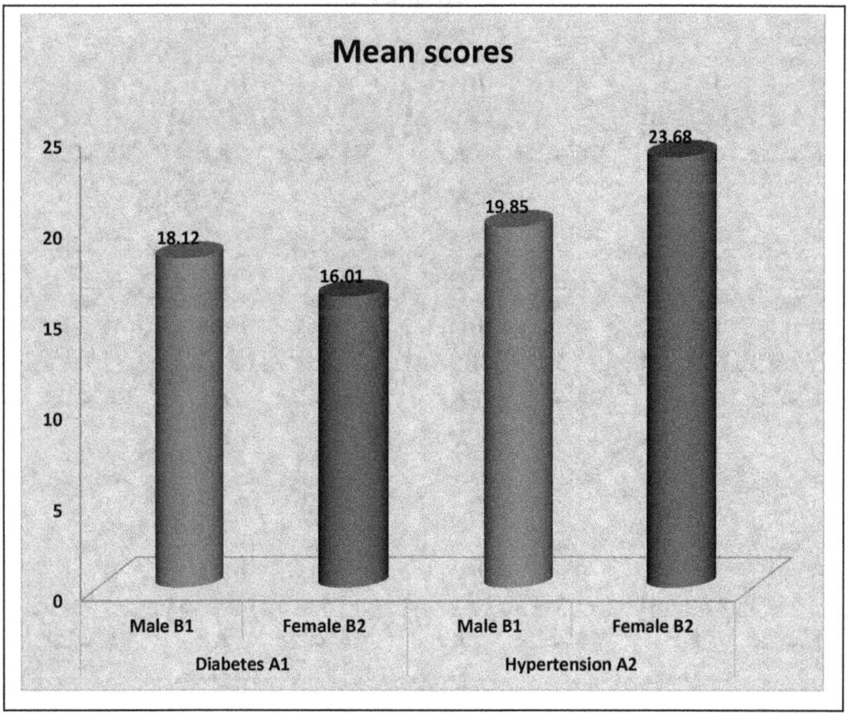

Table 190

Showing Mean, SD & Mean difference among interaction of diseases and hereditary status of patients for suicidal tendency factor Self- harm tendency.

Diseases (A)	Hereditary (C)	N	Mean	SD	Mean Difference
Diabetes A1	Hereditary *C1*	100	15.99	3.34	2.15
	Non- hereditary *C2*	100	18.14	3.93	
Hypertension A2	Hereditary *C1*	100	23.16	8.71	2.79
	Non- hereditary *C2*	100	20.37	6.29	

Figure no. 166

Showing comparisons of mean scores among interaction of diseases and hereditary status of patients for suicidal tendency factor Self- harm tendency.

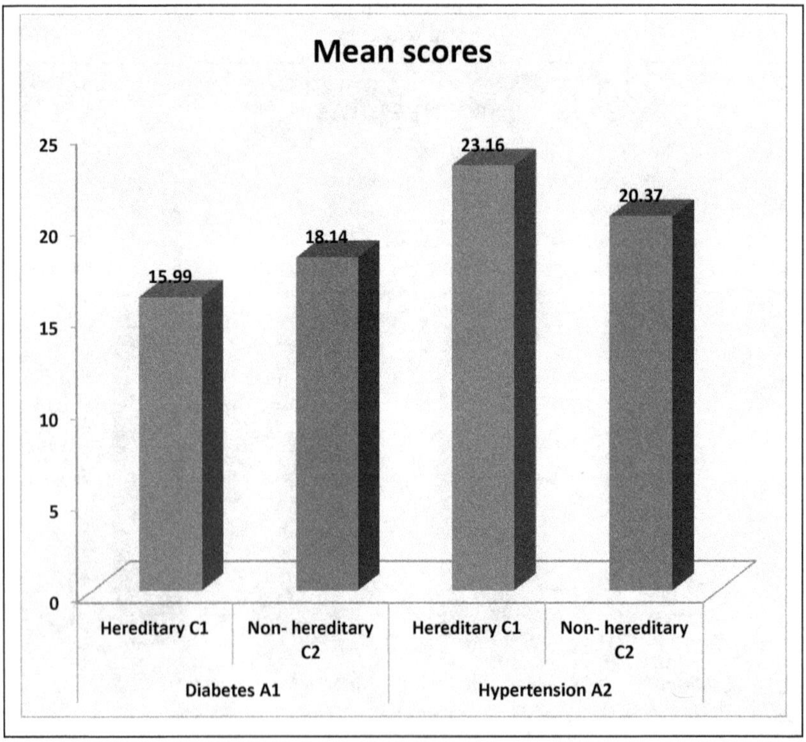

Table 191
Showing Mean, SD & Mean difference among interaction of Gender and hereditary status of patients for suicidal tendency factor Self- harm tendency.

Diseases (A)	Hereditary (C)	N	Mean	SD	Mean Difference
Diabetes A1	Hereditary *C1*	100	15.99	5.26	0.69
	Non- hereditary *C2*	100	18.14	3.63	
Hypertension A2	Hereditary *C1*	100	23.16	9.13	1.33
	Non- hereditary *C2*	100	20.37	6.66	

Figure no. 167
Showing Mean, SD & Mean difference among interaction of Gender and hereditary status of patients for suicidal tendency factor Self- harm tendency.

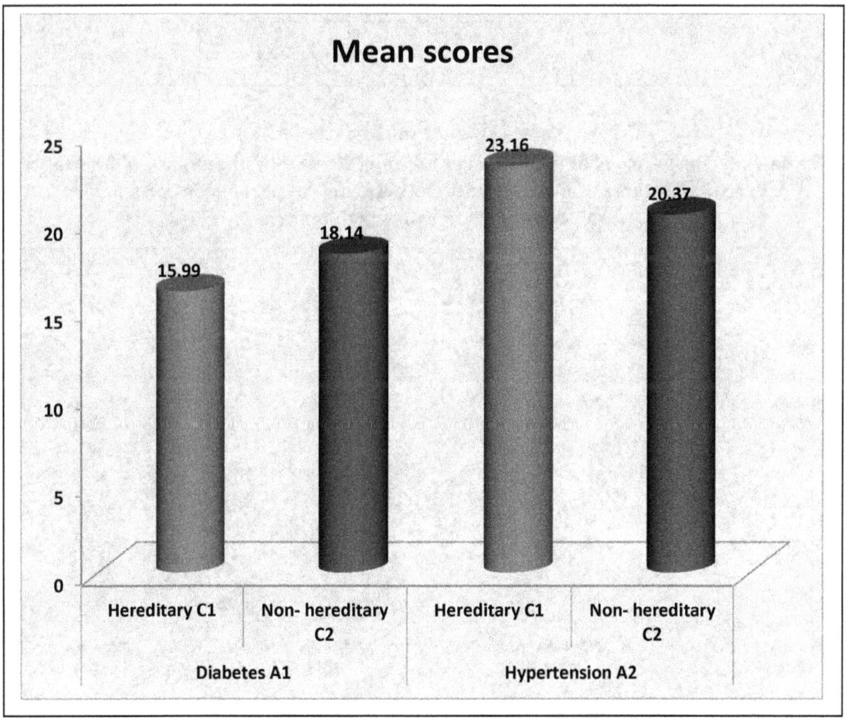

Table 192
Showing Mean, SD & Mean difference among interaction of diseases, gender and hereditary status of patients with diabetes and hypertension for suicidal tendency factor Self- harm tendency.

Diseases (A)	Gender (B)	Hereditary status (C)	N	Mean	SD	Mean Difference
Diabetes A1	*Male B1*	*Hereditary C1*	50	16.90	3.58	2.44
		Non- hereditary C2	50	19.34	3.62	
	Female B2	*Hereditary C1*	50	15.08	2.83	1.86
		Non- hereditary C2	50	16.94	3.88	
Hypertension A2	*Male B1*	*Hereditary C1*	50	20.38	6.08	1.06
		Non- hereditary C2	50	19.32	3.67	
	Female B2	*Hereditary C1*	50	25.94	10.02	4.52
		Non- hereditary C2	50	21.42	8.01	

Figure no. 168
Showing comparisons of mean scores among interaction of diseases, gender and hereditary status of patients with diabetes and hypertension for suicidal tendency factor Self- harm tendency.

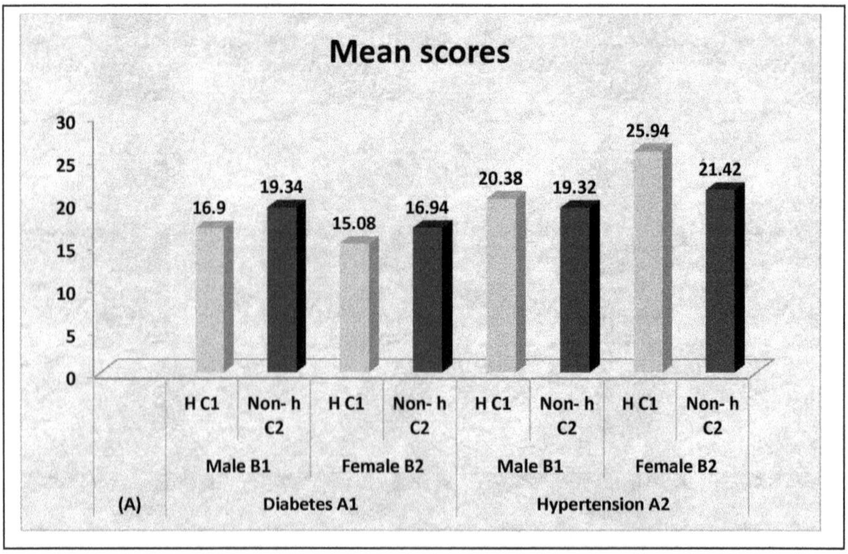

Main Effect:

Suicidal tendency factor Self-harm tendency with regard to Types of disease:

When the effect of disease type on suicidal tendency factor self-harm tendency in diabetic and hypertensive patients was found F(1, 200) =66.80, the value of F was significant (p>.01). The mean score for diabetes patients is 17.06 (SD = 3.79), while the mean score for hypertension patients is 21.76 (SD = 7.70). The difference between the two means is 4.7, according to Table 186 and Chart 162. Hypertensive patients, according to the findings, have higher characteristics of self-harm tendency.

Suicidal tendency factor self harm tendency with regard to Gender:

Tables 185 and 163 demonstrated the F value and mean score for diabetic and hypertensive patients, with the mean difference and F ratio stated as non-significant F(1,200) =2.23, p>.05. The male patients having a mean value of 18.98 (SD = 4.52) and female patients having a mean value of 19.84 (SD = 8.00). The mean difference between the two groups (Table No.187 & Chart No.163) showed a non-significant 0.86. According to the findings, female and male patients have more or less equal self-harm tendency.

Suicidal tendency factor self harm tendency with regard to Hereditary status:

The calculated F value for hereditary status was F (1,200) =.31, which was non-significant at .05. Patients with hereditary status have a mean score of 19.57 (SD=7.49) in Table No. 188 and chart No.164, while patients without hereditary status have a mean score of 19.25 (SD=5.35), with a mean difference of 0.32. Suicidal tendency factor self harm tendency are similar in patients with and without heredity status.

Interaction Effect

Suicidal tendency factor self harm tendency with regard to Types of disease and Gender:

The types of disease and gender are interacting significantly with each other, thus male and female diabetic patients, as well as male and female hypertensive patients, have different levels of suicidal tendency factor self harm tendency. The F value for the interaction of disease types and gender was also significant, F (1,100) =26.67 p<.01. As shown in table 189 and chart 165, the mean scores of male and female diabetic patients are (M=18.12, SD=3.79) and (M = 16.01, SD = 3.51), respectively, with a mean difference of 2.11 between the two groups of patients. The mean scores for male and female hypertensive patients are (M =19.85 SD=5.02) and (M=23.68 SD=9.31), respectively. The mean difference between male and female hypertensive patients is 3.83. The mean difference between the four groups indicated that all the groups of patients have different opinion towards self harm tendency.

Suicidal tendency factor self harm with regard to Types of disease and Hereditary status:

The value of F (1,100) =18.45 was a significant at ($p<.01$) for the interaction between disease types and hereditary status. As shown in table 190 and chart 166, diabetic patients with hereditary status have a mean score of 15.99 (SD = 3.34), while diabetic patients without hereditary status have a mean score of 18.14 (SD=3.93). 2.15 is the mean difference between the both of groups. Similarly, hypertensive patients with hereditary status have a mean score of 23.16 (SD = 8.71), while hypertensive patients without hereditary status have a mean score of 20.37 (SD=6.29). the mean difference between hypertensive patients with hereditary status and hypertensive patients without hereditary status is 2.79, which is statistically significant. All of the four groups has a distinct suicidal tendency factor self harm tendency.

Suicidal tendency factor self harm tendency with regard to Gender and Hereditary status:

The calculated value for the interaction between gender and hereditary status is F(1,100)= 3.08, which is insignificant at .05. The mean score for male patients with hereditary status is 15.99 (SD =5.26), while the mean score for male patients without hereditary status is 18.14 (SD =3.63), resulting in a mean difference of 0.69. The mean score for female patients with hereditary status is 23.16 (SD = 9.13), while the mean score for female patients without hereditary status is 20.37 (SD = 6.66). The mean value difference is 1.33. In all four groups, the mean difference is almost the same. As a result, the suicidal tendency factor self harm tendency s was similar in all four groups of patients.

Suicidal tendency factor self harm tendency with regard to Types of disease, Gender and Hereditary status:

In diabetic and hypertensive patients, F ratios for disease types, gender, and hereditary status are not significant (F (1, 50) =1.56, $p>.05$). Diabetic male patients with heredity have a mean score of 16.90 (SD = 3.58), while diabetic male patients without heredity have a mean score of 19.34 (SD = 3.62). The mean difference between the two groups is 2.44. Female diabetic patients with heredity have a mean value of 15.08 (SD=2.83) and female diabetic patients without heredity have mean value of 16.94 (SD = 3.88). Between the two groups, the mean difference is 1.86, which is statistically insignificant. The mean score for male hypertensive patients with hereditary status is 20.38 (SD =6.08), while the mean score for male hypertensive patients without hereditary status is 19.32 (SD =3.67). The mean difference is 1.06, which is statistically not significant. Patients with hereditary status including hypertension have a mean score of 25.94 (SD =10.02), while those without hereditary status as well as hypertension have a mean score of 21.42 (SD=8.01). The mean difference is 4.52. All eight groups of diabetic and hypertension patients have similar levels of suicidal tendency factor self harm tendency.

CPSIA information can be obtained
at www.ICGtesting.com
Printed in the USA
LVHW012248291122
734192LV00013B/477

9 781805 451860